HENRY VAN DYKE

A Biography

BY HIS SON

TERTIUS VAN DYKE

J. F. McCarthy
Oconomowoc
Wisconsin.

NEW YORK AND LONDON

HARPER & BROTHERS PUBLISHERS

1935

TO

ELLEN REID VAN DYKE

Elusive, vivid, delicious, strong,

who would not allow

her part

in the life of her husband, family and friends

to be praised.

ACKNOWLEDGMENTS

THIS book is *not* "a labour of love"—though I once abjectly feared it might be. For me it has proved an arduous but ever fascinating review of a life of which, as boy, youth and man, I have been vividly aware for forty years. During the last twenty years of that time I was an intimate confidant of Henry van Dyke as well as his frequent companion. I have been his pupil in the University and informally elsewhere. We have disagreed strenuously, but never been divided. He once told me: "You know I love you dearly, but you're about the most obstinate man I know." In 1905, without informing him, I made my first desultory jottings about him—just out of my own interest. In 1912 I continued these jottings more systematically. About 1920, when a number of his friends urged him to write his reminiscences, he first suggested that I might wish to record his life—if it were worth doing at all. Steadily I refused—not being convinced that he was in earnest. It was in the summer of 1931, when we were talking over the state of the world by the fire in "Green Door" with a thick Maine fog outside, that he said: "You have a real sympathy with me. You often disagree, but you do understand." For me that settled the question both as an opportunity and as an obligation—though I was unable to take up the work specifically until two years later.

Henry van Dyke, who captivated me as a human being long before I dreamed of writing about him, is the chief source of this book. As his biographer I am particularly grateful for the long talks we have had throughout the years in many places and various circumstances.

My mother and four sisters have greatly aided with personal recollections and intimate talk. My aunt, Mrs. Edith Gittings Reid, gifted interpreter of human beings, has been constant in faith, encouragement, counsel. I am peculiarly indebted to my wife, Elizabeth Cannon, who actively cheered me through the snowstorm of papers and doubts, endured me while writing, offered trenchant and uncompromising criticism after listening patiently to the reading, and when satisfied she had made her points, let me have my own way.

Dr. John H. Finley and Mr. Struthers Burt, who with myself are the Literary Executors, have been from the beginning fruitful in counsel and encouragement.

For several long and intimate conversations I am much indebted to Professor J. Duncan Spaeth, of Princeton University, who has written the article on Henry van Dyke for the *National Dictionary of Biography*. Dr. Varnum L. Collins, the Secretary of Princeton University, Dr. James Thayer Gerould, the Librarian, and Dr. Malcolm O. Young, the Reference Librarian, and Rev. Dr. W. B. Sheddan, the Librarian of Princeton Theological Seminary, have generously aided my researches.

Mr. John Hall Wheelock of Scribners who was intimately associated with my father, especially in his latter years, has gone out of his way to give me aid and personal encouragement.

Mr. G. F. J. Cumberlege of the Oxford University Press first gave me the important suggestion that this work must appear in a single volume,—with much interesting correspondence held in reserve.

Mrs. Ralph Downes (formerly Miss Agnes Rix), from 1913-1931 my father's invaluable private secretary, has been a willing consultant among his voluminous papers. Her careful preservation and organizing of those papers and the preparation of the volumes of newspaper clippings which she undertook at my suggestion in 1917 have greatly facilitated the task of research. Miss Joan Comins who followed her as my father's secretary and who has acted in that capacity for me has been steadily and generously helpful.

The Hon. Theodore Marburg to whom Henry van Dyke wrote: "It was through your friendship that I first became actively interested in the League of Nations idea," has freely shared his authoritative knowledge of League matters as well as his personal friendship with my father. Professor George Grafton Wilson, who became Counselor at the Legation in The Hague on the outbreak of war in 1914, has given me invaluable information and counsel about that period. My Princeton classmate, Mr. Joseph C. Green of the Department of State, has been most kind in arranging access to the Department records. I am indebted to others who kindly aided my work there.

Rev. M. Ernest Hall, for twenty years a missionary of the American Board in Japan, has kindly examined the report of my father's Japanese sojourn for me.

Others with whom I have talked and corresponded in America and abroad will be found mentioned in later pages. But the exigencies of space compel me to be content to say a general thank-you to unmentioned helpers. This is the fate of all who complete any task in this interdependent world.

The attempt to portray Henry van Dyke among the men of his day by mentioning the names of some who were close to him has certainly resulted in omissions. To reconstruct past years and then reduce the picture to the limits of one volume is an exacting task. Will any who have been wrongfully omitted forgive—and correct me?

I am especially indebted to Charles Scribner's Sons for their freely rendered aid and for permission to quote copyrighted material. Also to *Distinguished Families in America Descended from Wilhelmus Beekman and Jan Thomasse van Dyke,* by William B. Aitken; to the privately printed *The Raritan, Notes on a River and a Family,* by John C. van Dyke; to an incomplete series of printed sheets—the identity and authorship of which I have been unable to discover— entitled, *The Descendants of John and Mary (Currier) Ashmead in America,* which my father told me was an authentic report on his mother's family; to the author and the corporation of the Brick Church for permission to quote from *A History of the Brick Presbyterian Church in the City of New York,* by Shepherd Knapp.

It goes without saying that any van Dyke accepts full responsibility for what he writes.

T. v. D.

CONTENTS

Foreword

CLUE TO THE MAN

THE autumn of 1892 was a time of sickness and sorrow for Henry van Dyke. His heart was still bowed with grief at the recent sudden death of his father, the man whom he knew best, admired most and loved passionately. The responsibilities of a large parish and the unhappy theological controversies then harassing the Church weighed heavily upon him.

One anguished, sleepless night there came to him "suddenly and without labor" *The Story of the Other Wise Man*. Patiently, in the following months, he gathered the detailed knowledge that the telling of the tale required, and wrote it down with meekness and with joy. The story is that of Artaban who sets out to join the Three Wise Men in bringing gifts to the Savior's cradle in Bethlehem. He stops to help a man in need and arrives too late at the appointed place. His companions are gone. He follows after them, and again his inability to pass by a call for help makes him too late. The Child has been taken from Bethlehem to Egypt. He follows after, often losing the trail, but never failing to help needy folk as he was able, and never surrendering his quest. At last, after three and thirty years, with all but one of his gifts expended in deeds of mercy and with the years heavy upon him, he comes to Jerusalem. As his last gift is given in the service which he could never refuse the old man dies in the earthquake that follows the crucifixion. But he had found the King; for the King came to him in death.

Undoubtedly the unsought impulse which brought this story to Henry van Dyke and the patient toil and quiet thought with which it was written saved the life of its author. Undoubtedly too, its na-

[xiii]

ture as the answer to his own overwhelming need accounts for the well-nigh scriptural influence of the story as it has made its way round and round the world in English, in all the European languages, and in many languages and dialects of the Near and Far East.

What needs to be noted here is that, if it be ever possible to find the inner clue to a man's life, this story is the clue to the life of Henry van Dyke. It is the tale of a man who chose always to act in the living present, and who received the final answer to all his questionings not at the beginning but at the end of his journeyings.

As the author expressed the same truth in a quatrain a few years after the writing of the story:

"Who seeks for heaven alone to save his soul,
May keep the path, but will not reach the goal;
While he who walks in love may wander far,
But God will bring him where the Blessed are."

Without committing ourselves to any one scheme of interpretation but letting the man himself stand forth in his deeds and words, let us follow the story of Henry van Dyke's eighty crowded years. No attempt will be made to explain or justify that life by any formula. Let the man bear his own witness. Only so is there hope of truth. For as he himself wrote of the Other Wise Man:

"Now that his story is told, what does it mean? How can I tell? What does life mean? If the meaning could be put into a sentence there would be no need of telling the story."

ILLUSTRATIONS

HENRY van DYKE

I

GROWTH AND DECISIONS

The bars of life at which we fret,
    That seem to prison and control,
Are but the doors of daring set
    Ajar before the soul.

                H. v. D.

Chapter One

ANCESTORS

THERE is a daguerreotype of Henry van Dyke at the age of four arrayed for a fancy dress children's party. A slight but sturdy figure with a red soldier's jacket and brass buttons, white knee breeches and stockings and buckled shoes stands gracefully upon a little rug. His white gloved hands hold a sword and on his well set head a black three cornered military hat shines with gold braid festooned about it. Henry van Dyke was going to the party in the character of George Washington. The event deeply impressed him, for in after years he often spoke of it with the reminiscent humor which is never far removed from tender sentiment.

But we are concerned here, not with the party or the costume, but with the alert poise of the whole body and the steady gaze of the clear eyes. Even as a child Henry van Dyke was a compact, concentrated personality.

What lay behind him in the mysterious realm of heredity? What was the rock from which he was hewn, the pit from which he was digged?

.   .   .   .

The van Dykes of the Netherlands were a solid, sturdy family who had taken their name from the dykes near which they lived. It was the conviction of Henry van Dyke, who made some investigations, that the family never really lived in the city of Amsterdam, but came either from the island of Texel, or perhaps from the region of Harlingen in Friesland.

However that may be, in 1652 Thomas Janse van Dyke, almost sev-

[3]

enty years old, sailed from Amsterdam with his son Jan Thomasse, the latter's wife and seven children, to New Utrecht, Long Island, in one of the high-pooped ships like the Half Moon. As the late Dr. John C. van Dyke wrote of that time:

"On sea and land, in war, commerce, learning, art; in politics, liberty and religious tolerance, Holland was in the lead. Why did Thomas Janse, then an old man, wish to leave it? What was the impelling motive for crossing a stormy ocean to take up life in an unknown unexplored land?"

There is no answer. Perhaps as the same author suggests it was the influence of his son, an able energetic man who in 1657 became one of the nineteen founders of New Utrecht, owned one of the fifty acre farms comprising the town, added other acres thereto, and is variously recorded as "sergeant" and "a magistrate of Fort Orange and New Utrecht" and in his last year, 1673, was one of the "schepens" appointed by Governor Colve.

The son of Jan Thomasse, Jan Janse, may have been one of the children who came with their parents and grandfather to New Utrecht, 1652, or he may have been (as some say) the first of the American born van Dykes. In any case, his boyhood was spent on the shore of the Lower Bay and doubtless round about the Raritan Bay and River. John C. van Dyke paints a vivid picture of what that boyhood must have been:

"A boy's life on the shores of the Lower Bay two hundred and fifty years ago was, of course, never thought worthy of recitation in the chronicles; but it must have been an interesting life for all that. There was school to be attended, for the Dutch early established public instruction and the schoolmaster was second only to the domine in local importance. Besides this, there was farm work to be done, and chores about the house; but, even so, there was plenty of time for play. . . .

"In those days there were deer, elk and bear in the Long Island woods, and turkeys, pheasants, pigeons, rabbits were everywhere. It is not likely that the young Jan effected much slaughter among the larger game, but the rabbits, squirrels and pigeons were probably worried by fire from bow and sling; and perhaps many a 'possum was smoked out of a hollow tree and hustled to a finish by the dogs. Youth needs little teaching in such matters. The reversion to the hunter is natural and dominant in almost

[4]

every boy. But Jan the Third, like some of his later descendants, must have received not only inspiration but instruction from the Indians. There were redskins a-plenty on Long Island and they were all friendly enough with the Dutch. The boys of either the red or the white race are less reticent than their elders, and it is very probable that Jan and his companions soon got upon good terms with the younger Indians. The wood trails and the water ways, with game grounds and all the methods of hunting and trapping, were known to the young redskins and were soon picked up by the white boys. The spearing of fish from a canoe by torchlight, or through the ice in winter, the baiting and trapping of turkeys in runways, the setting of springs for muskrats, beaver, and mink, the chasing of young ducks with dogs, the treeing of coons and squirrels, the effective use of the bow and feathered arrow must have been known to Jan. . . .

"There can be little doubt that Jan the Third, as his father before him, knew something of the River. With its marshes and its meadows it was a great hunting ground. The wood ducks bred there and in October great clouds of mallard and teal swung up or down the stream, passing from lake to lake, while wild geese in V-shaped flocks honked their way down to the Lower Bay. The back country was the feeding ground for all sorts of game. The forests of oak and uplands of chestnut and hickory, the far-away blue mountains, the upper River, were haunts of the deer and the bear. The whole region was as yet unexplored by the whites, and consequently mysterious in its depths. Even the faint Indian trails that ran through the underbrush were uncanny in their windings and sudden disappearances. It was a new land and had the spell of the wilderness about it."

Jan grew up and equally settled down. He was married and spent the sixty-three following years upon his *bouwerie* in solid and apparently undisturbed contentment. Several times during his life New Amsterdam changed hands between the Dutch and English, usually in a more or less casual manner. But though Jan was at one time a lieutenant commissioned by the Dutchman Leisler and later was commissioned captain by the Englishman, the Earl of Bellomont, it is not recorded that he saw action for either side. Perhaps it was not necessary, the matter not looking important except to those who effected the changes or who read the news of it afar off.

Jan Janse was a sound man of parts. He was a magistrate and also a Deacon and later Elder of the Dutch Church. His will contains this sentence which the facts of his life proclaim not only an orthodox but an honest declaration of faith: "First I bequeath my soul to God who gave it, my body to the earth from whence it came . . . in certain hopes of the Resurrection and the union of my body and soul at the last day and of Eternal Life through the sole merits of my blessed Saviour Jesus Christ."

The next Jan in the family, being the son of Jan Janse, was born in New Utrecht. Sometime, probably between 1711, when he was recorded as a Deacon in the New Utrecht Church, and 1715 when "private Jno. Vandike" was listed in the 5th company of a militia regiment in New Jersey under Col. Thos. Harmer, he moved to Mapleton (Fresh Ponds) near Spotswood in Middlesex County, New Jersey. When New Brunswick was incorporated as a city and chartered by King George II he became one of the first aldermen. His was the great silver clasped and cornered Staats-General Bible still preserved, and a will which assigned to six sons a farm apiece totalling 2135 acres as well as other provisions for three daughters. The family life was still Dutch, basically adventurous, but on the surface stolid and orderly. The joys and problems of land ownership and management and family life and Church affairs occupied their time and strength. The Ten Mile Run cemetery near Griggstown has two brown stones bearing in English (mark of the changing cultural conditions) the names of this Dutchman and his Dutch wife each of them "upwards of 80 yrs. old" when they died.

Another Jan, the fifth of that name, lived on the farm at Harlingen inherited from his father. He served on various township committees and did much in the Church. Indeed his father and he—whose parts are not always distinguishable—appear to have been the leading founders and supporters of the Church.

With him enters a tragedy which clearly reveals the strong passions which underlay the orderly and peaceful external life of these early Dutchmen in America. His eldest son, known in the family tradition as Colonel John the Tory, was a magistrate and an officer in the British army. When the dividing axe of the Revolution fell he would not abjure his oath of loyalty. Neither Jan nor John, father

[6]

and son, could agree on a common cause. The father and the rest of the family took the side of resistance to the British. Colonel John, in a stormy interview, returned the farm he had received from his father and went to Nova Scotia, where he served in the British Navy. The tradition is that they never met again—two Dutchmen who saw their duty differently and each loyal to his convictions.

Six men bearing the name of "John Vandike" served in the New Jersey troops in the Revolution and among them was Jan the fifth, a private in Capt. Peter D. Vroom's Company, 2nd Battalion, Somerset County Militia under Colonel Abraham Quick. He and his second son, Frederick, then twenty-seven years old, fought in the Battle of Monmouth June 28, 1778. The son was wounded and the father killed in action in his seventieth year. Thus did the old man bear witness in his body to the conviction that made him disinherit his oldest son. Among the present family heirlooms is part of a gold watch taken from the dead body of Jan the fifth on the battlefield.

Frederick recovered and in December was married to Lydia Cole. He lived at Six Mile Run near New Brunswick. The record is scant, but doubtless like many a soldier home from war, he was happy to lose himself in the affairs of his family, his acres and his town. Of his three sons but one married. This was Frederick Augustus who was the first of the family to go to college and to enter one of the professions. He was graduated from the College of New Jersey in the class of 1812 and for more than 60 years practised medicine in Abington and Philadelphia, "taking a prominent and useful part in the early temperance movement in this country." He married Eliza, daughter of Thomas Anderson of Connecticut. His grandson, Henry van Dyke, wrote of him.

"My grandfather was a leading physician in Philadelphia; a doctor of the old school, with a ruffled shirt and a gold headed cane; a vigorous and determined gentleman who had for his idol in history Napoleon I and for his guide, philosopher and friend in medicine Dr. Benjamin Rush. He continued in robust health until the time of his death in his 86th year, during which year I remember that he took my father and me for a long walk around the family property near New Brunswick, leaving us both thoroughly tired out while he was still fresh as a lark."

The fourth of Frederick Augustus' six sons was Henry Jackson van Dyke born in Abington, Pa., March 2nd, 1822, on the corner of Washington Lane and the Old York Road. His boyhood was spent in his father's country home where he added to his inherited love for rural life and occupations. "The marked traits in his boyish personality (wrote Henry van Dyke in 1892) were physical courage and religious earnestness. There was nothing that he loved more than to ride his father's wildest horse, bare-backed, across the meadows; and the cunning animal soon learned that he could only dismount his young master by running through the orchard under the low-lying branches. But the boy's moral vigor developed no less early than his bodily daring. His religious impressions were profound and real. He united with the church while he was still very young, though neither of his parents were at that time professing Christians." He graduated at the University of Pennsylvania in 1843, after spending one year at Yale; and for two years lived in the family of Mr. David Stewart one of the old charcoal iron founders at Colerain Forge in central Pennsylvania. Young Henry Jackson van Dyke's occupation was preparing the sons of the household for college, but this by no means prevented his acquiring a passionate devotion to trout fishing on the spring fed waters of Spruce Creek. He completed his course at Princeton Seminary in 1845 having studied theology under the Reverend Albert Barnes and Dr. Thomas Brainerd, and immediately settled in the pastorate at Bridgeton, N. J., being married in that year to Henrietta Ashmead, daughter of Thomas Ashmead, Esq., of Philadelphia and his wife Catharine Lehman.

"He travelled all the country roads and lanes through a wide circuit, and hardly a week passed in which he did not go out to hold service in some school or farm-house in a remote settlement. At the same time he was a diligent presbyter, and neglected none of his duties in the general oversight of the Churches."

Early in the young minister's career at Bridgeton he came down with a "rheumatic fever" and was brought to his father's home for care. In a sudden crisis two other doctors were called in to consult and prescribed brandy at once. His father declared violently: "I would rather see him dead than see the accursed stuff pass his lips." Whereupon he turned and left the room knowing that as soon as he was gone the other doctors would give him the dose—which they did.

In 1852 with two little children Henry Jackson van Dyke came to the First Presbyterian Church of Germantown and here was born, November 10, 1852, Henry, baptized Henry Jackson van Dyke, Jr. The sudden death of the two elder sons in rapid succession made the recently installed pastor willing to leave; and in July, 1853, he removed to Brooklyn to the First Presbyterian Church in Remsen Street, where he served with brief interludes until his death in 1891.

Thus Henry van Dyke came into being on his father's side from a long line of solidly Dutch ancestry, "gentlemen farmers" he called them, and "out-door men," of upright and independent conscience, public-spirited and capable but never zealots or reformers, being at heart lovers of life and living chiefly in the private realm which in those days never reached the records. His grandfather and his father in their professional careers showed the same characteristics of stability, forthrightness and vitality.

At the rich dinners accompanied by a generous flow of wit and ebullient spirits with which the New York Knickerbockers of the 1880s and 1890s used to regale the winter nights, Henry van Dyke often spoke of the old Hollanders. The intention was often serious though the mood was that of laughter. On one occasion he perpetrated these lines which he claimed to have overheard in Sleepy Hollow:

A Song of the Typical Dutchman

They sailed from the shores of the Zuyder Zee
  Across the stormy ocean,
To build for the world a new country
  According to their notion:
A land where thought should be free as air,
  And speech be free as water;
Where man to man should be just and fair,
  And Law be Liberty's daughter.

[9]

Chorus

They were brave and kind and of simple mind,
  And the world has need of such men;
So we say with pride, on the father's side,
  That they were typical Dutchmen.

They bought their land in an honest way,
  For the red man was their neighbor;
They farmed it well and made it pay,
  By the increment of labor,
They ate their bread in the sweat o' their brow,
  And smoked their pipes at leisure—
For they said, then, as we say now,
  That the fruit of toil is pleasure.

Chorus

From a plain man's work they would never shirk,
  And the world has need of such men;
So we say with pride, on the father's side,
  That they were typical Dutchmen.

They held their faith without offence,
  And said their prayers on Sunday;
But never could see a scrap of sense
  In hanging a witch on Monday.
They loved their God with a love so true,
  And with a head so level,
That they could afford to love man too,
  And not be afraid of the Devil.

Chorus

They kept their creed in word and deed,
  And the world has need of such men;
So we say with pride, on the father's side,
  That they were typical Dutchmen.

When the English fleet sailed up the bay
  The small Dutch town was taken;
But the Dutchmen there had come to stay,
  Their hold was never shaken.

They could keep right on and work and wait,
   For the freedom of the nation;
And we claim today that New York State
   Is built on a Dutch foundation.

Chorus

   They were solid and strong; they have lasted long,
     And the world has need of such men;
   So we say with pride, on the father's side
     That they were TYPICAL DUTCHMEN.

. . . .

The Ashmead family of which his mother was a daughter, was first represented in this country by John Ashmead, the second of the name, born in Cheltenham, Gloucestershire, England, October 14, 1648, and there identified with the Society of Friends. Townsend Ward writes: "There is an ancient family in Spain, named Ashmede, as I believe the name is spelled there, which is thought by some to be of Moorish origin. Some one has said, the name possibly came from Achmet." Perhaps the ancestors of John Ashmead took refuge in England at the end of the 16th or beginning of the 17th centuries when hundreds of thousands of Moors were expelled from Spain under the edicts of Philip III. However that may be, the latest culture of the Ashmeads with whom we have to do was English.

The third John accumulated a considerable estate in Pennsylvania and built the first stone house in Germantown. His eldest son, the fourth John, died in his 45th year and leaves little on the record. Perhaps his generation was lying fallow for the astonishing activities of the next. For his two sons achieved, the one a career of high adventure, and the other a career of inventive genius.

Captain John, the younger (but in the direct line we are following), took to the sea, and his life is a romance of the first water in the West Indies and in the Far East. One of his adventures when in command of the "Eagle" in the Revolutionary War became a matter of international concern because of his claim that the neutrality of Holland and other aspects of international law were violated by the British. In 1795 Thomas Twining was a passenger from Calcutta on the "India" commanded by Captain John and gives a picture of him that is both rare and revealing: "Everything between the Captain and the officers and the crew (was) conducted in the most good-tempered and amicable manner. The latter enjoyed a degree of comfort which I had never seen on board a ship. Most of the men had a few private stores, and many of them took their tea in small parties about the forecastle. I was not surprised at their indulgence, for I learned, soon after sailing, that the young men whose genteel appearance I had noticed were the sons of respectable families of Philadelphia and Baltimore, who had come to sea under Captain Ashmead for the purpose of being instructed by this experienced seaman, preparatory to their being officers and captains themselves. While this system of harmony and decency was extremely agreeable, I could not perceive that it was less efficient, as regarded the duties of the ship, than the usual vulgar system of offensive severity called discipline. I had been now three months on board the 'India' and had not heard a threat used nor an oath uttered."

Captain John sums up his own career in the epitaph "written by Himself" and published in the *Franklin Gazette* of Baltimore, November 5, 1818:

"In life's hard bustle o'er troubled seas,
Through many a storm, and many a prosperous breeze,
Through summer's heat and winter's chilling blast,
From torrid to the frigid zone I've past.
Through sickly climes where each contagious breath,
Spreads desolation by untimely death:
One hundred voyages, through unnumbered toils,
I've sailed at least five hundred thousand miles;
Been taken, sunk, and oft times cast away,
Yet weathered all in this close port to lay,
Where a dead calm my wearied bark doth find,
Obliged to anchor for the want of wind.
Here, undisturbed, at rest I shall remain,
'Til the last trump calls up all hands again;
And what new perils I shall then go through,
No human reason ever yet could shew:

But the same power who leads through earth and sea,
Will doubtless lead me through eternity."

William, eldest brother of the seafarer, it may be worthy of note, was a great friend of the Indians who came to Philadelphia to present their complaints to the Colonial authorities. He became a noted blacksmith and wagon builder, "at that time one of the most lucrative of occupations rating secondary only to a professional career." He made a "plough with a wrought iron mould, instead of the customary board" which appealed so much to Lafayette that he bought four for his estate. With his son John he originated the famous "Germantown Waggons."

John Ashmead, the sixth of that name and son of Captain John, was born in Philadelphia in 1762, and married Arabella King Ryves in 1782. He was one of the pioneer wall paper manufacturers in this country. His son Thomas married Catharine, fifth daughter of George Lehman, who was a surgeon in the Revolutionary army. One of their children was Henrietta who married Henry Jackson van Dyke and became the mother of Henry van Dyke.

Thus there entered into Henry van Dyke by the devious course of ancestry the strain of blood that was immediately English (perhaps ultimately Spanish and Moorish), and in part German, to be added to the Dutch. Who can analyze the strains of the one blood that is in humanity? And who will pick out the threads of culture that appear in the fabric of life?

Chiefly Dutch and English in blood and tradition the culture into which Henry van Dyke was born was primarily American. Eight generations on his father's and seven on his mother's side had lived in America. The soil and the sea were in their blood and they found life good. But none of all these factors had more influence upon Henry van Dyke than the merry brown bearded, fearless man, whom he delighted to call "the Governor," the serious teacher and counsellor of his boyhood and youth, his inseparable comrade up to full manhood, the constant admiration of his whole life—his father.

Speaking of the determining factors in a man's life Henry van Dyke was accustomed to rank them in rising order of importance as: "first, heredity; second, environment; and third, choice, free-will."

[13]

Chapter Two

THE CHILD AND THE BOY

HENRY VAN DYKE, born in Germantown, Pa., on November 10th, 1852, came into a world of great personalities, well advanced into what is now known as the Victorian Age. Bismarck and Gladstone were beginning to dominate the European scene. Japan was shortly to be opened up to Western influence by Commodore Perry. The steam engine and other inventions were beginning their economic revolution. Europe and America were drawing closer together and the laying of the Atlantic cable was not far off. The Victorian novelists and poets as well as the older English literature was widely read, at least in American homes of culture along the Atlantic seaboard and the influence of Darwin's *Origin of Species* was soon to reach the colleges. The New England School of poets and essayists was in full flower. The United States though geographically huge was still small in population and remained an aggregation of communities until after the Civil War. The census of 1860 shows 41 states with a population of 31½ million; and it was not until May 10, 1869, that the Central Pacific and Union Pacific railroads met to span the continent. It was the beginning of a period of great changes and, in America, of rapid growth in all directions at once.

In the early summer of 1853 the Reverend Henry Jackson van Dyke, with his young wife and only son, Henry (the two older sons, Thomas and Frederick, having just died in their early childhood), removed from Germantown to Brooklyn, to undertake the pastorate of the First Presbyterian Church (Old School) at the corner of Remsen and Clinton Streets. The Church had been without a pastor for several years and was in a run-down condition with a small congregation and heavy financial burdens. The young pastor was a staunch conservative, stern and uncompromising in the pulpit, believing strongly in the dignity of his office but appealing equally to young and old through his ardor and natural human sympathy. He always despised sensational methods and on being twitted with his lack of success in attracting the crowd once replied: "If I were to advertise in the *Eagle* that at my Sunday morning service I would repeat the Lord's Prayer standing on my head in the pulpit, and deliver my sermon in my shirt sleeves, my church would be crowded to the doors, but whom would such a service benefit? Not the congregation—not the minister, and certainly not the Great Master of the human heart, whose promise still holds true that 'where two or three are gathered together in my name, there am I in the midst of them.'" His first six years were years of "an everyday ministry, persistent, patient, unflagging in its noiseless zeal," and resulting in the gradual restoration of the Church to its place among the leading churches of the growing city.

Brooklyn Heights at this time was basically a Dutch village just coming under the influence of the New England invasion, Henry Ward Beecher having begun his famous ministry there in 1847. Conditions at first were simple not to say primitive. As reported in James H. Callender's *Yesterdays on Brooklyn Heights*, Mr. Robert Commelin, a young Scotchman, wrote home on the 14th of October, 1854: "It has been very wet today and in going through the streets of the city you have to wade nearly knee deep in mud; the streets truly are in a very uncivilized state. You can readily believe what Dickens says in regard to pigs. You will see them going about the streets in every direction, especially in Brooklyn, seemingly belonging to no one, and wandering at pleasure, picking up scraps of food here and there."

Many of the institutions which were to play so important a part in the life of Brooklyn were just coming into being: The Athenaeum, the Collegiate and Polytechnic Institute, the Philharmonic Society and the Opera House.

The family life in which Henry van Dyke grew up was simple, intimate, and hospitable. Religion in the personal sense was its centre. Again and again Henry van Dyke throughout his long life spoke and wrote of that period with affection and gratitude. He has described his mother as "a lovely, well-bred and joyous American girl . . . a notable housewife, inheritor of a store of delicious old Philadelphia recipes, with a culinary genius which enabled her to train her own cooks, and a spirit of fine hospitality which made her home delightful to all who visited it,—and the guests were many."

"Through all her cares and toils she kept her youthful spirit and love of fun. . . . Her Bible was her daily companion. She never missed reading her chapter. Of her husband's prowess as a preacher she was rightly proud. She would certainly have gone to church from a sense of duty; but as it was she went with a glow of pleasure. Most prompt and ready in her kindness to the poor and the sick, she was never particularly engaged, so far as I can remember, in large public organizations for beneficence. I cannot recall her serving on committees or presiding at meetings: but she was very busy all the time in doing good to persons in need."

Of her influence he wrote: "It came not so much from what she said as from what she did. Her watchful care kept us in life and health. Her eager interest and fond pride in our work helped all unconsciously to hold us up to the mark."

By common consent and personal influence the father was the head of the household. Of him the wife and mother often spoke in the family circle as "my saint," a phrase no less indicative of her humorous possessiveness than of her womanly veneration. In 1854 Kate, a golden-haired blue eyed daughter was born but in 1857, like the two older children before her she passed from sight. In 1859 Paul was born who with Henry grew up in the Brooklyn home and died in the fulness of years in 1933.

Their father in 1890 dedicated to the two sons his book *The Church, Her Ministry and Sacraments* in these words: "To my two sons, who were the hope of my early manhood, and are the joy and crown of my later years." Of them he used to say with a twinkle in his blue eyes: "Paul was born good, but Henry was saved by grace."

Henry was a sensitive, adventurous—not to say pugnacious, child of light physique, but from the first of dominating will. As an infant he had tempests of rage which were frequently stilled by his father who held him in his arms while he walked quietly about the room. When his infant sister Kate was vaccinated he stood watching with flashing eyes and, as a drop of blood appeared on the baby's arm and she began to cry, he attacked the astonished doctor with concentrated fury.

As a child the scenery of Brooklyn, the bay, the life and the sounds of the streets, deeply affected the impressionable Henry:

"A nurse, whose hateful official relation was mitigated by many amiable personal qualities (she was a rosy Irish girl)—had the happy idea of going now and then for a day off and a breath of fresh air on one of the many ferry-boats that ply the waters of Manhattan. Sometimes she took one of the ordinary ferries that went straight over to New York and back again but more often she chose a longer and more adventurous voyage to Hoboken or Hunter's Point or Staten Island. We would make the trip to and fro several times, but Biddy never paid more than one fare. The other boats we saw were wonderful, especially the big clipper ships—far more numerous then than now. The steam tugs with their bluff, hasty, pushing manners were very attractive, and I wondered why all of them had a gilt eagle instead of a gull on their wheel-house. A little rowboat tossing along the side of the wharves or pushing bravely out to Governor's Island seemed to be full of perilous adventures. But most wonderful of all were the sea-gulls flying and floating all over the rivers and bay.

" 'Do they have gulls in Ireland, Biddy?' 'Sure,' says Biddy, 'an' they do be a hundred toimes bigger an' foiner than these wans. The feather of thim shoines in the sun loike silver an' gowld, an' their eyes is like jools an' they do be flying faster than the ships can sail. If ye was only seein' some of thim rale Irish gulls ye'd think no more of these little wans.' While this reply increases your determination to go to the marvelous Emerald Isle some day, it does not diminish your admiration for the gulls of Manhattan.

"These are memories of old times, the ancient days before the invasion of the English Sparrow; the good old days when orioles and robins still built their nests in Brooklyn trees, and the streets still resounded to the musical cries of the huckster's 'Radishees, new radishees,' or 'Old clo' and bottles, any old clo' to sell'; or 'Shad, O, fresh shad, North River shad.' "

In 1857, following the death of Kate, his father was forced to rest for a year. After a spring and summer alone in Europe, he spent most of the winter quietly with his family in Florida. There is a glimpse of Henry in one of his father's letters from Magnolia:

"My wife is well. Henry flourishes in the sand. He has just returned from a ride in the woods with a beautiful bunch of violets and other wild flowers. Among his new acquaintances are a tame deer and a little donkie about his own age."

On this occasion the journey was made to Jacksonville, the end of the railroad, in a Brown car (the predecessor of the Pullman). "It was," said Henry van Dyke on another journey to Florida seventy years later, "like a box car with bunks; I remember that everybody was impressed with the novelty of being able to lie down while travelling on a train."

When Paul was born in 1859 Henry felt both the dignity and duties of his own years, and greatly enjoyed being allowed occasionally to watch over the sleeping child. Perhaps this sense of responsibility accounts for his sage observation one day when Paul was crying: "He shouldn't have been named Paul," said Henry to the distressed parents, "but Saul,—for he hasn't been converted."

About this time began those unforgettable summer expeditions when his father took Henry away from the nurses and their charges who caught sunfish in the shallows of Lake George and mounting him on his back introduced him to the mysteries of the trout brooks. Thus was established in the boy a lifelong passion which, by the way of many little rivers, Lycoming Creek, the Kaaterskill, the Neversink, Rocky Run, the Pocono and the streams of the Green Mountains and the Adirondacks, developed into one of the most potent influences of his life.

Among the close friends of the van Dykes was the family of Professor Darwin Eaton, a youthful and happy spirit, who was a deacon and elder in Dr. van Dyke's church in Brooklyn, and held the chair of chemistry, astronomy, and mathematics in the Packer Collegiate Institute. Mr. Frank Eaton, the son, writes: "Your father was my junior by about eighteen months, but in our games we were quite equal. For two or three years we exchanged visits very often, playing indoor games, mostly with blocks and soldiers." The family of George L. Nichols were also close friends and neighbors and there began for both Henry and Paul a lifelong friendship with the sons and daughters of that household. Katrina Nichols and Henry van Dyke flying kites from the flat roofs of their Brooklyn homes were drawn into an understanding that was full of grace and meaning for both throughout their lives.

One of the first books read to Henry chiefly by his mother in the way of religious instruction was that old compendium of Bible stories "Line upon Line" of which he wrote many years after-wards: "My interest in the book was much stimulated by my fond belief that its title was 'Lion upon Lion,' and I wondered why the chapter about Daniel was the only one which seemed to come fully up to the promise of the title." Perhaps the form of that memory is a little influenced by literary considerations but it is essentially true in that the boy was by nature romantic and early developed a taste for personal adventure above everything else.

At the age of five his father taught him to read but it was not until his tenth year that he went to school. His first and probably most influential education, then, was obtained in his home. In what did it consist? First of all in the largely unconscious influence of an intimate family life organized around a serious purpose and involving much good conversation with many interesting guests (not that a child understood, but that he felt the purpose and manner of it). Secondly in the habit of reading which he speedily acquired from his father who kept and used a library filled not only with theology but also with poetry and fiction and essays. For five years more or less Henry van Dyke read indiscriminately "books of fairy tales without a moral", various inconsequential Sunday School stories and children's books, *Robinson Crusoe* and, as evidence of precocity, *Don Quixote* and Plutarch's *Lives*; of the last two he writes that they "appeared to me equally historical" and "seemed to open a new world to me, the world of the past." Many a Sunday was shortened by Bunyan's *Holy War* and Livingstone's *Missionary Travels and Researches*. The third element in his education at that time consisted in occasional contacts with an outside world which was somewhat lacking in the gentility he found in his home but which yet exerted a strange fascination over him. The direful hill to Fulton Ferry and the regions around the old farm house on Montague Terrace were his haunts.

"You see that little Henry van Dyke", said an old maid who lived nearby and kept a sequestered watch over the neighborhood boys, "he comes out of the house looking as if he had just been taken from a band-box. He goes back into it looking as if he had been picked out of the ash-can."

About this time Dr. van Dyke was passing into a stormy period of his pastorate. The Civil War issues were pressing upon the people. Abolitionism was rampant in Brooklyn. Dr. van Dyke was not in sympathy with the methods of early abolitionism; and he expressed his opposition with frankness. He did not believe that the Bible condemned slavery as a sin in itself and therefore he would not be forced to say that it was one. He pleaded and argued for the maintenance of the Union. But his position was too honestly democratic to be popularly understood and he received much opposition and some threats for being a pro-slavery and anti-Union man neither of which he ever was. "He always thought slavery was an anachronism and a menace of which the country should rid itself by peaceful means. He could not see in the Constitution any express denial of the right of a state to secede; but he held that the act of secession would be a dreadful and dangerous mistake. He was by conscience and conviction a Union democrat, like Horatio Seymour and George B. McClellan."

In January 1861 Mrs. van Dyke and Mrs. Eaton desiring rest took their two little sons Henry and Frank to Charleston, S. C. Mr. Frank Eaton describes those days:

". . . Of course the civil war was becoming more threatening every day, but that did not affect our boisterous young spirits. We were gay little traitors wearing proudly palmetto cockades, watching excitedly the construction of the famous floating battery, which by means of its porous palmetto logs, was sure to absorb any Yankee cannon balls and render them harmless. We had great sport too kicking football in the upper corridors of the hotel until the Manager ordered us to stop."

[20]

Early in March Dr. van Dyke joined them, coming to deliver the address before the Bible Society of Charleston.

"The first steps of the secession had already been taken when he reached the city, and the flag, with the rattlesnake upon it, was flying over the batteries that bristled around the harbor. The building in which the meeting of the Society was held, was so crowded that the speaker was obliged to enter by the window. He began his speech thus: 'When I accepted this invitation some months ago, I thought I was coming to speak in my native country; but as I sailed up your bay, I saw floating a new flag, with a strange, and not altogether pleasant, device. Before I address you further, I want you to understand distinctly that I, for one, am standing under my own flag, the good old Stars and Stripes.'"

The forthright courage of these words drew a spontaneous burst of applause.

A few days later the van Dykes went on a steamer around the harbor and Henry noted a rowboat filled with turkeys and other provisions lying at one of the wharfs. With a boy's interest in food he asked who it was for and was told that it was going to Major Anderson at Fort Sumter. Looking out in the harbor he saw with childish delight the stars and stripes floating in the breeze over the still silent fort. At Richmond, their next stop, his father was invited to address the Virginia Convention and pleaded eloquently with them not to forsake the Union. Of that heart-rending day Henry remembered only that he had liked "a tall, lean man with a beak like an eagle who took him on his knee and said: "My little man, are you a good Virginian?" "Why no, sir," stammered the confused but honest boy, "I am an American." Afterwards his father told him that the man was Governor Henry A. Wise.

Hardly was the family returned from the South when the fury of the Civil War broke out. Once Dr. van Dyke found himself at home with a mob outside at midnight demanding that he should at once display the flag upon his church and house on peril of death if he refused. Henry was in the room and has often recalled how his father's friends entered with serious mien each laying down his revolver upon the bare dining table. The boy never forgot the clatter of the guns and the look on the faces of the men. And especially he remembered the tones of his father's voice as he pleaded to be allowed to go out on the balcony to address the mob and how finally they had to hold him back while a spokesman dispersed the mob—but obviously not by carrying the message of the outraged and obstinate pastor: "Go tell them that I love my flag too well to hang it out at the bidding of a crowd of rioters."

In the fall Henry was sent with a few other boys to a school conducted by the Reverend L. S. Davison who soon became a vigorous abolitionist. Boys regularly visit the sins of the fathers upon the children and Henry found ample occasion for exercising his natural pugnacity. Often his mother wiped away the blood and bound up the wounds and encouraged him with her faith that he and his father were right. He was held under a stream of water from a street hydrant and "washed" to the point of exhaustion by a gang of boys to the tune of "dirty little democrat." Once he succeeded in knocking two teeth out of the mouth of a boy who called his father a copperhead. Finally Henry was removed by his father and sent to a small school conducted by the Reverend William Cleveland, brother of Grover Cleveland. With him he spent a happy and profitable year.

Of course, all his fight was not against other boys. The seeds of personal religion were stirring within the growing Henry. Being of an imaginative nature he was at one time much troubled by the mysterious fear that he might have committed "the sin against the Holy Ghost". Picture the delicately balanced child of passionate and earnest nature confronted with the harshly expressed theology of the day. It was as if David, before the conquest of the lion and the bear, had been compelled to meet the world's champion Goliath. Even of his adored father it must be confessed that there were those who found him somewhat grim and stern in the pulpit. But perhaps this reveals as all the more intimate the personal relation between this father and son; for Henry, after an inward struggle, went to his father with his problem and was told: "If you fear the sin you can't possibly commit it, for it is through the Holy Ghost that the fear of sin comes. And any sin of which we truly repent is no longer a sin against the Holy Ghost."

Relieved not only by these common-sense words on an appalling mystery, and encouraged by the friendly and affectionate manner always typical of his father in dealing with personal troubles, Henry revived swiftly. But, as always,

> "shades of the prison-house begin to close
> About the growing boy."

He had to win his way out not once, but again and again until his victories became a settled conviction.

When he was about twelve years old he did some childish thing which he felt was "very wicked." When he went to bed at night he lay there thinking of it and suddenly was overwhelmed with the sense of being lost. He tried to think how he could be saved and began to recall Scripture verses. The one that seemed to fit the case was: The blood of Jesus his Son cleanseth us from all sin. He got out of bed and said a little prayer on his knees and such a feeling of peace came over him that he knew he was saved and then and there resolved to hold fast that salvation. It may have been in connection with this incident that the boy wrote some verses which his father preserved with the notation that they were written when Henry was about twelve years old and were copied from his manuscript:

> "Spirit of the mighty Maker,
> Haste on earth to take Thy station,
> Make me of life a true partaker
> Chant the song of Christ's salvation.
>
> "Altho' my sins like scarlet be,
> Has Christ not promised intercession?
> With broken heart I look to thee,
> Oh! Cleanse my soul of all transgression.
>
> "Christ, the captain of our glory,
> For us, he died a cruel death,
> For us, he bore the sweat so gory,
> For us, he died a cruel death.

"Shall then a sacrifice so precious
That never can be sent again
Offered by a God so gracious
Be sent for wicked men in vain?

"Oh! spirit waft God's revelation
Across the great and mighty sea
Tell the news to every nation
Of heavenly bliss and glory free."

It was almost four years later after a prayer meeting in his father's church which had been addressed by Professor Eaton on "Our Responsibility to God" that he found himself ready to speak to his father about becoming a Church member in confirmation of that earlier decision. During those years the father had said nothing directly to him about the matter though he received his son into Church membership with an unaffected joy that indicated he had been watching over him with prayer. Thus simple and natural, but restrained, was the relation between this father and son in the things which both found vital. The root of that relation was comradeship. The branch for the man was joy and hope flowering in affection; for the boy it was admiration and trust also flowering in affection.

Many other things occupied the growing boy. Fishing excursions with his father to the then unpolluted waters of Coney Island Creek and Sheepshead Bay and summer escapades in which he led his younger brother astray; Monday afternoons in winter with his father to visit the old bookshops on Nassau Street and to eat oysters in Fulton Market; more books to read. Those of Captain Mayne Reid and R. M. Ballantyne by his own choice for unrestricted adventure, and Scott and Dickens at his father's suggestion. He never forgot the thrill of his father's reading aloud of Milton's *Comus* in the book-lined study.

At fourteen with the birthday gift of a dollar from a pleasant old lady he made his first purchase of a book. Significantly, for those interested in the smallness of beginnings, this was, at the suggestion of the gentle, lame book seller, a pirated edition of Tennyson's *Enoch Arden.*

In 1863 he saw the Nassau Baseball Club, organized by three Brooklyn boys at Princeton, inflict a crushing defeat upon the Excelsiors of Brooklyn. Many years later he wrote of it: "The Nassaus played good ball and behaved like gentlemen. At that time I discovered that Princeton was the college that I wanted to go to. Since then I have found many additional reasons, but as a matter of fact in chronological order that was the first."

In the fall of 1867 he entered the Brooklyn Collegiate and Polytechnic Institute, "the Poly", definitely to prepare for college. But he was still very much a boy although now to become an ambitious one. All the time that could be garnered from School was spent in self-organized activities. Of course a school in those days had no regular sports or athletic equipment. But the boys arranged baseball games in the open spaces of South Brooklyn, and Henry was a member of the Premier football club "which included such heavy athletes as Seth Low, Bert Mills and Frank Lyman." Between games they engaged in a chronic state of war with "the Micks" who came up from Furnam Street to make raids and forays. The battles always ended with the eternal cry of boyhood: "Wait till we ketch you alone down our street."

In winter there were trips by horse car to the Capitoline Skating Rink beyond Lafayette Avenue, often with the girls for companions. There Henry became a skilful skater, achieving the double Dutch roll, the grape vine, the spread-eagle and the waltz.

Now, too, the growing boy began to take a more mature interest in the girls. He recalls how he noticed through the tall iron railings of the Packer Institute "the supposedly studious maidens pacing demurely around the cast iron fountain or chasing one another along the paths among the flowering shrubs and bushes" and found it "a pleasant sight." The atmosphere in which the boy grew up was culturally that of romanticism. He was in the romantic years of a courtly and worshipful nature. He was in love with love, but though he dreamed he always acted too. There were notes passed through the fence, boy and girl friendships, and every once in a while the general passion burned to a momentary flame when a sacred trout caught in the brooks around Lake George or Elizabethtown was laid upon the breakfast table of a temporary goddess. The boy believed in romance but he also knew that an adventurous spirit and a worshipful attitude were vital parts therein and he acted accordingly. Romance for him lay not in day-dreaming but in action embroidered with feeling and thought after the manner of Sir Walter Scott.

In the spring of 1868 he went on a coaching trip among the Virginia Springs with his father. Four horses drew the coach and among their fellow-travellers were Dr. Moses Hogue, Dr. and Mrs. Basil Gildersleeve and Dr. James H. Brookes. One incident of this trip at White Sulphur made a deep and lasting impression upon the boy. He met what seemed to him "the finest, the most lovable, the most heroic, dignified figure of a man that I had ever seen, with a pointed gray beard and kindly eyes that had in them a smile of love and tenderness, and a face that bore upon itself the mark of suffering and pain." This was General Robert E. Lee who said: "My boy, would you like to have a ride on my horse?" and helped the eager lad to mount *Traveller*. Again and again in later years Henry van Dyke spoke of three men whose personality made vital impressions upon his own: they were, always first and foremost, his father, and then Lee and Tennyson.

With his entrance into the Polytechnic Institute there began to be added to Henry's characteristics of admiration, love of adventure and audacity, that of purposeful ambition. He became an earnest and successful student but never a drudge. To his teachers, the Principal, David H. Cochran, Spencer in Mathematics, Collard in Latin and Greek, Kellogg in English he has paid eloquent tribute. Recalling his schoolboy days he spoke frequently of three priceless gifts received from them: "the desire of knowledge, the power of concentration, the ambition to finish each day's task as well as he could." "Real education is putting a boy in possession of his own powers and giving him a share in the collective wisdom of mankind." But his teachers were not only those who held the formal position. There was his first fishing rod, a true "instrument of edu-

cation" under the direction of his father who "preferred to educate
his child by encouraging him in pursuits which were harmless and
wholesome, rather than by chastising him for practices which would
likely enough never have been thought of, if they had not been
forbidden." There was the first unforgettable two weeks camping
trip and the lessons learned from that famous old Adirondack guide
Sam Dunning and "one-eyed Enos, the last and laziest of the Saranac
Indians." The boy's education in the formal sense was made rich
and effective by his constant attendance upon the school of life.

On the 21st of June, 1869, he graduated from the Poly in the
classical section of his class, delivering an oration on the Patriotism
of Cicero and holding the office of Secretary among his classmates.

Is there not in Henry van Dyke's Lawrenceville Ode of June 11,
1910, "The Spirit of the Everlasting Boy," something truly descriptive of his sensitive, tempestuous but essentially happy boyhood?

> "O spirit of the everlasting boy,
>   Alert, elate,
> And confident that life is good,
> Thou knockest boldly at the gate,
>   In hopeful hardihood,
> Eager to enter and enjoy
>   Thy new estate.
> Through the old house thou runnest everywhere,
> Bringing a breath of folly and fresh air,
> Ready to make a treasure of each toy,
> Or break them all in discontented mood,
>   Fearless of Fate,
> Yet strangely fearful of a comrade's laugh;
> Reckless and timid, hard and sensitive;
> In talk a rebel, full of mocking chaff,
>   At heart devout conservative;
> In love with love, yet hating to be kissed;
>   Inveterate optimist,
>   And judge severe,
> In reason cloudy but in feeling clear;
> Keen critic, ardent hero-worshipper,
> Impatient of restraint in little ways,

Yet ever ready to confer
On chosen leaders boundless power and praise;
Adventurous spirit burning to explore
Untrodden paths where hidden danger lies,
And homesick heart looking with wistful eyes
Through every twilight to a mother's door;
Thou daring, darling, inconsistent boy,
How dull the world would be
Without thy presence, dear barbarian,
And happy lord of high futurity!
Be what thou art, our trouble and our joy,
Our hardest problem and our brightest hope!
And while thine elders lead thee up the slope
Of knowledge, let them learn from teaching thee
That vital joy is part of nature's plan,
And he who keeps the spirit of the boy
Shall gladly grow to be a happy man."

Chapter Three

PRINCETON COLLEGE YEARS

IT WAS a significant and fortunate decision that sent the sixteen-year-old Henry van Dyke to the College of New Jersey in the fall of 1869. His grandfather who was warmly interested also in Rutgers College in his native New Brunswick offered him a house there for his college course if he elected to go to Rutgers. But his father's influence and his own inclination were decisive for Princeton. Doubtless the fact that many of the best young men from the South were accustomed then as now to come to college in Princeton influenced the decision. Also there was the rising influence of President James McCosh who had come the previous year from Queens College, Belfast, and was beginning his distinguished career as a leader of thought and a builder of what he always referred to as "my college". The choice of Princeton was a far-reaching one, both in inner and outward events for Henry, as plainly appears in the record. Until the day of his death Princeton was one of the central passions of his life.

So thorough had been his preparatory work that Dr. Duffield said he could enter the sophomore class, but his youthfulness led his watchful father to enter him as a freshman. At once the young student struck his stride both as a scholar and in the other college activities of his day. His first report dated December 23rd, 1869, gives him an "average standing of 97.9. In a class of 56 members he ranks 2nd." Throughout their course the competition between J. P. Kennedy Bryan, who ranked first, and Simon J. McPherson, who several times divided second place with him, was keen but friendly, "with several others in dangerous proximity". Once the class of '73 (or perhaps one had better say a considerable portion of it) was thrilled when Bryan led with 99.6 and van Dyke and McPherson pressed him with 99.5. But the issue was not one of unrestrained personal ambition for honor. The young men were fast friends and always remained so; they were not without a canny desire to avoid unnecessary competition. In their senior year they put the three scholarship plums in a hat and drew for them, having agreed that it was not worth while to contend with each other. Bryan drew the right to compete for the philosophical prize (which each accounted the most desirable) and eventually won it. McPherson drew the historical, but reasons of health demanded his temporary removal from College. Henry drew and won the literary prize. Evidently their vigorous individualism was tempered with a sense of the need for cooperation.

One of his instructors, F. L. Dalrymple, who was registrar of the college and taught Henry mathematics in freshman year (and who still survives) writes that he "found him, to use one of Dr. McCosh's expressions, an 'apt student'" and that "I can truly say he was held in high esteem by the entire faculty as to both scholarship and deportment." But mathematics (geometry excepted) were always a *bête noir* to Henry and he quickly dropped the subject to concentrate on the classics and English literature and philosophy.

From the beginning he was well received among his class and college mates. The customary autograph-book in which members of each of the graduating classes during his college career wrote messages for him gives many side lights on the vagarious Henry.

A senior from North Carolina writes flowingly for the freshman:

"Your interest in the condition of my afflicted state and country has won for you my highest regards and has taught, or rather confirmed me in the conviction that it is far better for one to look beyond the narrow bounds of state lines, and regard the state of humanity rather than that of mere party.

"And then our ideas of country life—among the wilds and the hills—hunting, fishing, etc., are so very similar that I have always enjoyed conversation with you.

"You have just begun college life and you have begun it well. You

[30]

have taken a stand both in your studies and in the estimation of your friends which is flattering, and my advice would be to continue as you have begun."

Another commending his "industry and ability" adds:

"You do not allow yourself to become so absorbed in the cultivation of your mind as to coop yourself up like a hermit in your cell to the neglect of your bodily health. Your regular attendance upon the exercises in the gymnasium is altogether commendable, though I used to fear that the petticoats in the gallery had a great deal to do with your unremitting devotion to those swinging rings."

By sophomore year the boy had truly begun to find himself in the man. Henry van Dyke has hinted at this in the statement. "I can't remember just when I first read 'Henry Esmond'; perhaps it was about the beginning of sophomore year. But, at all events, it was then that I ceased to love books as a boy and began to love them as a man". Doubtless this development accounts for the outbursts and escapades of that particular year which are gently reflected in the autograph of a senior of '71: "That you may never have reason to regret your college course by misspent time, is my sincere wish." This was the year when Henry was President of his class and a leader in many extra curricula and some sub rosa activities. There was a particularly fine bonfire around the cannon where Olympian thunders and Plutonian gloom of eloquence "shook the arsenal and fulmined over Greece." He joined in an uproarious comedy with four of his college mates and two young ladies in which he acted the part of Timid, a dead shot. He was noted for his "terrible onsets of sarcasm at the table", and for his generally jaunty and audacious bearing. One of his great friends Newell Woolsey Wells, a Brooklyn boy of the Class of '72 wrote to him: "Your prowling qualities as a Night Hawk, your discordant nature as a Mean-Grinnist (a serenading quartette) your thieving propensity as a Ranger are only equalled by your good looks."

Many years later Henry van Dyke wrote to this same friend:

"Vividly return the old days when you and I were fellow students at the Jane Comfort University in Princeton (a boarding house at the corner of Nassau Street and Washington Road) and when the famous literary association known as the Night Hawks was in full bloom. I remember your exploits in the character of Nimrod, and the fat old cook, Caesar, with the little black dog, and the Lady Jane's remarks at table, always friendly but sometimes slightly acidulous. Them was the good days!"

In a college scrap book is found a poster with this legend in large type:

$50 Reward!

The above reward will be paid for the apprehension
and conviction of the person or persons who took
the gate and damaged the fences on the Seminary
and Library grounds.

Geo. T. Olmstead
Treas. Theol. Seminary

Princeton June 20, 1871.

On the margin of it was written, evidently after the lapse of a sufficient interval of safety: "They didn't catch us. H.v.D."

Such was one of the by-products of a serious mind that even to the end remained slightly incorrigible. The event takes its place in the singing traditions of Old Nassau. In the *Carmina Princetoniana* re-published in 1873 appears "The Triangle Song" by H. J. van Dyke '73 to the tune of "Marching through Georgia" one verse of which runs:

Well the old Triangle knew the music of our tread,
How the peaceful Seminole would tremble in his bed!
How the gates were left unhinged, the lamps without a head
While we were marching through Princeton.

But not all the fun was of the extempore night-prowling variety. Although some of these young men took no part in the crop of re-forms then springing up in college, yet they had a feeling for the power of sound ridicule and a few of them at least enjoyed a little horse-play on their serious studies. The sophomore course in English Literature with the text books, Craik's "English of Shakespeare" and March's "Origin and History of the English Language", struck several of them as a dusty and futile affair "refreshed only by an occasional fountain welling from the inexhaustible literary reminiscences and fine critical faculty of our guide and preceptor," Dr. John S. Hart, newly come to the chair of Belles Lettres and English Literature. So they proceeded to enact, as the bills record:

The Funeral Ceremonies
of
the late Julius Caesar
conducted by
The Sophomore Class of P'ton College
VI Kal. Jul. MDCCCLXXI

Personae

Pontifex Maximus (6 ft. 5 in.)
Samuel McLanahan

Gas Blowers

Brutus (Craik)	Samuel Wells
Mark Antony	J. Clarence Conover
Poeta	Henry J. van Dyke

While the body is burning (at Cannon) the bard
will pronounce his poem.

The verses composed and delivered by Henry ran:

Requiem

Canto I

    Here we come, great Caesar mourning,
    Killed by Craik's long notes was he—
    We, our grief and sorrow showing,
    Hither bear his statüe,
    It to burn with Roman customs,
    That his shades at rest may be.

Canto II

    He, great virtues had unnumbered,
    Which immortal Shakespeare sung,
    But by Craik they were up-root-ed,
    With the aid of Saxon tongue;
    With the aid of derivations,
    Which our hearts with grief have wrung.

[33]

Canto III
> May his slumbers ne'er be broken
> By the strife of learned men;
> But in peace and quiet resting,
> Freed from Geo. L. Craik's dull pen
> May his spirit fly to regions
> Where it may have rest again.

The following year under a pseudonym in the *Nassau Literary Magazine*, Henry followed up the horse play with a serious critique of the conduct of the English department. Much of what he wrote is virtually a premonition of his own activities thirty years later in that department of Princeton University:

"Nor have we fared much better during the past session. The course consisted, nominally, of 'Lectures on English Literature,' to be delivered by a gentleman of great learning and fine culture. The course consisted, really, of an interminable column of births, marriages and deaths, interspersed with 'Fancy Sketches', and selections from the 'Indelicacies of the early English Poets.' It gave us no philosophical view of the literature; no critical insight into the authors who came under our notice. It was about as strengthening to the intellect as a diet of very weak tea and very dry toast is to the body. It was necessarily 'crammed' for examination, and left us in the end wholly innocent of any knowledge in the department which it pretended to teach.

"It may be replied that ours is the best course possible under the circumstances. Is it so? Is it then impossible, during four years of study, to give us an insight into English Literature? Literature is 'the result of knowledge, learning, and imagination, preserved in writing.' Must we let these grand 'results' go, and consider only the writing in which they are preserved? Is it too much, for us to wish to be led by some wise and enthusiastic guide among those eternal monuments of Genius which embody the best thought of the English mind? Too much, too long for some brief communion with the intellectual kings and heroes of the race, instead of dallying in the antechamber among the valets and scandal mongers? These are questions, gentlemen of the Trustees and Faculty, which it interests you to answer. They are asked respectfully, but earnestly. We await your reply in a practical form—if it is possible to give us a course in English Literature in any degree adequate to the grandeur of the field,—in any degree adequate to the interest which we feel already exists among the students, only waiting for a spark to kindle it into enthusiasm, for your own sake and for ours, we ask you to give it to us."

Meantime Henry's father and mother and his brother Paul, now a lad of twelve, were by no means out of the picture. There were holidays at home with college friends as guests rejoicing in the mother's household hospitality. His father's fragmentary diary for '71 records on January 30th: "went to Princeton at 9:30, took basket of fruit to Henry. Put weather strips on his windows and door. Staid all night." One sees both the mother's and father's devotion in this most personal care. That Easter vacation Henry divided between a visit to Philadelphia with his mother and a fishing expedition to Smithtown with his father and Paul.

On June 17th his father records "wife and Paul went to Princeton", and on the 19th "wife returned leaving Paul with Henry". Imagine Paul, the quiet boy of gentle manner, never stalwart though always wiry, set down with his self assured and successful elder brother. How his mind on that visit must have been stored with memories of places, events and personalities in the great world of college. Perhaps this was one of the sources of the affectionate regard with which these two always looked upon each other—the elder with that slight tinge of conscious advantage which is the characteristic of elder brothers; the junior with the frank admiration that is the mark of an appreciative younger brother.

The summer passed in fishing from Elizabethtown as a center and ended with a rollicking trip to the lower Ausable Lake and over Mount Marcy and out at Indian Pass.

Versatile, ambitious, often troubled by intellectual questions, frequently restless and not a little affected by matters of the heart Henry entered upon his Junior year. He was conscious of his rapidly growing powers and working manfully to hold the mastery of them. Poetry and the fellowship of his friends, not forgetting the steady and cheerful comradeship of his father, were his chief delights. He and the daughter of one of his professors, a spirited, charming and high-minded young lady spent much time together and apart translating the songs of Heine and learning to know themselves and each other. Henry found satisfaction too in maintaining his scholarship and continuing his exercises with Indian clubs and on the flying rings in the new gymnasium under that fine athletic instructor and inspirer of young men, George Goldie. The life of the Halls in which he was actively concerned from the beginning claimed his attention. He was a representative of Clio in completing with Whig the treaty that debarred secret societies—an achievement dear to the heart of President McCosh. His mind was coming steadily to grips with the leading intellectual question of that time: materialism. That question was not finally settled for him until a number of years later though he found several resting places as he advanced on the long campaign and though the temper of his honest warfare therein ran true to the consecration of his boyhood days.

One of those resting places is pictured in the Junior oration with which he won the third medal:

"The question which must sooner or later meet every man who thinks, a question which must be answered in life if not in words, is, 'What will you do with Materialism?' This is no question for discussion in the cold light of simple reason. It is no abstract problem, no remote speculation. The answer to it must determine the whole motive, and movement of life. It must not come, then, from one side of man's being. The intellectual verdict may be irresistibly favorable. But this is not enough. There is in man a higher tribunal than the intellect. The intuitions of the heart are the links that bind us to those truths which are dearer than life; deny them, trample on them as we may, they are immutable, the eternal bed-rock of faith. By these intuitions, the highest earthly court of appeals, let this new philosophy be tried."

From this he goes on to condemn materialism as a "creed of negations" and to describe its fruits, and concludes:

"What, then, is the judgment which we pronounce upon this proud philosophy, as it stands, clothed in its own teachings, and crowned with its own fruits, before the bar of our inner nature? False, by all the higher intuitions of our being. False, by all the most sacred affections of the heart. False, by all the ties and interests of human society. False, by every yearning of man after the true, the beautiful, the good. False, finally and

[36]

forever, by the voice of Nature within and around us, proclaiming the immortal truth,—God is."

The young orator had taken thus early a stand on ground from which he never retreated though, as we shall see, he was hard pressed for it in 1876. How did he achieve this stand? In terms of external influence two things are worthy of note: The first is the lasting impress that the teaching and personality of President Mc-Cosh made upon him. The President's instruction in the intuitional philosophy and psychology were eagerly followed and absorbed. The pupil was deeply affected by his teacher's steady insistence upon direct intimations in the soul and by his observation that when you step on the bank to watch the flow of your current of thought the river is likely to run differently or perhaps to stop running altogether. In struggling with the problems of thought which Darwinism had raised he found strength in McCosh's declaration that the doctrine of the development of species was not necessarily contrary to religion and that a new apologetic would rise in which the very theories which were denounced as atheistic would become the defense of religion. It may be worthy of note here that in the final examination of senior year in the President's course Henry is marked "100 alone."

The second external factor which influenced Henry in taking the stand indicated in his Junior oration was that of his study and reading of English poetry. Shakespeare, Milton, Keats, Wordsworth, Cowper and, above all, Tennyson he read with delight. His sophomore prize essay on "The Ideal in Art" and his junior prize essay, "Pope and Cowper," contain many indications of that stand. And it is a significant fact that his Junior oration when published in the *Nassau Literary Magazine* was prefaced by these lines from Tennyson's *In Memoriam*

> "A warmth within the breast would melt
> The freezing reason's colder part;
> And, like a man in wrath, the heart
> Stood up and answered, 'I have felt'."

Attempting to look at that stand from the inside two things again seem to account for it: his strong conviction that to be a man was to hold all one's powers in the balanced service of a great ideal; and his discovery that he belonged by nature, training and personal choice, with the artists, the interpreters and enrichers of the mystery of life.

In July 1872 the van Dyke and Eaton families sailed in company to Liverpool. There were walking trips for the sons in England and Germany and Switzerland and family assemblages at convenient points. The Rhine and the Rhône and many lesser rivers received the walkers on their banks. The great organ at Freiburg "the voice of some great spirit that rose and fell, throbbed and died away through the mysterious darkness" deeply stirred the impressionable Henry. They climbed the Rigi, trod the Mer de Glace and walked from Fluelen on the Lake of Lucerne to Interlaken. In an Alpine dawn Henry climbed the Riffelberg to gaze upon Monte Rosa and the Matterhorn. With fascinated eyes he saw through a rift in the early mist: "far, far away, all green and gray and golden in the sunshine and cloud shadows, Italy."

It was a journey of unalloyed delight for Henry, planned no doubt by the wise old heads and youthful hearts of the elders. In articles and verses, in the *Nassau Literary Magazine* of his senior year, foregleams of many later travel-notes, he has recorded that delight. Thus began the journeyings to many parts of the world with which Henry van Dyke refreshed his tireless spirit throughout his life.

In the strength of that food from his European ramble Henry entered vigorously upon his senior year. His chief personal concerns were poetry, to which he was seriously considering devoting his life, the hammering out of his own philosophy, and the development of his power as a speaker.

He wrote two poems in obvious but sincere imitation of the Tennysonian manner; and published a number of verses in the *Nassau Literary Magazine* only one of which he has preserved in his collected poems; probably two others "The Rendezvous" and "The Parting and the Coming Guest" (later published in *The Builders*) were then written; and for a thesis on *The Tempest*, he composed "The Enchanted Island" which bears the following apologetic note: "Will Professor Hart pardon my 'pimpling out into poetry' or rather 'varses'. It wasn't my fault. The subject was irresistible. H. van Dyke." The verses were obviously written in response to an irresistible impulse and so well convey the point of view of their youthful author that they are reproduced here:

The Enchanted Island

An island washed by lapse of sapphire seas,
Whose waters flow beneath a southern sky
Of dazzling depth and richness. Every breeze
That blows is fragrance-filled, from Italy,
Or some warm land where summers never die;
Yet is its languor freshened by the spray
Of crested waves. The clime is endless May.

O'er all, enchantment flings a mystic spell;
Prospero, sitting in his ocean-cave,
Summons the spirits, dainty Ariel
And all his host, to do his bidding grave,
To raise the tempest, or to calm the wave.
Mysterious music falls, strange visions gleam.
They change and fade like figures in a dream.

Miranda,—sweetest wonder of the isle,
My fancy loves to paint thee bright and fair,
In maiden freshness, all untouched by guile;
Thy native grace is free and light as air.
The cool sea-breezes blow thy soft brown hair
Back from a broad, low brow. Thine eyes
Are wide and grey, and changeful as the skies.

Oh! happy tempest that to such a land
As this, and to a maid so wondrous sweet
Carries the Prince! From that deserted strand
Where he was cast, soft music guides his feet
To where she stands. Their glances meet
And as two roses blend in one rich scent
Two hearts in love are at that moment blent.

[39]

The fairy isles of unknown seas
  In modern times have vanished,
The dragon-kept Hesperides
  From modern charts are banished.
Even the school-boy laughs to read
  The myths of olden fable
And wonders if an Ariel's speed
  Were swift as news by Cable—

And yet, while lover's vows are paid,
  While lover's prayers are granted,
So long shall each beloved maid
  Walk in a land enchanted.
The power of love, in every heart,
  Revives the old delusion,
And truth and dreams, with magic art,
  Mingles in sweet confusion.

One of the theses of this year reflects something of the severe struggle through which underneath the outward motion and success of his college career his nature was passing. He writes of Iago as "proud of his subtle intellect," one in whom "the fiery desires of youth have burned themselves to ashes, leaving his soul charred and blackened and bitter . . . At the fountain head of his nature, lies the satanic envy—that passion through which the angels fell, that passion which first stained the earth with human blood, that passion which draws its strength from the master-motive of man's heart, self-love, and fills the springs of life with bitterness and death . . . He will believe nothing better of the world than he knows of himself."

But most revealing of Henry's inner struggle is his Chapel Stage oration entitled, "Drifting", delivered on November 23, 1872. Life, he declares, is not a river bearing all along. It is rather a vast ocean with shifting streams and varying currents, shoals and reefs, in which only a boat with a rudder and a guiding principle can safely navigate. With surprising insight and sympathy he faces the eternal mystery: "There are some shipwrecks in life, at whose contemplation our hearts are touched with purest deepest pity. Who has not dropped a tear over the grave of Robert Burns?

> 'Misled by Fancy's meteor-ray,
> By Passion driven;
> And yet the light that led astray
> Was light from Heaven.' "

And of Chatterton he says "we could almost question the goodness of that Providence which spread the fatal storm and darkness around his youthful life."

From this broad and sympathetic base he moves to his practical conclusion:

"Let no man forget his power over his own destiny. Let no man sit moaning over his fate, but let him arise, and make himself what he would be. Leave to theologians their speculations on the awful mysteries of predestination. Behind that veil we seek not to look. With no vain mournings over the past, with no wild questionings of the future, ——

> 'Act, act in the living present,
> Heart within, and God o'erhead!'

A fixed purpose and a strong will to make it be,—these are the powers that tell in the world. With the whole being consecrated to the great idea that shines starlike on the horizon of the Future, push out boldly into the unknown ocean, and, like that grand old discoverer who set sail four centuries ago, from the shores of Spain into a pathless sea, you shall behold, on the morning of some happy day, a new world rising from the deep."

Small wonder that in looking over some of the papers for use in this biography he wrote on this manuscript:

"Here is the same idea of *Free Will* that I have followed through despite Calvinism. H. v. D. Nov. 17, 1919."

But the mood of a senior year at college is by no means wholly forward-looking. There is the affectionate sentiment with which youth fondly dreams over the far-off events of two or three years ago. There is the delightful experience of feeling free to introduce

[41]

a premeditated explosion in a droning class room. There is the necessity which a healthy young mind knows to make a little fun even of that which is readily acknowledged as noble, "lest one good custom should corrupt the world." Agile youth in its moods is as changeable as Proteus.

With appropriate sentimentality and to a tune as tinkling as an old-fashioned music box Henry van Dyke composes his

Retrospect

"Bright days of my Boyhood, with sad, sweet emotion,
  My spirit turns backward to linger with you. . . .

"Light loves of my Boyhood, swift-winged as the Fairies,
  As seasons glide onward why must you depart? . . .

"Bright hopes of my Boyhood, how soon are you faded,—
  How soon your gay petals are withered and fall! . . .

"Is it wrong for my spirit so fondly to linger,
  Happy days of my Boyhood, in dreaming of you,
While Duty points forward, with stern warning finger,
  And Life's golden moments are fleeting and few?
Ah yet, while the great world comes nearer and nearer,
  And the last year at College is vanishing fast,
The days that are ended seem brighter and dearer:—
  Let me pause for a moment to live in the past."

He does not neglect to stir up a staid session of the President's philosophy class with the debonairly offered assertion that "so far as I am concerned, space is the absence of matter and time the absence of events." He perpetrates anonymously some verses jocosely protesting against the uncoordinated demands of the various professors upon the student's time:

"Ah! little do you know the strange delusion—
Each Prof. thinks his the only branch of knowledge.
Ah! little can you know in what confusion
Our young ideas are taught to shoot at College.

[42]

We're told to read, by way of recreation,
Gibbons and Darwin, Ueberweg and Taine,
Malthus and Reid and Smith, for variation,
Hallam and Butler to relieve the brain.

At nine we have a lecture on Astronomy,
At ten on Kant, Othello at eleven;
We pass from Greek and Latin to Economy,
We turn from studying rocks, to study Heaven. . . .

We feel that all our youthful strength is wasted.
Please place above our early graves this rhyme:
'Here lies a pious youth by "cramming" blasted,
An embryo sage that died for want of time.'"

He writes, with much of that *argumentum ad hominem* of which he was always a master, a reply to one of the college editor's attacks on the custom of conferring "floral offerings" upon the Junior orators. To Henry the custom seemed beautiful because it was a natural expression on the part of the orator's friends. The fact that the offerings could not be equalized and the possibility that they might influence the judges he treated with sarcasm. Henry van Dyke was never in favor of levelling down. He was by nature a leader and not a reformer.

At the opening exercises of Class Day, June 23, 1873, in the Second Presbyterian Church his Class Ode was sung to the air of "We meet 'neath the sounding rafters." Later around the cannon in the intimacy of the class (rendered, as is always unhappily the case, a little self-conscious by an audience), he spoke the part of reception orator to S. C. Wells' presentation. The occasion was hilarious, the idiosyncrasies of classmates were pilloried in a flood of unloosed oratory amid which they were compelled to stand silent receiving into their unwilling hands a symbol of ridicule. The fun was fast and furious and Henry let himself go with a will. In acknowledging the receipt of a pair of bellows for one intending to become a lawyer he even perpetrated a parody of his adored Tennyson:

[43]

"The lawyer bawls in court-house walls,
   Before the terror-stricken jury:
His arms he shakes, fierce gestures makes,
   The verbal cataract pours in fury.
Blow, Bissell, blow, set the wild jurors crying;
Blow, Bissell; answer, jurors, dying, dying, dying.

O hark! O, hear! how faint and queer;
   How very hoarse his voice is growing!
Yet, still he speaks, in husky squeaks,
   And still they tremble at his blowing.
Blow, let us hear the other side replying;
Blow, Bissell; answer, lawyers, lying, lying, lying.

O friends, they lie, and you and I
   Support them in their mad endeavor
To blow their gas, though hours pass,
   And lie forever, and forever.
Blow, Bissell, blow, no matter what you're saying;
And answer, clients, answer, paying, paying, paying."

And to the freshmen he offered this ironic counsel:

"Always reverence the Faculty. They are the incarnation and essence of earthly wisdom. Never apply the rules of common sense to any of their proceedings. They are intuitions. They are not contrary to reason, but above it. They are high, you cannot attain unto them."

Two days later in quite another mood Henry delivered the Belles Lettres oration which best records the serious achievement of his college years. Significantly, he elects to answer in the characters of two men—Goethe and Milton—the question "What are the relations of culture to life? Is intellectual development in itself the loftiest aim of man's existence, or is it but the means to a higher and nobler end?" In an accent always characteristic of him thereafter he declares:

"No vague and lofty generalization can ever equal the strong and immediate logic of a life."

He portrays the many-sided Goethe who worshipped himself and, as apostle of the religion of culture, proclaimed refined enjoyment to be the highest law of life.

"Not wishing the history of so lofty a being to be lost to posterity, he inscribed upon the pedestal an autobiography, which records all the vast events and influences of his life, from an attack of measles to a severe case of platonic affection for his neighbor's wife."

And yet, the young orator scornfully pointed out, this genius remained silent and actionless in the crises of the new Germany. Against this beautiful but craven figure he sets Milton.

". . . No man has attained to a higher degree of learning and mental power than John Milton. During the first thirty years of his life he was surrounded by all the ennobling influences of culture, and he drew from literature, music, and nature an almost feminine grace and refinement. But he never once elevated that Culture into a final end. He never once forgot that he had a place in the world, that he owed a duty to his Maker. And those years of study were but the preparation for the work of life. He stood ready and waiting for the call to action: and when that call came to him, as he was travelling in Italy, it found no tardy response. He says, 'I thought it base to be travelling for pleasure, abroad, while my countrymen were fighting for liberty, at home.'

Hard as it was for him to 'lay aside his singing-robes and embark on a troubled sea of noises and harsh disputes' he could do it, because it was *duty*. He threw himself with all his might into the conflict. He assailed the formalism and corruption of the Church in pamphlet after pamphlet, pouring forth resistless logic, burning scorn, sharp ridicule, crushing invective. He defended the Commonwealth, asserted the rights of the people, shattered the idol of divine tenure, proclaimed the freedom of the press, the liberty of thought. Even after his labors had cost him his sight he still continued. And in those last months of anarchy that followed the death of Cromwell, Milton still wrote with the energy of despair against the Restoration."

"Goethe", he concluded, "stands like a marble statue beautiful, cold, lifeless; Milton like a living man, imperfect, unsymmetrical perhaps, but strong and earnest; and the blows which he struck for Freedom and Truth still ring through the conflict of the ages. Their force can never die, for they helped to carry the banner of the race upward and onward."

Here speaks the essential spirit of Henry van Dyke. The accent and the objective are unmistakable. They are the words of a doer, a true poet.

The *New York Herald* of June 25th reports, "It was an eloquent and artistic effort and was frequently applauded." Henry was beginning to take up the power that he soon learned to wield so masterfully over the many audiences he addressed throughout his life. Perhaps his "eloquent and artistic effort" was achieved through faithful practise on spring evenings in the secluded nooks of Potter's Woods of which he later wrote that "there is one favored spot from which on a propitious evening, one may often hear the mingled eloquence of three speakers, each thundering away unconscious of the others' proximity."

And here it must certainly be recorded that the second classical oration of that Commencement on "The Power of a Dominant Purpose" was given by his classmate William Ward Van Valzah who less than twenty years later played a vital rôle in Henry van Dyke's career.

Not yet twenty-one, Henry was graduated second in scholarship rank to his friend J. P. Kennedy Bryan in a class of seventy-four. At the same time he won the 1859 Prize in English Literature. "Throughout his course," another friend, the Secretary of the class of '73, Dr. J. H. Dulles, has written, "he was a foremost man in the classroom, the gymnasium, and all class and college affairs."

The period of his residence was one of great growth for the college. He had seen the gymnasium, Reunion and Dickinson Halls and the Chancellor Green Library erected and the walls of the new John C. Green School of Science almost completed. McCosh at Princeton, like Eliot at Harvard, White at Cornell, Porter at Yale and Angell at Michigan was building the modern period of higher education in America. "There are now," records the *Nassau Literary Magazine* of June 1872, "368 colleges in the country of which twenty-eight are under State supervision. The whole comprise very nearly 50,000 students. One hundred and fifty-eight instruct males only, while ninety-nine admit males and females."

Of this fresh rising tide in the colleges Henry van Dyke was a part; and in it he himself had grown from a boy to a man. Already winning his way to several of the basic convictions of his career, he had proved himself master of his capacities in the whole life of the college. He was one of the natural leaders who are more interested in life than in any one specialty. His nicknames, Little Van, Uncle Benny, and Little Peacauk reflect the diversity of his nature. College photographs and statistics portray him as a light-boned, well-set youth, five feet, six inches tall and weighing one hundred and twenty-five pounds. His eyes reveal the steady and penetrating look always characteristic of him and his bearing is invariably that of unconscious self-possession.

He had learned much of how to use his bow. On what mark was he now to bend it? It is significant that in answering the class statistics he had left blank the place for recording his intended profession.

Chapter Four

PRINCETON THEOLOGICAL SEMINARY

ALMOST immediately, but perhaps not surprisingly, after his crowded and successful senior year Henry van Dyke began to run into the doldrums. The fresh breeze of college days died out and his sails were not yet filled with the wind of a career. The '73 class orator at Commencement had uttered the plan of cultural salvation on behalf of faculty and students thus:

"We have been taught 'Asia, Europe and North America are the three great stages of humanity in its march through the ages. Asia is the cradle where man passed his infancy under the authority of law, and where he learned his dependence upon a sovereign master. Europe is the school where his youth was trained, where he waxed in strength and knowledge and grew to manhood.' This is the land where he is to apply all that he has learned during the centuries that are gone. Thus it is that our own country is so full of opportunities for doing good."

But in retrospect this must have seemed formal and forensic to a man not yet decided on his course. Besides this was the year of one of the periodic financial panics and of increasing strikes in industry. Dr. van Dyke who in the spring of 1872 had planned to go to the pastorate in Nashville, Tennessee, and had even preached there for two months, was now back in Brooklyn to which he was more attached than he realized. In this he had also been influenced by the necessity that Mrs. van Dyke, then seriously ill, should remain under the care of a physician in New York. Deeply immersed in the difficult financial problems of his church and laboring mightily for the reconciliation of the Northern and Southern Presbyterians, Dr.

van Dyke was passing through a period of great depression. Henry felt keenly that he ought not to be supported by his father and said so to him. Half-heartedly he entered himself in the Columbia Law School, but his real interest was in writing and he did not matriculate. He declared himself ready to do anything at all until he found the way to follow up his basic purpose. In this emergency his father sent him for counsel to President McCosh who offered to recommend him for two things: the principalship of a high school in Cedar Rapids, Iowa, and a tutorship in the household of Henry J. Biddle, Esq. of Philadelphia. On McCosh's advice he applied for the latter and spent a busy and happy year preparing the eldest son for Annapolis and tutoring two younger children.

But this was an interlude, and the young man was eager to get at the shaping of his own future. In the fall of 1874 Dr. James Ormsbee Murray who had just come from the Brick Church to become Dean at Princeton supported his father in urging Henry to enter Princeton Theological Seminary as a preparation either for writing or for the ministry. Henry accepted this advice with the distinct understanding that he had not decided to become a minister and might not do so. Thus entered into the young man's life another wise and kindly man whose counsel on this and later occasions he followed with great profit.

Not yet twenty-two Henry began his studies at Princeton Theological Seminary in early September 1874. Four members of his college class entered with him, but though he found good companionship with them and others of the seminary faculty and students it must be noted that he was looking back somewhat regretfully to the gayer days of college. Like every honest and imaginative youth he felt the struggle involved in going down from the all-inclusive, and variegated moods of culture to concentrate on the basic issues of religion. The artist and the moralist, both of which were so vivid in his nature, had not yet had it determined how they were going to live together in one man. Each insisted on supremacy; the decision was being sought, but it was not yet formulated, much less consolidated in action. Consequently the choice of his career, which he regarded most seriously and insisted on approaching with entirely independent honesty, remained undetermined.

But more important still the motive power of a clear life objective was still wanting. His consecration did not fail, but his mind was deeply involved with the problems of rationalism, materialism, scepticism. And he entered soberly upon the contest with these spectres of the mind. It was not an ultimate and abstract solution that he needed. He never took much interest in dialectics. What he sought was the establishing of a base from which he might freely exercise his already proven abilities. The whole problem expressed itself broadly in the concrete issue: Was he to follow the amorphous career of a writer,—or more specifically of a poet; or the then clearly defined career of a preacher? He did not know; so he left the decision in abeyance and went steadily to work on the specific tasks of the day—Hebrew, and Greek, Old and New Testament and theology and sermon preparation and delivery. Meantime he experimented with his own pen and continued to read widely fiction and poetry and essays.

Evidently he must have underestimated the strain; or perhaps nature thought he would be all the better for a holiday. At any rate early in 1875 "typhoid or brain fever" (how vague but honestly inclusive are the old diagnoses!) necessitated his leaving the Seminary for the balance of the year. It was his first dangerous illness. High strung and slight in physique from an infant, he had passed through several minor childish ailments but had never been seriously ill. Now he must rest. It was typical of him that as soon as a period of care and repose in the Brooklyn home made it possible he set out with three other young men and his brother Paul, then sixteen, on a trip. They went to Jacksonville, Florida, thence to St. Augustine and up the St. John's River where they stayed on an orange plantation owned by a retired Methodist minister. From this base they exercised themselves, after the manner of young men of a sporting nature, chiefly in fishing and hunting. One tale comes down from that day: they had hired an old sloop on Lake George to fish for bass and were suddenly caught in a violent squall with all sails set. At a critical moment on a lee shore the crazy rudder broke and only the fastest action in cutting away one sail and in getting a big oar in position to replace the rudder saved them from certain disaster. Even the memory of the fish caught is obliterated in the vividness of that fateful moment!

Henry returned from this holiday of companionship and adventure restored in health and much revived in spirits. He held his place in his class and began to contribute correspondence and editorials to the influential *Presbyterian*, at a time which can only be described as the heyday of the religious press. The outward events of the next two years were few on the record and in memory. The life of the Seminary was externally serene, even academic. The catalogue says: "complete arrangements are made on the spacious grounds of the Seminary for gymnastic exercises, according to the most approved methods for sedentary men." But Henry was hardly sedentary. He was always interested in athletics: he still swung his Indian clubs and took active part in the ever popular impromptu games of football. On one of his frequent visits to the college he acted as a judge for the '79 crew in the First Annual Regatta of the Boating Association.

Various matters of public interest engaged his attention. He liked to keep abreast of what was going on. He attended some of the Moody and Sankey meetings in Brooklyn, and heard Professor Huxley's first lecture in New York. He went to the Centennial Exposition in Philadelphia and walked across the wires of the still incompleted Brooklyn Bridge. But the significant elements of these years were inward developments and they are well reflected in the poetry, articles and editorials that ran steadily from his eager pen, and in the more fragmentary records of several old notebooks. Among his teachers special mention must be made of the senior professor, Dr. Charles Hodge, of whom he has written: "His cheerful saintly character, his ability as a teacher, and his general wisdom made a profound impression upon me. He used to call me by my first name and give me excellent advice about the combination of loyalty with tolerance."

Theologically and artistically Henry, like his father, was orthodox. He attacked vigorously the "great masters of vituperative theology" who announced their mission "to destroy and spare not orthodoxy, creeds and church organization." "There must be," he wrote of religion, "an underlying basis of deep settled conviction; an organized body of principles, through which the emotional nature may pour its vivifying and energizing force."

With the irony of which he was always a master he comes to the defense of his father whom *The Independent* had attacked for displaying loyalty to the Westminster Standards, and adds a fable:

"A fox of the Congregational persuasion had the misfortune to lose his caudal appendage by an attack of trap; and, as he walked up and down and beheld the magnificent symbols of his Presbyterian relatives, his soul was filled with envy, and he said, 'Why do you adhere to those useless tails? It is far cooler and better to have them frittered away by a licentious interpretation.'"

Henry was a conservative, but even as a young man he could not endure the way in which many revivalists used the oxthodox doctrines upon the tender persons of children:

"It is time for Christian people to understand, and to say clearly and boldly, that any style of exhorting that terrifies little ones into hysterics by way of bringing them into the fold, is both cruel and wicked. The soul of a child is a delicate instrument; O! how slender and sensitive! And I, for one, can see neither wisdom nor righteousness in submitting it to the torturing touch of a rude and untrained hand."

Is there not in another of his editorials, on "The Home-Power," a reminiscence of his own boyhood experience and the evidence of a conviction forming thereon?

"It is enough to say in general, that the work of evangelizing children can be more happily, easily and thoroughly done by example and influence, than by any direct and formal teaching . . . That kind forbearance with the waywardness of youth, that unwavering hope for the future with which the old father has waited and watched by the career of his son, is not a wasted force. Silently, but strongly, like gravitation, its invisible cords hold the boy though all his wanderings, until at last, when the time comes, they draw him back into the paths of righteousness and peace."

To Henry, as to his father, the popular preaching of the day and the conduct of its leading exponents were anathema. Talmage and even Henry Ward Beecher at times, were regarded as distinctly dangerous figures in the Church. But equally the young theologue hated the abstraction from reality so often characteristic of some of the otherwise sound preachers: "Idleness or that over culture of the sensibilities of head and heart, with which elegant leisure is so often employed, produces a character which cannot understand, and therefore despairs and hates the real world."

The sentiment of reverence, the temper of worship, the avoidance of cant and pious profanity, the necessity of doing all things decently and in order in the Church were early typical of Henry van Dyke. He wrote approvingly of the Moody and Sankey meetings, of their obvious sincerity and fervor without false excitement. These men appealed to him as human beings motived by intense sympathy and as preachers of nothing less than the pure gospel. But the controversial preacher he regarded with scorn: "The honest faith of every man is entitled to respect and tender treatment. . . It is better to *convert* than to *controvert*. . . The man of controversy . . . has an uncomfortable habit of wearing his armor all the time."

Henry expresses his convictions about worship in an early editorial. How clearly it foreshadows his work as chairman of the committee that produced *The Book of Common Worship* thirty years later and revised and added to it after another twenty-five years.

"The emotions and actions of the soul in worship must find a sincere and beautiful form. Every element of its conscious relation to God must be honestly and becomingly expressed. The impulse of adoration must temper itself to the principle of reverence, and solemn worship must utter the longings of love, and glow with the fervor of young devotion. To accomplish this end is the one purpose of all the varied forms of divine service which the genius and art of the Church have devised. All true worship must have some ritual, however simple. When the form kills and buries the substance, that is ritualism."

The same idea is approached from the opposite side in one of his earliest sermons:

"Prayer that may rise to Heaven free and untramelled as a soaring bird, or the fountain waters that sparkle upward; prayer that utters itself in the glowing and consecrated language of our fathers in the faith, or prayer that falters from the heart, passes the lips in silence and wings its soft, tremulous flight upward, unheard by human ear to the all-merciful Father: —simple, direct, sincere prayer is the element of true and acceptable worship to God. *Without it,* all our chanted services and solemn litanies are as nothing and less than nothing. *With it* the humblest forms of worship, the most feeble utterance, the poorest places are holy and blessed."

The authentic ring of the later preaching and writing is already apparent in the themes and phraseology of these early sermons and articles:

"True religion is not external. It is vital and intimate. It is as deep as the beating heart that sends out floods of life to all the body; yes deeper; it is in the living will, so deep and central that we can never touch it, analyze it, know what it is, save that it is in us, and that it makes us what we are. True religion is no contagious tumult of the emotions caught from the crowd around us, and the feverish atmosphere of an excited hour. It is something between two only—a resurrection by the power of God; a covenant in the gratitude of man; a life in the consecration of a new purpose. You can never 'get' religion. It must get you, once for all."

How keenly he sensed the danger of spiritual blindness: "If you and I had happened to be passing along one of those country roads in Galilee and chanced to meet Jesus the Nazarene in his common dress, dusty and weary, with his company of fisherman-disciples we might easily have passed them by without a thought."

"To preach Christ," he said on a theme always dear to his soul "is to gather light from every quarter of the wide heavens and pour it upon the central truth that the man Christ Jesus was the Son of God, and that his death is an all-sufficient atonement for sin.

"That is the one truth which all men must perceive. And it matters not what particular ray of light reveals it to us, provided only we really behold it. . . . The arguments are full enough and strong enough to gain the assent of any unprejudiced mind."

And yet he had no hesitation in writing: "No theological terminology is worth preserving at the cost of freedom and popular power. There may be a ritualism of words as well as of ceremonies."

The sermon with the earliest date of preaching found among his papers (October 21, 1875 at Bryn Mawr, Pa.) is on *The Voice of God* with the text "Speak Lord, for thy servant heareth." Here he expresses the two native passions of his soul, for Nature and for personality. He is speaking of the Voice of God in Nature:

"Vague and delicate as strains of half-forgotten music, dim as the first monitions of a former life, are the emotions stirred by the voice of ocean, the sublime silence of the mountains, the circling of the stars . . . And surest of all our blessed Master heard and knew the voice of Nature. How beautifully has he caught its meaning and put it into human words. His teaching is full of poetry gathered from the mountain sides and lake shores of the Holy Land. He touched the lily of the valley and left it clothed in new grace and purity. The fruitful vine, the trees, the lambs, the swift winged birds, the waving grain fields mean to us something more and higher since Jesus has walked among them."

Henry van Dyke was by nature gifted with the pastoral touch and he was advancing in the exercise of it both as a writer and as a preacher. His vigorous and poetical style was constantly directed by a genuine human sympathy. His faith, rigorously orthodox in form, was fighting a mighty battle in the secret recesses of his mind. But as in college and ever after, he believed and practised that a man ought to "consume his own smoke." The old battle between Calvinism and free will was raging again in his mind. It was characteristic of him that he fought that campaign in private. One gets only glimpses of it in the practical conclusions that he uttered. In a sermon at Rocky Hill in December 1875 he said:

"Self examination can never save you, though you should turn your heart inside out until it is all torn and bleeding. Never mind the misgivings and evil thoughts of a morbid imagination. . . if you believe enough to go forward, if you trust Christ enough to obey him, you are safe."

On April 4, 1876, following a full examination, the Presbytery of Brooklyn unanimously licensed him and two other candidates to preach. *The Presbyterian* commenting on it said: "We announce his licensure with special pleasure, for Mr. van Dyke has been for some time a correspondent of our paper, and one of the most constant and acceptable of our editorial contributors. We are sure that if the promise of the past is fulfilled, his will be an honored and useful career."

In early May he went to Baltimore to preach in the First Presbyterian Church. His father before him on his presbyterial duties had been entertained in the home of Andrew Reid, Esq., a rosy Scotch Elder and city merchant. So it was natural that the young preacher was invited to dinner in the home on Mt. Vernon Place. He met the daughters of the household, the elder nearly his own age, and the younger several years her junior. At dinner only the elder was allowed to sit down at table with the young minister. Rumor saith that the younger, not a little rebellious at being excluded, peeked upon the formalities from the stairs. Let us simply observe the delicately impersonal enthusiasm with which a few weeks later the guest adorned the dignified pages of *The Presbyterian* with "Notes from Baltimore." "Standing on the border-line between the North and South, Baltimore blends the qualities of both into a character peculiarly her own. Temper the often over-harsh vitality of a Northern clime with a soft admixture of Southern languor, accent the sharp clearness of Northern speech with the gentler cadences of Southern intonation, mingle the energy and vim of the North with the courtesy and hospitality of the South, and you have that enjoyable compound called Baltimorean."

The van Dyke family now entered upon a busy period. The father's faithful pastoral and presbyterial activities carefully aimed to establish a spirit of reconciliation throughout the troubled Church were crowned by his election as Moderator of the General Assembly of 1876. Meantime Henry had been selected to deliver the Master's Oration in receiving his M. A. from Princeton College. He spoke on "The Allegiance of Culture."

"True culture," he said, "owes allegiance not to beauty, nor to utility; they follow in her train. Her loyalty, her service, her devotion are to truth. By virtue of her relations to truth she holds her power. To discover, to preserve, to impart the true, is the mission of culture to mankind."

Grace and vigor he described as the qualities of a cultured man and argued that in comparison with the culture of the German universities American culture was lacking in vigor.

Visiting the Centennial in Philadelphia in the early summer he wrote upon the contrast between American and French art. The article is of interest as indicating some of the standards on which he was beginning to settle in his own mind the contest between artist and moralist in his nature. He found the French pictures immoral, not so much because of their subjects, as because of the artist's treatment of them; and many of them he found sensational and equally deserving of condemnation.

In contrast with the French treatment and themes as there exhibited he rejoiced in the American pictures, especially in the appearance of a powerful and characteristic school of landscape painting. Thus appears in connection with his college oration on *The Ideal in Art* the clear expression of his theory of esthetics that insists upon the selective nature of genuine art and emphasizes the artist's duty to "elevate humanity." Deride it as the "uplift theory" if you like, at least it represents a standard based on a real view of life. And ever afterward that standard was characteristic of the artistic work of Henry van Dyke.

But summer was coming on and incorrigible fishermen had other matters to attend to. There was a three days' wagon trip jouncing over the rough roads of the Adirondacks. Dr. van Dyke, "the Moderator, a small package with a great deal in it, his venerable beard waving in the wind, and his dignity crowned by a patriarchal felt hat"; Dr. Wm. M. Taylor, "The Domine, brimful of jest and seasonable anecdote"; Mr. T. G. Hunt, "genial and jovial New York merchant"; and "two young sprigs of divinity," Henry and W. H. Miller, "who are commonly believed to travel with Hodge's *Outlines* in one pocket, and *The Presbyterian* in the other" made up the party.

Behold them in an open meadow taking forty pounds of trout on the fly. "If you could have seen the delighted Domine, as he whipped the water with one hand, and fought mosquitoes with the other; or the Moderator, when we were forced fairly to drag him away by the coat tails as night descended; or that young theologue, standing in water up to his knees, with a basketful on his back, a long string of fish in one hand, and his rod in the other, an easy prey to the voracious punkies and flies; if you could have seen this you might have appreciated the fascination with which the piscatory art binds its votaries, and the full meaning of a good day's sport in the Adirondacks."

There followed the rollicking journey of the Troubadours, a band of younger men, W. H. Miller, Charles McMullen, C. S. Lincoln, John Fox, Henry and even including Paul, "Little Coat Tails." By the forks of the Boquet to Beedes, past Ausable Ponds to Panther Gorge, by Lake Tear of the Clouds to the Iron Works, fishing in Calamity Pond, and thence through the Indian Pass to Scotts and back to Elizabethtown, they wended their cheerful way. Their deeds and their characters, are they not hilariously recorded in the book of the *Elizabethtown Post* by the amused father of the last two who welcomed them back to the rocking-chairs and broad piazzas of the Mansion House?

Perhaps the picture his father drew of Henry helps us to see that vagarious young man: "The next is the Warbler, sometimes called *Pea kauk,* owing to the exquisite sweetness of his voice just before rain. He is a very singular, or rather a very plural character. His complexion is that of the cameleon. His mind is like a well, with the truth at the bottom of it. His moods are various as the shade by the light quivering aspen made, and his singing is of a miscellaneous character. The most remarkable feature of his face is a luxuriant moustache that hangs over his ample mouth like the trees on Mount Marcy over Panther Gorge."

Nor was this all. The van Dykes did their fishing and camping thoroughly. Late August found them in "Hash Camp" on Ampersand Lake with Allan Marquand, Henry Marquand, and James C. Spence. And Henry turned the tables with a picture of his father for the *Post:*

"The Governor is undoubtedly the most important individual in the party. He has the most piratical beard, the shabbiest felt hat, the loudest yell, the biggest head, and the most fluent tongue in the country. He knows what he wants, and he knows how to get it.

He can make a camp more comfortable than any man in the woods. He can spin a long yarn without taking breath. His personal appearance is imposing. Could you see him late at night, as he stands by the fire, in his suit of red-flannel bed-clothes, his venerable head crowned with a white cotton night-cap, you would agree that he is ornamental. He is also useful. We shall not now specify how, further than to say that we have almost perfected arrangements for lighting the camp by gas, in which the Governor is to play the most important part. We have reason to believe that the flow will be constant. It is only necessary to attach a pipe."

These two inseparable companions regarded each other not only with admiring and affectionate eyes but also with the eye of keen and amused appraisal.

In a more serious article Dr. van Dyke (doubtless after observation of these particular young men) wrote on his return. "The time is coming, and now is, when the name of hunter and fisherman will not be considered inconsistent with that of Christian. Indeed, if we mistake not, the whole subject of sports and pastimes needs to be reconsidered, and settled upon a more consistent basis than that which our pious ancestors arbitrarily erected into a test of religion, if we would preserve the physical and mental health of our young people, and secure their allegiance to the church. We must recognize the distinction between total abstinence and temperance in things indifferent. We must not discard the moderate use of innocent amusements because drones and mere pleasure-seekers waste life in their pursuit. . . . More boys in proportion are killed by being coddled at home than ever were drowned or shot or eaten alive by mosquitoes in the woods. More young men are seduced to ruin by effeminate sentimentalism and carpet knight-errantry and the mammon-worship of our great cities, than ever were hardened in heart by the supposed cruelty of field sports. If the State of New York would preserve this whole region as a public hunting-ground, it would be a grand college of physical, mental, and moral culture, for ministers, lawyers, merchants, and overwrought students of every class."

Sermons as well as fishing tackle always had a place in the luggage of father and son and both of them are recorded as preaching here and there on their rambles. Fishing for men or for trout was natural to them. It was part of their religion.

Much restored by these excursions Henry returned to his studies and took up the intellectual problem which he had laid down for a time. Perhaps this was the time when he wrote the undated and unpublished verses, "The Isles of Rest" which conclude:

"So in Life's voyage to the Sea
Through toil and tumult, God will give
Sweet places of tranquillity,
That make it worth the while to live.
And thou, when such a time is come,
Rest and be thankful. Learn to say,
'This is a foretaste of my Home,
Towards which I'm drifting even today.'"

Here is a note of deeper maturity than that which found expression in the more militant but youthful oration of his college course on *Drifting*.

Fragmentary notebooks with quotations from a wide reading and with his own observations as well as a number of verses, published and unpublished, hint at the inner conflict of the three years since college graduation. Of that conflict he spoke but once and briefly (to me) and only one document bearing directly on it can be found. Poet as he was, Henry van Dyke never wore his heart upon his sleeve. His own problems were fought out alone and were mentioned only in the confessional of friendship. For the rest they were absorbed into the material for a growing sympathy with mankind.

Two quotations in his notebook, the first from Shakespeare and the other from Wordsworth reveal the temper of his mind in this and later struggles:

"Rightly to be great,
Is not to stir without great argument,
But greatly to find quarrel in a straw
When honour's at the stake."

and:

> "Happy is he who caring not for Pope,
> Consul or King can sound himself to know
> The destiny of man, and live in hope."

With the exception of four lyrics, *Wings of a Dove*, *The Fall of the Leaves*, *A Snow Song*, and *Transformation* which are in his Collected Poems, the verses of these days are unpublished. They are not good poetry (and he knew it) but they do portray the confused state of his thought and feeling. They are melancholy reading.

Some time, probably in the early winter of 1876, the crisis broke in Henry's mind. He found himself deprived of his faith in free-will. Curiously enough it was not before the stone wall of the abstractions of Calvinism that his mind faltered. It was his observation of human conduct, including his own, that led him to this very temporary conclusion. He sat down and wrote: "The Practice of Philosophy, Being a letter to the President of —— College from a quondam pupil, who finds it difficult to reconcile his theory of life with his manner of living." In it he declared that as a practical matter there seems to be no universal regulative belief supporting the doctrine of mind as an immaterial essence distinct from and superior to the machinery of the nerves and muscles and intuitionally recognized; and supported this thesis by four observations: 1, that young men choose their occupations for pecuniary reasons. 2, that men work, but chiefly for the increase of luxury. 3, that in the fundamental institution of society, marriage, the senses rule. 4, that in the amusements of society we see most plainly the instinctive homage which man pays to the body over the mind.

The letter concluded: "If indeed there be such a thing as a spirit distinct in its nature from the body, it is the lower, not the higher factor, the slave, not the queen."

Is not this precisely the conclusion of the realistic school of writers sixty years later? But for Henry it was not a conclusion; it was merely a mood evidencing the reality of his battle with the spectres of the mind. The letter was never sent to President McCosh. "I kept it, that was much better," said Henry van Dyke with a twinkle

[61]

in his eye when telling me about it fifty years afterwards. And this was quite true, for the only trace of this bitter struggle to be found in later years is his clear recognition of the mutual influence of body and mind when dealing with problems of his own or of other people.

Meanwhile the formulation of his misgivings was a relief—as so often to a troubled soul. And doubtless the deciding factors in his determination not to send the letter were his personal unwillingness to shape his life on a negative conclusion and his realization that, like many another youth, he might have exaggerated the importance of his own limited observations especially the *ex parte* views of a young bachelor upon the marriages of his friends. Something of the tension of the experience remained with him for a while and is reflected in the ironical and polemical note that occasionally peppered his writings—though it should be recorded also that that note was more or less characteristic of the day.

Henry was certainly not one to mourn or brood for long. He was for action and threw himself vigorously into his formal studies and his activities in the church world. He published an open letter to Professor Huxley accusing him of *ignorance* in assuming only three hypotheses respecting the past history of nature; of *insincerity* in identifying the traditional interpretation of the first chapter of Genesis with the Miltonic hypothesis; and of *arrogance* in taking for granted that the various interpretations of Genesis invalidate its witness while at the same time claiming infallibility for the doctrines of science which are notoriously changeable. He wrote sarcastically of "The Inconvenience of Dying a Theosophist" and of "Lenten Soup"; and he made some acute observations on the future of the Protestant Churches. Speaking of Dr. Schaff's plan for the recognition of all creeds in their relative aspects as a way to intercommunion, he called attention to "the exclusive claims deeply imbedded" in many of the creeds and declared: "The change if it comes must come spontaneously within each church; and the free union must be a result, rather than a cause." In another editorial contribution he wrote: "Doubtless, when the mission of the Protestant denominations, which is the many-sided development and propagation of Christian doctrine, is effected, they in their turn will give way to a higher form of religious life."

From his lofty and perilous stance on the slat-covered wires of the incomplete Brooklyn bridge he cast his eye upon Brooklyn plentifully besprinkled with steeples, and then upon New York. With no premonition of what would happen in a scant six years he wrote:

"With the exception of Trinity we hardly see a steeple until we look up-town. There they are plenty, especially on that sacred belt of land which has become the rallying place of fashionable congregations, where they meet in the rivalry of buildings and debts, as fashionable ladies meet in the rivalry of bonnets. They know a somewhat disagreeable version of 'Hold the Fort' up in that neighborhood, particularly when their guns are spiked with mortgages, and their nearest rival has opened fire with a double-barrelled choir.

Enough, cynical moralist, enough! Stay the flow of your misanthropic reflections, and feed in silence on the wonderful beauty of this sight. . . . Look over these populous cities, thronging with life; recall the manifold works of art with which they are filled, the temples of science and industry, the various contrivances to protect and sustain life in the inhabitants from day to day; and tell me if you can believe that all these marvellous constructions are the effect of nothing more than the blind, mechanical movements of gray matter, in the brains of little animals hardly six feet high!"

Three times during the year Henry went to Baltimore—to preach in the First Church, of course, but also to visit the Mt. Vernon place household and to see the brown-eyed maiden who demurely, in the fashion of the day, was reading all the novels of Scott, and, at least in consonance with the young minister's interest, not a little of the poetry of Mr. Tennyson. He preached elsewhere, in the Congregational Church at Newport, in the West Side Presbyterian Church at Buffalo, in the Third Presbyterian Church at Indianapolis, where he renewed his boyhood friendship with Frank Eaton, and in the Presbyterian Church at Emsworth, Pa.

At the end of April, 1877, Henry was graduated from the Princeton Theological Seminary but was still undecided as to his career.

He had received several calls to small churches but experienced no specific calling to accept any of them. His father, returning from a peace mission to the Southern Presbyterian churches with Dr. John C. Backus and William Earle Dodge, looked at his son with an understanding and sympathetic eye and offered to pay half his expenses for a year of graduate study in Germany. The idea appealed greatly to Henry, already an ardent admirer of the vigor of German scholarship; but he was doubtful whether duty demanded his acceptance of one of the Church calls he had received. In this dilemma he went to consult the venerable Dr. Charles Hodge who heard him patiently and then pushed his spectacles back on his ample forehead and said in his benevolent manner: "Well, Henry, I should advise Germany—and drink plenty of beer and come back about twice as big around the middle."

So the decision was made. Dorner, Bernhard Weiss, and Grimm were the names that drew him to Berlin.

Chapter Five

SCOTLAND, THE UNIVERSITY OF BERLIN AND EUROPE

IT WAS a full and cheerful shipload that sailed on the 4,000 ton S.S. Bolivia for Glasgow on June 16, 1877. A large number of the passengers like Dr. van Dyke were going as delegates from the various Presbyterian Churches to the First General Presbyterian Council to be held in Edinburgh. They were a distinguished lot but many had their families with them, including a full complement of youth, and all looked upon the voyage as a holiday.

"All the clergy on board the ship were boys together," writes one who made the voyage as a girl, "and from the venerable Dr. William S. Plummer to young Francis L. Patton, they were a jolly band."

Henry in his correspondence to *The Presbyterian* records the trial of Dr. Yeomans who was caught making sketches of the picturesque pilgrims and

"hailed before a court in which Dr. van Dyke sat as Radamanthus, and Dr. Archy Hodge was appointed to persecute the offender beyond the utmost limits of the law. He was charged with violation of the second commandment, with gross libels on his ministerial brethren, with heretical views in pictorial theology, and finally with having been seen by all the ship's company more than 'half seas over.' The most strenuous efforts were made to secure conviction; but through the skilful advocacy of Professor Patton, who proved in spite of the facts, that the sketches were not likenesses of anything in heaven above, or in the earth beneath, or in the waters under the earth, the prisoner was acquitted, with the decision which has become so familiar in our ecclesiastical courts, 'Not guilty, but don't do it again.'"

The young people had their own particular brand of fun in the nature of practical jokes, though Henry

"kept to himself a good deal, and was very sparing of his attentions, much to the aggravation of the young ladies, but he always joined the group when the boys played their pranks on us, and especially when the gong for meals sounded, and they would crowd the stairways to prevent our passing."

Five years later Mrs. Daniel J. Holden, who has written me her personal recollections of the voyage, was decorously welcoming Henry van Dyke at the conclusion of his first sermon as newly installed pastor of the Brick Church. The proprieties of the moment were suddenly suspended when he addressed her confidentially: "See here, if you won't tell on me, I won't tell on you."

They were dignified in those days; but even the young occasionally forgot to be serious.

Arriving in Glasgow four days before the Council opened, Dr. van Dyke went on to Edinburgh to help prepare for the meetings, while Henry set out for a tramp in the Trossacks,

> "Land of brown heath and shaggy wood,
> Land of the mountain and the flood."

His stanzas *Roslin and Hawthornden*, first printed in the Edinburgh *Daily Review* on July 10th, were composed on this walk. Pure and simple intensity marks both the religious feeling and the poetic expression of the lines.

From Edinburgh he and his father under the pseudonyms of Timon and Augustin wrote to *The Presbyterian* two illuminating letters about this first Pan-Presbyterian Council. It was a significant gathering, "three hundred and thirty-three delegates, from forty-nine different churches, with an aggregate of twenty-one thousand congregations, in twenty-five different countries," which gave distinct expression to the spiritual unity of the Church. The address of Dr. van Dyke as reported in the Edinburgh *Daily Review* deserves mention here for its vigorous statement:

"Whilst in one sense Presbyterianism was a republic, in the highest

[66]

sense it was not a republic, but an absolute monarchy with the Lord Jesus Christ on the throne," and for its liberal declaration that "the ministers of Jesus Christ must be ready to answer all questions which come up in the human heart."

Incidentally, speaking of the great literature of the English tongue which belonged as much to America as to Great Britain, he said that, although America had stolen much of it by the unrighteous refusal to establish an international copyright law, yet if his British hearers would be patient it would be repaid. One cannot help wondering, in view of later events, what young Henry was thinking as his father spoke.

There followed, inevitably for the van Dykes, a journey among the wild Hebrides. Chancellor Howard Crosby of New York University was the father's companion. And Paul trudged beside Henry. But the latter's chief companion, as he has recorded, was the romantic vision of Sheila that filled the air as he read William Black's *A Princess of Thule*.

"It was Sheila's dark-blue dress and sailor hat with the white feather that we looked for as we loafed through the streets of Stornoway, that quaint metropolis of the herring-trade, where strings of fish alternated with boxes of flowers in the windows, and handfuls of fish were spread upon the roofs to dry just as the sliced apples are exposed upon the kitchen-sheds of New England in September, and dark-haired women were carrying great creels of fish on their shoulders, and groups of sunburned men were smoking among the fishing-boats on the beach and talking about fish, and seagulls were floating over the houses with their heads turning from side to side and their bright eyes peering everywhere for unconsidered trifles of fish, and the whole atmosphere of the place, physical, mental, and moral, was pervaded with fish. It was Sheila's soft, sing-song Highland speech that we heard through the long, luminous twilight in the pauses of that friendly chat on the balcony of the little inn where a good fortune brought us acquainted with Sam Bough, the mellow Edinburgh painter. It was Sheila's low sweet brow, and long black eyelashes, and tender blue eyes, that we saw before us as we loitered over the open moorland, a far-rolling sea of brown billows, reddened with patches of bell-heather, and brightened here and there with little lakes lying wide open to the sky. And were not these peat-cutters, with the big baskets on their backs, walking in silhouette along the ridges, the people that Sheila loved and tried to help; and were not these crofters' cottages with thatched roofs, like beehives, blending almost imperceptibly with the landscape, the dwellings into which she planned to introduce the luxury of windows; and were not these Standing Stones of Callernish, huge tombstones of a vanished religion, the roofless temple from which the Druids paid their westernmost adoration to the setting sun as he sank into the Atlantic—was not this the place where Sheila picked the bunch of wild flowers and gave it to her lover? There is nothing in history, I am sure, half so real to us as some of the things in fiction. The influence of an event upon our character is little affected by considerations as to whether or not it ever happened."

The young probationer in theology preached in the Established Kirk but only after the senior Elder had arranged with his father for certain precautions:

"Ah'm not saying that the young man will not be orthodox—ahem! But ye know, sir, in the Kirk, we are not using hymns, but just the pure Psawms of Daffit, in the meetrical fairsion. And ye know, sir, they are ferry tifficult in the reating, whatefer, for a young man, and one that iss a stranger. And if his father will just be coming with him in the pulpit, *to see that nothing iss said amiss, that will be ferry comforting to the congregation."*

Here too Henry took his first salmon:

". . . at last we found a salmon that knew even less about the niceties of salmon-fishing than I did. He seized the fly firmly, before I could pull it away, and then, in a moment, I found myself attached to a creature with the strength of a whale and the agility of a flying-fish. He led me rushing up and down the bank like a madman. He played on the surface like a whirlwind, and sulked at the bottom like a stone. He meditated, with ominous delay, in the middle of the deepest pool, and then, darting across the river, flung himself clean out of water and landed far upon the green turf of the opposite shore. My heart melted like a snowflake in the sea, and I thought that I had lost him forever. But he rolled quietly back into the water with the hook still set in his nose. A few minutes afterwards I brought him within reach of the gaff, and my first salmon was glittering on the grass beside me."

[68]

In late August he and his friend, Allan Marquand, left for Germany. His father writing from Edinburgh (and later from Brooklyn to which he shortly returned), began a long series of affectionate and beautiful letters to his son which the latter carefully preserved all his life. They are the exquisite expression of what is perhaps the most significant as well as the most difficult of all human relations:

"I envy you," he wrote, "the freshness and impressibility of your youth—: no I do not envy but I cannot avoid an undefinable sadness when I think that our difference of age necessarily puts a gulf between us. I wish I were your brother and not your father; and then we would go and grow together. Sed Domini voluntas fiat."

The young men, studying German, went to Heidelberg for several weeks and then wandered through the streets and museums of Munich. At Nurnberg they visited the grave of Dürer; and, as old camping companions, tramped and fished in the Tyrol.

"Your tour through these new mountains must have been very enjoyable," wrote the father to Henry. "Those trout must have brought many an old familiar stream and springhole before you. I can see you 'in my mind's eye, Horatio,' with that Tyrolean oleander in your hat."

In the late autumn they went to Berlin and settled down for the winter's work being among the forty-two Americans of the 2,834 matriculated students of the University.

Henry was there to study New Testament criticism and Christology under Dorner and Bernhard Weiss but he not only followed their teaching assiduously, his artistic interests led him to follow also the teaching of Herman Grimm and to strike up a lasting friendship with him. The *Kulturkampf* was then in progress. Rome and Prussia struggled for control of the educational system. The popular idol of the university was Heinrich von Treitschke and, inevitably, Henry attended a number of his fiery and eloquent lectures. Henry's full correspondence to *The Presbyterian* and occasionally to others of the religious press bear testimony to his keenness as an observer and commentator on the current scene.

His early impression of Berlin is recorded:

"In two things Berlin is apparently without an equal,—soldiers on the

[69]

streets and statues on the housetops. The overwhelming ubiquity of the Prussian officer has, so far as I know, only one parallel, and that is in the general diffusion of caraway seeds in German bread . . . With respect to the lofty statues, there is reason to be thankful that an architectural fashion has spared our age from a closer view of these fearfully and wonderfully made figures. I stood in the broad, open square in front of the University the other day, and counted 70 life-size, but far from life-like, statues, poised in various attitudes of perilous awkwardness on the edges of the neighboring roofs."

He wrote of the clash between Haeckel and Virchow over the teaching of the development theory; of the religious outlook in Germany, bearing witness to his delight in intercourse with Dorner, "the kindly, unassuming scholar who stands probably at the head of living theologians"; and very fully of the Church conflict in Prussia. The study of the rising tide of Social Democracy—"half a million of men voted the social democratic ticket at the last election"— claimed his attention. He described German university student life and defended American athletic customs. "College sports as such," he said scornfully, "are practically unknown. Beer drinking and duelling are the only characteristic amusements."

His father watching and praying from afar wrote:

"I am afraid you are working harder than you need to do, or than is good for you. The object of your year abroad was not strictly study but health, recreation and general improvement. Don't go too deep into theology. Give philosophy a wide berth, and take German and literature as a sponge does water, by absorption. Try to come back fat and strong."

And again:

"This will be to you a most profitable year. Only don't forget to study Christology in the heart as well as in the head. Only one thing has kept me from shipwreck—*loyalty to Christ*."

To this advice Henry was by no means indifferent. Was it not given by the man whom he admired above all in the world? And yet his insatiable mind demanded of him the grasping of all knowledge within reach. And his nature insisted that where things were going on there must he be.

[70]

From the dinning of the tumultuous world upon his sensibilities Henry found relief, not only in his studies and visits with "the saintly Dorner, the sagacious Bernhard Weiss, the broad-minded Herman Grimm" whom he has called "the inheritors of Kant and Lessing and Goethe and Schiller," but also in companionship with his fellow students; in the services of the American Chapel, in which he and several others frequently preached; and above all in the hospitable home of Dr. and Mrs. Joseph P. Thompson. Henry's lodgings were just across the tree-shaded canal of the Potsdamerstrasse beside which dwelt this large-hearted and understanding couple. With Dr. Thompson he discussed the world of thought and of affairs and enjoyed the exploration of a carefully selected personal library. Mrs. Thompson offered him the rare and beautiful double gift, the attraction of a wise elder sister and the subtle guidance of a womanly mother. One sees again the dashing young man coming and going in that household in an atmosphere of lively stories and horrific puns, or more soberly cracking some metaphysical nut or chasing the derivation and meanings of words in the dictionary or enjoying a bite of supper after an evening's work. This experience was one of those draughts of natural culture irradiated by personality that makes the cup of life satisfying for any young man.

His father wrote him on Christmas day:

"This is the first Christmas in twenty-five years that our little family have not been together. We tried to keep up the old forms and have something like the old row in the morning. Paul and I had a pillow fight and presents were exchanged. But still it was not what it used to be and what I hope it will be yet again."

The dilatory Paul after his return to college wrote:

"I had a very good time during the holidays although we missed you *awfully*. We none of us cared to dress the rooms with green because you were not there to do it as you have always done. I think I realized more than I have before how far you were from us. However we comforted ourselves with the thought that half of your stay is over."

A couple of his mother's letters are found full of news of the Brooklyn neighborhood and little personal touches. She hopes he is not smoking too much; she loves the word pictures of his letters "they are so vivid and have such a charm about them"; she thinks a flower in his buttonhole must have looked so "refined and delicate" on some occasion. "What would I give," she exclaims with motherly pride, "for your education."

Through the dark of a northern winter Henry gave himself eagerly to his studies. The kenosis theory took a strong hold on his Christological thinking,—a hold which it always retained. He was thinking seriously of the ministry for his career and inclining more towards it. His father's letters follow him closely: "Keep your heart right and true towards God and all other things will regulate themselves in time. You are entering the ministry at a time when there will be need for clear and positive opinions. The negative preaching and the no-matter-what-you-believe philosophy of the past twenty-five years have raised up a crop of infidelity which we are beginning to reap."

"I do not wonder that you have doubts and misgivings about your fitness for the pastoral office. 'For who is sufficient for these things?' But I am very sure that apart from the question of your *calling* and *ultimate life work*, the very thing you need to *complete your education* is a few years of pastoral experience."

He answers Henry's questions about rationalism:

"I think we need more *rationalizing* in the interpretation and appreciation of the Gospel, in *this* sense, we need to show more clearly than most of the current evangelical preaching does that revealed religion is not contrary to, nor aside from, but supplemental to natural religion. The scriptures assume the light of Nature and the testimony of human consciousness and interpret both. The Gospel provides for the felt wants of men . . . The *pulpit* is your throne, and *preaching* is the sceptre God has put into your hand. Few men have had so long, and in all outward things, so advantageous a preparation for it, as you have had; and not many have made a better improvement of their opportunities. In nothing has God more bountifully answered my prayers."

In the spring vacation Henry went down to Italy into which he had gazed with dreaming eyes through the dawn mists on the Riffelberg six years before. He and Allan Marquand delighted their souls among the scenes of ancient history, vivified the knowledge and allusions of their studies; and, under the guidance of his companion, Henry learned to appreciate the old masters. From Henry's notes we get a picture of their pilgrimage. In Verona they sought "the house of the Capulets, and tried to imagine the splendor of the feast, and the impassioned tenderness of the lovers' stolen interview on the balcony. But the house was gloomy and dilapidated; there was no garden; and in the doorway of the court sat a withered, dingy crone, selling roasted chestnuts." They climbed to the topmost circle of the amphitheatre and basked in the sun watching the quick-darting lizards on the stones or the clouds drifting overhead and occasionally trying to recapture the days of Diocletian. In Bologna they gazed upon "Raphael's adorable St. Cecilia" and in Florence sought to live again with Savonarola in the Cathedral. Perhaps Rome made the deepest mark on the impressionable youths.

"Rome is not one city, but manifold; a Rome of ruins, a Rome of churches, a Rome of pictures and statues, and a living Rome of today. These cities are not divided from each other by any lines or demarcations. They are piled one above the other, mixed together inextricably. The fragments of an ancient ruin have been built by some long dead architect into a structure which has in turn crumbled into ruins; and these ruins have again been plundered for a new building, and so on, until at last we find the columns of heathen temples supporting the roofs of Christian churches, and the stones of an Emperor's palace heaped together to make the beggar's hut. If there should ever come an architectural Resurrection Day, what a wild confusion and strife there would be between the buildings of different ages as to the true proprietorship of the stony limbs which have been attached to so many bodies! . . ."

Present-day aspects of life struck Henry. He wrote of the lottery and of the Ghetto. He was especially charmed by the manners and customs of the people: "They are so quick, so pleasant, so facile; the children are so pretty, with their dark, soft eyes and gleaming teeth; one sees so many signs of happy, affectionate life among the

[73]

very lowest classes, that it is easy to believe there must be noble and admirable qualities in the race."

Back in Berlin again he put the finishing touches to his year's work. Already his studies were settling him to a vigorously Christ-tocentric theology. He was at work upon the translation of an article by Bernhard Weiss on "The Life of Jesus and Modern Criticism" which was published in the fall in *The Contemporary Review*. The article defended the historicity of the Gospel of John and stressed its importance in the understanding of the synoptics—a position in which its translator often said he heartily concurred.

In June two attempts were made against the life of the old Emperor William. Once Henry was but a short distance away strolling with a Sunday afternoon crowd along Unter den Linden. He wrote vivid accounts of it for the secular and religious press in America expressing great indignation for the crime. As he put it in a sermon about a year later:

"There is probably no sovereign in the world more famed and honourable than William, King of Prussia and Emperor of Germany. For his daily life is simpler and more temperate than that of his servants and the chief glory of his crown is an upright and noble Christian character."

All his comments on the affair are typical of the strength and weakness of Henry van Dyke's highly personalized way of looking at a man even to the disregarding of the social forces behind him.

Meantime his father wrote him at length about churches where his ministry might have an opportunity to begin, about a fishing trip to celebrate his return, and above all of an eager desire to see him again:

"No sweetheart will ever kiss you more lovingly than the old man who will meet you, God willing, on your arrival."

Henry made the Fourth of July address in the American Chapel. He was finding it difficult to conclude his colorful sojourn. He sent an unnamed photograph to his father asking his opinion on its merits. The older man recognizing the color of that fly responded to it warily:

"Who is this nymph," he enquires, "rising so suddenly upon my vision? From what part of land or sea does she come? Has she a sister, has she a mother, who is her father, and who is her brother, and what is she to *you* more than another? But if you must have an opinion here it is. The whole picture is neat and graceful. There is no hole in the lobe of the ear which may prove that the girl's mother had some common sense. The poise of the head is pleasing. The under jaw and the upper lip are somewhat heavy; but the upper part of the face is beautiful, and there seems to be a light and sweetness in the eyes. The expression of the silent mouth is upon the whole agreeable and might be still more so if I could hear what comes out of it. The eyebrows are arch and the forehead intellectual. The unknown quantities in the problem before me would greatly affect judgment of the known for better or for worse. If you want to hear more from me you must tell me more. The picture is returned according to your request."

But the whole affair was merely the momentary sentimentality of a young man on going away.

Henry made his farewells, and in midsummer departed for Scotland where he spent several happy weeks with family friends and preached in Edinburgh and in Broughty Ferry. Early in September the family met him at the pier in Brooklyn. His brother Paul had predicted his arrival "with an enormous beard hanging down on your chest and a form of aldermanic proportions." A full brown beard was there, though the form was hardly aldermanic. But a fine sporting suit of brown velvet in his luggage bore witness to the cheerful front which Henry presented to life.

Mrs. Thompson had written him on his departure from Berlin: "Bless the Lord that he has endowed you with the keenest sensibilities to suffering as well as to joy, and so taught you how you may save and bless. And the day of your rejoicing will come. And the work of the ministry is *the* work that pays even in this life."

"It might not be safe or wise," she continued, "and possibly not in good taste for me to give you all the pleasant things that were said about you in my little green room after you left. How that owly Professor W. spoke of you as a live man and how Mr. U. told me of the way in which you could mad him up in an argument, how Frau O. would go back again and again to the service in the American Chapel which made a deep impression and a new impression on her mind."

Henry and his father plunged at once into the Adirondacks,— among other things, to talk in the right surroundings. They spent several weeks at Ampersand and Henry began the taking of photographs with his new Tourograph—a hobby which he followed for many years. Still divided in mind as to whether writing or the ministry was to be his career he felt strongly the need of getting into action. He continued his contributions to *The Presbyterian*. From Syracuse, where he visited the Onondagas' reservation, he wrote: "There was a tumble-down cottage beside the road, and a little granddaughter of the forest playing under a booth of old boards. She was dressed in a blue gown, with a necklace of bright yellow beads around her neck. Her white teeth gleamed at us, and her little black eyes looked like huckleberries in a spoonfull of milk."

He preached in a number of churches, in Boston, in Syracuse, in Flushing and in his father's church. He saw Dean Murray of Princeton who urged him to help out in the vacant pulpit of the United Congregational Church of Newport, R. I. "But I don't want to be a candidate," protested the still uncertain Henry. "Well, go to help them for a month without being a candidate," insisted the Dean. Henry went, though he was not altogether happy in himself. The tension of indecision about his career bothered him. But he "consumed his own smoke" save in the inner circle of his friends where he moodily described himself as "a failure" and "a mistake." Within the month, on December 30, 1878, a unanimous call to the Newport Church was issued to him. Henry went to his father and to Dean Murray for advice. "You have got me into this," said the young man a little tensely, "so you ought to decide." The older men demurred but gently indicated that unless it were contrary to his personal calling they thought it well to accept. The young man considered, and on January 14th wrote a cordial letter of acceptance.

That it was no stop-gap choice is plain from his attitude on entering upon that ministry and is recorded in the poem that appeared a couple of months later in the *Christian at Work*.

The Bargain

What shall I give for thee,
　Thou Pearl of greatest price?
For all the treasures I possess
　Would not suffice.

I give my store of gold;
　It is but earthly dross;
But thou shalt make me rich, beyond
　All fear of loss.

Mine honors I resign;
　They are but small at best;
Thou like a royal star shalt shine
　Upon my breast.

My worldly joys I give,
　The flowers with which I played;
Thy beauty, far more heavenly fair,
　Shall never fade.

Dear Lord, is that enough?
　Nay, not a thousandth part,
Well, then, I have but one thing more;
　Take Thou my heart.

It was a basic life decision made against the background of a concrete opportunity. He had cut the gordian knot of hesitancy by a positive action. Go back to his college oration on *Goethe and Milton* in which he had exalted Milton's public service above Goethe's artistic self-preoccupation; go back to the early sermon in which he declared: "If you believe enough to go forward, if you trust Christ enough to obey him, you are safe . . . I believe not so much in the perseverance of the saints as in the perseverance of God"; note all through his student years, despite intellectual problems and personal doubts of himself, his inability to turn away from the idea of the ministry—and you will see the forces that were integrated in

[77]

that decision of his career. Even when he left the pastorate, twenty-one years later, to teach and write he was not forsaking the ministry. He was rather continuing the fulfilment of his first calling through what he had come to believe was a natural development within it.

Perhaps the immediate basis on which he decided to go to the United Congregational Church of Newport is reflected in a letter he addressed "to a young man whose doubts prevented him from becoming a Christian."

"The religion which is offered to you in the name of Christ has its source and centre in his person, not in miracles, nor in inspiration, nor even in the Bible itself. I can conceive of the Gospel being preached, and of souls being saved, without the mention of any of these things. . . . Come to Him in the spirit that cries, 'Lord I believe, help thou mine unbelief,' and you will find the guidance that you need."

This was Henry van Dyke insisting upon making his choice on positive, not negative grounds; meeting his difficulties directly by stepping into action; and bringing his religion to the test of beginning with Christ.

Chapter Six

THE CONGREGATIONAL CHURCH IN
NEWPORT

THE decision was a good one and it was time to make it. Henry was in great need of what his father had described as "a few years of pastoral experience to complete your education." In going to the United Congregational Church of Newport, Rhode Island, he was to fulfill that need for himself. Also he had something to give, and part of his trouble with himself had been the lack of a chosen place in which to begin. But the decision was a risky one as always for a high-spirited young man with a keen tongue, full of high resolves, and a bachelor. He was an anti-sectionalist and a Democrat plunging into a New England region when New Englandism was regnant. He was beginning his ministry in a church that had been divided and in a community where not a little of the theological gloominess of the day prevailed. In addition his own health was at the moment bad. With one accord the letters of his friends, young and old, breathe a sigh of relief at his undertaking a definite task, and join in friendly warnings. "Don't (as you put it) 'make an ass of yourself'," writes his Adirondack camping companion, Ned Mason. "Stop literary work aside from your sermon writing. Shut down on it altogether. There will be plenty of time for it, and you will be no worse a worker, when you have accumulated a couple of barrels of sermons. In the meantime you have not strength for so wide a diffusion of your powers."

Allan Marquand, his fellow student in Berlin, is rejoiced to see him settled down to his life work. "There must be a satisfaction about it—something like that of standing upon dry land after being tossed upon the briny deep—the deep as we have experienced it, sublime in its simplicity." He has heard Henry's health solicitously spoken of and adds, "Don't let it fall below the average. Take a little beer, for your stomach's sake. It will remind you of old times." "In my happy acquaintance with you in Scotland," writes Chancellor Howard Crosby, "I learned to respect your mind and to love your heart. I am sure God has furnished you for much usefulness, and I am glad if I see you occupying a defined field. . . . The water of the Word is a sweet water and ought to flow through clean conduits."

Mrs. Thompson from Berlin writes her "dear Herr Prediger."

"I was dreadfully sorry to hear you had been sick. Did they charge it to Brooklyn malaria or hunt up a grudge against the Berlin canal? I hear your dear Mama saying to herself she was 'glad he wasn't in Deutchland or even in Newport' and so she tipped around with a low voice but with satisfaction in her soul . . . In those old days in 36th Street one and another would say to my husband, 'How do you do so much work?' He had one invariable answer. 'I eat well, sleep well, and laugh well.' I can't improve upon those rules for holy living and I am glad to testify to my Herr Prediger's ability to *laugh well*. I am not so sure about the other points. But for pity's sake listen to the Frau Doctor, and don't let anything nor anybody keep you awake o' nights. If you have preached 'not much of a sermon' let it go and don't lie awake about it. Perhaps you are not a judge! But go to sleep."

Meantime, whatever his personal difficulties, Henry was preaching vigorously and effectively:

"We modern Christians are a timid folk. . . . We tremble at every new theory and watch the progress of science with jealousy and mistrust. If a man in England discovers a new kind of animalculae, or a man in Germany starts a new theory of the working of the brain, an instant protest goes up. 'That can't possibly be true. It's a malicious invention.' Or, 'That proves nothing against Christianity or the divine authority of the Bible.' Certainly not: who said it did? But why so restless, so fearful, so petulant, O Church of Christ bought with his blood. Stand firm and confident in thy faith. Enjoy the peace that Jesus has given thee. Say to every earnest seeker in every sphere of human thought, God speed, for all truth is God's truth and must be one. His revelation in Nature cannot contradict his revelation in Christ."

"I am thankful," writes a humble parishioner, "someone has come to us who absolutely believes what they profess and tries to help you."

On February 12, 1879, Henry had the happiness of being ordained in his father's Church in Clinton Street by the hands of the Brooklyn Presbytery. And on March 18th, following examination by the Council of Churches, he was installed as pastor of the Newport Church.

On the latter occasion his father delivered the charge to the pastor which was reported as being expressed in informal and affectionate terms and as the most impressive event of the evening. On the record of that service made by the Church Chorister, George H. Pritchard, is written "Dan Barnum, pumper." Dan was a simple-minded ward of the Church who was very proud of his part in the services and used often to say to the choir, "We did pretty well with the music this morning." On one occasion when Professor Horatio Parker of Yale gave an organ recital he remarked: "That fellow isn't much good. I pumped one number he couldn't play."

When Dr. van Dyke returned to Brooklyn after the installation he wrote Henry:

"You looked wearied out last night. And no wonder. The strain of such a service as you have gone through is very great. None can understand it but those who experienced it. But the very thing that makes it a strain and puts it beyond the comprehension of those who only see it from the outside, makes it glorious and blessed.

"You have been on the Mount, and need not be surprised at some reaction. But you will never come down to where you were before. You have received a baptism that will remain. Only be careful and use yourself gently while you are passing through these physically exhausting experiences. You have kind and considerate people, and above all a Master who requires mercy and not sacrifice. . . . Your mother is well. It was only excitement that ailed her at Newport. God bless you and make you better and more useful than I have been—which is not a very great wish."

Within a week Henry received a letter addressed to himself and to several other ministers of orthodox churches inviting them to join in a series of Sunday evening public discussions of "reasonable views of human salvation." The writer pointed out that he had been addressing "large and eager congregations (some of whom I am told were regular attendants of your respective churches)" on this subject. Henry replied promptly and unequivocally,—though with a touch of the forensic typical of the ecclesiastical manner of the day:

"I have neither time nor desire to preach upon any other theses than those contained in the Holy Bible. My views of human salvation are set forth in St. Paul's Epistle to the Romans. It seems to me my present duty to preach them as faithfully as I can from my own pulpit: and if in so doing, with God's blessing I should be able to give help to any one who is troubled with real difficulties, ancient or modern, I shall be gratefully content."

Henry van Dyke intended to be master on his own ship. Besides he was too much in earnest about his objective to be deflected by so specious an invitation to argument.

One matter did however usurp much of his time. For Henry was ever one

> "Greatly to find quarrel in a straw
> When honour's at the stake."

Dr. T. DeWitt Talmage, pastor of the Tabernacle, and a member of the Brooklyn Presbytery, was drawing great crowds to his services. His methods and speech were free and easy and attracted much public attention. It seemed to some members of Presbytery that they were injurious to the Church as a whole. Undoubtedly there was an element of rivalry in the affair between the "neighborhood preachers" and the "popular preachers." In any case the matter finally came to trial before the Presbytery, Dr. van Dyke being a leader in this procedure. Dr. Talmage was exonerated and Dr. van Dyke was greatly discomfited. The trial was open to the public and was widely reported in the press. To many the conduct of the trial was indecorous and ridiculous. Henry who supported his father in cherishing the ideal of dignity and decency in ecclesiastical proceedings was disgusted and offended. He expressed his indignation in a letter to the *Evening Post*. Furthermore, he felt that his father's good name had been impugned particularly by a reference reported to have been made after the trial in the Tabernacle pulpit. He came down from Newport with a carefully prepared appeal to join his father's request for a judicial investigation of the personal issue in the affair. But the Classon Avenue Church where he expected to find the meeting was locked and telephones were not then in general use. Before he could discover the new meeting place action had been taken by the Presbytery refusing his father's request.

Promptly Henry wrote a letter to the Presbytery couched in no uncertain speech: "You have . . . left the Presbytery in this position. Either it contains malicious and unjust persecutors whose character is morally rotten, or it contains a man who uses the pulpit and the communion to shelter him in slandering his brethren. I am not willing to remain in connection with such a body." He went on to say:

"I desire to sever my connection with the Presbytery of Brooklyn . . . and I humbly pray that you will absolve me from any future subjection to you and strike my name from your roll."

When this was read by the clerk at the next meeting the *New York Herald* reported:

"There was silence after this for several minutes. The brothers hemmed and hawed and looked at one another with questioning glances. It is not unlikely they would still be sitting there but for a happy thought of Brother Halsey of the Franklin Avenue Church, who suggested that as there were so few of the members present it would be well to put the matter over until the next regular meeting. A half dozen grateful brothers promptly and joyously seconded the suggestion and it was carried unanimously."

In April the Presbytery returned to Henry his letter describing it as "disrespectful" and urging him to take "further consideration." He replied:

"I am still more unwilling to have any further relation with the Presbytery of Brooklyn, and must therefore leave you to take such practical action in the case as may commend itself to your wisdom and discretion.

"Permit me to inform you of my reception into the Rhode Island Congregational Association at its last meeting."

In June the Presbytery on the basis of this information dropped his name from their roll.

Meantime Dr. van Dyke was prepared practically to withdraw from all participation in proceedings of the Presbytery of Brooklyn under existing circumstances and was even ready to join the others in the same case as himself, in applying for a new Presbytery.

The real issue was perhaps too delicately idealistic and the personal rivalries were too greatly exaggerated in those slogging days of ecclesiastical affairs. The whole matter was thoroughly aired in the newspapers and the Presbytery placed a high valuation on technical peace. The judicious were grieving while the ungodly scoffed. The indignant van Dykes and the minority who stood with them saw that the issue was futile in terms of action. Besides there were more important practical matters which claimed their attention. Finally the elder van Dyke on January 20, 1881 addressed a letter to the public reviewing his position and action and concluding:

"If I have done any wrong I will be sorry for it when the wrongdoing is proved. Only let me not be tried and condemned unheard by a judge who has avowed his purpose to drive me to the wall and assassinate my reputation. If the Church I love better than myself so ordains, I will relegate my vindication to the final judgment and wrap myself in the love of those who know me and in the peace of a conscience void of offense in this matter to God and to man."

There the matter rested with Dr. van Dyke and his Church which sustained him, withdrawn from activities of the Presbytery for ten years. In April 1889 a resolution declaring that "the true intent of the resolution refusing to grant that request (for a judicial investigation in January 1880) was the entire vindication of Dr. van Dyke from all the accusations alleged to have been brought against him, and that the Presbytery now so construes the action then taken" was offered in Presbytery. It was unanimously passed with Dr. Talmage rising to vote for it, and Dr. van Dyke and his Church were heartily welcomed back to their place in the Presbytery.

Throughout the two years while this rumpus was at its height Henry took it much to heart. It struck him in two vital places: his loyalty to his father and his ideal of the purity and dignity of the Church. Unfortunately also it came at the beginning of his pastorate so that he was often torn between pastoral activity and Church controversy.

The depth of religious conviction with which he entered upon his ministry is expressed both in the reality and simple fervor of his preaching and in his parishioners' appreciation of his pastoral services. One elderly man wrote:

"I have been a professing Christian *more years* than Mr. van Dyke has. But to my regret be it said, his closer acquaintance with Christ is so evident as plainly to qualify him to *lead me* in Divine things."

In all this Henry was greatly helped by the strong support of the leading officers and laymen of his church. Edwin D. Morgan, Ex-Governor of New York was a staunch personal and public friend. The Pastor Emeritus, Dr. Thatcher Thayer, was renewing his youth at the young pastor's flame and urging him to heed his health by baiting his hooks for trout (evidently he did not know he was dealing with a confirmed fly-fisher!), to "avoid all embroglios, ecclesiastical, literary and social" and to come as a "comfort to your poor old Domine who needs your help."

But the yoke was not yet light upon Henry's neck.

His ever loyal and forthright friend, Katrina Nichols, then Mrs. Spencer Trask, wrote him:

"You spoke in your letter of the fatigue it brought you in thinking of how much there is to do and trying to fulfill your trust. Do not try to do too much. Do not reach too far.

"Do not, Henry, please do not try to make yourself stronger and firmer when God has given you the talent he has. There is hate enough in the world—we need more lovers. There is character enough in the world—too much preaching and teaching. We need more beauty, more helping.

"It sometimes seems that you are doing an absolute wrong not to fulfill the beauty in your soul—and when you tell me that you will not write more poetry I do not think you modest and strong. I think you hard and an unfaithful steward. I am so glad I am not one of your congregation . . . and really, apart from any association with you, the poem 'Just to give up and rest' [which Henry had written and sent her] would do me more good than all your philosophy."

That counsel was characteristically couched in universal terms but its intention was very particular. Henry made a wry face but took the medicine manfully. He wanted very much to be at peace in order to do his work well. He cut down on his contributions to the religious press, and sought to complete his own education by gaining pastoral experience. Meantime his insatiable mind could not wholly occupy itself with personal and local things. He was deeply conscious of the westward trek that followed the Civil War and of the growth of the United States. Encouraged by Henry Mills Alden, Editor of *Harper's Monthly Magazine*, Henry and his friend W. S. Macy, the artist, went in September 1879 to Dakota and Manitoba to prepare an illustrated article on the huge wheat farms of the Red River Valley. This was Henry's first magazine contribution being printed as the leading article in the May 1880 issue. That he was somewhat dubious about its effect on his ministerial career is evident because at the last moment he wrote Mr. Alden asking that his name be withheld in connection with it. What a commentary on the popular view of a minister's position! Mr. Alden wrote him that his request was too late and added: "Really, however, the article will do you only credit. It helps a clergyman, moreover, even in his distinctive mission that he is able to touch human life in its more objectively practical places."

The article revealed Henry's ability to grasp a new situation, set forth the salient facts, describe it in vivid and pictorial language, and raise practical questions as to its significance. He pictured the gigantic wheat farms as "the army system applied to agriculture" and raised a question of decidedly modern flavor:

"Does this large farming pay for the country? It absorbs great tracts of land and keeps out smaller farmers. It employs tramps, who vanish when the harvest is over, instead of increasing the permanent population. It exhausts the land. The cultivation is very shallow. There is no rotation of crops. Everything is taken from the ground; nothing is returned to it. Even the straw is burned. The result of this is that the average crop from any given acre grows smaller every year, and it is simply a question of time under the present system how long it will take to exhaust the land."

Winnipeg, eight years before, had been a cluster of homes around the Hudson Bay Company's fort. Now it was the metropolis of the Northwest with a population of over seven thousand. Henry watched the colorful scene along the main street, the middle of which was a sea of mud in which wagons were frequently bogged. He saw:

"German peasants, the women in dark blue gowns and handkerchiefs, the men marked by their little flat caps; French half-breeds, with jaunty buckskin jackets, many-colored scarfs around their waists, and their black hair shining with oil; Indians dark, solemn, gaunt, stalking along in blanket and moccasins; Scotch and English people, looking as they do all the world over, but here, perhaps, a little quicker and more energetic."

The companions went further to the end of the railroad at Bismarck for a hunting trip in the Bad Lands of the Little Missouri. By wagon train they proceeded to camp on the Knife River in the region where Sitting Bull was still a fear to the sparsely settled inhabitants. Returning by way of the Hot Springs of Arkansas, Henry met a philosophic citizen who advised him as a measure of safety to leave his gun in his trunk and added the sage counsel: "Whatever you do, don't make remarks on a game, or look on at a fight; more people die of that disease out here than of any other."

Back in Newport he settled down to knowing all his people and especially devoted time to the growing boys and girls, and their preparation for coming to the Communion. He found a not uncommon fear prevailing among them lest they eat and drink damnation at the sacrament. This he set himself to eradicate as inconsistent with the real meaning of the Gospel. He gathered the boys and girls in classes for instruction and he joined them in play. He was a familiar figure on the winter ice sail-skating and doing figures of eight, grape vines and diamond twists.

He wrote an article for *Harper's Magazine* on "The Gospel History in Italian Painting" which criticized with equal fervor the ascetic and stilted expression of the Byzantine School and the sentimentalism of the late Italians, while speaking with enthusiasm of the realistic presentation of ideally conceived figures and scenes. Quite in accordance with these activities he led a movement for the redecoration of the uninspired interior of his Church, which resulted in the notable work of John La Farge. The gloomy minded spoke of it as "the Apostles and buttercups." But the young minister and the real leaders in the Church knew what they were doing. As spring came on he used to go trout fishing with an old fellow of the town. The old man always took more fish than his youthful companion and one day gave him a piece of advice which was often recalled: "Domine," he said solemnly, "the trouble with you is that you don't expect to catch fish while I do."

On a foggy afternoon in early June 1880 he took a walk along the cliffs with his friend, Edward Potter, conducted an evening meeting in the Church with some feeling of distress, and on returning to his rooms in the Church House felt violently worse. He sent for Dr. Rankin, his friend and personal physician, and fainted in his arms. Henry was put to bed with a severe attack of typhoid fever. His father was summoned and a mulatto nurse, to whom Henry always referred with gratitude for her natural simple kindness, was set to watch the patient. It was a close call but by the end of the month the corner was turned. Dr. Howard Crosby who had continued his interest in him since the excursion in Scotland, wrote: "How I wish you were well, and I could have a good 'set-down' talk with you. Yours is one of the suggestive minds that it is a treat to talk with," and added the hope "that, when restored, you will not attempt the work of two men."

Several times during his convalescence his father preached for him and finally in August they went off together to try new fishing grounds in Nova Scotia. His father was always subject to the lure of angler's guides and this expedition was no exception. Recalling the trip twenty years later Henry wrote: "The harvest had been well gleaned before our arrival, and in the very place where our visionary author located his most famous catch we found a summer hotel and a sawmill. 'Tis strange and sad, how many regions there are where 'the fishing was wonderful—forty years ago.'"

But the effect of the trip was beneficial. Henry resumed his work again with unabated zest and vigor. His sermons embody his rapidly solidifying convictions. He insists upon facing the vital issue of life in universal terms:

"That false and flowery optimism which goes into silly raptures over the perfection of humanity and the beauty of nature, which strives to ignore sin and forget sorrow, this sweetly refined theorizing of a few fortunate people who because they are well fed and clothed proclaim the universal welfare of the world under a reign of vague love which winks at crime and is ignorant of punishment,—this selfish, self-complacent, sentimental doctrine is untrue and poisonous. It is a tenuous, rose-colored bubble of fancy, which must shiver into nothingness at the first touch of reality. . . . Like two vast and evil angels, sin and sorrow stretch their black wings over the world and threaten us with despair and death."

In place of this bubble he offers the reality of Christ.

"This then is the Gospel I would proclaim to you today. Not a gospel of the Church though I believe with all my heart in the Holy Catholic Church and reverence her as the body of Christ. Not the gospel of morality though I believe there is no religion without goodness. Not the gospel of a theological system though I have one and hold to it. But the Gospel of Salvation in the goodness of Jesus Christ the living personal, divine Redeemer. *He* is the theme of our preaching the centre of our faith, the master of our life. To his love we must confide our souls for this world and the next."

This core of personal religion he declares must include the missionary spirit which is the true spirit of liberal Christianity.

"Send it out to all mankind, strive with all your might to bring it in contact with every form of human existence, and then you will see it delivered from all narrowness and formality, a living power in the living world."

[89]

Another conviction was solidifying for Henry. In May 1881 he went to Baltimore and endeavored to persuade Ellen Reid to marry him. The days slipped by but she wouldn't say yes. Henry was at his wit's end. There was Sunday and a sermon at Newport inevitably approaching. Hopefully he wired his father to ask if he would arrange a substitute for him. But his father, whether from a stern insistence on duty or for other reasons, replied that he would preach for Henry in Newport if Henry would preach in Brooklyn. That meant a half day's delay in returning, so Henry accepted. But it wasn't enough and Henry preached in Brooklyn and returned to Newport under a cloud of uncertainty. In June he went back to Baltimore and found the Reid family in the country. Among the woods of the Maryland hills the consent was finally given. And there too, one may imagine, began the processes of that poetic alchemy which fourteen years later produced "The Maryland Yellow Throat":

> "Along the shady road I look—
> Who's coming now across the brook?
> A woodland maid, all robed in white—
> The leaves dance round her with delight,
> The stream laughs out beneath her feet—
> Sing, merry bird, the charm's complete,
> *Witchery—witchery—witchery!*"

Henry was in the seventh heaven. Later Mrs. Reid taking Ellen with her went to stay with her elder daughter, Mrs. Edgeworth Bird, on the island of Martha's Vineyard. The boat that summer often bore Henry over those charmed waters.

The church work flourished along with the now thoroughly resurrected pastor. Mrs. Thompson wrote: "God bless you and *her*! and the Church. I am so glad you are not a lost man, but a right up and down natural and good man!—and I hope and pray all things may work smoothly now."

On a late August Sunday, President Chester A. Arthur was in the congregation that heard Henry van Dyke preach on Jacob's wrestling with the angel. The sermon is significant in that it clearly indicated that the young preacher, like Jacob, had come out of his night of wrestling and was now facing a rising dawn. That his own happy personal situation had much to do with this psychological result need not be denied. The preacher himself would have been the last to gloss it over. It was characteristic of him to stress the value of "vital feelings of delight"; and in a sermon on the previous Easter he had said: "Not only is the physical an integral part of our being, but our soul itself is endowed with powers which can only be developed and satisfied by relations with an outward world of realities." From the earlier struggles of his youth and these later wrestlings of his manhood, Henry was emerging into the sunlight and he was heartily glad of it. In the shadows he had learned much, but he found nothing to be ashamed of in the delight with which his whole nature greeted the rising sun.

During the summer an invitation came to occupy the pulpit of a London Presbyterian Church with a view to a permanent call. (Occasionally there is a reverse *English* on these calls to preachers between America and Britain). But Henry, though naturally flattered, was for living in America and besides he was busy at Newport. He was a leader in the movement of ministers, permanent and summer residents to put an end to Sunday concerts at the Casino. His pastoral activities in people's homes and in the "terrible intimacy" of the pulpit, endeared him to many. He had become a commanding and respected citizen of the town.

On December 13, 1881, Ellen Reid and he were married in the First Presbyterian Church of Baltimore surrounded by a gay assemblage of friends. They returned shortly to Newport and lived in the house of Mrs. Berry a widow who kindly and no doubt delightedly took the young bride marketing with her and otherwise instructed her in the arts of New England housekeeping. If the bride was then, as she still insists she was, "a bewildered young idiot" there is no evidence of it. All went happily as a wedding bell. The town busybodies, as always, were an occasional thorn in the side. Some people are so constituted that if they can think of anything harsh they feel it their duty in all honesty to express it. But the forward motion of the life and work swallowed up their effect. More than forty years afterwards the organist, Horatio B. Wood, wrote Henry van Dyke. "I have always remembered the interest in the organ which was taken by yourself and Mrs. van Dyke. The little Chopin prelude is always associated with you both in my mind." Henry was preaching realistically and in a high spirit. The sermons that survive on paper reveal his strenuous endeavor to deal with practical issues and equally display his deep human sympathy. One series especially displays his Christocentric emphasis: "The World's Need of a Divine Saviour; The Old Testament Predicts a Divine Saviour; Jesus Christ claims to be a Divine Saviour; The Church Acknowledges a Divine Saviour."

On the side Henry continued his usual studies of art and morality which issued in a paper on "Art and Ethics" in the *Princeton Review* for January, 1883, and a brief article on "The Moral Influence of Tennyson" in the *Christian At Work* for June 1882, and a fuller article on "Milton and Tennyson" in *The Presbyterian Review* in 1883. The two latter were the first of many studies of Tennyson which, aided by the interest which his wife shared with him, resulted seven years later in his notable volume on *The Poetry of Tennyson*. Also there were days off when together they climbed down to Tommy's Rock and "all unnoticed by the idle, weary promenaders in the paths of fashion, hauled in a basketful of blackfish."

Meantime several church calls came to the young minister. He began to feel that his particular work in Newport was completed and that a new field was desirable. But he was not ready to say yes to any of the opportunities that were offered.

As an incorrigible fisherman and camper he had before him the thrilling experience of introducing Ellen to the mysteries of fishing tackle, guns and the woods. She was to become "my Lady Greygown." In the late summer they went to the Adirondacks and in camp on Tupper Lake in September were joined by Ellen's brothers Harry and Andrew. Henry shot two bucks. The fish were plenty; and everyone was having a fine time. On September 21st a guest paddled into camp. It was George Rowland, nephew of Governor Morgan. He bore a message informing Henry that the Brick Presbyterian Church of New York desired his services as their minister. Henry was tickled at this unconventional way of calling a minister, and naturally much inclined to accept. But the memory of what he had felt about New York churches as he crossed the cables of the Brooklyn Bridge five years before was not easily overcome, and despite his own successes he was seriously doubtful of his ability for so large an undertaking. He went to Elizabethtown to think it over and take advice. Here he found a letter from his father full of practical counsel and affection. The elder man hopes he is enjoying the golden autumn weather and that he will not return to Newport without a full vacation. "The only anxiety I have for you is your health—and there is no ground for anxiety about that if the means are used to keep well."

"This call," he continued, "is a crisis in your life. It is a curious coincidence that I was born in 1822 and called to Brooklyn in 1852. You were born in 1852 and called to New York in 1882. You are nearly as old as I was when I came to Brooklyn. You are stronger than I was at that time, and far ahead of my attainments at that time . . . I will not advise you in any paternal way, but I want to help you to a wise decision. I can do that better face to face than by letter. I will only say now that while I am profoundly thankful to God for the great favour you have found in the eyes of his people I am not surprised at it. It is what I have expected from the beginning. I know that the 'congratulations' and the worldly gabble you will hear about it will not puff you up, and that the responsibility of the question will press heavily upon your soul. You must not expect most people to understand much or to sympathize with your feelings, nor to look at it from any but a worldly point of view. But I can sympathize for I have been there. Commit your way to God and He will direct your steps.

"Give my love to Ellen. I hope you succeeded in getting a deer. Next year if we live we will have a camp. After all that is the only way to hunt."

From Elizabethtown Henry wrote to Dr. William G. T. Shedd, who had moderated the Church meeting issuing the call; to Dean Murray who had first sent him to Newport as pulpit supply; and to Dr. Howard Crosby who had known him well since 1877, and to his father.

[93]

Take the letter to Dr. Crosby as typical:

". . . Meanwhile I am in fact quite overwhelmed with doubt and in perplexity. It is certainly a responsible position and probably a very difficult one. I cannot persuade myself with all reasonable self-esteem that those people are justified in their choice. And certainly if they are wanting or expecting a 'star' to shine or a magnet to 'draw' I would not consider it for a moment. I shrink with an unconquerable repugnance from any such work and its inseparable rivalries and jealousies, and could never undertake it.

You know something of me, and probably much of the church. Will you befriend me with a frank and just opinion as to my probable line of duty? Do you honestly think that I could serve the church of Christ better there than in some other place? The temporary considerations of salary and position need not enter for a moment into the question, for I am now better off in these respects than I need or deserve.

We have had a glorious trip through the wild woods, plenty of game and fish, and *otium without dignity*, far from the frivolous haunts of men."

None of those inquired of would express a direct counsel; but all indicated that it was a case of the right man for the right place. One is struck by the practical sagacity and spiritual purpose of all concerned. Dr. Crosby writes of past difficulties in the Church and declares: "They desire just such a man as you are, faithful, independent, sound, sober-minded and thoroughly versed in the Scriptures." Dean Murray in two letters declares, in reply to Henry's question, that no "sensational preaching" is desired. "They do not want the Church filled by any clap-trap methods. I can speak on this point with emphasis . . . Perhaps I ought to remind you that any such position may involve something of the nature of risk. But we must not confer too much with flesh and blood." It must have greatly delighted Henry to have him add: "The Session will I am sure rally round you, and are an exceptionally fine body of Christian gentlemen." That indeed was prophecy! Dr. Shedd wrote in the same vein and added: "I shall be an attentive and teachable hearer of the word from your lips, and disprove the somewhat common assertion that a clergyman is a bad parishioner."

Dr. Morgan Dix, Rector of Trinity Church, (whose wife was a cousin of Mrs. van Dyke) and many others wrote hoping that Henry van Dyke would accept the call.

Meantime the Newport Church held a meeting and appointed a committee to persuade him to remain. But on October 21st he accepted the Brick Church call. The decision was inevitable. Henry van Dyke was a man of his own time and the call to the vigorous and growing city was irresistible. He was a lover of the streams and woods but he was also a lover of men and he had a passion for being at the centre of human life and activity. Besides it was well understood that the vacations for fishing and other purposes were to be long. The basic decision was solemn and serious as befitted a man who had become a minister only because he could not prevent it.

On November 5th he preached his farewell sermon in Newport on the text: "I determined not to know anything among you save Jesus Christ and him crucified."

"Not in the Rabbi's chair instructing the ignorant and wayward, not on the monarch's seat guiding and controlling by his authority, was Jesus Christ enthroned and crowned with victory; but on the blood stained cross when he conquered sin and death and offered his life a ransom for sinners.

"As I think of the future", he concluded, "with all its trials and temptations and dangers I have but one word to say. It is the word of the same Gospel I have tried to preach, my *last word*: Christ died for us."

On November 12th he preached his first sermon in the Brick Church, on the word of Peter: "I ask therefore with what intent ye sent for me." The sermon stressed the part that the hearers of the gospel have in its effect and concluded with a simple statement of the duty and responsibility of the preacher. Like Peter, he declared himself ready to preach to Cornelius the same gospel that he had preached in Judea and Samaria, "the simple gospel of a crucified and risen Saviour. . . . This is the only gospel that I have to preach. In its service I am your servant. And I pray that in spite of my own weakness and ignorance and insufficiency, the Gospel of which I am the messenger may be able to enlighten and comfort and save you . . . May it be my privilege to draw water from the wells of

[95]

salvation and bring it here even to one thirsty longing heart! I ask no higher joy, no greater reward than this."

Burdened with the weight of the decision, and the sense of responsibility, and under the doctor's orders he and Mrs. van Dyke went to Montreal where they spent a few weeks at Christmas time sleighing and tobogganing before going to New York.

The Newport experience was never forgotten. Henry van Dyke has recorded some of the lighter impressions of those days in "A certain Insularity of Islanders". His personal relation to the Church and the friends there was still fresh in the last years of his life. At Newport he had passed out of the fatiguing introspection of youth through the peace of resignation into a vital joy. You may trace that course clearly in his poetry. "The Bargain," and "Bitter Sweet" are the prelude to the later songs of joy. But already the joy was present. He was prepared to launch his little boat on the mighty deep, the ever raging tides of New York.

II

NEW YORK AND WIDENING INFLUENCE

This is my work; my blessing, not my doom;
Of all who live, I am the one by whom
This work can best be done in the right way.

H. v. D.

Chapter Seven

BEGINNING AT THE BRICK CHURCH

IN EARLY January 1883 Henry van Dyke and his southern wife settled themselves in the Manse at 14 East 37th Street, a half block away from the brick and brownstone Church on Fifth Avenue and 37th Street. They were warmly welcomed by many, but special mention must be made of the Ex-Governor and Mrs. Edwin D. Morgan. They had been summer visitors and parishioners in Newport and Mr. Morgan as chairman of the Brick Church Committee on a new pastor was primarily responsible for their coming to New York. Mrs. van Dyke had been told that New York was the paradise for ministers' wives and, indeed, both found themselves at once overwhelmed with hospitality and kindness. They entered with elation and hope upon the seventeen years that were to test all their qualities. But neither of them could see that far at the beginning. In fact, Henry van Dyke had said to his father that he would try it for five years. The call had been "unanimous" but four important men had absented themselves from the meeting when the call was issued. It is significant that before formally accepting the call Henry van Dyke had seen to it that the four had united with other Churches. He did not propose to start with the handicap of a divided house. On December 11, 1882, he was received into the Presbytery of New York by letter from the Rhode Island Association of Orthodox Congregational Ministers and on January 16th, he was installed as pastor of the Brick Church. His father preached on "the unsearchable riches of Christ" and all who had parts in the service were venerable members of the Presbytery. The Church in those days was in the hands of the elder men and we may note that even in seeking coun-

[99]

sel as to his decision to accept the call Henry van Dyke had appealed solely to his fathers in the faith.

The newspapers almost without exception while referring to his qualifications emphasize his youth. The *New York Times* said:

"The new pastor of the Brick Church is a young man of fine presence and strong personal magnetism. He is about 35 years of age, tall and slender in build, with handsome and intellectual features and a young, fresh and vigorous voice which he uses very effectively. His thick brown beard which completely covers the lower portion of his face, gives him an appearance of mature dignity well in keeping with the long black gown which he wears in the pulpit. As a preacher he is earnest, graceful and entertaining. He talks to his hearers in a plain and straightforward manner, and impresses them with his own sincerity."

The pastor was thirty years of age—not "about 35"; and he was short, not tall. But perhaps the beard, and other considerations, accounted for the added years. The impression of tallness he created in the pulpit was due to his graceful and commanding carriage; a small platform on which he stood within the pulpit had something to do with it. But the "young fresh and vigorous voice" was ever a notable feature of his vivid personality.

The Brick Church had been transferred from Beekman Street in 1856 and planted in what was then an outlying district. Shepherd Knapp in his full and discriminating *History of the Brick Presbyterian Church of New York* says of it:

"In the middle of the nineteenth century Murray Hill was suddenly seized upon and developed by people of position and means, who there set about the transformation of a region of almost open country with scattered suburban residences into a district of city streets with costly houses built in solid blocks."

Dr. L. D. Bevan who had come to the pastorate from London in 1876 left in 1882 with some dissatisfaction at the conservatism of Americans compared with Englishmen and feeling that "clergymen (in America) are well paid and kindly treated, but they are not expected to work for the good of their fellow men, except in certain defined lines." Henry van Dyke was well aware of this tradi-

POISE AT 4

GOOD BEHAVIOR AT 10

PURPOSE AT 32

ON HOLIDAY AT 38

GLIMPSES OF HENRY VAN DYKE

THE AUTHOR OF "LITTLE RIVERS"

tion, but we shall see how he overcame it by the sheer force of personal leadership and intellectual power.

Meantime on February 14th Governor Morgan died. It was a genuine personal loss to the pastor and to the Church, not to mention here the loss to the State and the Nation. Henry van Dyke bore eloquent tribute to him as a strong man, an honest man, a good man, a Christian man. And then turned to the particular task immediately before the Church. The Church roll including those who were attendants of the Mission Chapel in West 35th Street contained about one thousand names, but it had long been unrevised and New Yorkers then as now were always on the move. Inexorably the roll was reduced to 650 of which 350 attended the Mission Chapel, leaving 300 for his own congregation. This was drastic but salutary. With literal scriptural accuracy and effective appeal Henry van Dyke used to speak of them as "Gideon's band"; and together they girded themselves for the work.

It was the purpose of the new pastor to employ all the aid that art could bring to the services. At the first trustees' meeting after his installation the appropriation for music was increased by nearly twenty-five percent. Furthermore, it had been understood when he came that a complete renovation of the interior of the Church would be undertaken promptly. "The old interior which had stood practically unchanged since the erection of the Church, some twenty-five years before, was dignified, but it could not be called beautiful. According to the standards of taste that had arisen in the interval, the bare walls, the white plastered ceiling, the plain, unornamented character of all the fittings and furniture produced an effect of coldness and severity which to many of the younger generation was positively repellent."

The death of Governor Morgan who had been without question the leading member of the Church and who had been particularly interested in this plan was a great blow. But after the first hesitation no one held back. The Church officers voted to go ahead, the laymen undertook to raise the necessary thirty-thousand odd dollars, and Henry van Dyke expressed the purpose and faith of the Church in a memorable sermon on "The Love of God's House." The pastor was convinced as he had also been in Newport that the beauty of a house of worship was a vital part in its serviceableness. And, as at Newport, John La Farge was the artist chosen. From June 4th to October 28th the services were held in the lecture room while the renovating work was going on. On October 28th in the now beautiful interior Henry van Dyke preached on "The Joy of the Christian on Entering the Lord's House."

"The building or adornment of a church is not like the building or adornment of a dwelling-house," he said. "It is not a work of private ostentation, but a work of public beneficence . . . For it stands with open doors, and, if it be a true church of Christ, offers its privileges to all who will receive them."

The artist had done his work superlatively well. The effect was that of the warmth and richness of the early Italian Churches of the eighth to the tenth centuries. Shepherd Knapp writes:

"The prevailing tone selected for the broad surfaces of the walls was a soft or broken 'Pompeian red', while the color of the woodwork and upholstery of the pews was somewhat similar . . . lightness and variety were secured by the use of mosaics of various colors, relief work in majolica, embroideries, and colored glass in windows and lanterns. But the most important work was done in the ceiling and the cornice. There the richness of sombre colors on a background of weathered gold, the wealth of varied and intricate design, the significance imparted by a pervading, yet unobtrusive use of Christian symbol and inscription, produce together an effect of great and enduring beauty, and make this work of Mr. La Farge one of the most important examples of Church decoration in America."

The organ and choir gallery had been moved from behind the pulpit and placed at the east end, at the rear, of the Church.

The house of worship was ready and the church and pastor were still more united by their common delight in it.

Furthermore, Henry van Dyke was casting in his lot wholeheartedly with his people. Almost at once he established the principle that nothing new should be done by the session without a unanimous vote. This delayed some things that he wanted to do but it kept the Church together and made for the rapid growth of confidence.

In fact, the picture of the pastor and session loyally sustaining each other and growing together in wisdom and grace is an unforgettable one, and is the secret clue to the Church's achievements during the whole pastorate. With immediate respect and rapidly growing affection the young pastor looked upon his Ruling Elders and they upon him. And out of that relation sprang life long friendships. Indeed, the most notable single feature of all those years was the personal relationship achieved between pastor, officers and people. The fragrance of it still survives, like lavender in the record, though in life it was full of good red blood.

In December 1884 Hamilton Odell, Clerk of the Session, wrote a personal note to Henry van Dyke's father:

"I can't help telling you of the superb pulpit work that your 'boy' the junior Doctor, is doing. We are getting the Gospel without interruption or dilution, and it is given to us with prodigious plainness and power. The last preparatory lecture was intensely and immensely good, and has made much remark.

There is no division of opinion in the Church.

You have heard all this before, I dare say, but it will not displease you, I am sure, to be told it again."

In acknowledging the letter his father voiced his warm but discriminating judgment:

"It was kind of you to write your note of yesterday. While it does not altogether surprise, it gratifies me greatly and fills me with a thankfulness which I cannot express except to God. The young Doctor, as I early discovered, has a straight-grained mind, a clear insight, and a natural gift of expression which education has largely developed. Above all these, he has an honest heart refined by divine grace and truth. And now it is a blessed thing to know that he brings all his endowments and attainments to the feet of Christ and consecrates them to the preaching of the gospel 'without interruption or dilution.'"

The young pastor was pouring out his high-strung strength without stint both in the specific work of his Church and also a little too freely in outside affairs. Everything that concerned people interested him and he found the adjustment of his pace to his physical powers difficult. New York appealed to him mightily and she was welcoming him with enthusiasm. A little later we shall note the diversity of his activities. For the present let us simply observe that his voice in the pulpit, on the platform, in council, and at the dinner table was only silent when he was reading or writing in his study on the top floor of the Manse.

In the winter of 1884-5 he had put an end to the desultory Sunday afternoon services of the Church and launched an informal Sunday night preaching and singing and praying service that had proved very successful and had aroused not a little evangelistic fervor throughout the Presbytery. If the truth be told he had somewhat neglected his summer vacations—a dangerous proceeding for a man of his nature and interests. He had spent some time at Elizabeth-town and Saranac Lake with his wife and infant daughter Brooke who was born not long after his coming to New York. And there is a photograph of him arrayed in his jaunty German velvet sporting suit on the little steamer on Moosehead Lake. But the expression of the face is more sober and dignified than befitted the raiment and occasion.

In early March 1885 a son was born but within twenty-four hours, following a midnight struggle with father and doctor wrestling for his life in wisdom and love, the child died. It was a great sorrow and many were the hands stretched out to the parents in sympathy. The Pastor in restrained but feeling words preached the following Sunday on "Sorrow not as others who have no hope"; and went soberly on about his tasks. That summer he realized his ideal of keeping the Church open all summer, thus establishing a practice which has only occasionally been interrupted in the past fifty years. Settling Mrs. van Dyke and their lively little daughter in one of the old haunts of the van Dykes, Pine Hill in the Catskills, he came to the city for weekends. Some of his Church officers besought him to spare himself, but he would not.

As the winter work began he felt wearily dissatisfied and somewhat querulously questioned his own usefulness and the attitude of the congregation toward him. Finally, he addressed a letter to this effect to the Session and asked for the calling of a congregational meeting to dissolve the pastoral relation, and with his wife and daughter went to Baltimore. The Session saw the issue clearly and wrote him that:

"It was affectionately and unanimously resolved that in the opinion of the Session the ground on which Dr. van Dyke's proposed action is based is entirely unfounded and imaginary; that in their opinion also, there has not been within many years past so much reason for both pastor and Session to feel encouraged and satisfied with the prospects of the Church as at present; and that the Session are unwilling by any action of theirs to aid in a course which seems to them to be founded in mistake and prejudicial to the united interests of both pastor and people.

"Inasmuch as in the judgment of the Session the misjudgment or misapprehension of their pastor respecting the condition of the congregation grows out of his ill health induced by his uncommon labors during the fall, it is

"Resolved that he be requested, at his option, to take an absence from the pulpit, or to receive assistance in preaching and pastoral work."

This firm and affectionate document and several clear and sympathetic letters notably from Frederick Billings, George de Forest Lord, John E. Parsons, Dr. W. G. T. Shedd, and from his father who signs himself "the old Governor," drove out the fog of doubt. Dean Murray of Princeton, a former pastor of the Church, took some of the Sunday services and Henry van Dyke's brother Paul, recently returned from graduate study in Germany, led the Wednesday evening meetings of the Church.

Henry van Dyke gradually stepped back into his work chastened, as he always was by every break in his stride, but nevertheless—and not without reason—encouraged by the demonstration of genuine affection it called forth.

About this time occurred what he has called "one of those psychical changes which come over a man". In that change, and especially in its later developments, his Princeton classmate William Ward Van Valzah played an important part. Dr. Van Valzah was then just regaining his own broken health and entering again upon the practice of medicine. He was a parishioner of the Brick Church and later became an office holder. On the evening of January 8, 1886, he attended the first dinner of the Holland Society where Henry van Dyke made an uproarious but essentially serious speech on the Dutch virtues. As Henry van Dyke himself described it to me thirty years later: "Something hit me in the back of the head and I let everything go." The speech was a tremendous success. As they walked home after the dinner Van Valzah said: "Van, why don't you preach like that?" That question marked a turning point in Henry van Dyke's preaching and in his whole attitude to public speech. He realized that he had approached his public appearances laboriously. Particularly in preaching he had felt the weight of constraint and had been too much concerned over form and style. Here was a rebirth of the sense of freedom which he gladly accepted. From that night he dated the full exercise of his powers of public speech and was ever grateful to the man whose question brought his new freedom into life. As a matter of fact it did more. By helping to remove the anxiety with which he prepared for public appearances it added considerably to his working power in all directions. It was one of those small but significant occurrences that marks the beginning of great growth.

Chapter Eight

PREACHING AND PASTORAL WORK

GRADUALLY the Brick Church began to fill up and revive. The sap of direct earnest preaching and lively personal enthusiasm flooded its veins and the stalk straightened up and began to bear fruit in social service.

Henry van Dyke was by nature and conviction a preacher. He believed with all his heart that the centre of the minister's work was the proclamation of the Christian message. The programme that issued from the message was to be built not by the minister alone but by both minister and people. In its particular proposals it was to be formulated by the Session, i.e. the Minister and Ruling Elders of the Church. Here unanimous consent before action was the governing principle. His preaching was aimed to provide the ferment out of which the programme was to be developed. And in turn his preaching sprang from a constantly renewed knowledge of peoples' needs tested on the altar of a vigorous personal religion and continual Biblical study. As he expressed it in a note about himself for the decennial record of his Seminary class:

"I have travelled in England, Scotland, Holland, France, Germany and Italy, on foot, by horse and by rail; have visited every eastern state from Maine to Florida and westward as far as the Little Missouri and northward as far as Winnipeg; have lived in an army camp, on the plains, in a lumberman's shanty in the woods, with German peasants in the Tyrol, and Scotch in the Orkneys; have tried to see life on many sides, cast a line in many waters, preached everywhere, as opportunity offered, in Berlin, in Edinburgh, the Highlands, London, the south and the west. Men are the same everywhere, and the Gospel fits the world."

Devoting himself to a flood of pastoral needs he began immediately to visit all the members of his congregation twice a year and to preach out of what he learned in the process.

The 250 surviving sermon manuscripts from the first ten years of his pastorate bear ample witness to the practical, personal and positive nature of his preaching. Many of them show signs of the interrupted though always thorough nature of their preparation. Written during the early years in full, and later in abbreviated form, they are set down now with this pen and now with that, and again with a lead pencil or a blue one. Here and there pages of various sizes are inserted. One can almost see him jumping up from his desk to answer a call or settling himself again to resume his writing. Adequately to describe his preaching in objective, themes and manner, would be to write a volume. Let us simply note a few outstanding characteristics.

God, the individual soul, and Jesus Christ were to him the vital realities. Throughout his preaching, not only during the first ten years of his New York pastorate, but before and after them, this emphasis stands out. Henry van Dyke was totally unconscious of himself as a member of any particular social class and he refused to approach men from the point of view of class distinctions. In a sense this seems to have been a weakness—a blind spot. But it was in reality a deliberate artistic choice. He chose to emphasize in his dealings with men the eternal problems of the soul rather than what he felt were the secondary issues of class struggles. Superficially he appears to have been very much a man of the age in which he was living. But when you go underneath the conventionalities of brownstone fronts and all the paraphernalia of a prominent New York pastorate you find a devout and fiery heart. The Brick Church Session in 1933 summing up the Church's remembrance of those first years says:

"Installed as pastor in his thirty-first year, Henry van Dyke at once brought new courage, vigor and hope into its life and work, through the power and distinction of his preaching, the insight and force of his leadership, and the attractive friendliness of his human contacts."

Henry van Dyke had a passion for men, and New York stepped naturally into his heart.

"I tell you," he declared vehemently at the installation of Dr. James H. McIlvaine in the Church of the Covenant in 1888, "this is a town worth working for and working in. This community—so eager, so active, so broadminded, so generous, so quick to respond to every appeal to its heart—is worth serving in its highest interests, and I would to God that we were better able for such a lofty work." He was a minister but never a conventional one; for the humanity of the man was always his first characteristic. His emphasis on eternity was not abstract but concrete:

"The journey is part of your life as much as the arrival . . . time is quite as real as eternity, indeed it is a part of eternity without which it would be incomplete. We cannot bear to have this pilgrimage of ours from the cradle to the grave slighted or belittled. . . . We want a religion that is good for two worlds . . . There is no more bitter and grievous error into which a Christian can fall than the error of other-worldliness."

The positive, practical note is outstanding. He scorns the fault-finder who can never be the redeemer; the infinitesimal believers who shake and hesitate and sink.

"The present age . . . is too much given to introspection and analysis. Its coat of arms is an interrogation point rampant above three bishops dormant, and its motto, *Query*".

Speaking of religious somnolence he says:

"Religion is the most dangerous of all narcotics but the best of all stimulants."

—which is a little more adequate than the modern half truth: "Religion is the opiate of the people." The practice of religion is for him a steep ascent; natural, in the sense that it is simple and within the reach of any man who honestly desires it, but never natural in the sense that it is easy. Christianity is intended and fitted for a child, and can be received by a child, and kept from childhood to the end, but only upon the condition that there shall be recognized in it an element of progress as well as of permanence. He ridicules the easy-going habit of whitewashing evil characters:

". . . The first requisite of this art is to find a character which has generally been regarded as black, and then by plastering it liberally with excuses, by passing over its manifest defects and diluting its concealed or imaginary virtues into a watery coat of praise sufficiently abundant to cover the whole figure, to exhibit it in shining splendour as the true effigy of a wronged and neglected hero.

Examples of recent masterpieces produced by this process will readily suggest themselves to your memory. There, for instance, is our old friend Henry the Eighth, whom we are invited to consider as a man of tender and capacious domestic affections, whose chief misfortune was that they were so often misplaced. And there is Mistress Lucrezia Borgia, who is represented as an unhappy and ill-used lady of profound attainments in chemistry, whose experiments for the good of the human race were sometimes a little careless and did not always result according to her benevolent intentions. Even Judas Iscariot has found his defenders and admirers. Goethe has suggested that he was a hasty and enthusiastic man who attempted, by betraying Christ to the rulers to bring out at once the clearest proof of His divinity. Several other writers have taken up this same idea. And Thomas De Quincey, in one of his well-known essays, has tried to prove that Judas was an earnest and impulsive believer, one of the first heroes of Christianity whose only fault was that he made a mistake as to the best way of calling out his Master's power and establishing His kingdom in the world. In view of such extraordinary efforts to revamp ruined reputations it would hardly be a surprise if some one should write an 'Apology for Apollyon', or propose to set up a statue of Beelzebub as a public benefactor."

"Come and see!" he cries in the words of the Samaritan woman. "That is the first Christian sermon. It is uncommonly short—just three words. It is amazingly plain. Every man can understand it. But it is so divinely full of beauty and power and meaning that it reveals to us in an instant the secret of the religion of Jesus and the history of its progress."

He drives the message home not only by personal appeal, but also by direct application:

"Yes my friends, you wealthy people, you prosperous people, you people of honor and influence among your fellowmen, you must lay aside all thoughts of pride and patronage when you enter here, you must come to ask a blessing without which you are lost."

Henry van Dyke laid great stress on the freedom and responsibility of the individual. The ability of any man to become a new creature in Christ Jesus was really the core of his message. Having wrestled mightily with that issue in his earlier years his conclusion was now in position to be the cornerstone of his preaching. This was particularly notable in a day when the clouds of foreordination and election hung heavy over the Presbyterian landscape.

Not only is the Bible against fatalism, he declared, but "our souls are conscious of the power of contrary choice in all the serious moral issues of life. . . . Much has been determined for you by causes beyond your control; your circumstances, your inheritance, your talents; but one thing has not been determined, and that is what use you will make of them." Speaking directly on the much abused Presbyterian doctrine of election he said: "A split dollar will no more pass for a good coin than a divine election will save a man without obedience."

With his strongly personalized view of men and institutions and under the strong influence of the Presbyterian tradition that the powers that be are ordained of God, Henry van Dyke's preaching on social issues took a specialized—some would say a *limited*—form. The matter is important for a right understanding of the man. Let us examine it on the basis of what he said and what he did.

From the beginning of his pastorate he was well aware of the terrible contrasts between the rich and the poor in New York. One of his first observations in the pulpit sprang from one of these personal investigations which he frequently made alone: "The difference between east and west of 3rd Avenue", he said, "is like the separation between Dives and Lazarus". When the redecorated church was opened and a distinguished congregation was assembled he said:

"May God forbid that we should ever hear our Church called a rich man's church, or a poor man's church. It is neither. It is just a church of

[111]

the Lord Jesus, where the simple gospel of the Cross is preached for all who will hear it; where the young and the old, the strong and the weak, the learned and the unlearned, the rich and the poor, all meet together and bow before the Lord, for he is the maker of us all."

And he went on to predict that in such a church minister and people would be united in the warmth of kindred hearts and common labor.

Speaking of Christianity and crime, as he frequently did, he reminded the Church that:

"The most densely crowded spot on the face of the globe today lies just below you in the Fourth Ward of our beautiful city: 290,000 human beings to the square mile; 1,500 persons in one house . . . Out of such places as this comes at least 80 per cent of the criminals. And on top of this we build our houses of comfort as it were on the thin crust of hell."

He pleaded and worked for preventive measures especially among children, and for specific reforms in the treatment of prisoners. He was a leader in the People's Municipal League to the infinite scorn of the *New York Sun* which concluded an editorial on "Dr. van Dyke's Mistake":

"We nominate him as the fit Mayoralty candidate of the lay and clerical politicians of the Municipal League; and we shall gladly assist in accomplishing his defeat, thus withdrawing him from his present distractions and returning him to entire devotion to his holy profession."

In the 1884 presidential campaign when Blaine was running against Cleveland a meeting of ministers in New York offered an address to Mr. Blaine in which their spokesman incontinently referred to the democrats as the party of "rum, Romanism and rebellion." Henry van Dyke had been invited to join in that meeting but though Mr. Blaine had been in the Brick Church congregation the previous Sunday he had promptly and peremptorily declined. Following the meeting he wrote a vigorous letter to the *Evening Post* protesting "against every attempt, even though futile, to make the Holy Church of Christ a bob to the tail of any political kite." A few sentences from that letter express clearly his attitude:

[112]

"With the political significance of this meeting we need not trouble ourselves. I have not a word to say now in regard to any of the parties or candidates. When I go into active politics I shall retire from the ministry. But in regard to the religious aspect of the meeting I wish to utter a clear, definite, earnest protest. As private citizens these gentlemen have a right to vote, talk, speak and write as they choose. But when they meet as clergymen, in their official capacity, claiming to represent churches, or denominations, and publicly endorse any political party or any individual candidate, they are, in my opinion, forgetting the high duties and responsibilities of their calling, injuring the cause of pure and undefiled religion, and, perhaps unconsciously, but none the less really, endeavoring to make Christ the servant of Caesar, and a small Caesar at that."

In a symposium on "Shall Clergymen be Politicians?" in the February 1885 issue of the *North American Review* he opposed Henry Ward Beecher, arguing that it was superfluous,—the clergyman having no special fitness or training for it; that it was disloyal,—a nonsectarian state implying a non-partisan church; and that it was injurious,—since the *odium politicum* would replace the now extinct *odium theologicum*. The distinction that he attempted to make between the Church's rightful concern in local or national affairs and direct political activity was summed up, as so often with him, in a word. There is an undated and incomplete manuscript of a speech made in Boston, "The pulpit in Politics and Politethics", which appears to belong to the year 1890 in which for the first time is found this word "Politethics". He asks:

". . . what relation has the pulpit to the organic life of the community and the state? Has it anything to say to human beings as citizens? Is there any sphere of national and civic life in which it has a part to play and a duty to perform?

It seems to me that there is: and that the very reason which ought to keep the pulpit out of Politics ought to send it into Politethics. I must ask you to pardon the appearance of the strange word. It is said that no man ought to come to Boston without something new. And this may perhaps be excused as my humble offering to the *genius loci*.

Politethics means the morality of government and citizenship. It is the ethics of the state and its members as such. It is based upon those great moral principles which ought to regulate human society and deals with those simple duties of justice, obedience, loyalty and charity which belong to all citizens. It is concerned principally and primarily with the ends of governments, and touches upon the means only as they are evidently and necessarily connected with the ends. Its one standard of judgment is, not the political necessity of any party, nor the financial expediency of any measure, but the right and the wrong of national and civil action.

Now in this sphere the pulpit has a place and a duty, and it is bound to acquire the knowledge and cultivate the courage for its performance.

I believe that the object of preaching is to make men really good; and that it is a part of this object to make them good citizens."

The most notable illustrations of the application of this principle will appear in the account of his later preaching in the Brick Church. For the present let us note that while Henry van Dyke was convinced that the Church had a concern in certain aspects of public affairs he was equally sure that the field of government was being too greatly enlarged. He was an "old fashioned democrat" believing in a government of men rather than of laws, and this conviction inevitably colored his preaching and other activities. "What we want," he declared, "is only a strong, clean, simple and strictly limited government which shall have for its one object to secure to every man and woman enough for life, liberty and the pursuit of happiness."

He regarded the new census "as a moral factor in the life of a modern nation," but was very anxious lest it become an impertinent inquisition invading private life. "If we try to find out too much we get less real knowledge."

Henry van Dyke's attitude toward poverty and wealth and the social unrest that was rampant in New York is clearly set forth in one of his early sermons on "Property and theft from a Christian point of view."

". . . We do not believe that the Bible makes any confusion between property and theft or encourages us to set up equality instead of righteousness as the law of society. Christ and His Apostles teach us that the only way is to live honestly, to deal justly and to love our neighbors as ourselves. This is our faith and we must prove it by our works.

There are now two readings of the parable of the Good Samaritan.

Our modern theorists tell us that when the proud Levite and the bloated priest had passed by, a benevolent Communist came down that way and began to whisper in the ear of the wounded man: 'My friend, you have been much in error. You were a thief yourself when you accumulated your private wealth, and these gentlemen who have too hastily relieved you have only begun in a rude way what must soon be accomplished on a large scale for the benefit of the whole community.' Whereupon we are to suppose the sufferer was much enlightened and refreshed and became a useful member of society.

But Christ tells us that it was a Samaritan, a man of property, riding on his own beast and carrying a little capital in his pocket who lifted up the stranger, bound his wounds, brought him into a place of safety and paid for his support. And He says to every one of us: 'Go thou and do likewise.' Which reading of the parable do you prefer? Which do you follow? It is a serious question. For of two things you may be sure: first, if God has given you possessions in this world they are your own: second, He will certainly hold you to account for what you do with them.

If we really want to help the world we must get back to the kind of teaching that St. Paul gave the Ephesians: *Let him that stole, steal no more,* that is reformation; *but rather let him labor,* that is industry; *working with his hands the thing that is good,* that is honesty; *that he may have,* that is property; *to give to him that needeth,* that is charity."

This was individualism all right, but it was not quite *laissez-faire* doctrine. It was liberty qualified by one kind of accountability. As a matter of fact, Henry van Dyke was preaching *accountability to God*, while the rising socialism was demanding *accountability to men*. (The phrases are used for convenience of emphasis.) Meanwhile the teachings of Herbert Spencer, popularly understood to mean that progress was inevitable, were directing the formation of the economic scaffolding of the age. "Infant industries" were becoming "big businesses", and money making in New York was a popular and respectable game.

Against the beast, "the frantic haste to be rich and the insane thirst to get money without earning it," Henry van Dyke fought with all the weapons in the armory of individual ethics. And for reinforcement purposes he labored diligently in the development of all sorts of charities and set forth their appeal in moving statements.

Along with Parkhurst, and Rainsford—a host of other less conspicuous men fought beside them—he cut a gallant figure.

The *New York Sun* took particular delight in harassing him: "It is the dissatisfaction with what is possessed, and the eager desire to get something more that keeps society from stagnation," declared that Spencerian oracle in commenting on Henry van Dyke's attack on "the dollar worship which prevails quite as much among those who desire wealth as among those who have it." And in replying to Henry van Dyke's observation that "not enough has been said of the organizations of great pecuniary interests into trusts and trades and unions, which avowedly have no more conscience than a bull or a bear, but seek only to defend and promote their selfish interests", the same oracle declared:

"Our point was that the average of dishonesty is likely to be greater among the many than among the few. It may be true that such corporations are not 'in harmony with the spirit of Christianity', as Dr. van Dyke contends. But neither are the methods of business generally in harmony with the spirit of Christianity. If the spirit was satisfied there would be no rich Christians, Dr. van Dyke; there would be no greed of gold."

But Henry van Dyke was not to be diverted from what he conceived to be his business. He wrote the *Sun*:

"A reasonable appetite for the rewards of labor is the quality of an honest man. A gluttonous greed of gold is the quality of an evil beast. This simple and Scriptural doctrine will be preached in the Brick Church to all comers, whether they own five dollars or five millions."

Doubtless this was a little too simple in view of actual conditions; but at least the preacher was expounding the coordinated ideals of liberty and responsibility. And, without arguing the point, it may be suggested that such preaching is capable of being more effective in the Church than is propaganda for any one cut and dried social theory. Certainly for one who believed, as Henry van Dyke did, that education is basic to all enduring reform, this approach to the problems of human relationship was natural. Indeed, there is some justification for believing that the preaching of liberty with responsibility is truer to the spiritual facts of human life than other ways of preaching that are determined by sociological theory.

At any rate, Henry van Dyke and the session and members of the Brick Church acted on their convictions. The record of parish work is a notable one. Not only were hearers pouring into the Church for its services, they were going out as partners in the work. The mission work established on the West side in 1858 and installed in a fine chapel in 1867 with Reverend J. J. Lampe as pastor, was growing steadily. In 1888 the Mission was organized as the self-governing Christ Church. "Thus was completed", writes Shepherd Knapp, "an undertaking in which the Brick Church, disregarding its own feeling in the matter, and seeking with singleness of purpose to act for the best interests of those who had formed its mission and of the Church at large, had set an example of unselfishness and established a precedent in the management of so-called 'Mission' enterprises, whose influence has been far-reaching."

Among the numerous organizations promptly established to carry on the work two deserve special mention: first, the Pastor's Aid Society composed of the young men of the Church whose object was "to promote acquaintance and cordial sympathy among the young men of the congregation, and secure their cooperation in the general work of the Church." Through informal monthly meetings in the Pastor's house this society rapidly became a great force in the Church's life and work. The Sick Children's Aid Society offered a parallel opportunity to the younger women of the Church, continuing and developing a work for children begun under the pastorate of Dr. Murray. Miss Mary Ziese, the visitor sustained by the Society, was for almost fifty years an outstanding Churchworker in this field; as was also Miss Margaret E. Kinnie in work for boys.

In 1892-4 the work of the Brick Church was carried into a new field. The old Church of the Covenant on Park Avenue and 35th Street was running into difficult times. So was the Brick Church. Both were suffering from the northward trek of parts of the volatile New York population and from the pressure exerted by the rise in value of real estate. In 1891 there appeared in the *New York Tribune* the following characteristically expressed letter:

[117]

"Sir: Every now and then some idle, or busy, body amuses himself by starting a report that one of the clubs is thinking of purchasing the property of the Brick Church, at the corner of Fifth Avenue and thirty-seventh Street. The report resembles the head of the person who circulates it—there is nothing in it.

"The property is not in the market. None of our many fine clubs is rich enough to buy it. It is a good thing, in a great city like ours, to have some things which are not for sale. One of the first of these ought to be a church which is doing a useful work. The more valuable the property is, the more glad we are that it is devoted to the service of religion. Yours sincerely,

Henry van Dyke".

The two Churches voted to unite their forces in the Brick Church, meantime organizing the memorial chapel of the Church of the Covenant on East 42nd Street as a self-governing Church with the title of the Church of the Covenant and continuing to give financial and other aid from the augmented Brick Church, as was being done with Christ Church on West 35th Street. It was a great achievement with many ramifications including the passage of an act by the Legislature. In it pastors and people not only exercised great faith and tact but exhibited profound foresight and courage. They put a check on the flight of Churches and established their work as a permanent force in the life of the city. It is not without significance that the final achievement of the union by the transfer of property and action of the Presbytery was accomplished in the absence of Henry van Dyke who in January 1894 had been compelled to go away for rest and change.

Henry van Dyke and James H. McIlvaine became equal and coordinate pastors of the Brick Church; and with Reverend J. J. Lampe continuing at Christ Church and the Reverend George S. Webster at the Church of the Covenant, to mention only the ministers, the parish work was organized for its fullest effectiveness. In 1894 Henry van Dyke coined a phrase for the bond existing between the three Churches which proved a blessing to a not always easy relationship and which has proved influential in many other places. He called the Churches "Affiliated Churches." Never was there a better illustration of the power of words, for the phrase served constantly as a check upon those who liked to think of themselves as benefactors and as a friendly hand to those who were ashamed of any feeling of dependency. As a matter of fact it was a true phrase, for the benefits exchanged between the churches, though not similar, were in accordance with the capacities of each and redounded to their mutual good.

In 1896 the two coordinate pastors of the Brick Church addressed a letter to the Session offering their resignations. The dual pastorate had been frankly experimental. It was now found to be unsatisfactory all round. Dr. McIlvaine, with a magnanimity as rare as it was beautiful, wrote a letter insisting upon his own retirement and suggested that Henry van Dyke remain as sole pastor of the Church.

At a meeting marked by friendliness and unanimity the Church gladly agreed to this procedure. The report of the meeting is a model of Christian courtesy and sagacity. *The Evangelist* in an editorial entitled "A Remarkable Bit of Church History," concludes its commendation of the meeting by telling of a young man who remarked as he came out of it: "Such a meeting as that purifies and strengthens a man in his inmost heart; it makes me proud and glad to be a member of the Brick Church."

Throughout all this delicate and strenuous work the relations between pastor and officers remained astonishingly friendly. There were as was inevitable vigorous exchanges of opinions and tense moments. One note concerning an involved issue of policy is signed in evident disgust: "Deacon—Elder B, General Cook and Bottle Washer and General Soup." Henry van Dyke was very strict about what he considered his prerogatives. On one occasion the Trustees ordered that the church bell be not rung for the Sunday morning service. One of the Elders, hearing of it while he was shaving in preparation for going to Church thought it might be well to inform the pastor. So he called Henry van Dyke on the telephone. "That's too bad," said the latter in a significant tone, "because the bell is the only way I know when church is to begin" and hung up the receiver. Hastily wiping the soap from his face the Elder rushed to the Church and ordered Henry Jenkins, the colored sexton, to ring the bell. The congregation was there and the hour for the service had already struck but there was no minister. As the bell notes from the steeple floated out Henry van Dyke came quietly into the pulpit and began the service as usual. Such were his views of his rights even in small things. No one who knew him can doubt that he would not have appeared unless the bell had rung.

Meantime Henry van Dyke's public interests had been increasing steadily. Well qualified to be a willing apostle to the Gentiles, he was an acceptable and frequent guest at all sorts of functions. His zest and humor were contagious. The human touch never failed him. He always refused to accept:

"The falsehood of extremes"

and sought to unite warring factions in the harmony of common action. He agreed with his father's saying: "The Sadducee is always a more agreeable, and generally a nobler man than the Pharisee." A speech at the New England Society dinner ended:

"Let us choose for the supporters of our republican shield those old fashioned figures of Jonathan and Diedrich and between them put the cavalier, and on the shield itself let us blazon no proud symbol of a privileged class, no red hand of universal license, but the steadfast, serene, self-poised figure of liberty."

At a police dinner where he "felt very much as Daniel may have felt in the lion's den, perfectly safe but somewhat embarrassed," he spoke eagerly of this "great, strong, laborious, generous, abused, maligned town of New York." He pleaded for increased means and ease of transportation to solve overcrowding; for cleanliness as a health precaution; and for home rule on the ground that "municipal government is business and not politics" and ought not to be "bandied about at Albany."

At the dinners of the various Dutch societies he held forth with a great flair of imagination on various personalized virtues and defended the rights of commerce. Always humour was an ingredient of his speeches: "Let me make this discourse like a kiss, which you know, consists of two heads and an application."

At the Sons of the Revolution dinner he responded to the toast of

"George Washington" in words that embedded the seed of his great oration on Washington delivered a number of years later:

"Germany produces specialists", he said, "America produces men. The German asks, 'How much do you know?' The American, 'What can you do with what you know?'"

In this devout minister and whole hearted citizen of New York lay the capacity for the dragon slaying forays of St. George along with the good nature of the popular knickerbocker. This was not due to the wearing of a chameleon's skin; it was due to the irrepressible humanity of a man who liked life and who believed it could and ought to be kept livable. The strict theoretical logicians frequently found his words and his conduct unsatisfactory. But the paradoxes they discovered were the paradoxes inseparable from a man who insisted first last and all the time upon speaking and acting as a human being.

When Henry van Dyke's decision to remain as pastor of the Brick Church was announced in 1896 the *Mail and Express* in an editorial on February 21st said:

"Dr. van Dyke, though still young, stands in the front rank of the preachers of the metropolis. In his person profound scholarship, persuasive eloquence, dialectical skill, the brilliancy of wit and the poetic soul, unite with a universal sympathy and with all the lovable characteristics of humanity to make the admired preacher the beloved pastor. Preaching the fatherhood of God, he recognizes none the less the brotherhood of man. His leisure hours and his vacation jaunts have enriched current literature by the produce of his versatile and graceful pen. A profound student of Hebraic and classical literature, a Tennysonian scholar and critic; a descriptive writer whose pictures of nature, of life and character have for his readers a perpetual charm; poet, lecturer, philosopher, citizen, friend—there is hardly a chord in the gamut of metropolitan life which he does not touch, and touch in melody."

Chapter Nine

LIBERTY IN THE CHURCH

BUT we must go back in the story to keep up with our man. For the facets to this dynamically versatile American were many and each one had a ray to flash from the human heart behind them all.

In the affairs of the Presbyterian Church, Henry van Dyke promptly took an important part. Following in his father's footsteps as a devout and faithful presbyter he entered gladly into the inheritance that was his as the son of a former Moderator and as the pastor of a strong church. Within eight years he was well known throughout the whole Church.

The truest portrait of him in his church activity appears in one of the brilliant phrases with which Harvard University conferred the degree of D. D. upon him in 1894:

"Presbyterianorum sententiis libere adsensum nec serviliter addictum" (freely subscribing to the Presbyterian doctrines he is not slavishly subject to them).

"This tickled me clear to the backbone", said Henry van Dyke recalling the occasion. It was in fact a just description of a man basically loyal and passionately devoted to freedom. The whole story is long and significant, but for purposes of the present volume it is necessary to omit much and to concentrate on two matters: creed revision and the Briggs heresy trial—in both of which the central issue was the attitude toward the Bible.

The doctrine of development, the evolutionary theory, was having an important effect on American thinking, and historical and literary criticism of the Bible was beginning to prove disturbing to the accepted view of orthodoxy throughout the churches. How far matters had gone may be seen in the words which Henry van Dyke's father, who had always been a tower of conservatism, spoke in his charge to Dr. Francis L. Patton when the latter was inaugurated in 1882 "Professor of the Relations of Philosophy and Science to the Christian Religion" in Princeton Seminary.

"We not only submit it (the Westminster Confession of Faith) to all the crucial tests science and philosophy can propose, but we intend to aid in the process and see that it is fairly conducted. Let all ascertained and accepted facts, all demonstrated truth, be cast into the furnace; if our creed cannot walk into it without the smell of fire on its clothes, *let it be burned*."

The General Assembly of 1889 overtured the various Presbyteries asking: Do you desire a revision of the Confession of Faith? If so, in what respects, and to what extent?

Henry van Dyke was sure that a revision was both desired and needed. Indeed, all his preaching had been pointing unconsciously in this direction. Now he threw himself whole-heartedly into securing the vote of Presbytery for revision. One thing in particular about the Confession as it stood troubled him greatly both as a pastor and as one who had grown up in a household, and was now the father of a household, where death had entered among the children. Many strict Calvinists took the Confession as teaching that by God's decree some infants at death are condemned to eternal punishment. Henry van Dyke revolted from this idea with passion. For months he had been meditating upon it and finally on November 3 and 10, 1889, he preached two strong sermons, "No children lost" and "All children saved", in which, deliberately refusing to fix the age of responsibility, he argued and pleaded that the damnation of non-elect infants was an impossible conclusion from the Gospel. At the same time he declared that for practical use a shorter, more complete, simpler and more satisfactory statement of faith than the Westminster Confession was possible and desirable.

"In that creed," he said, "there would certainly be room for four great truths: The fulness of the Fatherhood of God; the salvation of all dying infants; the universality of the Gospel; and the consequent duty of the Church to proclaim it to all men in love and sincerity. For the declaration of such a creed as that by the Church I love, I do not hesitate to pray constantly and fervently."

A few months later these sermons, with the references to the immediate situation in the Presbyterian Church omitted, were published under the title *God and Little Children*. They had no small influence in establishing the emotional current that carried forward the struggle for revision.

Meantime the Presbytery of New York by more than four to one voted for revision. The issue could no longer be called the movement of a few disturbers of the peace. The following General Assembly appointed a Special Committee on Revision of which Dr. Henry J. van Dyke of Brooklyn was a member. But the opponents of revision in New York and elsewhere had only begun to fight. On January 27, 1890 in the Presbytery of New York, Henry van Dyke made a speech which had wide repercussions throughout the Church and the press. He pleaded for Confessional change including two principal features. *"First,* to blot out the doctrine of reprobation or antenatal consignment to hell; *second,* to prepare a new, brief, simple, Scriptural creed, as a supplement to the revised Confession." With all the force of cogent debate, unequivocal language, and restrained passion behind it, he made a thoroughly come-outer speech. Reprobation, he argued, is superfluous, unscriptural, unevangelical and, to cap the climax, "horrible", a word which Henry van Dyke showed Calvin had used in speaking of this doctrine although unwilling to surrender the doctrine itself. On behalf of a shorter, simpler, more Scriptural creed for popular use, he said: "We want a creed that will lay a massive emphasis upon the love of God for the whole world, the atonement of Christ for all mankind, and the free, sincere offer of the Gospel to every creature." In concluding he pictured the possibility of the failure of the Church to approve these proposals and issued his challenge:

"I know not what course others may pursue, but for myself there is only one course. I intend to keep right on disbelieving and ignoring that doctrine, and if necessary denying it, by teaching that there are no infants in hell, and no self-imposed limits upon God's desire to save men, and that no man is lost save for his own sins. I intend to teach that God's love is universal, and that Jesus Christ is the Saviour of the world, and that whosoever will may come unto him and take of the water of life freely. Is that Calvinism? I do not know. I do not care. It is Christianity."

It was a fighting speech. Henry van Dyke had thrown down the gauntlet to the Presbyterian Brahmins. It was like proposing Arminius for membership in John Calvin's Church. Behold, had he not uttered blasphemy in refusing to accept one of the doctrines of the remorseless logic of Calvinism?

Inexorably that speech constituted Henry van Dyke the active leader of the revision movement in the Presbytery and gave him a wider place in the affections of people who were not interested in Calvinism but had some hope of Christianity. Take some of the words of an editorial in the *Times-Union* of Jacksonville, Fla.

"Not only religious, but secular journals note and applaud the stirring declaration of intellectual independence. It was an utterance which marks a new era in religious thought for thousands, since surely if there were not thousands who believed in infant damnation, there would have been no reason nor courage in Dr. van Dyke's emphatic renunciation of it.

He will take rank in history among the great names of earth and his followers will be numbered by millions. It is strange what cowards men are! They carry for years in their hearts a silent protest against some error, some grave wrong, moral or political, fearing to break down some old superstition, but just as soon as one is brave enough to speak the truth, thousands of lips which otherwise would have gone mute to the grave, begin to applaud the hero. One of the crimes and blunders of the age is the fear to speak the truth, let the result fall where and on whom it may. And the public will soon follow the genuine truth-teller."

Henry van Dyke was made chairman of Presbytery's committee on the Proposed Revision of the Confession of Faith. Perhaps the heart of his vigorous leadership of this cause is to be found in what he said when a pacifically inclined but yet firm Calvinist suggested in Presbytery that a footnote might be added to the Creed explaining that the love of God was also a doctrine of the Church. Instantly

Henry van Dyke was on his feet protesting: "I object to putting the love of God in a footnote!"

The opposers of revision throughout the Church were many, and not the least influential of them was President Francis L. Patton of Princeton College. Henry van Dyke was always a great admirer and friend of Dr. Patton but on this issue they contended against each other with all the power at their command.

The strict Calvinists published an article in the New York *Observer*, said to have been prepared in substance by Professor Shields of Princeton and approved by Dr. Patton, which referred to Henry van Dyke's defiance and attempted to point out that his quotation from Calvin was inapplicable and even that it was merely one "of many popular superstitions in regard to the life and work of John Calvin." Henry van Dyke promptly replied in a letter which the *Observer* said: "We print . . . with great pleasure", but on which Henry van Dyke has noted: "The *Observer* was very reluctant to insert this and only consented when I said that otherwise I would print it with my correspondence in regard to it in the *Tribune*."

It is not necessary to go into the scholarly exposition of the Latin of Calvin by which he justified the conclusion that Calvin was voicing his own belief when he said that "God precipitates into eternal death harmless, new-born children torn from their mother's breast."

Dr. W. G. T. Shedd said of this reply that it was sufficient and conclusive and *The Evangelist* reported that "Competent judges, and among them one eminent opponent of revision, have declared that Dr. van Dyke's vindication is complete."

In concluding his letter Henry van Dyke wrote:

"I will give one hundred dollars to the Babies Ward of the Post Graduate Hospital, or to any similar institution that you will name, if any one will produce a passage from the works of John Calvin, in which he unequivocally declares his belief (as Dr. Charles Hodge and Dr. W. G. T. Shedd have done), that all dying infants are elect and saved."

The next issue of the *Observer* contained an editorial concluding: "The offer to give a hundred dollars 'if any one will produce a passage from the works of John Calvin in which he unequivocally declares that all dying infants are elect and saved', might be followed by an offer to give one thousand dollars if any one will find such passage in the works of Peter, Paul, John, James or any inspired author."

Neither the actual offer nor the canny imaginary offer were taken up. But the controversy inexorably continued.

During these troubled days Henry van Dyke and his father were constantly united in thought and action and were frequently together in consultation. The older man had kept pace with the development of his son and the son had gained from his father the rugged and stedfast qualities of the veteran. How they admired each other's work and how promptly and generously they expressed themselves to each other! And now they were drawn closer together by enlistment in a common cause. The manner in which they sustained each other in their particular responsibilities—the elder as a member of General Assembly's Committee on Revision struggling to prepare revisions that the Church would accept and yet unwilling to sacrifice the future interests of the Church on the altar of a one-sided and enforced harmony, and the younger contending in the Presbytery of New York for liberty with harmony—is a picture of unforgettable beauty.

In early May, 1891, the elder Dr. van Dyke, then in his 70th year, was elected to the chair of Systematic Theology at Union Theological Seminary in New York. *The Evangelist* commenting enthusiastically on the appointment said:

"If any think him too old to assume new duties they have but to hear him in conversation or in debate to be sure that his strength is not in the least abated. He is as full of life and vigor as when in the prime of manhood. Indeed he is of that sort of temperament that never gives up and never grows old; so that, although in the course of time he may pass away like other men, yet we are sure that he will not anticipate the time. To such a veteran may be applied the famous saying of the old guard at Waterloo:—he 'can die, but will never surrender.' "

On May 24th, while Henry van Dyke was acting as Harvard University preacher, Henry J. van Dyke preached twice in his own church in Brooklyn. During the evening service a sharp attack of pain in the heart failed to stop him. Afterward the doctor diagnosed it as angina pectoris and warned him of the danger. He refused to be alarmed and spent Monday about his affairs and seeing friends in New York. At the conclusion of an evening at home with his wife the end came. To the hastily summoned doctor and friend, Dr. S. Fleet Speir, he said half-humorously "Well, doctor, you can call it what you will, I am ready to go" and went swiftly as he had always hoped he might. Henry van Dyke asleep in the preacher's rooms at Harvard was awakened in the wee small hours to receive the message from a telegraph boy. Sorrowfully he returned for the services; but unshaken, he took up immediately the burden of his work. The latest description of these inseparables that can be found is in a biographical sketch by Dr. George L. Prentiss, founder and first pastor of the Church of the Covenant and later professor in Union Theological Seminary:

"I used to admire the beautiful relation which existed between Dr. van Dyke and his two sons. He was their comrade and dear friend, as well as their loving father. One of my last recollections of him is his look of honest pride and joy, as he sat on the platform beside ex-president Cleveland and Mr. Choate, listening to a glowing address by his son Henry, on the public charities of New York."

This was on May 1, 1891. It is a true picture of their relationship as the elder comrade joined the encompassing cloud of witnesses to watch his son run with patience the race set before him.

The movement for revision was rightly adjudged by its opponents to be the entering wedge of a great liberalizing movement in the Church; and an opportunity to hold up revision soon appeared. With the aid of other conservative members of the Presbytery of New York, a heresy trial was launched against Dr. Charles A. Briggs. It began in April, 1891, with a committee appointed to consider his recent address at his inauguration in Union Theological Seminary. Henry van Dyke was appointed a member of this committee but promptly refused to serve "owing to pressing engagements connected with pastoral service." When the matter came on the floor of Presbytery he was a leader in winning the dismissal of the case 94-39. The *New York Tribune* reports him as arguing that the supreme authority of Holy Scriptures was not called in question and as pleading for liberty with orthodoxy.

"Liberty first. And why? Because without liberty there is no true orthodoxy. A man cannot be taught to believe and think right without liberty. Orthodoxy must flourish in an air of freedom; and the best way to defend the Bible is in the open air, and in the light of facts; and that is the way I want to see it defended. . . . That is the position of a conservative."

The *New York Sun* never missing an opportunity to criticise him said:

" 'A boy said in Sunday school once,' said Dr. van Dyke before the New York Presbytery, 'that the lions didn't eat Daniel because they didn't know how good he was. We know, of course, that the reason the lions didn't eat him was because they did know how good he was. We know how good Dr. Briggs is—now, don't let us eat him. He submits and appeals to the Bible as the only infallible rule of faith and doctrine. Can we look upon such a man as our enemy?' And upon this broad ground of universal charity to the morally virtuous the charges of heresy against Dr. Briggs were dismissed.

It is hardly necessary to suggest that such an argument is no argument at all in a trial for heresy. Few members of any Protestant Church would be so bigoted as to deny that the Lord has other sheep that are not of their fold, and every Protestant denomination appeals to the Bible as the only infallible rule of faith and doctrine, but that does not make all Protestants Presbyterians. It would seem that Dr. van Dyke is a better politician than a logician."

But the *New York Herald* more sympathetically said:

". . . One sentence in the address which that remarkable young man, Dr. van Dyke, delivered on Wednesday can be particularly commended to Presbyterians and all other church people who fall by the ears about words and doctrines.

'This great city,' said Dr. van Dyke, 'wants the bread of life. Don't let us give it the stone of controversy instead.' "

Meantime Henry van Dyke as chairman of Presbytery's committee on the Proposed Revision of the Confession of Faith went on with this work. On November 23, 1891 the recommendations of the committee were adopted. To put them briefly in the words of the preamble they aimed at a "revision which shall really revise" as the fruit of "a wide and deep movement in the Church" and provided for:

"First the frank, explicit, and unhesitating declaration of the living faith of the Church in God's loving and true offer of salvation to all men, through Christ, by His Word and Spirit. Second, the clearing of our Confession of Faith from the possibility of a fatalistic misinterpretation."

The *New York Sun* continued its opposition in an attack logically impeccable and in a form highly personal. Accusing Henry van Dyke of undertaking "to whip the devil round the stump" the *Sun* declared:

"The Presbyterians will make nonsense of their creed if they follow the advice of Dr. van Dyke and the New York Presbytery . . .

If Calvinism wins, the Confession will remain. If it is defeated, an entirely new creed and system of theology must be constructed from the foundation and a radically different Presbyterianism substituted for the Presbyterianism of the Westminster Confession."

The fact was, of course, that a revolt was rising against this exclusive emphasis on the Calvinistic portions of the Westminster Confession. Other strands in the complex document were being discovered as historical studies were bringing new light to bear on the nature of the Bible. The revisionists took their stand as Presbyterians on the section of the Form of Government that called for acceptance of the Confession of Faith "as containing the system of doctrine taught in the Holy Scriptures", and argued that a better understanding of the Bible now made it needful to revise parts of the Confession. The strict Calvinists were convinced that the revision of the Confession was only a mask for an attack upon "the Word of God."

Henry van Dyke was playing a leading part in what he considered a legitimate attempt to keep the Church of which he was a minister abreast of the thought and work and life of the day. In three sermons from his pulpit in February 1892 he set forth the issues: "The Bible against fatalism; the liberty of man by the decree of God";

"The Bible against chance; the sovereignty of God in his World"; and "The Bible against a selfish religion; election to service." The ecclesiastical issue was whether the hitherto accented Calvinistic interpretation of the Bible was to be made obligatory, or whether the freer interpretation, which was also included in the Confession, was to be allowed in the interests of a Biblical approach to theology rather than a theological approach to the Bible. Henry van Dyke summed up the issue in a paper he read before several ministerial associations in which he cited instances to show that "the practice of conforming Scripture to theology is both ancient and modern, that it has been followed in many fashions and by men of all schools and that it results in a corrupted text, a coloured translation, and a crooked exegesis." From this he concluded: "First, that there is very much less in single texts of the Bible than theologians have tried to draw out of them. Second, that there is very much more in the whole Bible than has ever been put into any system of theology. Third, that the Scripture itself is our best interpreter."

Everywhere the controversy was making divisions. Paul van Dyke, Henry's brother, who since 1889 had been an instructor in Church History in Princeton Theological Seminary felt it. Under pressure to sign an agreement to "interpret the Westminster Confession in the sense usually accepted" he indignantly resigned his work into the hands of the Board of Directors asking that his name be not considered in connection with the future of the Department of Church History. Some of the students wrote the Board enthusiastically asking for his retention. Meantime he received two calls from churches. Henry van Dyke who had been a member of the Board since 1884 came from New York to take active part in a stormy session. The Board refused to hear the students and granted Paul van Dyke's request while refusing to accept the reasons he had assigned for his action. Under Henry van Dyke's insistently persuasive leadership, however, they recorded their appreciation of Paul van Dyke's work in his department, in optional classes, and in the religious life of the Seminary, and expressed gratification at the great affection and high esteem in which Mr. van Dyke was held by the students. Paul van Dyke accepted the call to the Edwards Church in Northampton. The

[131]

brothers retired from their successful rearguard action in the strong-hold of Calvinism. At a later meeting of the Board the letters contain-ing the gist of the controversial issues were ordered removed from the minutes and preserved on the files of the Board.

The trial of Dr. Briggs during November and December 1892 was long and bitter. Henry van Dyke was popularly accounted "the leader of the Briggs forces" but he preferred to describe himself as "a Christian Presbyterian who believes in a short creed and a large work" and when asked if he were a liberal or a conservative replied passionately "I am a comprehensionist". The last stanza of a poem written in 1892 tells the story:

> "Something to learn, and something to forget:
> Hold fast the good, and seek the better yet:
> Press on, and prove the pilgrim-hope of youth,—
> That creeds are milestones on the road to truth."

The reports of the trial in the press were full. The headlines of the New York papers included: "A Hubbub in Presbytery"; "The Great Heresy Trial"; "Still Wrangling"; "The End Draweth Near: Brethren of the Presbytery: About Ready to Disagree."

To cut short a long and painful story every charge against Dr. Briggs was dismissed on December 30th by the small majority of six votes. The defense had won but it proved to be only the first skirmish in a long campaign and the margin was too narrow to be at all decisive.

One incident during the trial deserves mention for it serves to bring out the objective of the leaders of the defense. On December 16th it was reported that "a peace coterie" had met at Henry van Dyke's house. Pointing out that the Briggs case and the case of Henry Preserved Smith in the Presbytery of Cincinnati would both come before the next General Assembly in May the *Mail and Express* said:

"It is an essential matter in the plan of the peace combine to see that the liberals are in control at this assembly. That is the aim of the gathering of noted liberals in this city, and the dinner party at the house of the energetic, ambitious and eloquent pastor of the Brick Church was its inception. Another matter no less important to come before the next assembly is the final action on revision of the confession. The proposed revision is not extreme enough to satisfy the liberals, and the combine will go in to defeat the present report, with a view to securing a new committee and of adopting a short creed."

What had happened was that Dr. George Alexander and Dr. Wilton Merle Smith, both of New York, Dr. Teunis S. Hamlin of Washington, Dr. Charles Wood of Germantown, and Dr. A. V. Raymond of Albany had met privately with Henry van Dyke to talk over the distressing situation in the Church and had planned a memorial to be circulated among the ministers of the Presbyterian Church entitled *A Plea for Peace and Work*. Thoroughly disgusted with the controversy which lay athwart the Church's path they proposed to appeal to all who desired peace on an inclusive basis.

The document was not partisan. As one conservative from South Dakota wrote:

"Although certain extremists may *misunderstand* or *misconstrue* one or two phrases in the Plea, I think it expresses the *conservative* idea adequately; and tho' I have been in one *swirl* that for a time gave conservatism a tossing, I am willing to allow my name to be used in a cause so evidently Christian as this Plea proposes."

Nevertheless the whole incident was accounted by those who favored exclusive acceptance of the strict Calvinistic accents of the Confession as merely a step in the strategy of the revisionists; while still more, who feared that the Bible was being undermined by the Higher Criticism, considered the *Plea* a mere obscuring of the issues in the interest of an impossible peace. Undoubtedly the document was capable of such an interpretation. In a time of controversy truth is usually neglected and only debating values are taken into account. In anticipation of the publication of the *Plea* on February 17, 1893, with 235 signatures, the mutterings swelled into a storm not only in the Church but in the press. The ever ready *New York Sun* was in the forefront of the hullabaloo with an editorial headed: "It will not work."

"It is understood that a concerted effort to compromise the Presbyterian controversy over the Bible by a sort of hedging process is to be made under the leadership of Dr. Henry van Dyke. He is the pastor of the Brick Presbyterian Church in Fifth Avenue, a church formerly anchored in the strictest Calvinistic orthodoxy, but which now gets more consolation from his elastic and genial doctrines. . . .

It is a very clever plan, for Dr. van Dyke is a very clever man. He is also a minister who likes to have all things pleasant about him, and with his cheerful and genial nature he contributes to make them so. He is a very polite man, and in the refined society in which he moves it is obligatory to avoid subjects of conversation that tend to provoke harsh disagreement. If President Patton resents the treatment of the Bible by Dr. Briggs, the polished pastor of the Brick Church would have them talk about something else when they meet, the weather, for instance, or the last college football game. . . .

The issue is squarely drawn, and it must be met squarely at Washington, or the Presbyterian Church will forfeit the public respect. Dr. van Dyke's scheme of compromise and evasion cannot work."

But the press as a whole saw greater issues than party victories at stake. The Hartford, Connecticut, *Times,* writing of "the Troubled Waters", said:

"Dr. van Dyke does not believe the Bible is exempt from errors. His many brethren, in and out of the pulpit, who have in recent years been accused of heresy, are with him in this conviction. They see, what is the truth, whether the rigid sectarians see it or not, that many of the old beliefs which have been regarded as fundamental to 'orthodoxy' in theology, cannot longer maintain their hold; a new and greater day is breaking."

Henry van Dyke had refused to serve on Presbytery's first committee to consider Dr. Brigg's address, had consistently refrained from preaching about the ecclesiastical troubles in his pulpit, had been working tirelessly for an inclusive peace, and had finally been drawn, much against his will, into the heresy trial. Now he found himself in a peculiarly delicate situation. Dr. J. J. Lampe since 1867, minister of the Brick Church mission (which in 1888 was constituted as Christ Church, one of the affiliated churches of the Brick Church) had been a member of the committee prosecuting the

Briggs case. It was understood that this committee intended to appeal the case they had lost in Presbytery to General Assembly. Henry van Dyke addressed a friendly and affectionate letter to Dr. Lampe beseeching him not to take this step:

"You are a member of the Committee of Prosecution in the case which has just been tried in the Presbytery of New York. You have doubtless observed the verdict of the Presbytery in that case has been framed with the utmost care; first, to avoid committing the members of the Presbytery to a personal agreement with the theories of the defendant or the manner in which they have been expressed; second, to do full justice to the Committee of which you are a member and to refrain from any assertion of the Presbytery's authority to control your future action.

As a member of the committee which framed this judgment I wish to say to you frankly that our desire in framing it was to make peace. I appeal to you personally to cooperate with us in that desire.

If the case is now carried up to the General Assembly it will in my opinion, result in a bitter civil war in our church and work incalculable injury to the cause of Christ. It will mean simply that an attempt is to be made to enforce the theory of the 'Inerrancy of the Original Autographs' as a test of orthodoxy in the Presbyterian Church. This as you know, will result in the condemnation of a very large number of our ministers, including myself and others, who accept the Bible as it is as the word of God and our only infallible rule of faith and practice, but know nothing about the 'original autographs' and are not willing to make any affirmation concerning them."

This letter was endorsed upon the author's copy of it by the personal signatures of all the officers of the Brick Church but was sent without that endorsement (as Henry van Dyke has noted upon it) "to avoid all appearance of pressure."

Dr. Lampe's reply simply affirmed that the Committee would do what they thought best in the circumstances, and shortly thereafter notice was given of the appeal to General Assembly.

Regretfully but without hesitation Henry van Dyke laid the issues of the conflict and his own position in it before the Brick Church in a sermon "The Bible as it is" preached on January 22, 1893. The sermon began with a plea for allowing men of differing opinions to

[135]

exercise their constitutional liberties within the Christian purpose of the Church. "Absolute uniformity in any association of men means the absence of thought or the presence of hypocrisy." Contests seldom do any good; often do great harm; and are bitter and harmful in exact proportion to the smallness of their cause and the absence of real necessity for waging them. Besides the majority of Church members and "working ministers" are tired of conflict and want to preach and practice plain Christianity.

Next it pointed out in reference to the Briggs trial that the verdict of Presbytery was not an expression of agreement with all the positions of Dr. Briggs but a refusal "to condemn as a heretic, and drive from the ministry, a man whose sincere faith, earnest piety, spotless life, great learning, and Christian devotion we all know and love. That was a fair verdict of acquittal, based not on the grounds of partisanship, but on the grounds of comprehension."

The prosecution, the sermon maintained, had attempted to introduce a new test of orthodoxy, "The inerrancy of the original autographs of the Holy Scriptures, as distinguished from the Holy Scriptures which we now possess." *As a private opinion,* though incapable of proof, non-essential, contrary to the Confession, and unconstitutional Henry van Dyke claimed that this theory should be permitted while he declared for himself "I do not see how it is possible for me to affirm or deny anything in regard to a subject on which I have absolutely no information." But as a test of orthodoxy he denounced it as utterly inadmissible.

Finally the sermon stressed the duties of the moment as: refusing to withdraw from the Presbyterian Church under the threat; studying to be quiet and mind our own business; mildly but firmly opposing every attempt to impose new tests of orthodoxy or to restrict the liberty hitherto enjoyed by those who sincerely subscribe to the essential and necessary doctrines of our Church; and turning from the paths of fruitless controversy and devoting our energies to the work of plain religion.

The crux of the issue at stake in the Church was whether or not the exclusively Calvinistic interpretation of the Bible as fortified with the new theory of inerrancy of the original autographs was the final authority. Henry van Dyke clearly took the position that "there is only one (authority)—the Holy Spirit, who speaks to our souls through the Bible, and the conscience, and the testimony of the Church."

The Brick Church encouraged by the receipt of many letters of enthusiastic approval distributed something over 5,000 copies of the sermon among ministers and elders of the Presbyterian Church.

Mr. Winthrop S. Gilman who took an active part in this distribution wrote to Elder Albert R. Ledoux:

"All the innuendos and the slurs of the press, secular and religious, (not to mention the *falsehoods* which will react most favorably in the long run), cannot defeat the cause of Christian liberty and progress of which by God's singular providence Dr. van Dyke has been made the champion. It is a most happy circumstance that one so gifted intellectually and spiritually as he is thus brought to the front. His courageous spirit, his *clear perceptions* and his remarkable talent for explaining matters have made him a most powerful agent in crystallizing the thought of a very large body of devoutly loyal Presbyterians throughout our land. I do heartily rejoice in what I acknowledge to myself is the success of his great labors for a peace after the Gospel pattern."

That this judgment was sound was witnessed by the letters that the preacher received. Take a few samples from all sorts of people—liberals and conservatives. From North Carolina a minister wrote:

"You have voiced the sentiments of all the 'Lower Critics'. We are weary of controversy. . . . Personally I am a conservative and believe in Verbal Inspiration. Possibly this is due to my extreme obtuseness. Howbeit I am not in sympathy with the new test to be imposed upon my brethren unless they agree to it."

From India:

"As a foreign missionary I feel strongly upon the matter. I cannot consent to be forced into the approval of a theory regarding our Scriptures which I am in the habit of condemning in the Mohammedans as to theirs."

From Professor Henry Preserved Smith under accusation in the Presbytery of Cincinnati:

[137]

"Thank you for the courageous stand you have taken on behalf of liberty. At the risk of being considered officious let me express the hope that you will not leave the Presbyterian Church. That Church needs you very much not only for the opportunity of usefulness in your immediate charge, but even more because of the influence you can exert in the Church at large."

From an elder in Washington, D. C.

"I thank you for the position you have taken before the Church and the thinking world. . . . After the storm has passed . . . our Church, her ministers and office bearers will not only be freer, but more catholic, more evangelical, and have more of the true evangelistic and Christian spirit than now and the Bible will still be the Word of God, the message of salvation for a lost world."

From a pastor in the state of Washington:

"If dispassionate discussion, lucid argument, language devoid of invective, profound regard for demonstrably essential doctrines, courage of conviction, indifference respecting things indifferent, and unknown and unknowable, and a peace-loving and peace-making spirit, are possessed of any potency for influencing the members of the Presbyterian Church, then your sermon, adorned as it is with these pleasing features, is destined to do much toward quieting disturbances, allaying bitterness, and causing brethren to love as brethren, be courteous, be Christ-like. Amen."

From Richard Watson Gilder, editor of the Century Magazine,

"May an outsider commend your words of bravery and of wisdom uttered yesterday from your pulpit?"

From a pastor in Ohio:

"You served the cause nobly in New York both in the trial of Dr. Briggs and in your own pulpit; but have had almost as much power out here in Ohio."

In the questions raised by creed revision and the heresy trial Henry van Dyke contended as a lover of peace. He was not above enjoying the fray when the issue was joined, but his objective even in the heat of controversy was the restoration of the peaceful basis on which alone the life and work of the Church could progress. The one thing he was unwilling to do as a presbyter was to surrender the Church into the hands of any one party in it. Against that he was fully prepared to fight. Believing absolutely in the Bible as "the only infallible rule of faith and practice" he declined flatly to leave it to the tender mercies of those who thought it ought to be hidden from the new light of truth. For him the Bible became increasingly significant the more the light of truth beat upon its pages. On these issues he was a fighting man of faith, insisting that the Confession must be approached through the open Bible rather than the Bible approached through a static conception of the Confession.

Meantime the burden of responsibility and emotion was bearing heavily on him. His ever beloved friend Dr. George Alexander of the University Place Church who was contending by his side for liberty wrote:

"Never mind misapprehension and suspicion. Your Father's son ought to be able to endure a great deal of that. We must all take our share of it till the clouds roll by. Your righteousness will come forth as the noon day. I am learning that one must battle beside his friend to know him—and love him."

In the midst of these many distractions a difficult decision had to be made by Henry van Dyke. He was called in the spring of 1893 to succeed Dr. William J. Tucker, recently elected President of Dartmouth, in the Bartlett Professorship of Sacred Rhetoric at Andover Seminary. To a man so deeply devoted to preaching, with the pen of a ready and eager writer, and so desperately overburdened in his present position the call presented many appeals. It was understood that there was no objection to his keeping his standing in the Presbyterian Church so that he could not be accused of fleeing for safety before the theological storm.

Another element that joined with the insistence of the Andover call to make the decision difficult was the depleted state of Henry van Dyke's health following his ten years of arduous labor. In fact all along, the Session had watched their pastor with affectionate concern. In 1888 they had packed him off for five months and the trustees had increased his salary. "Your one great business now," Hamilton Odell, Clerk of the Session, had written "is to gather yourself together and in the language of the plains to 'git up and git.'" And on several other occasions they had generously provided substitutes in the pulpit. A careful physical examination in 1893 showed him to be organically sound but nervously exhausted and he was suffering greatly from distressing symptoms. His condition was reflected in the anxiety and hesitation with which he approached the decision. William Earl Dodge wrote him:

"Your best medicine is now put up in half pound doses which are to be taken 'on the fly' in Long Island. . . . Yesterday, the opening day, was an ideal fisherman's day and the trout came to me as if they loved me. And I know they would like your theology better than mine. . . . My only fear is when you are a little 'down' in health and spirits and tired out by the unreasonable and absurd men of the New York Presbytery even a 'lodge in some vast wilderness' would tempt you. In this crisis you cannot be spared. No one is more needed."

Evidently Henry van Dyke was having trouble in facing the decision squarely. To the great distress of his Elders he even questioned the loyalty of the Church. Dr. Albert R. Ledoux addressed him an earnest letter in affectionate terms:

"Dearly beloved brother,
My text is I. Cor. 14:3. 'He speaketh unto me *edification* and *comfort* and *consolation*.'
A layman may sometimes preach and this is one of the times. I feel it a duty to say one solemn word after my hour with you last night,"

and he went on to remind him of the complete loyalty of the Church and of her achievements in the very words which Henry van Dyke had himself used at the 125th anniversary a few months before. "No pastor," he wrote, "ever had such a *personal* congregation! None such a diminutive bump of self-esteem!"

Dr. Odell wrote: "I think it will do you good to go to my house and permit Mrs. Odell to talk to you as only a woman in *dead earnest* can."

After the services on April 9th he went with his wife to Northampton to talk with his brother Paul expecting thence to go on to Andover to look over the situation. But the Brick Church was in determined and serious mood. A congregational meeting, following the example of the session, adopted vigorous resolutions declining to let him leave, expressing warm confidence and affection, and protesting that "his resignation as our Pastor will work serious and lasting injury to our church, and that we solemnly and strenuously protest against the action of the Seminary which is calculated to do us this great wrong." To this was added the offer of "such leave of absence as may be necessary to effect his restoration to health and strength," and the promise of "such assistance in the pastoral work as may be found to be for his best interests."

That ended the matter. The Andover call was declined. Henry van Dyke and his wife were solidly agreed that they must stay in New York.

A wire was sent to Dr. Henry M. Booth who, as a number of times before, had held the reins in the Brick Church during the pastor's absence, announcing his immediate return to preach on the following Sunday. A letter was addressed to the congregation in which he wrote:

"The work which I have been permitted to do here for the last ten years, although arduous and exacting, is one to which I am profoundly attached. When you say unanimously that its continued prosperity still demands such service as I can give, and that a resignation now would work injury to the Church, *that settles it.*"

A flood of joyful letters poured in upon the pastor, and the crisis was happily past. New York had a part in the result, for Henry van Dyke was ever a lover of that tumultuous and mighty city. But the real victory was won by that band of faithful and devout men who were the heart of the Brick Church and with whom Henry van Dyke rejoiced to live and work. As he had put it in the historical sermon in observance of the 125th anniversary of the Church:

"It is the custom of ministers in preaching their anniversary sermons, to give an account of their labors, to tell how many discourses they have delivered, how many visits they have made, how many baptisms, weddings and funerals they have performed. I shall not follow this custom, for I do not feel that I have done anything to speak of. I will only confess that I have worked hard, both from necessity and from inclination. But my purpose to-day is to tell what you have done during these ten years, for this is your church, and you have made it what it is.

"Ten years ago, if report speaks truly, you were somewhat discouraged. You had a nominal membership of less than three hundred; a congregation which half-filled the church in the morning and varied from fifty to a hundred in the afternoon; a floating debt and a sinking revenue. But you had also a company of people who were devoted to the church and willing to work for it in the face of discouragements."

From this he went on to describe the work done mentioning those "strong and generous men" called from us by death, "E. D. Morgan, Frederick Billings, S. H. Witherbee, Charles G. Harmer, John C. Tucker, George de Forest Lord, and many more"; and speaking also of Winthrop S. Gilman, Benjamin F. Dunning, John E. Parsons, Hamilton Odell, William N. Blakeman, A. R. Ledoux, Daniel J. Holden, Henry L. Butler, W. D. Barbour, Adam Campbell, Hector M. Hitchings, George W. Comstock, Daniel Parish, Lucius D. Bulkley, William B. Isham, W. W. Van Valzah, Edward W. Davis, Caldwell R. Blakeman, Edward W. Davis, Jr., William F. Dunning, Shepherd Knapp, Isaac N. Phelps, John A. Stewart, Charles A. Miller, Cornelius B. Gold, Benjamin H. Bristow, Frederick H. Billings, Jr.

These church officers and a host of other workers who must here be nameless held Henry van Dyke to New York, to the Brick Church, and to the continuance of the pastoral form of his struggle for liberty in the Church.

Chapter Ten

FAMILY, VACATIONS AND TRAVEL

HENRY van DYKE'S time and energy were by no means wholly exhausted in the work of his parish and the Church at large, or in the lecture and speaking engagements that were steadily increasing, or in the mass of writing that kept piling up on his table. He was by nature an outdoor man with a well-established habit of taking outdoor holidays—not only as an aid to fitness, but because he enjoyed them. For a number of years he was a familiar figure in the afternoons riding vigorously on the bridle paths of Central Park, and only surrendered it when the exercise proved too violent for a man who was spending his nervous energy so generously in other ways. He was not one to amble even when on a horse. "Dr. van Dyke", said the *Herald* "has the rather spare figure of an athlete and looks springy on his feet. His blue eye is keen and good natured and his honest belief in the practice of outdoor sports evidently does him good." In the spring he would run off trout-fishing on the least provocation, at first in Long Island and later on the Swiftwater. The summer vacations were long; at least he managed to be away a good deal of the time between Sundays, and added to this a stretch of several weeks in camp beyond reach of anything but personal messengers. For the sake of the whole family, now including two daughters and two sons, he rented a summer cottage, "Brightwater", at Westhampton, Long Island, conveniently near New York. Here he refreshed himself and became the inseparable companion of his little children. In New York he was to them a somewhat mysterious figure going and coming from his book lined study, seeing streams of callers and, except for the enthusiastically welcomed evening

[143]

story hour and the Sunday afternoon walk, wrapped in an aura of aloofness intensified by their Sunday morning view of him in the beautiful pulpit. And yet though he was regarded with awe he always remained human. Three children can never forget one Sunday stroll on Fifth Avenue with their frock-coated and silk-hatted father. The Sunday atmosphere of brown stone respectability was in the air and began to settle upon the minister's children until decorum was all and in all. Suddenly their father rushed up to one of the tall hydrants, placed his hands upon it, and neatly vaulted over it. The children at first were too startled for utterance, but a moment later, as their father with perfect dignity took off his hat to some smiling acquaintances who had seen the event from afar, they burst into laughter and all four holding hands passed chattering down the Avenue.

Children are natural imitators of the people they admire and the minister's children soon were aware of the books that issued from their father's pen. A publishing house was organized and many were the books of stories and poems that were written and published in the nursery. Unsuspecting callers were waylaid with high pressure salesman's methods and persuaded to buy. Several amused publishers from the mysterious outside world fell victim. And great was the rejoicing in the nursery when the father added an unnamed amount to the funds thus procured and purchased a duplicator that greatly increased the size of the editions. There was also a *daily* newspaper published "every rainy day."

At "Brightwater" no one seemed freer from a sense of responsibility than Henry van Dyke. He was full of plans for spending time out of doors. There was a catboat "The Patience". Oh, what summer hours she spent, at times spanking along over the crisp wavelets of the inner bay with a port in view, but usually drifting through summer calms in profitable idleness nowhere in particular. How eager was the crew that boarded her on a breezy Sunday morning when it had been determined that we *ought* to go to church across the bay. There was a flat-bottomed row boat in which the children explored the shallow waters below the house. There were crabbing expeditions and fishing for snappers off the red bridge over the Channel, beach parties, and now and again an expedition to the mysteries of that nameless, "lazy, idle brook", where a small boy once exclaimed: "Wherever you see one of those big smiles on the water, I believe there's a fish"—a faith which the father promptly justified by filling his creel with a dozen shining trout.

On the fourth of July there was always a carefully supervised celebration with fire-crackers under the tall white flagpole with the stars and stripes aloft. And as the evening stars came out Henry van Dyke would be found setting off pin wheels and red fires and rockets amid a delighted chorus of Ohs! and Ahs!

There was a cow in the meadow who "gave us milk with all her might," and chickens including three admired bantam roosters, and the black spaniel, Roderick Dhu, "faithful and true his whole life through," not forgetting that true James Whitcomb Riley character, —"Webb, the daily man." And there was Jessie, the beloved Scotch nurse, with her Gaelic songs and a conscience that would have done credit to a Highland Manse. Now and again the genial and dignified Dr. and Mrs. van Dyke, Senior, would be there for a visit, or the ever popular Uncle Paul van Dyke would come with his infectious laugh and his warning to rioting youngsters: "One, two, three—no chocolate." The mother's care was perpetually around the children, but the father was the natural leader on all expeditions and the spokesman for the dreams and nonsense that poured out of a cheerful but by no means docile family life. He used to tell endlessly a series of stories about Frankie Frog and Tommy Lizard and the Little Girl that lived in the well, all of whom became vivid personalities in the children's lives. How bewitching were the strange voices in which they spoke and the wild adventures in which they were involved. His eldest daughter once wrote down some memories of those days which are freely drawn upon here.

"Of the making of rhymes too," she wrote, "there was no end. Sometimes at the dinner-table my father would sit perfectly quiet for ten minutes, apparently wrapped in thought, while we chattered and discussed the doings of the morning or planned for the afternoon; and then if we stopped for a moment and looked at him we would see a smile dancing on his face, and a new-made nonsense rhyme was recited much to our delight. We often tried to persuade him to write a book for children, but although he seemed to have plenty of time to make it up, he was always too busy to write it down."

Another recollection of the father among his children is associated with the Swiftwater in the Pocono Mountains in Pennsylvania. Here in the spring when "the flocks of young anemones are dancing round the budding trees" he used to go for a few days fishing. Dr. Richard Slee, then at work in his laboratory beside the stream, writes:

"My early recollection of your father dates to your early childhood. You may recall the fact that it was his custom to bring his little group of children to Swiftwater and although you may not know it he left you frequently in my care over Sundays when he returned to his church. At this time I can say that I have never known a more charming, well bred and obedient little flock. You may recollect that one of the treats that you children greatly enjoyed was a box of sugar peppermints reposing on the hat rack outside of the dining room at Swiftwater from which each child was permitted to select exactly one peppermint after their dinner and I can say that I do not recall that any of you children violated the trust reposed in you by your father."

By the Swiftwater the children, who were perhaps not so virtuous as a good man's memory records, played and followed their fishing father along the banks. Never can they forget the day when one after another, in places ruinous to the fishing, each slid unintentionally into the cold water, beginning with the big sister and ending with the littlest brother. The angry sound of the reel as the fisherman resigned his morning's sport was all the rebuke required—or given.

There too befell the incident when Henry van Dyke returned from a trip to New York without his beard. Two small boys hearing the carriage approach rushed out to meet him but seeing an unfamiliar face refused to be embraced and were reconciled only after two days' experience assured them that the father himself was unchanged.

One day the ever watchful father observed in one child a natural interest in birds. Characteristically he drew out and directed that interest. The boy received a treasured copy of Mabel Osgood

[146]

Wright's "Birdcraft" and a sheaf of colored plates. He became known in the family as the "bird-struck boy" but it was not until he became a man that he fully realized what his father had done for him.

On the banks of the Swiftwater stood the great butternut-tree beneath which the two boys and their father had a picnic lunch cooked over a little improvised fireplace with "Douglas, the beloved doll that the younger lad shamefacedly brought out from the pocket of his jacket." The following spring the younger lad, Bernard, died and the father wrote:

"Well, the fireplace is still standing. The butternut-tree spreads its broad branches above the stream. The violets and the bishop's-caps and the wild anemones are sprinkled over the banks. The yellow-throat and the water-thrush and the vireos still sing the same tunes in the thicket. And the elder of the two lads often comes back with me to that pleasant place and shares my fisherman's luck beside the Swiftwater.

"But the younger lad?

"Ah, my little Barney, you have gone to follow a new stream,—clear as crystal,—flowing through fields of wonderful flowers that never fade. It is a strange river to Teddy and me; strange and very far away. Some day we shall see it with you; and you will teach us the names of those blossoms that do not wither. But till then, little Barney, the other lad and I will follow the old stream that flows by the woodland fireplace,—your altar.

"Rue grows here. Yes, there is plenty of rue. But there is also rosemary, that's for remembrance! And close beside it I see a little heart's-ease."

It was the first break in the family circle that directly affected the children. The infant son that had opened and closed his eyes upon the world in a day was known only as a reflection in the father and mother. But now a playmate was gone. How that loss was made lighter for each by the common sharing; and how each child was led out of the sense of shame that death brings, let family memory cherish. The place of the lad in the family circle was never forgotten; but the ranks closed up, and relations were strengthened and bettered by the spiritual leadership that concerns itself with things temporal as well as with things eternal. The summer was passed in fresh scenes. The promise of a bicycle which had brightened the last days of the little lad but which he would not now need was fulfilled for another child. And the elder brother was made to rejoice in his first camping experience in the Canadian forests. It rained most of the time for ten days under canvas and the eleven year old boy carried one arm in a sling but the wood magic was there and also several trout whose size it would be an act of treason to define.

The memory of all those years is not one of cloying sweetness. There were bitter hours. All children fight and rebel—at least all these did. Perhaps it was part of the process of learning about life and discovering themselves. And wooden saints do not make the best parents. But the things that stand out in the perspective of the years are the constant natural teaching for which there always seemed to be time in the family, the bond of genuine affection that could not be broken, and the lessons from happy experiences that brought meaning into the required tasks. The father was feared at times, in the Victorian manner; but chiefly he was loved with passion because he was best known as the elder playmate.

These were the years too when Henry van Dyke and "My Lady Greygown" would settle the children under competent care and disappear into the woods with tent and blanket rolls. The Adirondacks were becoming too civilized, so they betook themselves to the Canadian rivers and forests. There was a trip up the Ristigouche on a horse-yacht, but the Lake St. John region was the usual camping ground, and there Ferdinand, the French Canadian guide, joined Sam Dunning and one-eyed Enos and Joe LaCroix, and others who came later, in that band of woodsmen and *habitants* who provided the matter out of which Henry van Dyke produced many a philosophical essay and moving story. There was something about these men, especially the Frenchmen, that appealed mightily to Henry van Dyke: their manners which rose out of primitive passion; their natural reverence; their childlike love of song and laughter; their simple devotion to adventure in the wilderness.

My Lady Greygown shared this fascination though she was not by nature or early experience a camper. She was essentially the companion, the model fisherman's wife, able to wait patiently in camp and welcome the late-comer with smiles and generous exclamations when the fish were displayed. Capable also of taking a *smaller* fish now and then, but quite content to grace the canoe and to bring out the little beauties of their surroundings. Thus her feminine instinct, without visible effort, rejoiced the way of her husband. And these trips proved for both sources of refreshment and renewal from which they returned with vital wisdom for living in the more difficult surroundings of civilization. Henry van Dyke never wrote on these early camping trips, but he came back with many odd jottings in notebooks and on scraps of paper many of which were not used until years afterward.

But the immediate objective of these excursions was fish—in particular the land-locked salmon or ouananiche. On the back of one of the children's letters tucked in a notebook is recorded in detail four days fishing on the Metabetchouan River in 1894: thirty-five ouananiche weighing one hundred and thirty-three pounds. Usually the fate of these fighting fish was decided by a four ounce rod with tiny flies and gossamer leader. Henry van Dyke loved his tackle and delighted to pit skill against strength and speed. Once at least, when the rod case was inadvertently left behind, he made a great catch with what was left of an old spliced rod and he has described how the humble grasshopper served on an occasion when all flies failed.

Now the account of the fish that he caught and the wonders that he saw are they not recorded in the book of *Little Rivers* and *Fisherman's Luck* and vicariously attributed to the characters in many thrilling tales?

Four times in his early years at the Brick Church Henry van Dyke crossed the Atlantic to ramble alone with fishing rod and note book in the Scotch highlands; to spend a Norwegian honeymoon with My Lady Greygown; to join his friend Allan Marquand on a Della Robbia hunt in Italy and to visit Tennyson at Aldworth; and, with his little daughter Brooke as companion, to seek health and new knowledge in Egypt and Italy.

No one believed more profoundly in work than Henry van Dyke. But equally no one believed more delightedly than he in play. Profitable idleness was as much a part of his creed as strenuous work. Indolence was among the virtues, but only in its root sense of freedom from anxiety or grief.

From the summer of 1893 until the spring of 1894 Henry van Dyke had chiefly to practice that virtue. But he practiced it after his own fashion which was to let his creative mind lie fallow for future crops while failing not to gather in the harvest of the days gone by. In fact, it is important to note in recording the brief but not infrequent halts in the activities of his immediate career that these breaks usually coincided with the need for writing down the ideas which continually thronged his mind. So soon as the pressure of immediate duties was taken off, he began naturally to write.

But the break in 1893 was more of a crisis than this. Undoubtedly his strenuous efforts on behalf of creed revision and liberty in the Church had seriously imperilled his health. He was working faster than his constitution could stand. But when the doctors told him that he had only a year or so more of life before him he remarked: "In that case what I need is a new doctor" and turned to his friend and classmate Dr. William Ward Van Valzah. Dr. Van Valzah became his personal physician, established a policy of physical moderation, a strict dietary regime, and provided an abundant sympathy. The outcome was a triumph of common faith, medical skill and honest cooperation. Henry van Dyke summed up the achievement when he wrote on February 18, 1933 in reply to a friendly letter from Dr. William V. V. Hayes: "I always think of your uncle, Dr. Will, with gratitude, and wish that he was still with us. He was a beneficent tyrant endowed by God with the healing gift. Undoubtedly he saved my life forty years ago."

The summer passed quietly with his family at Amherst, Massachusetts, where Henry van Dyke spent long afternoons driving a pair of horses with a surrey load of singing children around the hills or loafing with his friends.

His restless mind he occupied with writing "The Source" (later published as the first story in the *Blue Flower*) and in seeing *The Christ Child in Art* through the press.

In the autumn, being alarmed at certain symptoms in his heart, he consulted his friend Dr. M. Allen Starr who sent him to the Virginia

Hot Springs. Thence Henry van Dyke, who could never pass up the chance to make his joke, wrote Arthur H. Scribner: "I expect to have the douche of a time for about a month. But a man can stand anything for the sake of getting well."

By January 1894 he was ready to put the finishing touches to his recovery. He sailed for Europe with his ten year old daughter Brooke. On the steamer Mr. and Mrs. Andrew Carnegie easily persuaded them to be their guests on a leisurely voyage up the Nile. Each Sunday by Mr. Carnegie's order the dahabieh was tied up to the bank by some little village where there were no ruins or curiosities to attract tourists. Amid all the vivid impressions of that memorable and happy trip Henry van Dyke always cherished that unspoken courtesy and often referred to that act of devout feeling from a man not at all inclined to ecclesiastical habits. At this time, too, began a life-long friendship with the scholarly and ardent British fisherman and sportsman, William Radcliffe.

In early April with a mass of notes on Egypt and the Bible, stacks of photographs, renewed health and a thrilled daughter, he returned to the Brick Church. On April 16th from the text "the simplicity and the purity that is toward Christ" he renewed his preaching to a crowded Church: "After ten months of absence from the place and the work that I love best in the world this is the text with which I would take up again the ministry of Christ among you."

Chapter Eleven

THE CALL TO WRITE

EVEN when he had answered the call of the ministry in 1879 instead of undertaking a literary career, Henry van Dyke had not turned his back on writing. In Newport and especially in New York his pen was the pen of a ready writer. Nor was this a divided allegiance. At first, as we have seen, his writing of articles and verses was chiefly the exercise of an obvious talent that demanded use, and his themes were mostly religious in the more specific sense. But even when his writing talent in the stricter literary sense began to blossom, as it did early in his New York years, still there was no divided allegiance.

There were, it is true, brief times of questioning,—the inevitable fate of a man of artistic temperament who refused to act until he was thoroughly convinced. In the winter of 1885-6 a number of events combined to bring up for him in a new form the old issue between the ministry and literature as a career. It was not truly the question of the central motive of his life. That had been once for all determined in 1879—though faith being alive and not dead must live from day to day. He was indeed a "dedicated spirit." But what form should his service take? The burden of pastoral responsibility combined with his as yet unadjusted physical powers, an urgent invitation to a London pulpit, the sorrow that possessed him at the death of his first born son, and the natural craving of the artist for unlimited time, weighed heavily upon him. In the summer of 1886 he let himself drive before the sea of troubles and took refuge in a trip to England and Scotland. In "A Handful of Heather", written in 1893, he has recorded some intimations of that inner struggle during which the white haired Mistress of the Glen gave such needed help. From this trip he returned refreshed and steadied. The outcome was a foregone conclusion so soon as he regained his perspective.

During his student days, when the moralist and the artist in him were as yet unintegrated, he had worked steadily at their fusion. His formal studies and, above all, his conversations with Herman Grimm, his youthful ramblings through picture galleries with his friend and fellow student, Allan Marquand, his visits and correspondence with Holman Hunt, his devotion from a boy to the poetry of Tennyson, all helped him to the conclusion that art and morality were complementary and not opposing activities of the genuinely religious man. In a number of articles, addresses and sermons he now set forth this thesis with power. He declared his faith that for the sake of life itself a moral standard can and should be applied to the character of the artist; to the temper and purpose of his art; and to the influence of his work.

"The highest element in the best art is always moral, and fitted to make men and women better as well as happier . . . Immoral art is one of the most evil influences in the world . . . Virtue may be adorned and made attractive by a pure art. Truth and goodness are not complete until beauty is added to the trinity of excellence."

The thesis was for him an expression not of abstract theory but of urgent concern with the well-being of people as well as an unaffected delight in life. Vigorously as he attacked the popular theory of art for art's sake Henry van Dyke never favored censorship in art. In accordance with his belief that one positive act or word was of more value than endless regulations and prohibitions he pleaded for more moral sense, that often indefinable but always recognizable "feeling in our hearts." It is significant that *The Christ Child in Art*, published as a handsome illustrated book in November 1893 begins with a preface which distinctly views the province of art as that of helping to create a noble and lofty life and that the book itself concludes with a direct plea in the face of actual conditions for the preservation of Christian homes. This was not because Henry van

Dyke was "always preaching." It was because of his faith that the highest art must ever play a vital part in the purposes for which man was created. The recognition of this faith is vital to understanding his work in the Church and also in the field of literature. Later we shall see how it occasioned many conflicts with the rising literary school of the 20th century.

In a sermon first preached in 1888, entitled "The Light of God's Countenance," he has a long passage on the gospel of gloom in literature. After referring specifically to certain books and writers of the day he says:

"No man can breathe an atmosphere like that which fills the literary world today without danger of infection, any more than he can live in a malarious country without being in peril of a fever. I do not believe there is one of us that has not felt its depressing, debilitating influence,— not one of us that has not been overcast by its shadow at least for a time, —not one of us that is not liable, should great disaster or trouble come upon us, to sink more or less permanently into its gloom. What shall we find to protect us from so great a danger, what safeguard, what sure remedy, what unfailing prophylactic of despair?

There is but one thing that can help us with continual comfort, and defend us from the dark miasma of graveyard philosophy, and keep alive in us that inward happiness and heart of joy upon which our power of vigorous and useful work depends, and that is faith in a personal, powerful, beautiful and good God."

Henry van Dyke's literary creed was an expression of his religious faith. His writing originated at the same source from which he drew his preaching. But while his preaching found ample scope in a liberal interpretation of Presbyterianism, his writing sought out the Gentiles in the broader reach of the same basic emotion. In fact, his actual literary work and interests originated as buds on the tree of his preaching which in turn, though it stood in the pulpit, had mighty roots that drew sustenance from a much wider range of life than that within ecclesiastical bounds. Being in love with life and a welcome and colorful figure at all sorts of gatherings, organized and accidental. Henry van Dyke's preaching tingled with the full sap of life itself. He was neither a professional literary man nor a professional clergyman. His preaching and his writing both were vital expressions of what he saw and knew and felt. Like every man who leaves behind him a large record of accomplishment he belonged to his age. But he belonged to it as one who believed in its aspirations and hopes and shared in its work and conflicts.

Doubtless his extreme spiritual sensitiveness, his wide human relations, and his industrious reading made him aware of the rising tide of American thought and literature. And certainly the concern that this tide should ennoble and not debase life caught his alert interest. Books had always fascinated him since the days when as a child he had sat enthralled in his father's library. And with a natural talent for writing fostered by constant exercise and by a continuous study of words it was inevitable that he should enter the field of literature. These natural qualifications and interests were greatly stimulated by his associations with literary people. In the spring of 1887 he was notified by William Hamilton Gibson of his election to the Authors' Club; and he was becoming a familiar figure in the formal and informal gatherings of writers who delighted each other with stories and criticisms in the corners of clubs and in publishers' offices and at luncheons and suppers.

It was his custom to dine with his friend Hamilton W. Mabie on the last night of each old year and frequently other writers were included in the party. There were few things that Henry van Dyke enjoyed more than good table talk. The spirit of these gatherings appears in a doggerel invitation written by his own hand:

> "My dear George W. Cable
> Do you think you will be able
> To take your dinner here
> On the last night of the year?
> Some literary fellows,
> Who haven't got 'the yellows',
> But still are sane and jolly,
> Will come to take pot-luck,
> And eat a bit of duck
> Beneath our Christmas holly.

[155]

We shall sit down at seven.
No Pharisaic leaven
Of envy or of guile
Our feasting shall defile;
But we'll give thanks to heaven
For all its blessings given,—
For all the things ideal,
And also for things real,—
For friendship, love and duty,
For pleasure and for beauty,
And likewise for our grub!
And then we'll seek the Club
To bid farewell the parting Year,
And welcome in the New with cheer.
So I hope that you'll be able,
To make one at our table;
And whether you come by cable
Or ride down on your bike,
Don't fail
   Your friend
   van Dyke."

Perhaps the first thing that gave him standing in literary circles was a sermon "The National Sin of Literary Piracy", preached in the Brick Church on January 7, 1888. In this sermon Henry van Dyke took up a matter which had long troubled thinking American men and to which he had heard his own father make reference in an address at Edinburgh in 1877. This was the American practise of printing pirated editions of foreign author's books. To a man of principle such a procedure was a shame and Henry van Dyke described that shame and pleaded for its removal in vigorous terms. Pointing out that the question was not one of politics, of economy, of national courtesy but, as Lowell had said, of right and wrong, he recalled Henry Clay's effort to bring it home to public conscience, and proceeded to show that "it belongs to the department of Applied Ethics, which the Church can never afford to make an optional course. It is a subject in regard to which the pulpit has many reasons for speech, and no apology for silence. The preacher is moving straight along the line of practical Christianity when he invites you to consider the National Sin of Literary Piracy; its nature; its punishment; and its cure."

"The sin, my brethren", he declared, "lies in the stupefying fact that ours is the only civilized Christian country on the globe which deliberately and persistently denies to foreigners the same justice which it secures to its own citizens, and declares that the intellectual property of an alien shall be forfeited and confiscated the moment it touches our shore or crosses our border."

The punishment for this sin "is the perversion of national taste and manners by the vast circulation of foreign books that are both cheap and bad" and also "the partial atrophy of our native literature" and above all "the weakening and degeneration of the popular conscience."

For its cure he besought the people to join with publishers and authors in bringing pressure to bear on the government to join the international copyright union.

The sermon at once proved a powerful reinforcement to the cause of international copyright in the United States, and Robert Underwood Johnson and Richard Watson Gilder of the Authors' Copyright League promptly enlisted Henry van Dyke's personal aid. He preached the sermon again in the New York Avenue Presbyterian Church in Washington on February 12th. "Although the weather was stormy" reported the *New York Tribune*, "Mrs. Cleveland was present and there was in the audience a fair representation of Congress." The sermon was printed as a pamphlet and received a wide distribution in Europe as well as in America. "Everyone on the committee heartily appreciates the way in which you have come to our aid," wrote Mr. Johnson. "The sermon will do more good than merely to help in passing the bill. It will reinforce the high moral ground which the League has taken and help shame people back to a less material view of politics." The Chace bill was introduced in Congress in March 1888 but it was not until three years later that it was finally passed. Meantime Henry van Dyke continued speaking and writing vigorously on the issue and in the end shared in the real moral victory achieved.

In the fall of 1889 Henry van Dyke published in *The Poetry of Tennyson* the fruit of his twenty years reading and study of the poet, much of it used from time in time in magazine articles. From his fourteenth birthday when he had purchased for fifty cents a pirated edition of *Enoch Arden* he had been an eager reader of Tennyson. And ever since his college days he had been studying and writing about his work. In the first preface to the little volume Henry van Dyke carefully defined his object:

"One thing that will not be found here is a biography of the poet, or a collection of anecdotes in regard to his private affairs . . . For my own part, I am of opinion that the best biography of Tennyson will always be found in his works. His poems are his life."

Declaring himself frankly a Tennysonian and concerned for the utterance of a man's "deepest convictions in regard to art and religion and human life" he said:

"I should be sorry to have any one take it merely as a collection of critical essays. It does, indeed, contain a certain amount of work which belongs entirely to criticism, and some of which has never been done before. The analysis of the changes in *The Palace of Art*; the history of the order of production of *The Idylls of the King*, and the attempt to show that they are not an allegory; the full table of Biblical allusions and quotations in the poems of Tennyson, these are contributions to the careful study of the technique of a poet who has become a classic in his own lifetime. But beginning with the second essay in this book, I have not hesitated to express with freedom, and with such clearness as I could attain, those opinions in regard to the meaning of life and the province of art, without which it is not possible to form any true judgment of the value of a poet's work. I do not desire to sail under false colours, or even under a dubious flag. There need be no doubt, at least, in regard to the standpoint from which this book is written."

The preface concluded with the question:

"In the future, when men call the roll of poets who have given splendour to the name of England, they will begin with Shakespeare and Milton,—and who shall have the third place, if it be not Tennyson?"

The volume was in fact literary criticism on the thesis that the prime business of poetry is the ennobling of life. Henry van Dyke's father writing him enthusiastically about the book grasped this fact from the standpoint of the born preacher when he said:

"The theology or rather the Christianity of your book is all that could be desired, and will add to your confidence as a preacher of the gospel. Indeed, it is the best kind of preaching for a class who cannot be reached by more formal sermons."

A few months before the volume appeared Henry van Dyke wrote Tennyson enclosing some of the articles and received the following reply inscribed with the poet's pen:

> Aldworth
> Haslemere
> Aug 20/89

"Dear Sir:

I thank you for your kind and able articles which you have sent me. That on the two Locksley Halls is also good.

I should be very ungrateful, if I were not grateful for the good wishes and warm congratulations, that have reached me on my eightieth birthday. As a general rule however I think it wisest in a man to do his work in the world as quietly and as well as he can without much heeding the praise or dispraise.

The report (which you quote) that I dislike Americans is wholly without foundation, though it is true that I have protested against the manner in which some of the American publishers have pilfered my work.

> I am,
> Very faithfully yours,
> Tennyson"

The book received wide and for the most part favorable and even enthusiastic notice in the press though there were those who, debonairly disregarding its carefully described standpoint, insisted upon condemning it for what it did not pretend to be. And in particular the tentative claim to third place for Tennyson among English poets aroused, as it was calculated to do, considerable protest.

It is not the business of the present biographer to attempt to evaluate any work of Henry van Dyke—or even to defend it against attacks. But it may not be without interest here to note that Walt Whitman—so often assumed by his later imitators to be the antithesis of Tennyson—wrote an article in *The Critic* for January 1, 1887, bearing enthusiastic tribute to Tennyson as a man and a poet:

"Yes, Alfred Tennyson's is a superb character, and will help give illustriousness, through the long roll of time, to our Nineteenth Century. In its bunch of orbic names, shining like a constellation of stars, his will be one of the brightest. His very faults, doubts, swervings, doublings upon himself, have been typical of our age. We are like the voyagers of a ship, casting off for new seas, distant shores. We would still dwell in the old suffocating and dead haunts, remembering and magnifying their pleasant experiences only, and more than once impelled to jump ashore before it is too late, and stay where our fathers stayed, and live as they lived.

May-be I am non-literary and non-decorous (let me at least be human, and pay part of my debt) in this word about Tennyson. I want him to realise that here is a great and ardent Nation that absorbs his songs, and has a respect and affection for him personally, as almost for no other foreigner. I want this word to go to the old man at Farringford as conveying no more than the simple truth; and that truth (a little Christmas gift) no slight one either. I have written impromptu, and shall let it all go at that. The readers of more than fifty millions of people in the New World not only owe to him some of their most agreeable and harmless and healthy hours, but he has entered into the formative influences of character here, not only in the Atlantic cities, but inland and far West, out in Missouri, in Kansas, and away in Oregon, in farmer's house and miner's cabin.

Best thanks, anyhow, to Alfred Tennyson—thanks and appreciation in America's name."

Meantime Henry van Dyke went on with his hobby of collecting first editions of Tennyson and Tennysoniana (of which it was said that he already had the finest collection in America) and entered upon a voluminous correspondence with Tennysonians in America and abroad. Tennyson himself sent him some autobiographical notes and corrections for the chronology. In the new preface to the second edition in 1891 Henry van Dyke made acknowledgment of the help he had received, added two new chapters, lengthened the title to the chapter "Milton and Tennyson" to include the phrase "a comparison and a contrast" as a special concession to one of his critics, and, with something of an air of justifiable triumph, concluded by quoting Thomas Bailey Aldrich's poem which ranked Tennyson third after Shakespeare and Milton. Mr. Aldrich on granting permission for this quotation wrote him on April 16, 1891:

"Though I hate to copy my own things, I have copied these lines with peculiar pleasure; first, because I greatly like your book about Tennyson, and secondly, because the last paragraph of your Preface gives courage to the first stanza of the poem, placing Tennyson's name third in the list of great English poets. Your prose and my verse must have been written nearly simultaneously, though your volume was, I believe, printed first. If the late E. A. Poe were alive he would not leave me a poetical foot to stand on, with his confounded 'coincidence'!"

On the morning of August 18, 1892, Henry van Dyke went as the invited guest of Tennyson, then eighty years old, to Aldworth. The pages of an old notebook and the memory of several conversations about the visit keep the event vivid. For Henry van Dyke it was not only a pious pilgrimage but an experience of a simple English household life flavored with good cheer and made bright with a common faith and enthusiasm. Met at the station by Lady Hallam Tennyson, he was driven three miles, mostly through wooded lanes and over-arching trees with the berries of the mountain ash gleaming from the edges of the wood, and for a short stretch across an open down bright with purple heather. The grey stone house set in green trees stood in a slight depression on the ridge of Blackdown. In the drawing room Lady Tennyson "delicate and refined—one thinks of a piece of rare and frail old lace" met him. For a half hour while resting upon the sofa she spoke with him simply and naturally in a low and gentle voice of spiritual things. Then Hallam Tennyson, "broad shouldered, fair haired, strong and direct", took him up to the booklined study, a large light room having a very broad window on the southern side with a glorious view of the valley and the whole range of Southdown, and a bay window on the west before which stood the poet's wide writing table. On one end of a lounge near the southern window were scattered several books, one of them, "the Gospel of St. Paul the Apostle" face downward, open, as if it had just been laid down. Tennyson greeted him with a cordial grasp of the hand and a kind word of welcome and bade him sit beside him.

"His face is long, dark, powerful. The forehead is high, the temples straight with the veins showing clearly; the nose aquiline, the mouth large with a strong chin, a little projecting; the eyes brown and dreamy with drooping lids, but full of fire. He wears a black velvet skull cap, the hair that escapes beneath it is thin now, but still dark, hardly showing any grey, and the moustache which curls inward at the corners is of the same colour; the beard is greyer, thin at the sides, but fuller and a little longer on the chin. He was dressed in dark grey."

"I have not thanked you yet for your book as I want to," began Tennyson. "You have praised me in some things very highly—to the very top of the mark,—but I don't agree with you in some things. In some of your judgments I think you are wrong. . . . You don't like *Maud*. Now *Maud* is one of the most original poems I have ever written. I want to read it to you this afternoon if I am able to read."

In this connection it is of interest to note that W. J. Rolfe had written Henry van Dyke on October 20, 1891:

"Your book was mentioned in the course of my talk with Tennyson, who said that his people wouldn't let him read it until they had torn out some leaves! I told him I hoped he would be allowed to read the whole book if you sent him the new edition as you probably have done. He seems particularly sensitive to criticisms of *Maud*, which must be a pet work with him."

After a family lunch, with Tennyson and his guest, both of whom were spare eaters, grumbling cheerfully together about their diets and with much other conversation, the poet retired for his rest while the guest listened to some phonograph records of Tennyson's reading of his own poems. About four o'clock the guest went up to the study. The grey day had turned rainy and dark. Tennyson asked for candles which his son brought, setting them beside him on the writing table. Tennyson held the book close to his eyes with his face outlined dark and strong against the light. He read in a rhythmic chant, his voice a little higher pitched than his talking, true and sustained. There was a touch of Lincolnshire in his accents. Before beginning to read *Maud* he said: "I want you to feel what the poem means. It is dramatic. The war is only an episode. It is meant to show the power of love in a nature that is morbid—with a touch of insanity in it—and selfish. It makes him unselfish at last. You mustn't forget that it is not the poet who is speaking; it is the hero who has the strain of madness in his blood. He begins with a false description, 'Blood-red heath'—there isn't any such thing in the world. But he saw it blood-red because his eyes were morbid."

Then he began to read, continue the note book jottings, the best parts of the poem, throwing an incredible force and passion into it. *O father, O God, was it well?* Voice rising to almost a shriek of protest. The invective against the age of peace hot with condensed passion. Alternatives of mood. All *lyrical. Faultily* faultless, *icily* regular—heavy emphasis. *The broad flung shipwrecking roar* and the *scream of the maddened beach* splendidly contrasted. He stopped here to say "The fools found fault with that. But a man of science came out and said he had heard such a *scream* eight miles away." . . . *Luminous, gemlike, ghostlike, deathlike* he read rapidly with pulsations of accent as if the face were alternately growing and fading on the sight . . . *Caught and cuffed by the gale*—you saw the trees first bent and then tossed from side to side. . . .

The mad scene—the inconsequences of it—true picture of madness—touches of reason but disjointed.

At dinner the guest was asked to say grace and the conversation ran upon poetry especially that of Wordsworth, and upon the poetry of Charles and Frederick Tennyson. "Have you got my brother Charles' sonnets?" asked Tennyson.

Yes, replied the guest.

[163]

"And have you got my brother Frederick's poems too?" with a smile.

Some, but not *all* of them.

A hearty laugh from Tennyson. "Yes, they are very abundant indeed."

Tennyson told the story of the man who, having piloted the elderly Duke of Wellington across a crowded street, expressed profuse gratitude to the Duke declaring he should never to his dying day forget the great honor. To which the Duke remarked simply: Don't be a damned fool, sir.

And the guest told the American story of the poet who retorted to a fulsome admirer: Don't slop over.

After dinner the lights were taken away and they sat watching a thunderstorm playing across the valley.

Later the guest sat with Hallam Tennyson and his wife in their third story sitting room, she sewing, and the two men smoking pipes while the conversation ran on children and their training, books and men and women.

In the morning the guest was invited to conduct prayers in the drawing room and later he went up to the poet's study and again listened while Tennyson read among other things *Wages*, the "small sweet idyl" from *the Princess, The Northern Farmer* (*new style*) [of which Henry van Dyke noted "full of humour, you cannot help laughing at it"], part of the *Passing of Arthur*, and *The Ode on the Death of the Duke of Wellington* which "ended with a solemn calm triumphant note."

The poet talked of his new volume, told the story of Akbar and read the poem of St. Telemmachus.

"At lunch Tennyson was a little tired, the pains in his face (rheumatic gout) troubled him so that he could hardly eat. But he was good humoured. Even his growls were playful. There is great simplicity in his manners. Even his gruffness is kindly. There is no bitterness in him. He is fond of telling stories, and tells them well. He is still living in his work and is looking now for new subjects for poems."

The poet bade his guest goodbye and went up for his afternoon sleep. Henry van Dyke made his farewells and Lady Hallam Tennyson drove him to the station.

A few days later Henry van Dyke received a letter from Lady Tennyson enclosing in Tennyson's handwriting the lines from the *Ode on the Death of the Duke of Wellington* for which he had asked:

> "Not once or twice in our fair island story
> The path of Duty was the way to Glory."

and also the lines which Tennyson himself had chosen and which Henry van Dyke kept framed with the Mayall photograph of Tennyson in his library

> "Love took up the harp of life, and smote on all the chords with might,
> Smote the chord of self that, trembling, passed in music out of sight.
> August 24, 1892   Tennyson"

On October 6th Tennyson died and Henry van Dyke, deeply moved, wrote his memorable lyric "In Lucem Transitus" of which E. C. Stedman wrote him:

"If you were English (which we are glad you are not) and the laureateship went to the best of the elegists thus far, it is scant praise to say that you would enter upon the succession. Your three stanzas speak for us all, at last, unpremeditated and noble as they are. How fine it is for a poet to know his theme and—to feel it!"

And five years later when this lyric was published in Henry van Dyke's first book of poetry, T. B. Aldrich wrote him:

". . . but the page that holds the brief monody on Tennyson is the page to which I shall most frequently turn . . . When those stanzas first appeared I could not resist the temptation to cut them out of every newspaper that brought them to my hand. I must have ten or twelve copies of the lyric stowed away in various pockets."

The Poetry of Tennyson came out in a third edition in the early winter of 1892 with a much enlarged chronology and with what

Henry van Dyke described as "an altered and improved estimate of *Maud*."

"I should be very much ashamed," he wrote, "if I felt any shame at confessing a change in critical judgment produced by the reception of new light. In this case the new light that came to me was Tennyson's own wonderful reading and interpretation of the poem."

Of this revised edition William Winter wrote Henry van Dyke on December 8th,

"Your book about Tennyson is lovely in spirit, noble in thought, and lucid and reverent in style. You show yourself to possess the first requisite for a good critic, a good heart. It was Coleridge who said it, and a truer word was never said. I have been deeply impressed by your fine discrimination and your reverent feeling, in all that you have written about Tennyson. Your writing has the prodigious, the incomparable excellence of being perfectly clear."

The revision of his judgment was typical of Henry van Dyke's critical work, and may be interestingly traced through the twelve editions and twenty printings into which this book passed before it was finally gathered with other later work into "Studies in Tennyson," Vol. XII of the collected works in 1921. Henry van Dyke's admiration for Tennyson was a lifelong passion. On April 11, 1929, four years less one day before his death, he wrote at the invitation of his friend Ferris Greenslet an introduction to Houghton Mifflin's six volume edition of Tennyson's poems. The same steadfast admiration for Tennyson the man and the poet is there, but the critical claim for third place among English poets is moderated: "Tennyson still stands, with his friend and rival Robert Browning, foremost in the front rank of modern English poets."

But Henry van Dyke had not only something to say as well as he could say it about literature, he had also things that he wished to say through the medium of literature. His studies of Tennyson were in a sense a preparation of himself for his own writing. In December 1891 his first story "The Oak of Geismar" (later known as the "Story of the First Christmas Tree") was published in *Scribner's Magazine*. This was followed by the "Story of the Other Wise Man" in *Harper's Magazine* for January 1893. And "The Source," "A White Blot," "A Christmas Loss" (later called "The Lost Word"), "A Lover of Music," and "Vaillant Coeur"—the two latter the first of his French-Canadian stories—were all published in Magazines before the end of 1899. Meanwhile the poetic passion so apparent in his youthful days but which had produced not a line for more than ten years until it had burst into clear flame on Tennyson's death, began again to seek expression in a flock of poems—chiefly nature lyrics. It is the general custom nowadays to condemn the lyrics of the eighteen-nineties as mere exercises of escape for city writers who dared not consider the realities of their actual surroundings. To read the magazines of that day is to recognize the truth of the charge in some instances. But it will not bear examination in the case of Henry van Dyke; for his double passion for the city and for the country was rather the natural systole and diastole of a heart in love with life itself. He was not an escapist in the modern pathological sense but one who sought to unite the joy of the natural man and the duty of the civilized man—which is more of an undertaking than theoretical critics realize.

The first of the lyrics to attain popularity was "An Angler's Wish" beginning "When Tulips bloom in Union Square." Richard Watson Gilder promptly wrote:

"You bold bad van Dyke,
> This came to me at my home-desk and fell right into the midst of a weighty sentence in our Tenement House report on 'agglomeration of nationalities', and the devil knows what. I didn't want to be interrupted, and before I knew it I'd read every blamed word —and wanted likewise to go fishing! It just ripples!"

There followed a number of songs out of doors of which the poems about American birds in particular expressed a fresh note.

"It is delightful even now" wrote T. W. Higginson, "to have an American poet who does not write about larks and nightingales! (At a picnic the other day I was offered potted larks from little English cans and thought of sending one to my old friend Mrs. M. . . . who has lately relapsed into that diet!)"

On April 10, 1897 John Burroughs wrote him:

"You have builded well in those bird songs and in the others too. I think I have told you before how much I liked the sparrow and the hermit thrush poems. The Yellow-throat and the Whip-poor-will poems are fit companions for them. How I should like to have quoted them in my 'Birds and Poets'. They are the best we have upon their subjects by far. I am beginning to repeat your Angler's Wish, and in May I hope to realize the dream."

Frank Chapman, the ornithologist and bird lover, quickly enlisted the poems and the personal assistance of their author in the early work of the Audubon Society. At the first public meeting of the Society on December 2, 1897 Dr. Chapman records that Henry van Dyke was the principal speaker addressing an audience of about 1,000 "doubtless the largest number of people that had ever assembled in this country to listen to an address in behalf of bird conservation."

The first long poem from the pen of Henry van Dyke was "The Builders," an ode read at the Sesquicentennial of Princeton College on October 21, 1896, and which gave the title to his first book of poems published in April 1897. The little volume was warmly and discriminatingly received by most of the critics. Stedman and Mabie were enthusiastic about the bird and flower lyrics, but less sure of the artistic value of the gnomic, meditative verses. Of the Ode, Stedman wrote:

"It is, in truth, no mean associate of the remarkably fine discourse pronounced by Professor Woodrow Wilson . . . Portions of Dr. van Dyke's ode, such as the grave and impressive second strophe, and the apostrophe to the Nation in the ninth, are strongly imaginative, and the celebrant may congratulate himself upon having succeeded in the most difficult of a minstrel's tasks."

Little Rivers published in 1895, and which Henry van Dyke has called "my first offense in the field of literature," began like the streams it describes in many small springs on the highlands of his experience as a fisherman, a traveller, and a lover of reading. For ten years or more before its publication one finds it trickling through his notebooks and gleaming in the printed correspondence which he wrote from England and Scotland in 1886 or full-orbed like the article on Ampersand published in 1885. But perhaps the earliest foregleam of the book itself as a whole is found in a sermon on "The River of God" preached on October 5, 1890. The note that lies beneath the many melodies of *Little Rivers* is there clearly uttered:

"The rivers are the emblems of life and fertility, of joy and peace. Nothing in the world is more beautiful than those living streams which make their way across the surface of the motionless and impassive earth, now swiftly and musically, now slowly and silently, but always moving with an onward impulse, always bringing the influence of life and refreshment into the region through which they pass. How infinite is the variety of their beauty. Some are cradled among the pine trees that clothe the silent hills; ice-cold springs trickling through the mosses of the forest, blending in the rush and roar of mountain-brooks, gathering force and volume as their waters are united in the deeper valley, until at length the highland river clears its way through the long slopes of woodland and the sharp ridges of rock, impetuous, clear, joyous, with dancing rapids and leaping falls, broadening, deepening, but never ceasing, as it flows toward its home in the sea. Others spring full-grown from the bosom of the great lakes; the sources of their strength are fed in silence and stored in the vast secret reservoirs of nature, and when the river comes forth it is at once a mighty tide like the St. Lawrence, spreading itself as a sea in motion and bearing the huge ships lightly on its breast. Others like the Nile and the Euphrates, the Amazon and the Mississippi are continental in their wide relation, and extended careers; gathering into themselves the tribute of many streams, travelling in the greatness of their strength through many lands, they become the feeders of nations, the highways of commerce, the mothers of cities, as they sweep onward, slow, steady, majestic through the thousands of miles of their appointed course.

But it is not always the largest rivers that are the most famous or the most beautiful. The sacred Jordan, the yellow Tiber, the silvery Arno, the castled Rhine, the placid Thames, the stately Hudson, have a glory and a beauty which depends not on the length of their course nor the volume of their waters. And there are other rivers, less celebrated in history and less widely sung in poetry, obscure and humble streams, which may have a higher place in our affection and a clearer picture in our memory than any of their more famous sisters. The river that flows by the town where you were born, the currents on which you have journeyed with those who were dear to you in the days of youth, the wild stream beside whose banks you have pitched your summer tent and on whose virgin waters you have floated in the light canoe,—every river has its own individuality, its character, its charm, and when we enter into it we cease to think of it as a mere water-power, it becomes to us a thing of life, a companion, a friendly influence. . . .

Now the Bible, which touches nature and life on every side, has much to say about rivers. It begins in the Book of Genesis, where it is written 'And a river went out of Eden to water the garden,'—for Eden itself would not be complete without a living stream as part of the picture. It closes in the Book of the Revelation, where the inspired apostle John says 'And he showed me a river of water of life clear as crystal proceeding out of the throne of God and the lamb,' for not even Paradise would be perfect without a pure flowing stream and the musical voice of many waters. From Eden to Heaven the river has a part to play in the life of man: and the Bible uses it as a spiritual type, a mark of deep significance in the picture-language of nature."

When the book appeared Hamilton W. Mabie promptly welcomed it:

"It is a volume of peculiar charm, full of life, sentiment, hope, health, and beauty. For Dr. van Dyke has both the heart and the touch of an artist; he feels instinctively the charm of the world of woods and waters; he has a loving companionship with all sound human living, and he has the magic of style. 'Little Rivers' is not only 'a book of essays in profitable idleness,' it is also a book of literature. It has the freshness, the felicity, the ease and frankness of first-hand work. Its ways are by little and great streams, in near and remote quarters; but its charm lies in its intelligent observation, in its quiet humor, in its mood of fruitful idleness, and in its constant and tender reverence for human character and vicissitude."

Henry van Dyke had now taken his place with that new group of American nature writers for whom Charles Dudley Warner, John Burroughs and John Muir had led the way. But the book not only made its appeal to nature lovers, it bore its message to all sorts of people. Fishermen like Dean Sage, Gilbert Parker, John Burroughs and the Englishmen, Edward Marston and Wallace Radcliffe wrote enthusiastically. President Charles F. Thwing wrote:

"I try to be a bit of a fisherman myself, and at times as we read, I was tempted to get out my tackle, put on my rubber boots, and slouch hat, and go up into the attic and make a cast. But this piscatory longing was not so great as was the literary delight in these pages."

Brander Mathews wrote:

"Why do you send me your book at the very time when I ought to give every moment to the works of Lope da Vega and Calderon and other dramatists I have to lecture about? I had to give up reading Fitzgerald's version of the 'Alcalde of Zalamea' just to reread your book—and I don't know how far you are responsible for the neglect of my duty (a subsidiary variety of sin that gave added zest to my enjoyment of your pages).

And why I should want to look at your chapters a third time, I don't know,— for I am not an outdoor man myself and I never caught a fish in my life. But when I open your book, the charm works, and I cannot choose but read your fish-stories. And the worse of it is, that I find myself really believing them,—or some of them. I can't say more, can I?"

"Down in Gloucester harbor the other Sunday night," wrote Bliss Perry, "I was reading aloud from 'Little Rivers' to a friend who was cruising with me, and the skipper was smoking his pipe and condescending to listen. He is a graduate of a lobster boat and a shore shop, and after I had finished the second chapter he volunteered: 'Say, Mr. Perry, that fellow *can* write; yes sir, he writes *right to the point.*'

"Who says that Massachusetts is not a literary centre still?"

"It is as good as Stevenson, and can a Scot say more?" wrote a minister from Thurso, Scotland, who subscribes himself as "one of Mr. Barrie's Auld Lichts."

Despite his earlier decision Henry van Dyke was finding himself irresistibly led into the field of literature. But he was entering this field, not from the mere ambition to write, but because he had a message he wished to convey. That he was not alone—though in the minority among literary men,—in that purpose, and how he himself viewed that purpose is well illustrated in letters exchanged with

George E. Woodberry in 1898. Mr. Woodberry writing about *The Toiling of Felix*, Henry van Dyke's ballad of labor just printed in a small private edition, said:

"I thought it quite the best poem you had written and developed to its full capacity both of thought and form. The moral of it is, of course what I must firmly believe; and, much as is said against using poetic form to enforce views of duty, I never could see anything in that line of argument. Doubtless they will say that only proves my intellectual impulse to be more than the artistic, and denotes slavery to academic tradition. But so it is—and in the present state of 'artistic' production I am content to be left out of it."

"I respond to what you say," replied Henry van Dyke, "about the possibility of *literature* and *morality* living together. An author is *not* a preacher, but I can't see why he should let the preacher monopolize all the best subjects. There are no themes in the world so real or so interesting as moral conflicts and problems. There are only two ways to handle them. The moral and the immoral way. I fail to see that the latter is any more artistic *per se* than the former."

Furthermore, while Henry van Dyke believed that literature and morality belonged together though the author was to be clearly distinguished from the preacher, he was equally emphatic that the pulpit was something quite different from "literary."

In a letter to the Editor of the New York *Observer* published in the issue of January 12, 1898, he wrote:

"I should be very glad if it were possible for me to accept your kind invitation to prepare an article for *The Observer*, on the question, 'How far should the pulpit be literary?'

"I do not believe that the pulpit should be literary at all. It should be evangelistic. But it is possible that a man who knows something about literature, may be able to do some decent work in an evangelical pulpit.

"One of the first things that a preacher should try to do, is to deliver his message in clear and simple English. An acquaintance with the world's best literature, which is always clear and simple, will certainly help him to gain the power of lucid and direct speech.

"Another point in which a knowledge of good literature may be of help to the preacher is in guarding him against flippancy and irreverence.

The man who reads nothing but the daily newspapers is very likely to fall into a frivolous and vulgar habit of speech. The sermons of such a man often present in their style a strange and disquieting contrast with the dignity and elevation of the language of texts taken from that Book which is a 'well of English undefiled.'

"Another point where a preacher may receive assistance from literature is in establishing a certain kind of sympathy and harmony with his hearers. The familiar treasure of good books written in English, offers material for a standard coinage of illustrations and allusions which will pass current on a gold basis among all people of thought and intelligence. . . .

"But if I keep on in this way I shall write the article in spite of myself. The intention of this letter was simply to thank you for your invitation, and to tell you that I am so overwhelmed with engagements of all kinds, that I cannot fairly undertake anything more."

As an artist Henry van Dyke was strenuous in the defense of his poetic principles and very clear in his understanding of himself and in the recognition of the uncertainties of writing poetry. A letter he sent in response to an invitation to deliver the Phi Beta Kappa poem at Harvard is a good illustration:

"Your kind letter of January 7th is duly received. You may be sure that I appreciate the honor of an invitation to appear as the poet of the Phi Beta Kappa Society of Harvard University at its annual meeting. But perhaps the sincerity of my appreciation is the very reason which makes me feel unable to accept the invitation. In a certain sense I am a very young poet, having only just begun within the past two years to attempt serious work in that art. My working relations with the Muse have not become so familiar as to lead me, even in the slightest degree, in the direction of contempt for her unchartered liberty and caprice. I can never count upon being able to begin a poem at a certain date, and, having begun, I am still less able to foresee whether, or when, it will be possible for me to finish.

The one safe-guard which I desire to preserve is the resolve never to undertake any poetical contract until the Muse has promised or provided the goods for delivery. This is the only security against routine work. If I had something ready I should be most happy to accept the invitation of the Phi Beta Kappa Society, but, failing this, I must decline, for your sakes as well as for my own."

But he was not only a devout artist, he was also genially competent in the various business transactions of an author. He believed absolutely in the value of his work—except in those occasional moods from which all creators suffer—and he managed his literary affairs with a steady hand. By no means the least interesting of his letters are those he wrote to his publishers with whom his relations were always healthy and frequently pungent. He did not consider that his work was done when he had written an article or a book. He concerned himself with its format, the illustrations which he frequently supplied from photographs he assembled and sometimes took himself; and he made suggestions about the advertising and marketing of his work. He took great interest in the details of publishing and found genuine delight in his relations with the men who were primarily responsible for these things. In all this he was not so much a worldly man as a man of the world interested in the making and selling of books as well as in the writing of them. How human are such letters as these:

To the Editor of Scribner's Magazine:

"You insist, like an editor, that *Au Large* shall be changed to *Au Petit*. You ought to supply your contributors with some of that stuff which Alice of Wonderland took when she shrank so fast that her chin bumped her foot. Well, how much do you want to cut out, and where will you thrust in the fated shears? Specify your pound of flesh! Mark it with a red pencil, symbolic of blood. Take my tender moralizing, take my delicate allusions, take my fresh quotations, take all, all for your cruel altar,—but leave me only the title and pay for it on that scale, and then I'll see whether there is sufficient balm in Gilead to enable me to stand the strain on my literary sensibilities."

Or again:

"I have finished one of the 'woodland tales,'—a story that I have known for years and tried to write a good many times, but without success until this summer. If you like it, it is at your disposal. I want five hundred dollars for it. This does not measure the work it has cost me. But it is about what the price would be for an instalment of a serial story. I am going away next week for a long stay in the woods, and would like to place this bit of work before leaving. Pray don't understand me as intending to hurry you in the matter. But as soon as you make up your mind about it, won't you let me know?

Perhaps I ought to add that this story belongs to a group of four,—if I can ever get the others written, they will follow this one; and the man who likes this will have the chance of saying whether he likes the other three or not. This is either a warning or an encouragement."

In 1898 his status among American writers was recognized in his election by the Academy of Social Science Association to the group of literary men which took part in the formation of the National Institute of Arts and Letters.

A true picture of the man at this period of literary burgeoning amid heavy pastoral responsibilities is found in one of the notes that he frequently dashed off to his beloved sister-in-law Edith Gittings Reid:

"It is a thing to be ashamed of, Edith dear, that I have not written before now to thank you for Vassari's Lives which arrived about ten days ago. But a new poem has been coming to me, and to be honest, I have been going about this busy world like a man in a dream. A terrible lot of things of the regular order has been done; but how, the Lord only knows. . . . Ellen and the children have been happy with Christmas expeditions. I have had little or none of it, until this morning which was spent over in the tenement district west of Eighth Avenue where there is a family of five little ones who shall have a merry Christmas for Bernard's sake and in his name . . . In March, if nothing prevents, and if the now invisible and incomprehensible lectures arrive to me, I am coming to Baltimore, and we will have a good time together, and that sweet baby Doris shall be baptized."

Henry van Dyke was turning steadily toward writing and literary studies. But he was not turning away from his life purpose.

Chapter Twelve

YOUTH PRESENTS ITS CLAIMS

IT WAS not long after his coming to the Brick Church that the schools and colleges and theological seminaries began to put in their claim for a share of Henry van Dyke's time and strength. Being young in years and of a youthful spirit the appeal was irresistible to him and many were the college sermons and addresses and conversations with young people that were crowded into his strenuous days. His own school, the Brooklyn Polytechnic, was the first to summon him and it may be of interest to note that after Princeton two of the first colleges at which he spoke were Wellesley and Vassar. Soon he was a familiar figure also at Yale and Harvard, Cornell, Williams, Amherst, Virginia, Columbia and Union. The Brick Church generously and intelligently shared their pastor with these institutions recognizing that it was the natural outworking of his influence among young people in their own parish. Dr. Francis G. Peabody wrote Henry van Dyke on March 17, 1890, asking him to obtain the approval of the Brick Church for his appointment as one of the five preachers to Harvard University:

"Harvard University, with its 2000 young men is, for the first time in the history of education, abandoning compulsion in religion and presenting religion as a privilege and an opportunity. It must therefore present religion in its most manly, modern persuasive form. It looks over the country, without reference to sect or name, for the men who can thus bring most closely to young men the truths of religion. It asks you to come, not because it has any claim on you whatever but because you seem to be one of these men."

[176]

And Dr. Lyman Abbott who was one of the five preachers wrote him:

"There are not too many men in the American pulpit that can win both its attention and respect. I believe you are one of the not too many," and went on to describe his own experiences in the capacity of preacher at Harvard: "The fifty or sixty who called on me at the Wadsworth gave me more insight into what educated young men are thinking about, more knowledge of really modern thought than a year of study in books could have done. They are so earnest, so genuine, so clear sighted and, when they are really convinced that you do not think any honest earnest questioning unusual and are not to be scared by it, are so frank and candid!"

Henry van Dyke found this a true word and often spoke with peculiar delight of his experience on this and later occasions as one of the Harvard preachers. It was the pastoral side of his service that especially appealed to him. Tucked away in some folders in a closet is found a bundle of the notes from which he spoke. Most of them are set down on the letter paper of the ministers' room and scattered through them are lists of appointments to talk with students —evidence, if later generations need it, that he spoke not as an angel from another clime but as a man who first listened to his hearers and then spoke the meditations of an elder brother. Take a few sentences from these pages to illustrate the simple direct nature of his talk:

"Jesus Christ is God's call to us to be true men". . . .
"Nicodemus was a good Pharisee, a rare kind of man but not impossible. In other words he was a man living in a false system, but a living man, whose life did not come from the system, as he thought, but from another source". . . .
"The word that I have chosen for today is *preach*. It has suffered a good deal of injury through misuse, this ancient word. So that it has come to be the reverse of praise when we say of a man, as Charles Lamb, said of Coleridge, that he is always preaching. But if we will get back of our own unfortunate experiences, and think what preaching really means,— the proclamation by a man to his fellowmen of the truth which he believes with all his heart,—we shall see that it is indeed a word of spirit and life.

[177]

. . . There are a hundred, yes a thousand, ways of preaching; but the essential thing is that every one of us who believes anything should feel that he is bound in some way to make it known to his fellowmen. . . . No man," (he warned his hearers), "ought to enter the ministry if he can honestly and fairly help it." . . .

"It is a great pleasure to come back, quietly and naturally, into the place that you have given me in your college life; to find the fire burning and the door on the latch in the preacher's rooms: and to feel that I can say to you again, 'Come in, at any time, on any errand, for I want to serve you, and even if I can't do that, I want to know you, and have good fellowship with you as men.' " . . .

In the *Home Journal of Boston* there is a description of his appearance and manner:

"A man in a silk gown comes out at a side door in the alcove and goes up into the oaken pulpit. He is on the younger side of middle age. His hair is dark. He has a full dark beard. He is not of large build. He appears to be a man of good stock; of fine quality of nerve; of a generation cleared of survivals from rude forefathers; of such intermixture of the feminine nature as to ensure the manliness that is keen in sensibility, and quick in sympathy. He has the style without the heartlessness which society imparts. That is the first impression . . .

The preacher's delivery is natural and it is his own. No school could impart it. It might be styled the successive surcharged delivery, fearful to imitate and imitated with fatal facility. The speaker goes on reading or talking in a quiet tone, and then suddenly the mental battery is overcharged and there ensues outbursting speech. It is unlike anything heard from the Unitarian pulpit, where repression prevails, resulting in twenty minute sermons. An hour's discourse from Dr. van Dyke would seem short to the audience. He is eloquent. You perceive that he speaks out from his heart. He is genuine. He is possessed by the preacher-spirit, without which a discourser is but an essayist.

Harvard manages the Appleton pulpit well. It has called the doctor."

Henry van Dyke speaking of these experiences has often recalled that Dr. Eliot said to him: "You are almost the only man who comes here and says: *Come to Jesus.* We want you to say what you believe. It would be no good for you to preach like a Unitarian minister."

And then Henry van Dyke always added: "You know 'faith in the Eternal' on Eliot's lips signifies just what 'Come to Jesus' does, but the latter means far more in an appeal to all sorts of men." The story is still current that once as Henry van Dyke came out of the pulpit Dr. Eliot remarked: "That sermon could do no harm."

The students heard him gladly and many were the letters they wrote him with such expressions as this:

"It all dates back to that one evening in Wadsworth House when you cared enough for a poor blind boy to bring him back to himself. I don't believe you will ever know here, with what reverence and tenderness his love goes out to you—you who brought Christ into his dull soul."

In 1893 Henry van Dyke gathered up ten of the sermons which he had preached first in his own church, and nine of them in the college chapels at Harvard, Yale and Princeton, to make a volume, *Straight Sermons to Young Men and Other Human Beings*. Dedicating the sermons to Phillips Brooks, to whom all American preachers and pastors are debtors, he explained in the preface that their aim "is nothing else than to help people to be good, which is the hardest and finest thing in the world. Their gospel is simply this: that the sure way to be good is to trust and follow Jesus Christ, the Son of God." Being addressed particularly to young men he had "tried to write these sermons, not in a theological dialect, but in the English language."

The same year he was invited to deliver the preaching lectures on the Lyman Beecher Foundation at Yale but had to postpone them because of ill-health. In the spring of 1896 he fulfilled his promise and delivered the lectures "The Gospel for an Age of Doubt." They came fresh from an eager evangelical conviction like a white dove flying into the black thunder cloud of literary gloom. "During the twelve years in which I have heard the Lyman Beecher Lectures," wrote Professor George B. Stevens of Yale, "the Lectureship has never touched a higher mark than just recently; but— what will, I think, please you more than any praise—I will add that it has never been more substantially useful than this year."

When the lectures were published in the autumn with a long appendix of quotations from the literature of the time a storm of criticism broke forth. As was to be expected the formal theologians and the meticulous logicians found them unsatisfactory. The serious debate centered around the question as to whether the age could justly be described as an age of doubt and whether the central thesis of the course, the offering of the gospel of a Person as a solution for the difficulties of the day, could be maintained. That the book was an honest attempt to get at the crux of religious difficulties appears clearly in such a review as that of S. D. McConnell in *Christian Literature*. After vigorously insisting that the age was an epoch of confidence and hopefulness rather than of doubt he concluded:

"It would be easy enough to show the inconsequence of his argument for the doctrine of the Trinity. One could drive a coach and four through his doctrine of the Kenosis. But who should do so would simply manifest his own lack of spiritual vision. In what the author says illogically and in the teeth of his Confession is God's truth as a man of God sees it. It is the truth for all ages. It will be seen and welcomed by the men of our time chiefly because it is not an age of doubt."

A flood of letters descended upon the author. Washington Gladden wrote:

"I have now read it and want to bear testimony to its just value. I do not always follow you, but I find the thought virile and stimulating everywhere. It is a masterly piece of work. . . . But what are you Presbyterians going to do? . . . It seems to me that Creed Revision must have been going on in some quarters at a lively rate."

John Fiske wrote:

"Such a book is, to my mind, a valuable harbinger of the higher and broader intellectual life which the next generation is to enjoy."

From Britain, R. F. Horton wrote:

"There are so many of us both in America and England who have been led to the same general attitude that you will have a chorus of gratitude for the brilliant way in which you have presented it. I cannot sufficiently express my admiration of the enormous acquaintance with contemporary literature which is the great feature of the book . . . I feel a peculiar obligation to one who gives me the sense of having just read all the new books and caught the authentic spirit of the age in which we live."

And ten years later James Stalker wrote:

"May I add that I frequently recur to your *Gospel for an Age of Doubt* and that in speaking of it to young ministers I generally find that they are well acquainted with it. It is one of the recent books from your side of the ocean which have laid a hold on this side."

The following letter with its gentle remonstrance bears the same witness:

"The great law of progress in theology,—John Robinson's 'more light to break out of God's Holy Word' and ever-unveiling Providence—that, I think, you have given us all an illustration of, whose literary charm and singular cogency will make a most helpful and permanently valuable contribution to our theological literature. Let me thank you for it, though you will care very little for any thanks or appreciation of a 'benighted prelatist' and believe me always

Your friend and brother,
H. C. Potter."

But among all the letters from high and low, from discouraged and rebellious folk, from an old retired sea captain who had long fought the sea and fatalism, from simple folk ship-wrecked on the rocky coast of orthodoxy,—among all these letters perhaps Richard Watson Gilder's midnight scrawl came closest to describing the mark at which Henry van Dyke had aimed. "It is," wrote Mr. Gilder, "a sort of lyric theology;" and on the back page of his letter he added these lines:

"Thou Christ! My soul is hurt and bruised!
With words the scholars wear me out;
My brain o'erwearied and confused,
Thee, and myself, and all I doubt.

"And must I back to darkness go
Because I cannot say their creed?
I know not what I think; I know
Only that thou art what I need."

[181]

While Henry van Dyke had had no idea of presenting a system of theology in his lectures the tenor of the comments of those who read them made him feel their incompleteness. During the next couple of years he hammered out on the anvil of University sermons and lectures another volume: "The Gospel for a World of Sin." Disclaiming any intention of presenting a theory of the Atonement, he sought to teach that there is no theory broad or deep enough to embrace or explain the fact of a loving and suffering God; but that if each man sees his little arc of experience in right relation to the centre, he sees it as part of the truth.

"The Message of the first book," he wrote, "was this: Christ saves us from doubt, because He is the revelation of God.

The message of the second book is this: Christ is the revelation of God, because He saves us from sin."

Only a few letters about this second book are found, possibly because Henry van Dyke moved a few months later from New York to Princeton; but more likely because people write easily about their doubts but only with reluctance about their sense of sin. But there are two letters, one from William Dean Howells and one from Margaret Deland, from each of whom Henry van Dyke had made a quotation in his book. Mrs. Deland wrote in part:

"It is a deep satisfaction to me to find that you endorse Dr. Lavender's words about the sense of sin; I know that some persons have felt that the idea which I tried to express was irrational or irreligious—and yet I was certain that it was not either. I once heard a poor, humble soul who had gone down into the gutter, and then, through the help of the Salvation Army, climbed out again, say to me: 'Sometimes seems to me like as if, if I hadn't sinned, I wouldn't have known any God. I didn't know Him in them days when I was respectable, anything like the way I know Him *now*!' This was a deep saying; I think it first taught me the hope that there is in the intolerable consciousness of sin."

Mr. Howells wrote:

"I have your book, and have read the pages for which you take a text from me. It is a great growth from so small a seed, and lifts its branches and strikes its roots into heights and depths that the seed never dreamed of.

The problem you deal with is one of perpetual fascination, perpetual mystery. Our whole life here, the life of the whole race on the earth, cannot solve it; but your path through the shadow is crossed with fore-gleams of supernal light.

I thank you for your gift."

These volumes were Henry van Dyke's first and last essay in the field of theology. When, after six and seven reprintings he gathered them up with a few changes in the Avalon edition of his works twenty-five years later, he confessed that if he were writing them again he might press some arguments and conclusions less absolutely but declared that his central conviction of the gospel of a person was unchanged, so "why change the form in which it was uttered?" The fact is that these lectures were the fruit of long struggles with the sense of sin and the problems of doubt, struggles which had begun in his youth. In the form of their approach they bear the strong impress of his great teachers, especially McCosh and Charles Hodge at Princeton and Dorner and Bernhard Weiss at Berlin. Several times in the last weeks of his life he said that these books contained the unchanged essence of his personal faith.

Are not the concluding words of the first volume the true utterance of a man of action who believed that the function of thought is to prepare the way for, or to interpret, action?

"Let us not miss the meaning of Christianity as it comes to us and claims us. We are chosen, we are called, not to die and be saved, but to live and save others."

"A short creed and a long service," as he cheerfully expressed it, was truly the mark at which he aimed.

Throughout these years he had delivered a number of addresses variously expressing his view of the function of art as that of ennobling as well as delighting human life. The most important of these were several lectures on Tennyson. In March 1898 his first formal series of literary lectures were given at Johns Hopkins University on "Three Nineteenth Century Poets and Prophets: Words-

worth, Browning and Tennyson." In them he summed up the years
of reading and meditation which had begun in his college days and
which was now given expression in face of his keen realization of
the need of the age for spiritual guidance. The lectures achieved
a *success d'estime* largely through the vitality and charm with which
they presented and interpreted the message of the poets. The press
reported that "Never in the history of public lectures here have the
citizens attended in such numbers." As a matter of fact many were
unable to find a place in the hall.

After the lecture on Wordsworth a curious incident occured which,
in view of later discoveries about Wordsworth may be worth recording. An elderly gentleman informed the lecturer that he was
a grandson of Wordsworth and took from his pocketbook a paper
which he said was a manuscript of one of Wordsworth's unpublished poems. "But I didn't know he had a grandson," said Henry
van Dyke. "By a French marriage," replied the stranger. One may
imagine Henry van Dyke's astonishment at this unexpected answer
which he could not follow up at the moment because so many people
were waiting to speak to him. He did, however, make an appointment for the stranger to call upon him the next day and waited
vainly for him several hours. "The man never came or sent any
word," he said in telling the story afterwards, "and I have always
regretted that because I did not take his name and address I had to
let this chance slip through my fingers." It will be recalled that it
was eighteen years later that the knowledge of Wordsworth's relation with Annette Vallon first became public. But whether this
stranger was what he represented himself to be or an imposter is
an as yet unsolved mystery.

In the Commencement season of 1898 Henry van Dyke completed a year of almost unbelievable activity in schools and colleges,
as well as in his church, by preaching the baccalaureate sermons at
Columbia, Princeton and Harvard and delivering the Chancellor's
oration at Union. The call of youth for his specific services was accompanied in Henry van Dyke's own mind by a turning toward the
literary enthusiasm of his own youthful days. But the turning, it

cannot too often be said, was not a returning to a divided mind about his career but a new conviction that through literature and lecturing he had something to say to his age that could not be adequately uttered in the pastorate.

Before we turn to the change that came in 1899 we must follow the course of his last years of work in the Brick Church. For he approached that change with the honest gusto of a man who loved the world and rejoiced in new fields to conquer but who yet remained a "dedicated spirit."

Chapter Thirteen

POLITETHICS AND THE PASTORAL TOUCH

THROUGHOUT the multitudinous activities of these years Henry van Dyke somehow managed to keep a sense of proportion. He was not an institutionalist but his vigorous loyalty to the Brick Church never wavered. His strong and inclusive ministry was the unifying force of his diverse interests. The loyalty to him of his church officers provided the base from which he could freely exercise his talents as a natural leader. And in the exercise of that leadership he took great delight. To a man of his qualifications and general popularity the public aspects of his ministry might well seem the only important ones. But it was not so with him. Behind his public career, which unfolded with an uncanny recognition of news' values, was a very human heart constantly in close grips with the issues of life. In the case of a man whose outward appearance was always gallant and clear-cut, even debonair, and whose utterances were so simple, clear and natural, it is not always easy to recognize the dishevelled struggles and the solemn midnight vigils out of which he often came. "Not a sermon comes into this pulpit," he once said, "which the preacher has not first tried upon himself to see if it fits."

The Brick Church, like a number of other New York Churches with strong and magnetic leadership, experienced great growth in the eighteen-nineties, both in influence and numbers. Much of this was due to the utterance of the pulpit. The *New York World*, in an editorial "The New Pulpit," on November 29, 1896, said:

"One of the interesting phenomena of our time is the new and changed activity of the pulpit. The preachers seem newly awaked to their power as public teachers.

[186]

When in one day Dr. Dix preaches on the relations of classes and masses and Dr. Parkhurst takes up the moral side of the monopoly question and when such pulpit orators as Dr. MacArthur, Dr. Henry van Dyke, Mr. Dixon, Dr. Rainsford, Dr. Huntington, Rabbi Gottheil, Mr. Peters and others habitually preach upon matters of immediate and living importance, instead of discussing the niceties of creeds and splitting theological hairs over questions of eschatology, it is not too much to say that we have fallen upon a new era in preaching."

Henry van Dyke saw his pastoral duty not only in terms of ministering consolation to troubled souls, but also in terms of calling men to action for the public good. Pointing out in a sermon that the two extremes of popular policy: "Damn the public" and "Down with the rich" were equally unfruitful he continued:

"It is hard to be earnest in a frivolous society. It is hard to be decent, spiritually-minded and full of true charity in a mercenary age. To be out of fashion is to be uncomfortable. There is such a thing as a moral atmosphere, and when it is saturated with the invisible germs of an epidemic it is not easy to be well and strong. Even those who do not take the disease are affected by its presence. The whole tone of their health is lowered and they must take care to make an effort or they will break down."

On February 24, 1895, Henry van Dyke preached to the Sons of the Revolution in the Brick Church a resounding sermon: "The People Responsible for the Character of their Rulers." Not only the central thesis with its clear-cut emphasis on this overlooked source of reform; but the particular comments which the preacher made on Civil service reform and especially on the spoils system as then threatening the recently elected municipal government of New York attracted much attention. The newspapers amid a storm of controversy at once called the names of the men to whom indirect reference had been made in the sermon. One suggested that the boss referred to might well take for his own the advice of the colored brother who said to the preacher: "If you want to succeed, you preach Him Crucified and let dis vexed question of hencoops entirely alone." And another concluded a vigorous attack upon Henry van Dyke by saying:

[187]

"A capital subject for Dr. van Dyke's next political sermon would be The Wickedness of Humbugging the People under the Pretence of Reform."

Dr. Parkhurst wrote:

"Permit me to thank you for the ringing words which you spoke in your church last Sabbath. It marks an era in political history, that matters of municipal and national interest are coming to be treated increasingly as lying within the jurisdiction of the pulpit and the church."

And Richard Watson Gilder generously wrote:

"That is a noble address and I honor you for it. You are a brave and useful citizen and a good man as well as a distinguished preacher. I would rather be a useful citizen and a good man than merely a distinguished preacher, but to be all is to be something unusual and most exemplary in these times."

In the sermon as preached in the Church Henry van Dyke evidently made a slighting reference to the proposed income tax law as part of the class legislation which he condemned. The incident drew at least two letters of strong praise for the sermon as a whole but of polite remonstrance for the slighting reference,—one being from Dr. Rainsford. When the sermon was printed the reference was omitted; and the incident is mentioned here only because it is a typical illustration of the limits of Henry van Dyke's approach to problems of social reform. It may be looked at as the reverse side of his strength in the preaching of personal liberty and responsibility. But it was nonetheless a defect. In fact it may be justly said that he habitually underestimated the power of environment in determining conduct. The forces external to the individual himself while recognized in a general way were seldom followed through to their consequences in social policy. In this very sermon he had condemned "The degradation of the poor by overcrowding in great tenements, and the enervation of the rich by exclusion in luxurious palaces," but in none of his sermons and addresses is there indicated any proposal for social control of these conditions. But with equal frankness it must be said that, with a few exceptions, of whom

[188]

Washington Gladden was outstanding,—this attitude was character-istic of the ministry at the time.

Two weeks before the presidential election of 1896 Henry van Dyke in a sermon "Politics and Politethics" uttered from his pulpit a direct attack upon the free coinage of silver. Arguing that the question was not a political but a moral issue he denounced the democratic-populist campaign as an appeal to class envy and a divisive force throughout the nation and declared that it was based on a quest for temporal advantage rather than for ethical principle. It was not honest, he said, because it would establish a double weight and measure in our country; because it would enrich one set of people by impoverishing another set of people; and because it would force everybody to take an immense and unjustifiable risk.

The sermon lacked nothing in pungency of phrase; and it boldly set forth the courage of the preacher's convictions for which he found no want of support among men whom he admired. Read today, while it still echoes tight as a drum on personal ethics, the sermon discloses an inability to sound those hinterland notes that echoed from Bryan's silver trumpet. The country was beginning to face a condition that could not be adequately met with a theory—even with a theory of right and wrong perfectly sound in terms of personal morality. It was not long before Henry van Dyke, though he never altered his views on sound money, found himself standing shoulder to shoulder with William Jennings Bryan on a far reaching issue. This, too, was characteristic of him. For an eager sympathy with men as individuals; a courageous readiness to accept the challenge of a need; a willingness to change his own views always dominated in his mind despite the absolutist thinking in which he had been rigorously trained.

Two Sundays before the municipal election at which Tammany was defeated Henry van Dyke preached with his usual vigor on "Crime, Citizenship and Christianity."

"We have no divine system of politics," he declared, "but we have a divine law of politethics . . . the absolute supremacy of moral law in

[189]

every sphere of life. . . . Here is the curse of our country and our city: that the ignorant classes sell the ballot and the educated classes neglect it."

Pointing a warning finger at the great increase in crime and at the political corruption that rots the moral fibre of the people he concluded with the declaration that "The only lasting reform of political evils must come through the awakened consciences of individual man. . . . For every idle word, for every deed done in the body, yes, and for every vote cast or withheld every man shall give account of himself to God."

To Henry van Dyke war in itself was always a hateful thing. It ran counter to everything in which he believed. But his thinking was such that he recognized it as sometimes a grim necessity in which the duty to fight was laid upon men. When the Venezuelan boundary dispute with Great Britain arose he responded eagerly to President Cleveland's forthright action because he believed it to embody national righteousness. But when the threatened war turned into a movement for an arbitration treaty his whole heart rejoiced. To the *Evening Post* he wrote a letter which is, so far as can be discovered, his first public expression on peaceful international relations:

"The threatening clouds of the Venezuelan question have parted to disclose, not the fiery comet of war, but the peaceful star of the arbitration treaty—the brightest light that has dawned upon the nineteenth century. It would be a great pity—nay, more, it would be an unspeakable shame—if men should not recognize the meaning of this light, nor hail the clearness of its rising with generous and universal joy. It foretells the immediate and immense reduction of the possible causes of wholesale bloodshed; it pledges the two mightiest nations of the world to seek peace instead of strife, and to think long before they strike; it brings the principles of justice, which have been acknowledged between man and man, to bear directly upon international relations; and it distinctly foreshadows the coming of that day when reason and right shall prevail over passion and might.

Surely to oppose such a treaty as this is to fight against the very cause of progress and the inmost spirit of the Christian religion. If by any chance it should fail of confirmation in the United States, the men to whose action, or inaction, that failure might be due would bring contempt upon their country's name and cover themselves with deep disgrace. It is the opportunity of a national lifetime. For if England and the United States confirm this treaty and make it a reality, they will stand together at the head of civilized nations, whose first appeal is not to the God of Battle, but to the God of Peace.

In every place of worship in our land thanksgiving should be offered to the Divine mercy for the dawning of this great light, and fervent prayers that human folly may not be suffered to dim nor to extinguish it before it has blessed mankind with the sweet reasonableness of its beams."

But the treaty failed of ratification by the Senate; and meantime the Cuban issue was rapidly bringing the United States to a crisis with Spain. The vast majority of high-minded Americans saw in the trouble between their country and Spain only the moral issue of the liberation of the oppressed Cubans. On May 1, 1898—the first Sunday after the formal declaration of War—Henry van Dyke preached "The Cross of War."

"Between man and man," he said, "the nation decides. But who shall decide between nation and nation? There is, as yet, no court with power to enforce its decisions. When arbitration is made final by universal agreement, or when the dream of a world empire is at last realized, such a court will exist. But until that time, war remains, under certain conditions, the only means of securing justice, liberty and order."

Is there not in these words the intimation of the direction that his own generous activity in another field of public service was to take twenty-five years later? The War with Spain, he felt, was an inescapable duty. "To put an end to a long record of robbery in peace," he went on in the same sermon, "and rapine in war; to deliver a fair portion of this continent from the incubus of the most obstinate barbarians who exist outside of Turkey; to bring liberty to captives, and to let the oppressed go free; to secure permanent peace and righteous order to the remnant of a cruelly broken race; to uphold the honor of our country as an unselfish and powerful friend of the downtrodden; perhaps to bring the oppressor herself, through re-

[191]

pentance, to a better mind, and send her forward to a new and nobler career—these are high, generous, Christian aims."

To an appeal for books for the library of the Battleship *Texas* he responded by sending among other books a copy of his *Other Wise Man* with the inscription:

"To the officers and crew of the United States Battleship *Texas* who have proved that courage and mercy may dwell together, and that there is no inconsistency between deep faith and good fighting—this book is presented with sincere respect by Henry van Dyke."

Not only did he support the war against Spain but the same convictions that led him to sustain that national action equally led him to oppose the great popular movement for the annexation of the Philippines which burst forth when the war was victoriously ended. His sermon "The American Birthright and the Philippine Pottage" preached on Thanksgiving Day was the outstanding declaration of the American pulpit against imperialism. In measured and cogent paragraphs he argued that annexation was unconstitutional, that it was inconsistent with republican principles, that the American record with the Indians and negroes was evidence of the nation's incompetency for the responsibilities entailed, that it would involve a heavy burden of military service, of taxation and of strife with European nations, and finally and chiefly that it would call for the surrender of our American birthright of glorious ideals.

All the way through the sermon were biting sentences like these:

"The cry of today is: 'Wherever the American flag has been raised, it never must be hauled down.' The man who will not join that cry may be accused of disloyalty and called a Spaniard. So be it, then. If the price of popularity is the stifling of conviction, I want none of it. If the test of loyalty is to join in every thoughtless cry of the multitude, I decline it. I profess a higher loyalty—*allegiance to the flag, not for what it covers, but for what it means.*

There is one thing that can happen to the American flag worse than to be hauled down. That is to have its meaning and message changed. Hitherto it has meant freedom and equality and self-government, and battle only for the sake of peace. Pray God its message may never be altered."

Mr. Bryan wrote him:

"I have read your sermon in full and am delighted with the vigor of your style as well as with your ideas on the subject of imperialism. Your reference to the meaning of the flag leads me to send you an extract from my remarks on hauling down the flag."

Mr. Bryan also came to see him—a visit which amusingly enough, called for not a little explanation on the part of Henry van Dyke when some industrious newspapers advertised it according to their own predilections.

The sermon was widely quoted in the press and circulated in a pamphlet. It was so amply quoted by one Senator that the *Nashville Banner*, under the heading "Stolen Oratory," denounced the "gross plagiarism" and added: "Probably the tone of Senatorial eloquence would be generally elevated if this practice of borrowing from the pulpit should become more common." The incident finally resulted in the printing of the sermon in full in the Congressional Record.

Letters of approval for the sermon came to the preacher from leaders of thought and government officials. And Henry van Dyke joined a group of leading Americans from many parts of the country in a long petition to the Senate asking for the amendment of the Treaty "to the effect that the United States shall not annex the Philippine Islands or Porto Rico, or permit their inhabitants to become citizens or compel them to become subjects of the United States without their free consent and the further and express authority of Congress."

"I don't see," wrote Edward S. Martin, "how you escaped being appointed a member of the new commission to run our 'colonies'."

It is gratifying to think that, though the conviction which the sermon expressed and which the petition followed up did not prevail in the heat of political conditions yet they may have played some part in the formation of public opinion that has since solidified in the American movement for Philippine independence.

But Henry van Dyke was not only using his pulpit for urging Christian participation in public affairs. The public aspects of his ministry were much bruited in the newspapers but they were only a small part of his preaching and pastoral activity. The themes of his sermons during these years bear witness to this: Confessing Christ; Christianity a Household Religion; Death in Life, and Life in Death; Egypt and the Bible; The Importance of the Visible Church; Christ's idea of what it means to be a Christian; Foreign Missions; Publicomania, etc., etc.

His concern with questions of worship was continuous. Gradually he had been enriching the order of service in the Brick Church. The use of the Lord's Prayer by the congregation had been introduced but only when it was understood that those who objected to it might remain silent. (What an evidence of the hard Protestantism amid which his ministry began!) Furthermore, he had broken with the often painful custom of funeral orations; and declined to burden the observance of the communion with an address. In 1888 he had inaugurated the custom of holding a service in the church on the morning of Christmas Day at which, during the latter years of his pastorate, he was accustomed to read a new story or poem of his own. The clear beauty of the varied musical tones of these readings, now light and swift, *staccato* in terms of sudden action; now full and resonant with a rhythmic description, interpreting the simple but infinitely poignant tales was unforgettable. Certainly it made a lasting impression on the preacher's elder children; deeper, perhaps, than most of the sermons, although during sermons too those children would not have been denied their right to sit in the minister's pew for all the occasional anguish of the experience. The stories and poems read for the first time at these Christmas services were The Other Wise Man, The First Christmas Tree, The Last Word, Vera, the Legend of Service, and the Toiling of Felix.

On March 2, 1897, there met in the Brick Church at Henry van Dyke's invitation a number of Presbyterian leaders who formed the Church Service Society for the purpose of studying the present conduct and the past history of the worship of the Church and preparing such forms of service for an orderly worship "as may help guard against the contrary evils of confusion and ritualism and promote reverence and beauty in the worship of God in His Holy House." Although, as the press both religious and secular indicated, the Society faced many difficulties and much vigorous opposition, nevertheless it marked the beginning of a movement that later achieved its objective in the Presbyterian "Book of Common Worship for voluntary use." In that work Dr. Louis F. Benson, the first President, and Henry van Dyke, the first Vice-President of the Society took a large part.

Meantime, he was working quietly on the matter of creed revision which had been buried temporarily under the storm of heresy trials. Many are the references in letters to his fitness for succeeding to his father's place in General Assembly's Committee, when the issue should come to life again.

On April 23, 1899, in a sermon on "The Progress of the Church" he suggested ten points that might be included in a fresh statement of faith. These points as reported in many careful newspaper accounts were as follows:

1. The fulness of the Fatherhood of God, in whose image and likeness every human soul is made.
2. The eternal Sonship of Christ, who is the brightness of the Father's glory embodied in a veritable human life.
3. The all-sufficiency of Christ's atonement to take away the sin of the world and reconcile us to God.
4. The living presence of the Holy Ghost as the source of all truth and goodness in every soul that asks for Him.
5. The sovereignty of God dwelling in His world and working out His will here and now.
6. The liberty of every human soul to decide whether he will work against God and perish or with Him and live forever.
7. The supreme authority of the Holy Scriptures as the record of God's progressive revelation.
8. The power of faith in Christ to join the soul to God who delivers it from sin and makes it holy.
9. The absolute necessity of love and good works as the proof of

faith whereby every believer becomes a witness for Christ to all men.

10. The immortal life of love made perfect—which is heaven.

But the thing that claimed the lion's share of his time and effort was the development of the Brick Church and its two affiliated churches. In these matters he was the vigorous and far sighted leader of an enthusiastic and consecrated band of workers. The bond that united Henry van Dyke and the whole staff especially Dr. George Sidney Webster and Dr. James M. Farr was not only the unity of a common task but a sincere personal liking. In 1900 Dr. Webster published a day book, *The Friendly Year* made up of selections from the sermons and other writings of Henry van Dyke. Dr. Farr often recalls the story of his call to join the work of the Brick Church. It was a "wild winter night when he was preaching at a little mission church on the west side. He was going to preach on the Prodigal Son. There were only a dozen or twenty people scattered about the little room. Then the door opened and a muffled figure, covered with snow, entered. 'Here is my prodigal' thought the young preacher; but when the man removed his wrappings, he was startled to recognize the well-known features of Henry van Dyke. The young man was thrown a bit off balance, but there was nothing for it but to go ahead with his sermon, and so he fervently exhorted the distinguished minister of the Brick Church to abandon the error of his ways and embark upon a new life. That the sermon was not without effect was evident when he was invited to preach in this place (the Brick Church) the following Sunday afternoon. After that service, Dr. van Dyke took him to the Manse and, before a wood fire in his study, talked to him about the Brick Church and what it stood for and what kind of help he wanted a young assistant to render. It was a talk which warmed the young man's heart, as the fire in the hearth warmed his body."

In the winter of 1897-8 the *New York Times* reported that eight Presbyterian churches were having the unusual experience of more or less difficulty in finding places for all who wished to worship in them. Among these was the Brick Church. With eight hundred and fifty members, ninety-four having been added in 1897, and with a waiting list of nearly two hundred persons who had applied for sittings the church was regularly holding services with people on chairs in the aisles and sitting on the pulpit steps.

On the fifteenth anniversary of his pastorate a new organ with a plate inscribed "in gratitude for the ministry of Henry van Dyke" was dedicated, and the works of Chaucer and Jeffries were presented to the pastor with a letter that said in part:

"The highest eulogy which those who work can receive comes from their work when well done. That your labor for us is deserving of all praise you cannot fail to know. It is pleasant to be permitted to point to it at this time. You found us few in numbers; weak, despondent. Today our numbers are full, our church is strong; we look with all confidence to the future.

In God's providence, the change is due to you. But in a better sense than from the material side has the Church progressed under your ministry. Its activity has made rapid strides; its usefulness has widened in innumerable directions; its people, in common attachment to you, have been drawn into closer common life for the upbuilding of the Kingdom of God.

We have shared your successes; we are proud of the high position which you have achieved. Your fame has shed luster on us.

We must not forget that all has not been sunshine during these fifteen years; clouds at times have crossed the sky. We have felt in our own sorrows your gentler touch; for you too have been called on to mourn."

In his report in the Brick Church Year Book Henry van Dyke speaks of the situation with characteristically mingled satisfaction and questioning:

"How much of Christian life and work has been promoted by these services, at which so many people have been present, cannot really be known by anyone except the Judge of all hearts. Only some of the outward results are reported here. They are enough to give us hope and encouragement, but they are not enough to make us satisfied with ourselves; for it is certain that we have come far short of what we might have done if we had all been more faithful to our privileges, opportunities and duties."

But he does not fail to note that the Brick Church had contributed "the largest sum given for Christian work by any Presbyterian church in America, and probably in the world." And he speaks with satisfaction of the work of the two affiliated churches:

"Last year we gave them $10,000. This year we want to give them as much if not more. We send our best young men and women to work in their Sunday Schools, Boys' and Girls' Clubs and Sewing classes. In the Sunday Schools there are nearly 1,200 children, in the churches more than 800 members, and through these agencies we have access to more than 500 families in the heart of New York's densest population."

The Philadelphia Press began an editorial on "Is Presbyterianism Declining" with the words:

"We hope that our brilliant contemporary, the *New York Sun* has received a copy of the last annual report of the Brick Church, of that city. If it has not we have no doubt that Dr. van Dyke, on request, will send it one. It will be found well worth consulting next time its religious editor feels moved to add another chapter to his serial 'on the decline of Presbyterianism in New York City'."

But perhaps the most significant witness to the nature of Henry van Dyke's seventeen years in the Brick Church and the thing which accounts for his later returns to its service in times of crisis are the bundles of letters long forgotten in detail by their recipient which were found among his papers. In beautiful penmanship and graceful phraseology, in almost illegible writing and fearful grammar, these letters from all sorts of people express gratitude for strong and ready help in the multifarious pastoral office. By the fire in his study, in the hospitals where on several occasions it is recalled that he had to appear wrapped in a sheet against infection, in the homes of rich and poor he moved steadily. "Dear Domine" wrote his particular friends and others contented themselves with beginning "Ever beloved pastor" or sprinkling "Dear Dr. van Dyke" through their pages.

Lest the voice of thanks be lost in the rush of the career let us read a few sentences. A stern and noble Elder of few words writes after the settlement of a delicate issue in the church's history: "I must express to you my appreciation of your forbearance, good judgment and of the admirable manner in which you have met the exigencies of a very trying situation."

A young foreigner whom he was helping to a useful career in the ministry writes from the seminary:

"I am thankful specially for your prays of me, whose help have made me strong in my duties to the Lord, to the nation, to the country and to myself, and today I am glade to reporte you after having most horrible time, now I am a successful student of the word of God, in my class being compounded of 50 members I am the fifth in them, of course that is great mercy of the Lord and as product of your prays of me."

One who was himself often called to walk through physical anguish wrote gallantly to Henry van Dyke of his conduct throughout the hard months of the heresy trials:

"In the pulpit you showed to us one and all how loving and charitable you could be and yet how fierce in everything which pertained to the great foundations of our one undivided and holy faith. Ever through this stormy life you walk surely because while holding fast to the hand of our dear Saviour your right hand is ever ready to uplift and sustain the down trodden and the suffering."

"There are certain things," wrote another man, "which might seem self-evident to you, which you have suggested to me and which I have tried to live—for example that God can take an unprejudiced view even of our sins, that stoicism is different from Christian patience, that hope is an element in courage, and that even in the far country of sin and sorrow, a man may come to himself. Words like yours about these things are not mere memories but facts which I know to be true."

"Will you not pray with me," writes a mother, "for the conversion of my two sons. In these days when there are so many who would lead our young people away from the dear old Bible doctrines, I rejoice to know of those who still labor to build up, not destroy the foundation of belief. Pardon a stranger but my heart is very full of these thoughts and hopes, and I bless God for your work, though I only know you through your writings."

The minister of a church who writes that his life "has been up-rooted by ill-health and by a certain cataclysm of soul that has left the roots of my faith lying around loose and broken on the surface" goes on: "Am I Hermes of the 'Lost Word'? but what John shall drive Apollo's priest away?

God bless you. One thing I believe:

> 'He who walks in love may wander far,
> But God will bring him where the blessed are'."

Following a service in which an offering was received for Home Missions the Secretary of the Board wrote:

"One subscription card has reached us which shows that the first amount put down was $100; further on in your sermon the contributor's enthusiasm kindled to such a degree that he erased the first and made it $250, and when you reached the climax he erased the second subscription and made it $500."

One day Henry van Dyke found on the desk in his study at the Church a letter from a girl who was ending an eighteen months' hospital experience and who wrote in a depressed spirit and uncertainty about the future asking if he could give her a word of encouragement,—and his autograph. There was something about the request or the mood he was in when it came that made him sit down and write. As he finished there came a knock at the door and his constant friend Hamilton W. Mabie came gently in. It was but one of numberless such meetings. The two inseparables took up their conversation where it had last been left off, but were interrupted a moment later when Henry van Dyke had to go for a few minutes to a meeting on the floor below. When he returned Mr. Mabie with the freedom to which each was accustomed in the other's study was holding in his hand "The Footpath to Peace" which Henry van Dyke had written for the sick girl. So it befell that it was first printed in *The Outlook* and after that it was printed and circulated in many ways and in many parts of the world. From letters scattered throughout his correspondence are many tales of the message it bore. Two girls in college read it nightly for their evening devotions. It was used as the theme of Sunday school classes. It was posted in one of the stables of the New York police department, and on a tree in one of the White Mountain hotel parks. Booker T. Washington thanking him for his letter about "Up From Slavery" adds: "May I tell you how much I have been helped by your 'Footpath to Peace' and that I am putting them into the hands of as many of my friends as I can."

The few and simple words written for the sick girl are these:

"To be glad of life because it gives you the chance to love and to work and to play and look up at the stars. To be satisfied with your possessions, but not content with yourself until you have made the best of them. To despise nothing in the world except falsehood and meanness, and to fear nothing except cowardice. To be governed by your admirations rather than by your disgusts; to covet nothing that is your neighbor's except his kindness of heart and gentleness of manners. To think seldom of your enemies, often of your friends, and every day of Christ; and to spend as much time as you can, with body and spirit, in God's out-of-doors. These are little guide-posts on the footpath to peace."

When the formal call to become Professor of English literature in Johns Hopkins University reached Henry van Dyke on January 4, 1899, he was strongly drawn to accept. The conviction that he had something more to say through writing, his growing concern with young men, the claims of his family, his own heavily burdened days —all made the invitation attractive. When it was discovered that he was giving the matter serious consideration his own parishioners and his colleagues in New York protested vigorously in person and by many letters and the newspapers discussed the matter, some with more and some with less illumination. On January 27th he addressed a letter to the Session and Congregation in which he said:

"A call to a University Professorship of English Literature has brought before me the question of my future line of most useful work in the kingdom of God.

It is not a question of giving up the preaching of Christ. I have no intention of doing that. His service is as wide as the world, and He is the master of all good workmen.

The question that comes to me now is simply a question of transferring the heavy administrative work of the pastor of a large city church, into other and more competent hands, and devoting myself to a life in which there shall be more liberty and the time to think and to write. After earnest consideration, and seeking light from above, I think that this is the line along which I can do my best and most lasting service to my fellowmen."

The Session rebelled and unanimously adopted a resolution refusing to call a congregational meeting for dissolving the pastoral relations as Henry van Dyke had requested. And the congregation met and unanimously endorsed the Session's action. Henry van Dyke yielded, though in his letter on February 5th he wrote:

"I still believe that a man may serve God and his fellowmen by writing as well as by preaching. I still wish and hope to be able to do some honest work in literature. But the call to Johns Hopkins University, attractive for many reasons, must be respectfully declined. Today's duty lies here."

The ultimate outcome was inevitable as this letter indicates. Henry van Dyke was ready to go, not because of a change in his convictions, but because of his recognition of the change in the form of his activities which the honest exercise of his talents demanded. Stories and poems and essays were flowing from his pen. *Fisherman's Luck* was published in the fall of 1899. His literary and artistic views were widely quoted and discussed both with approval and disapproval in the press. The newspapers discussed his fitness and unfitness for every college or university position that was unfilled. The *New York Sun* could see nothing in Henry van Dyke's purpose except the abandonment of the ministry and said so in no uncertain terms. Meantime Henry van Dyke held to his views. He set forth his faith in "the gospel of escape into life." He ridiculed the idea that the genuine Puritan spirit was crippling American art. He shared Stedman's confidence in the "virile chastity of the Saxon mind." In an interview about writing in the *Ram's Horn*, he said:

"The fact is the story method is the one used by Christ more than any other. He taught, not theological dogmas, but the great fundamental facts of life—and that means religion, for man's deepest instincts are religious— in parables. The parables are inspired short stories. Christ fully recognized the psychological principle that what most moves men to action is not cold, didactic discourse, but truths vividly and warmly presented through the imagination."

And he went on to disclose one of the immediate sources of his own literary interest:

"Each summer I go up to a sparsely settled part of French Canada and camp out for several weeks. My voyageurs or guides are simple, illiterate fellows, yet each evening they gather round the camp-fire and entertain themselves and us by stories—in part fairy tales, in part folk lore, in part their own adventures and experiences. That proves quite conclusively to me that the love of a story or tale or narrative is one of the deepest instincts in the human heart. So I believe that fiction is here to stay—that it will never lose its popularity."

At the first public meeting of the National Institute of Arts and Letters, speaking on "Books, Literature and the People" and distinguishing the people from the public he defined literature "as made up of those human writings which translate the inner meanings of nature and life in language of distinction and charm, touched with the personality of the author, into forms of lasting interest." And spoke of four elements that enter into good work in literature:

"An original impulse—not necessarily a new idea, but a new sense of the value of an idea.
A first hand study of the subject and the material.
A patient, joyful, unsparing labor for the perfection of form.
A human aim—to cheer, console, purify or ennoble the life of the people. Without this aim literature has never sent an arrow close to the mark."

In the *New Haven Register* on a visit to Yale he spoke of another aspect of his purpose:

"In my opinion the future welfare of our country depends upon the thoroughness and inspiring quality of the work which is to be done the next 30 years in the colleges and universities of the United States. It is here, not in Germany, nor France, nor England that the Americans are to be trained who shall lead our country in science, statesmanship, literature and religion. The man who puts his work into an American college now puts it where it will do the most good."

As a matter of fact the Princeton movement to secure his services had long been under way and the practical steps of endowing a chair for his occupancy were rapidly nearing completion. On January 31st President Patton wrote him that he had explained the situation to President Gilman of Johns Hopkins University and that the Princeton call only awaited the foregone conclusion of the Trustees' action.

III

PRINCETON, THE UNITED STATES, AND ABROAD

We'll keep the honour of a certain aim
Amid the perils of uncertain ways,
And sail ahead, and leave the rest to God.

H. v. D.

Chapter Fourteen

PRINCETON FINALLY GETS HIM

EVER since that day in his boyhood when he first watched the Nassau baseball nine play in Brooklyn Henry van Dyke had had a peculiar affection for Princeton. And it may be truly said that from his earliest student days the college had heartily reciprocated that affection. The form of the mutual affection changed somewhat during the years, as all genuine emotions do, but its intensity was a constant element in it. Princeton was always in his thoughts and many were the articles he wrote in his early manhood about her campus life, her athletics, her teachers. He referred joyfully to the growing number of Princeton College men who were coming into the pastorate in New York City. Hardly was he settled at the Brick Church when President McCosh wrote him in June 1883 of plans for making the department of Philosophy a very comprehensive one in Princeton College and inquired if he would be willing to accept the chair of Moral Philosophy in the new development. Henry van Dyke promptly, but regretfully, and with a touch of humor at the end, wrote that while "my personal preferences have always been for a literary and scholastic life . . . at the same time I am sure that you will agree that under the circumstances and in so brief a time it would be altogether improper, indeed morally impossible." Again in 1887 Dr. McCosh wrote: "The Committee does not seem to be ready to appoint a colleague to Dr. Moffat. I am of opinion that you are the fittest man. If I knew you would favor the proposal I would start you." But Henry van Dyke was too busy in New York to become a faculty member, though not too busy to accept a large share

[207]

in enthusiastic alumni activities. That same year he became President of the Princeton Club of New York, and as a delegate to the Conference of a committee of trustees and alumni he introduced the resolution which inaugurated the plan by which some trustees are regularly elected from the alumni. In June he made an address at the founding of the Art Museum in Princeton pointing out prophetically that "It does not inaugurate, but it does mark and emphasize a new era, not in the history of the College of New Jersey, but let us now say in the history of Princeton University."

When President McCosh resigned there was not a little talk of Henry van Dyke and of several others for his successor; but when Dr. Francis L. Patton was elected it was Henry van Dyke who spoke the welcome on behalf of the alumni at the inauguration, sounding the word of forward-looking conservatism, referring again to "the University at Princeton," and declaring that "It were better that this institution should close its doors tomorrow than cease to stand inflexibly for Christ and His truth."

Many were the Princeton dinners at which he addressed the alumni in hilarious manner but always ending on a note of gratitude to Princeton and confidence in her future as a small but potent University. He declined as a Princeton man to "identify piety with dyspepsia." The mild confusion which followed as he began a speech in Latin turned into roars of laughter when he remarked casually: "I should continue to address you in this language which is most natural and easy to all Princetonians, but for the fact that we have with us the graduates of other colleges, and our delight in their presence must not cause us to forget the misfortunes of their early education." And many were the chuckles among his hearers when he mentioned "the Board of Trustees—the power not ourselves that makes for righteousness," or proved his own loyalty by remarking: "In 1783 my grandfather was about to go to college and I never for a moment thought of letting him go anywhere else than to Princeton." And many were the impromptu exchanges at college men's dinners between Henry van Dyke and Chauncey M. Depew whom he called "the founder of the Yale School of after-dinner speaking." When James W. Alexander's carefully prepared list of speakers for a Princeton dinner began suddenly to evaporate with telegrams of excuse he sent a messenger to Henry van Dyke with a joyfully honeyed letter which ended:

"If you have a prayer meeting, come afterwards. Your meeting will be a grace before meat. If you are engaged at dinner bolt it(metaphorically) and smoke a segar with us. If you have the grip, seize your antipyrene and give us a chance to help you shake it off—the grip not the antipyrene.
But *do, please come.*
I am on my knees. Please send word 'yes' by bearer to save me from coming to see you tonight to stay with you until you relent."

On the margin was drawn a kneeling figure in abject supplication.

In letters from Princeton men during this time one notes the growing feeling that he ought to be part of Princeton's campus life. A. P. Whitehead wrote him in 1890: "Please say to Mrs. van Dyke that I do not approve of your acting as Mayor of New York City [a reference to his activity in the People's Municipal League] nor accepting the Presidency of Lafayette College nor of any position for you outside of clerical life but one, and that readily suggests itself to graduates of Princeton College who have the true interests of Nassau Hall at heart."

And in 1893 James W. Alexander wrote him:

"I see no reason why I should not confide to you that I had hoped that the time might come when you could be offered a Professorship in Princeton University, and that you would accept it. This is not an official but an individual aspiration, but I know of others who sympathize with it, and if it were not for certain ecclesiastical clouds, which I trust are only temporary, hovering over us, I should be at work in earnest in the matter. Inasmuch as I have no right to speak for anybody but myself, you are not called upon to express any views on this topic."

In 1894 at the funeral of President McCosh, Dean Murray and Henry van Dyke made brief addresses—the latter speaking in affectionate terms as one of the President's "boys"—indeed always a favorite one.

On March 20, 1895, his friend, Professor William Milligan Sloane, wrote:

"It was most satisfactory that at the recent meeting of our committee on the 150th anniversary of Princeton, Doctor Patton should have proposed you as the poet of the occasion. He did it handsomely. The proposition was received with enthusiasm and the vote was unanimous. We are all sure we have made a good beginning in this our first act."

"The Builders," an academic ode was read in Alexander Hall on October 21, 1896, when Woodrow Wilson also made his famous oration "Princeton in the Nation's Service," and the presence and words of President Cleveland brought lustre to the celebration. Of "The Builders" Edward Dowden wrote in the *Saturday Review*:

"To compose an ode for a public occasion which shall be more than rhetorical, is a rare achievement; Dr. van Dyke's poem, The Builders—builders not merely of material but of spiritual fortunes—was happy in its central idea, and the work of a skilled literary craftsman; it soared steadily and settled at last on a lofty point of rest."

And later from Dublin he wrote the author:

"The Princeton Ode seems as I read it not less but more excellent than as it reached me from your lips in Alexander Hall. I don't know whether you care as much as I do for Lowell's poem about the scholars that went out as soldiers in the civil war; but it is by the side of Lowell's 'Ode recited at the Harvard Commemoration 1865' that I think 'The Builders' should be placed."

Princeton was now well launched on her fresh career as a University and it was fully obvious that Henry van Dyke was a potent figure in that development.

In 1898 he was elected a trustee of the University but when it looked as if Johns Hopkins might get him several Princetonians felt that it was time for prompt and vigorous action. Convinced that Henry van Dyke would no longer remain in the Brick Church two of the Church officers, Charles W. McAlpin and John A. Stewart joined other Princetonians, Moses Taylor Pyne, James W. Alexander, C. C. Cuyler in carrying through the plan which had the strong support of President Patton and Dean Murray. The endowment for the Murray Professorship named in honor of the Dean was raised in an incredibly short time and warm letters of appeal and welcome came to Henry van Dyke from all the men mentioned above.

On March 11, 1899, the Board of Trustees unanimously elected him Murray Professor of English Literature and Henry van Dyke accepted the same day he received the letter, gratefully acknowledging the provision that the time of entrance upon his new duties should be left to his convenience.

A week later President Patton wrote him saying:

"The time of your entering upon the duties of the Chair was left to your own convenience; and no attempt was made to define those duties.

Indeed it was felt that the circumstances attending the erection of the chair were so peculiar that the Board could very well leave to your own discretion the settlement of the question as to what services you should render the University in connection with the Professorship.

I appreciate very fully the reasons indicated in your letter to me written some weeks ago which would make an academic position attractive to you. I quite understand that in giving up the attractive and eminent post as pastor of the Brick Church in order that you might secure the leisure for carrying out your plans for literary work you should naturally seek to have your position here as free as possible from the irksome forms of professorial work. I beg to assure you that you need have no misgivings on that score. I feel quite confident that your own desire to be useful to the University and to meet the reasonable expectations of the students will of itself suffice to settle to the entire satisfaction of the Trustees the amount of service that you shall render as the incumbent of the Murray Chair of English Literature. . . . If you care to offer an elective course on some period or phase of English literature to the senior class for one term you would find it very agreeable work and I am sure that you would have a most enthusiastic body of pupils. Then we should hope to hear you in the chapel pulpit as often as you would be willing to preach—I should hope about three times a term."

Such were the conditions—or rather the lack of them—in the Princeton call. What mutual confidence they imply in each other on the part of the faculty, trustees and the new professor!

"Is one to congratulate Princeton upon your going there, or is there nothing in it?" wrote William Dean Howells before the matter was fully settled. "Literature will not be the loser in any event, for if you do not teach it, you will still make it." And a little later, William S. Rainsford of St. George's Church wrote to congratulate him upon his recent Chicago address on "Democracy and Culture":

"In season and out of season, to impress on our best men the imperative duty of giving some of their time directly to the service of their country—this is most certainly the duty of the hour. So few of the clergy seem to see this. They keep pottering away over relatively unimportant things.

I hope you will keep this up at Princeton, for in the schools and universities are our best chance, and in them I verily believe today the spirit of the Lord God is working."

George P. Fisher of Yale writing about the *Gospel for a World of Sin* adds:

"I am glad that you are to take up the academic life, for one reason: the demand of the pulpit, 'the great hebdominal wave,' as old Dr. Fitch used to call it, is so exacting, so severe upon the *physical* man, that I am sure that it is safer and better for you to release yourself from the yoke, and to write sermons and preach them when you 'feel like it'."

But Henry van Dyke was not one to leave the Brick Church without, as he expressed it, some one at the helm. He proposed to stay until his successor was found and ready to begin work. And he went on with his preaching and pastoral and administrative work with unabated zeal. If anything were needed to show that his decision to go to Princeton involved no change in the purpose of his work this last year at the Brick Church would settle it. The work went steadily on. Forty-five new members were added to the roll. The affiliated churches continued to grow. In the Presbytery's dealing with the teaching of Professor A. C. McGiffert, Henry van Dyke again took a vigorous stand for liberty of scholarship and peace on an inclusive basis. The personal note of freedom and responsibility and the broad note of non-sectarian Christianity sounded steadily in his own pulpit and wherever he spoke. As he found opportunity he wrote the French Canadian tales that were taking form in his mind from his camping experiences. In November 1899 Dr. Maltbie D. Babcock of Baltimore accepted the call of the Brick Church and in early January 1900 was ready to take over his duties. Henry van Dyke's farewell sermon was, perhaps prophetically, never delivered. The emotional and physical stress were too much for him and he had to be content with sending from his bed an affectionate letter for the service.

At the congregational meeting Mr. John E. Parsons presented the Session's resolutions which included these simple and affecting words:

"Mere expressions of eulogy of Dr. van Dyke are as unnecessary as they would be distasteful to him. His seventeen years of labor known to all tell their own story. He came to us in the first flush of early manhood; he has stayed to give to us the best of his years and the warmest affection of his heart. . . . We thank Dr. van Dyke for his work; but he has bound us to himself by ties which are stronger than those of gratitude. Our hearts have responded to the affection which he has shown for us. It is as friend even more than as pastor that Dr. van Dyke has become endeared to us, and our hearts are sore this night when we think that a relation which has become so precious is now to be sundered.

It is not we alone who grieve that Dr. van Dyke shall go. While he has spared no effort for us, he has made himself useful as a citizen, influential in our body of the church, wise as a teacher, and conspicuous as a leader of the coming generation upon whom most largely depend the future of the church and of the community. Fame has come to Dr. van Dyke. His name has become a household word in many homes. Honors have been showered upon him. And not a little of the lustre has been reflected upon us.

It is hard to say farewell. God grant that all that Dr. van Dyke has done for this church and people may be requited to him a thousand fold. In the succession of pastors of the Brick Church there have been many noble names; men who were notable in doing the work of the Church. To not one does it owe more than to Henry van Dyke."

The severing of the pastoral relation was a hard wrench for him. His heart was heavy at parting. It seemed as if everyone had to see him or write him to express their feelings. J. Cleveland Cady wrote of the scene in Presbytery when official action was taken ending the pastorate. After referring to several "extremely interesting and affectionate" speeches that were made Mr. Cady wrote that a certain leading member of Presbytery who had been in vigorous opposition to Henry van Dyke on many issues spoke:

"Rev. Mr. . . . to my amazement, got up and wanted to express his feelings. (I trembled.) He said that 'he had known both your father and yourself, and while he rarely had the good fortune to agree with either of you, *you were two of the best friends he had ever had!'* I could have applauded when he got through, for it was delightful."

But not only was the leaving hard. As usual before getting into action in a new undertaking Henry van Dyke was passing through a period of uncertainty about the future. At the age of forty-eight and without any period of repose in which to gather himself together he was making a fresh start.

His ever-watchful friend Hamilton Mabie tried to see him and failing in that sent a note:

"I am immensely relieved that you are at last disentangled from New York. Now life will begin; your best work is ahead; don't doubt that. I visited Aldrich two days ago and if you could have heard the things said about you by men whose opinions can't be bought by friendship you would have dismissed all doubt about your work. You will take a start presently and get strength rapidly. If I could I would go to Princeton at once. I must see you soon. This town will be empty without you."

It is well to note the struggle that went on behind the scenes in Henry van Dyke's life for it is out of these struggles that his clear-cut confidence and vital utterances issued. No mistake is more vulgar than that which misjudges his career as that of a man blessed (or cursed) with unmitigated success.

Finally he joined his family who had been installed several months previously in Professor William Milligan Sloane's house, "Stanworth" in Princeton. On February 8th he delivered his first lecture at the University beginning a short course on Wordsworth, Tennyson and Browning. The lectures were at once popular and resulted immediately in a greatly increased reading of poetry by the students. When he concluded the course he addressed a crowded room with men standing around the walls in these words:

"Gentlemen, I wish to thank you for the courtesy and interest with

[214]

which you have listened to my virgin attempts as a University lecturer. I am very conscious of the fact that I am not yet perfectly at home in the class room, but I hope to do better next year. I have had rare good pleasure in giving these lectures and only hope you have had a measure of it in listening. I myself am in danger of falling in love with the vulgar art of teaching. I am proud to have delivered my first course to you, and again express my gratitude for your kindness in enduring me so patiently."

Meantime he was preaching almost every Sunday, frequently in the University Chapel and occasionally in other colleges or churches.

In April with a gift sent him by three hundred of his friends in the Brick Church he bought the Conover homestead on Bayard Lane, a colonial house, dating back to the Revolutionary period. The following September he moved into the house as one who had come home at last, and named it "Avalon." It was the first house and land he had ever owned and he rejoiced unaffectedly that here at last was a home which he and his family could call their own.

For Henry van Dyke Princeton was not only the new adventure of teaching and the continuance of his ministry, it was also the establishment of a home from which he could freely go forth and to which he could return and where he might gather up the literary harvests of the past and of the future.

Chapter Fifteen

TEACHER OF READING AND FRIEND OF YOUNG MEN

BEING a man of tremendous physical and mental vitality Henry van Dyke was never able to limit his interest in life and only seldom could he shut down on his activities. He burned the candle at both ends and in the middle. He was a true exponent of "the strenuous life." Looking over the record of those Princeton years in the newspapers one wonders how he survived it all. Two things may be said to have saved him from shipwreck amid the stress of constant action: first, and most important of all, his basically cheerful faith; second, his remarkable ability to concentrate exclusively on the matter before him and to decide quickly. His mind was the perfect servant of his will. Add to this his well-established habit of taking days off, when he laid aside every responsibility, and one sees how his slight but well-set frame was able to endure the drive of the dynamo that it housed.

First in his activities he now put his relationship with the students at Princeton. His one-term lectures to succeeding senior classes delivered alternately on British Poetry and Prose of the 19th century and the seminars that accompanied them were his chief occupation. Into them he poured constant study and from them he drew infinite delight. The work was much more than that of giving set lectures and preparing men for examinations. His vigorous convictions about literature and his own literary work introduced a fresh and lively note in lectures and seminars. His reading of poetry and prose was often followed by an outburst of applause, occasionally by a significant silence; and a "locomotive cheer" frequently marked the conclusion of a course. His lectures were never twice the same. In the university and elsewhere they were constantly being hammered out on the anvil of use. Besides, being delivered to new groups of men amid the kaleidoscopic changes of American life, and being given out of the conviction that good literature had a living message for the day, they were constantly developing new emphases and acquiring new material. Louis D. Froelich while he was a student of Henry van Dyke's in 1906 contributed a short paper to a symposium in John Wanamaker's *Book News* describing him in the class-room:

"Happy is the lecturer who can hold the attention of men who are ready and willing to be interested. But a genius is that lecturer who attracts and closely engages the attention and wit of all the men in his class. Such a genius is Dr. van Dyke. In a class of about three hundred men, he keenly delights each and every member . . . he seems to be speaking directly to each individual man. . . . He has the power to present men and ideas in a light in which they have not been viewed. He is able to bring into the bright, sharp flame of definite expression the smoldering, struggling, dull glow of general impressions.

His manner and personality in lecturing are as strong, decisive and sympathetic as is his subject matter. Not only his words, but his face, voice and general bearing bring out exactly the ideas he desires to communicate. His own hospitable and friendly smile, and soft quality of voice in describing the humor of Lamb make one feel instinctively that this humor was gentle, kindly and warm. His manner is intense in his disgust for snobbery and shams, when portraying Thackeray's hatred for these things. In reading from the books of the men he is describing, the pathos and feeling with which he renders selections from Dickens, his vivacity in others from Thackeray, his oratorical power in some of the lofty passages from Macaulay and Carlyle, do not fail to inspire men with the power of literature . . . Dr. van Dyke gives true pictures of his literary men. He does not tell all their virtues and then stop. He shows the other side of their characters and works. He does not try to advance literary theories as excuses where no excuse exists. His literary men are judged by the same code of laws and morals as are ordinary men. In this common-sense, fair-minded attitude he wins an interest for men of letters because they are human, and for himself because of his manliness.

Aside from the influence of his lectures as an inspiration for a greater love of literature, their influence as aids for a higher and more useful life is pronounced. Morals are not tacked on. They are far more effectively, though none the less clearly, shown by Dr. van Dyke in his descriptions of the noblest deeds and sentiments of Christian manhood as exemplified in the lives and teachings of the greatest literary men of the world. By presenting the best in life he stimulates to emulation. He points out with the intimacy of an old friend, the highest ideals for which men should strive, the practical ways in which they may be useful and ennobling to their fellowmen in the life beyond the college walls. It is in these short talks that men get the deepest inspiration, and from these that they will carry with them the most lasting impressions for good from the class-room influence of the personality and power of Henry van Dyke."

Outside of the class room he was frequently called on by the students for informal readings and discussions on the campus; and he was always ready to bring his literary friends to Princeton for the Seniors' Monday Night Club. Many were the stated and irregular gatherings of undergraduates by night in his library when he took down various books from the shelves and when, amid the fragrance of pipes, the conversation flowed easily on literature and life.

When the Seminar was at work on the short story as an English prose form he introduced a letter in which Mark Twain had written him:

"It probably costs you nothing to write a short story [imagine Henry van Dyke rising to that fly!] but I find that it costs me as many false starts—and therefore failures—as does a long one. And as the right start—the right *plan*—is the only difficulty encountered with either, consider what a rascal for time-expense the short story is to me. Ten years and five failures—that is about my luck. I had it with the one in the Christmas Weekly. And yet that one is so light and frivolous and looks so easy, and as if it *couldn't* be started on a wrong plan,—but I discovered four wrong ones in ten years. I have hardly *ever* started a story, long or short, on the right plan—the right plan being the plan which will make it tell itself without my help—except after three failures. I think you are safe to tell the advanced class that only the born artist can expect to start a story right the first time."

From the beginning Henry van Dyke was, as he called himself "a teacher of reading" rather than a professor of English Literature.

[218]

His own studies and reading were carefully used in his lectures to arouse his students to read and reflect for themselves. He was full of plans to direct the particular interest that any student developed, and he spent much time on the questions that individual men brought him.

Take as typical of the objective in his work these brief words spoken at the Rice Institute in 1912:

"Literature is that one of the arts which works with the least costly of all materials, words, to embody the most precious of all human possessions, ideas. Any language that has expressed noble thought and feeling in lucid form becomes classic. Any race that has succeeded in producing real literature, by virtue of that production, becomes immortal. The one thing that does not die is the well-chosen word whose soul is the well-born thought.

Literature is the most humane and intimate of all the arts. It comes closest to the common life of man. Good books help us to understand our own hearts. They open the world to us. They are revealers and interpreters, friends and counsellors. They liberate us, at least for a little while, from the slavery of time and space. And while the other arts in their perfection are not always accessible to those who are not rich in this world's goods, the best literature is usually the cheapest. . . .

Literature cannot be taught. There are things in our universities that we call 'chairs of literature.' Those who occupy them, if they are doing their duty, are simply 'teachers of reading', that is all. Literature cannot be taught any more than any other of the higher arts can be taught. You cannot make a literary man by instruction in a class room. You can correct his grammar. You can correct his spelling; that is to say, you can do something in that direction as long as the 'Simple Spellers' remain in abeyance. But you cannot make him a writer, any more than you can make him a sculptor, unless Nature has bestowed the gift.

The best that we can do for Literature in our universities is this: to cultivate an appreciation for that which is finest and most humane in the writings of the past; to teach young men and women to know the difference between a book that is well written and a book that is badly written; to give them a standard by which they may judge and measure their own efforts at self-expression; and to inspire in the few who have an irresistible impulse to write, a sincere desire to find a clear, vivid and memorable form for the utterance of the best that is in them.

[219]

This is something which I think the university may well propose to itself as one of its high objects: to promote the love of good literature, and to endeavor that no one shall obtain an academic degree who does not know *how to read*,—to read between the lines, to read behind the words, to enter through the printed page into a deeper knowledge of life."

In a letter to the *New York Times* in the same year he protested vigorously against the attempt to systematize and standardize the work of college English departments by which "masterpieces of vital literature were swathed and smothered in voluminous annotations, like mummies in a museum," defended "the use of English literature as a factor in a liberal education," and concluded:

"The best reward of thirteen years of service as a teacher in the English Department is to hear a fellow say to me, now and then, that he has learned to love reading, both prose and poetry, and that he has begun to collect a little library of his own favorite books."

Professor Charles A. Downer, writing enthusiastically about this letter said:

"You seem not ashamed, if I understand you aright, to justify the study of literature, in part at least as a noble pastime, as something of eternal interest to the human being. I hope it will not become in our colleges and universities a mere division of biology."

The result of the practice of such an ideal was electric. His courses were among the most popular in the University and several times at the undergraduates' request he felt obliged to offer optional courses. From a mass of letters of gratitude which still survive, these quotations must here speak for many.

"I am so overwhelmed by your kindness," wrote one man four years after graduation, "that I am put to it where to begin, or what to say first. . . . Better even than your letters themselves, I think, is the knowledge that the consideration you always showed me came from a real substantial kindness of heart and an interest that was genuine. . . . In the meantime you have played, at different times, a much more vital part in my life than you probably have any idea of; and possibly the knowledge of that fact may give you some pleasure."

[220]

From North China a missionary wrote a long letter in which he says:

"Your lectures at Princeton were full of mental meat for me and made me a devoted student of Tennyson; while your sermons helped me to decide to tackle the hardest work that I could do for God—which decision meant for me to become a foreign missionary."

Another man just about to be married asked for an autograph in one of Henry van Dyke's books which is to be "the corner stone of our library," and adds:

"As a test of the books we purchase we are making the rule to buy nothing which we do not intend to read more than once. This is not wholly because our funds are none too large but because we wish our books to be real companions in our home."

A young Japanese teacher from Tokyo wrote:

"I love Princeton, specially I feel very proud of that I have had you as my teacher. I was cherishing a desire to study your works and I have collect your books so far within my reach, and I read them, and would know better of you."

"If every one," wrote another who was already succeeding as a teacher and writer, "could put into teaching what you do, even a quarter of it, I think the vexed question of teaching wouldn't be vexed any more—although I have never been able to see how you did it at all, in connection with all the rest of your busy life."

A father wrote shortly after his son's graduation:

"I thank you most heartily for your great kindness to my son. He went to Princeton with no definite life purpose and plan, tho' not without worthy aspirations. In you he met a wise friend and counsellor and an inspirer of wishes and purposes which have given definite aim to his life. For your friendship and help so generously and wisely bestowed, I cannot sufficiently thank you. I have often wished that some able writer would draw the likeness of the 'Student-Professor' as the famous Professor Tholuck of Halle was called, and show to the teachers of our land that the personal friendship, influence and inspiration of the Instructor is even

[221]

more valuable than the facts which he teaches. I am thankful, very thankful to you for being such an inspiring teacher-friend to my son."

The liberal terms on which Henry van Dyke had taken up his part in the Princeton Faculty were full of danger for his relations with his colleagues which was not lessened by his immediate successes with the students. Nevertheless his own generous recognition of the work of others and the forbearance of those who performed some of the more irksome committee duties sufficed to keep those relations in the main happy. There were indeed dark days. Henry van Dyke was never quite able to relate his ideal and the actual Princeton. Being constantly conscious of the needs of men and never self-conscious in action, he was accustomed to look upon his own activities objectively as the fulfilment of the service which his talents could render. He had no sympathy with those who could see nothing in the actions of their fellowmen but the exercise of unrestrained personal ambition. His own career, like that of all men who achieve success on the field of public action, might look insatiable to an undiscriminating eye. To him it was quite simply a matter of living up to the responsibilities of his talents. At the same time, as a genuine artist, the filaments of his nature were sensitive to every light and shade and any breath. Perhaps the nub of the matter lies in the laughing comment of President Patton who once said of certain troublers of the peace in that Israel: "Well, you see, Henry, they are consecrated to a fierce democracy."

Unhappily, too, the resignation of President Patton in 1901 and the newspapers' habit of mentioning Henry van Dyke for all academic vacancies caused him no little suffering. As his close friend Dr. John DeWitt wrote him:

"I have thought a good deal about you since Dr. Patton's resignation, and have recalled our conversation of several weeks or rather a couple of months since in which, when I said that I hoped that being ten years younger than Dr. Patton, you might be his successor you replied that the proposal of your name when the time came by your friends would be a painful thing to you, as your present position was just to your liking and the only move you expected to make from your present house was the last move to the cemetery. Of course many people have thought of you for the Presidency of Princeton. But that this should be twisted by a few people into 'an ambition' on your part is—well, I trust it is not more than a slight, as it will not be more than a temporary annoyance."

Another friend Dr. George L. Spinning clearly perceived the issue when he wrote in a long and cheerful letter:

"Furthermore we don't think you ever thought of it [the Presidency] or would touch it any more than you would touch a live electric wire. We need no assurance on this point so long as we believe in your sanity —and upon this viz.: your clear judgment of things in general and of the vocation for which God has given you a special endowment we bank heavily.

The natural endowment determines the vocation—and we think you know this, and mean to follow the divine purpose in the use of your talents."

As a matter of fact Henry van Dyke's attention to public affairs at this time was entirely concentrated on the Church. He had been summoned back to the Brick Church in late 1901 upon the crisis following the death of Dr. Babcock and was acting pastor there for a year. The matter of creed revision was again demanding his careful attention. In 1900 he had been appointed to General Assembly's committee and he looked upon that appointment not only as an opportunity to do valuable service for the Church which he loved but as a filial duty to carry forward the work in which his father had been engaged and which had been wrecked at the General Assembly in 1892. In May 1902 he was elected Moderator of the General Assembly as the obvious leader to promote the needed revision and to prepare a book of forms for public worship. As Henry van Dyke often said to me with an honesty which the record supports: "I have never desired any office except Moderator of the General Assembly in order to carry through the revision,—and I didn't raise my hand to get that." When the Princeton Presidency was filled by the election of his colleague, Woodrow Wilson, no one was happier over it than Henry van Dyke. For the chapel services in October, 1902, he wrote and offered the prayer with which the new President was inaugurated.

The positive side of Henry van Dyke's relation with his colleagues in the English Department and elsewhere was always happy. There were frequent visits back and forth and mutual exchanges of congratulatory notes on things done.

Especially close was the relation with Professor Stockton Axson. The two men were heartily in sympathy with one another in their approach to literature and teaching, and happily the relationship of their courses—they alternated in conducting the courses in English Prose and Poetry—drew them much together. They became fast friends. Henry van Dyke often spoke of Axson as "a sane, enthusiastic, clear, steady teacher—a believer in the glorious service which good literature renders to life."

Dr. Theodore W. Hunt who had been a young instructor when Henry van Dyke was a college student, was now head of the English Department and their relationship continued to be affectionate. The note that Dr. Hunt wrote Henry van Dyke when he was about to leave for public service at the Hague in 1913 contains words that well represent their relations and incidentally bears witness to the great-heartedness of the writer:

"But the loss to us in the University and especially in the English Department—how shall I speak of it! It is simply irreparable. During these years of your distinguished service you have given to us the benefit of your national and international repute as an author and made us all justly proud of our academic relation to you as colleagues. While I have been the official head of the department you have been acknowledged by us all as our real intellectual and literary head. . . . Personally, dear doctor, I will miss you more than I can tell, and shall ever look back with profound gratitude and satisfaction to the long friendship of over forty years that I have had the privilege of enjoying."

From the beginning Henry van Dyke took an active part in the religious life of the University. He had come from the Brick Church with much the same purpose as Dean Murray, his predecessor in both places, had come before him. This appears plainly in the words that Henry van Dyke spoke at the unveiling of the Murray Memorial in the chapel, November 10, 1901:

"When he left his New York pastorate in 1875, to accept a professorship in this institution of learning, he had no intention of giving up the ministry of Christ. On the contrary he knew that he was going into it still more deeply. For if there is any place where the preaching of plain religion,—pure, reasonable, helpful, and ennobling,—is needed today, it is in our universities. Christianity must keep its hold on the educated young men who are to lead the Twentieth Century. Christianity must prove its power to lie in close contact and fellowship with science, philosophy and literature."

To this aspect of his task Henry van Dyke addressed himself vigorously and sympathetically. He frequently conducted the daily chapel and spoke for the Philadelphian Society (the college Y.M.C.A.). He preached often at Sunday chapel and delivered several baccalaureate sermons. He was not a systematic preacher but attempted always to speak directly to an immediate need. The themes of some of those sermons reveal his approach: "Positive Religion"; "What is Man?"; "The Things Law cannot Reach"; "The Gospel for an Age of Machinery"; "The Contagion of Virtue".

Take two brief paragraphs from his sermon at the 160th anniversary of the University. How simply and nobly they draw together the too often unreconciled ideals of free scholarship and genuine faith:

"I have no extravagant and fantastic notion of what is possible for an academic institution to do in this modern world,—no expectation of miracles, or sudden transformations of society. My thought moves along sober lines, within reasonable limits. I believe the Christian university will do its best work by being stedfastly true to the purpose of its foundation, by making its chief aim the promotion of disinterested study and the development of noble character by standing in the world for religion and learning.

You cannot put Christianity into the curriculum, but you can keep it in the daily life and spirit of the university. You cannot make scholars by a system; but you can develop and improve a system favorable to scholarship. You cannot restore the physical conditions, nor even the intellectual conditions of university life to what they were a century ago, but you can make its essence the same now as it was then—a vital discipline for the promotion of knowledge, learning, virtue and faith."

[225]

"Think daily of Christ," he concluded a baccalaureate, "and hold Him as your Saviour and Lord in your heart of hearts, for so your ideal will remain bright and stedfast among the confusions of life, and your courage will never fail in the conflicts of life, and you also will be true gentlemen, purified, fortified and ennobled by the contagion of His virtue and the inspiration of his praise. And so God bless you, Class of 1906, and may you all fare well."

How keenly he observed the life of undergraduates may be noted in a short article he wrote soon after coming to Princeton:

"The actual state of vital religion among students . . . seems to be sound and vigorous. Something it may have lost in meditative insight, in spiritual fervor; but it has gained much in steadiness of purpose, in breadth of brotherhood, in manly simplicity, and in everyday working power. Infidelity is discredited. The fascination of doubt has waned. Science, having won the fight for liberty, no longer appears hostile to faith. Within the last generation the thinking youth of America have experienced a great revival, at least of the will to believe. Christianity reasserts its eternal fitness to the vital needs of man. Never have the students in our colleges shown so deep a sense, or so frank a recognition of religion as an essential element of normal and noble manhood."

He recognized clearly that religion in the colleges was an issue with two sides: "The quality of the ministers who have come out of the colleges have always borne a close relation to the quality of the ministers who have gone into the colleges."

And how accurately he put his finger on two of the great difficulties in the chapel system at Princeton: "a semi-required, semi-voluntary chapel system is a hybrid humbug, and the students know it," and added: "The preachers who come to speak in the college pulpit could greatly increase, in many cases, the value of their services, if an opportunity were given them to come into private conference with students."

The academic years 1907-1911 were unhappy and difficult years for Henry van Dyke. His always delicate sensibilities felt keenly the fret of small handicaps in his university work. He heard too much of the inevitable gossip of a small town and fell into distressful periods of brooding over it. He could not forget the windy rumors of his ambition for the Presidency which, despite his denials and the clear record of his conduct in 1902 and since then, were still blown about in certain quarters. Being a man of action and passionately determined to do his work in an atmosphere of peace he suddenly, without consulting anybody, resigned his chair on February 27, 1907. The effect was instantaneous. The Faculty met and wired him in Boston this unanimous resolution:

"The members of the University faculty have heard with the deepest regret of the resignation of their colleague and friend, Dr. Henry van Dyke. They earnestly request him to reconsider his present determination and to remain in the Professorship he has adorned with rare distinction and to continue in our midst his manifold work which has proved so beneficent and valuable to this University as well as to the cause of letters, religion and good citizenship generally."

A universal howl of protest went up and petitions from undergraduates and alumni and friends of the University poured in upon him. Lifted from the slough of despond by the unexpected demonstration he withdrew his resignation, gratefully relieved at the generous reassurance that Princeton and he still belonged together.

But unhappy days for Princeton were approaching and in the difficulties that ensued Henry van Dyke was of necessity involved by his convictions. There was considerable feeling abroad that the social life and the intellectual life of the undergraduates were not in harmony, and many believed that the upper class club system was militating against the real purpose of the University. Certainly club matters were occupying plenty of time and energy among the undergraduates. Meantime President Wilson, who had certainly been elected to that office as a reformer, was leading vigorously toward democracy and scholarship. His new Preceptors, that remarkable band of young teachers whom he assembled, and the system of small group discussions through which they worked, infused new strength and also brought into the open certain weaknesses in the campus life. There was however considerable difference of opinion as to how best to deal with these questions. There were those who favored radical steps and those who believed that an internal reform, while admittedly slower, would be more effective.

In the issue of the *Alumni Weekly* following the Commencement of 1907, it was announced that the residential quadrangle plan (a plan founded on the English college system and first proposed by Charles Francis Adams of Harvard in a Phi Beta Kappa address at Columbia) had been adopted by the Board of Trustees. At once the Faculty, undergraduates and alumni were divided into two camps. There was not a little feeling that the plan had been autocratically foisted on an unconsulted Princeton constituency which added bitterness to the opposition to it. The main issue, however, was whether so radical a step was needed. Some desired radical measures—but not this particular one. There is no doubt that in proposing the plan President Wilson was convinced that he was leading in the direction of genuine social democracy and scholarship for Princeton. Even in the heat of the conflict the real leaders of the opposition did not question this. But it would be equally false to describe the struggle, as some have done, as a contest between a system of special privilege and democracy. As a matter of fact one of the issues for which many of the opposition were contending was the democratic principle of the right of the students to direct their social life for themselves rather than to have a system of social relations conferred upon them. Many of the opposition favored reform but believed that reform to be effective must be self-reform. This was Henry van Dyke's position, and regretfully, for he was a staunch admirer and supporter of the President, he took his place in the opposition following correspondence and conference with him. On July 10th he wrote a long letter which was published in the next issue of the *Alumni Weekly* on September 25th, which concluded with these words:

"Is it really necessary or prudent to give up the American university organization, under which Princeton has prospered, for something alien and unknown? Is it wise to use a remedy for present evils which may be more dangerous than the disease itself? Is it not highly probable that careful consideration and united discussion would find a democratic and efficient way of dealing with the troubles which have grown up around the present club system, without radically transforming the constitution of the University at a single blow?"

So determined was the opposition to the Quad scheme,—by no

means all of it motived by high principles,—that the adoption of the plan was withdrawn and the matter properly became one for general discussion. Unhappily that discussion continued with what Henry van Dyke described as "truly academic ferocity." Personalities and all sorts of issues were entangled in it and the atmosphere of Princeton became most distressing. The President carried his fight for the Quad system to the alumni on a lofty plane. The immediate issue soon became the placing of the new buildings for the Graduate College on the campus or apart from it. When the President succeeded in having the trustees reject a large gift for that college given with the provision that it be built on a site off the campus the storm broke out afresh. Henry van Dyke was invited by the Princeton Club of Philadelphia to discuss Princeton problems with particular reference to the rejection of this offer. He did so in no uncertain words carefully pointing out that:

"Attempts to study and solve the actual problems of student life have been blocked. A resolution offered in the faculty for the appointment of a committee, headed by the President to consider the conditions of student life and suggest the best way of promoting its unity, democracy and scholarship, was rejected by authority. A resolution of Grover Cleveland to the same effect, in the Board of Trustees, met with the same fate. The proposal to build a Students' Union or University Hall, and the offer of money for that purpose, was not considered. The building of the Graduate College has been indefinitely postponed. For what reason have these things happened if not for one related directly or indirectly with the plan to reintegrate the University by Quads?"

Arguing that the Quad scheme was unnecessary, un-American, undemocratic, unpractical and perilous to the Princeton spirit he declared:

"It has been no pleasant task for me to make this speech. But Princeton has long been the dearest place on earth to me, and believing her now to be in grave peril, I feel that my duty to speak out is inevitable."

And he concluded by pleading that the Quad scheme might be finally withdrawn and attention centered on four major problems:

"First, to perfect our excellent new curriculum and to develop our wholesome manly student life. Second, to complete and endow our promising preceptorial plan. Third, to justify our name as a university by the creation of a real graduate college. Fourth, to reunite, restore, and revive the Princeton spirit."

Throughout the speech he had avoided direct reference to Princeton supporters of the Quad scheme, and had accurately attributed its paternity to Charles Francis Adams. But there could be no doubt about the Princetonian against whom the argument was directed nor was there intended to be any doubt.

"What a splendid sportsmanlike speech that was of yours the other night," wrote Struthers Burt. "Outside of its brilliancy the very courage of it at such a time as the present should appeal to every Princeton man who is a sportsman, and I hope most of them are. Not all, more's the pity. I can't particularly say why this connection appears to me, but somehow men who know the big places and the woods do things and think things that other men don't."

But despite the issue between them neither the President nor Henry van Dyke suffered any break to occur in their personal relations. On this particular issue they were like those professors in another institution of whom one of them once said: "All my colleagues love one another sincerely, which is good; but equally they detest one another's opinions—which is also as it should be."

Gradually it began to appear that the radical reform of the Quad scheme could not be inaugurated at Princeton. But amid the clouds of that defeat Woodrow Wilson's political star shone clear. Henry van Dyke with his record free of personalities in the Princeton battle honestly and enthusiastically supported him. This made for misunderstandings with some other Princetonians but was quite typical of Henry van Dyke, who loved the swirling tides of a fight on a plain issue but loathed the treasuring of personal animosities.

In fact the official subsidence of the Quad battle with Woodrow Wilson's turning to the gubernatorial campaign in New Jersey left a Princeton still much inclined to divide on the old battle lines. Once more Henry van Dyke found the atmosphere intolerable to him. On November 24, 1910 he sent his resignation to the Secretary of the University "for the same reasons which led to my resignation three years ago." As a matter of fact the reasons though technically the same were now far more serious. That hoary bogey of his "ambition" for the Presidency was coming up again but chiefly he was in an utterly dejected and wrathful state over Princeton conditions. He put up a "For Sale" sign on "Avalon," which the undergraduates promptly tore down and he restored; and in a vigorous letter to the *New York Times* supporting Woodrow Wilson he made a reference to his own impending departure from Princeton. The two upper classes held a mass meeting and protested, sending their class officers to intervene personally. Henry van Dyke received them warmly but remained obdurate. The trustees tabled the resignation and sent a committee to confer. The committee suffered many things for Henry van Dyke was fighting on an issue which involved himself but which he declared "represents a principle by which I am ready to stand or fall whatever it may cost." A proposal that he should assume an additional office carrying with it the direction and charge of the religious interests of the University was held to be impossible of consideration until the *odium academicum* was gone and the University united in its work for the new curriculum, the preceptorial system, and the Graduate College. In pressing for these three things Henry van Dyke was actually demanding the obliteration of the old battle lines over the Quad scheme. He was determined to see the thing through. To Hamilton Mabie, always his familiar confidant he wrote:

"It is a good deal to ask a whole hour of your time but things have come to a pass where serious steps must be taken. Avalon is to be sold —a new life is to be attempted, and at fifty-eight that looks rather serious, doesn't it?

But you see, somehow or other, in the midst of all this wreckage, I still count on your affection, and I would like to have a real hour with you before I go."

Meanwhile Moses Taylor Pyne who had played an important part in bringing Henry van Dyke to Princeton in 1900 continued his generous and sympathetic efforts to meet the issue. And Henry van Dyke agreed to the request of the senior class and began his course with them although his resignation still stood.

Finally a new committee of the trustees consisting of Mr. Pyne, Cleveland H. Dodge and Dr. J. M. T. Finney wrote him the following letter on April 20th:

"The Committee appointed by the Board of Trustees to confer with you regarding your resignation earnestly ask you to withdraw it. We do this not only on account of our personal affections for you, but also in the interest of Princeton.

We have the highest appreciation of the benefits you have conferred upon the University during the twelve years in which you have held the chair of English Literature, and we should view your leaving Princeton with the greatest regret. You have been of the highest service, not only as a lecturer and teacher, but as a wise and sympathetic advisor to generations of Princeton men, and a warm personal friend to their elders.

We sincerely deprecate the rumors of which you spoke, that you have been seeking the Presidency of Princeton University, knowing that they are entirely false and unwarranted, and we trust that you may not give them any further consideration.

We assure you that the false position of which you complain no longer exists, and that we desire the benefit of your counsel and experience more than ever.

It is our desire and purpose that Princeton, holding fast to her traditions of a regulated collegiate course, shall give herself without distraction to the three specific tasks which are before her: the maintenance and development of the new curriculum, of the Preceptorial System, and of the Graduate College."

And on May 10th after full consultation with his friends Henry van Dyke replied:

"Your esteemed favor is duly received. I thank you for your references to my work as a teacher of reading. It has always been a pleasant work to do. Its reward has been a happy fellowship with twelve successive classes of Princeton men. If I have rendered them any service, I am sincerely glad.

It is gratifying to note that you recognize that the perennial rumors of my seeking the presidency of your body are 'entirely false and unwarranted.' I do not know where they originated. But your frank disavowal now should put them to rest, and relieve me from the recurrent annoyance of being considered as a candidate for an office contrary to my desires and altogether out of my line. The prospect of this relief is welcome.

The last subject touched by your letter is the most important. The reasons for my resignation have never been concealed, nor personal. They have to do with the spirit and policy of Princeton for the future. Regarding peace and work as essential to the life of the University, I have ventured in the course of these long conferences which you have invited, to put a certain pertinent question. Your last paragraph is in reply to this question.

If I understand you rightly, the phrase 'without distraction' is meant to express your wish and intention that Princeton shall not be distracted by factional rivalries and conflicts. You purpose that she shall move forward, under a guidance disregarding academic politics, to accomplish her three specific tasks as a university, in an atmosphere favorable to manhood, scholarship and religion.

Understanding you thus, with the consent of the Board of Trustees, I will gladly accede to your wish and withdraw my resignation. This is a double pleasure because it makes the way clear at last to return an affirmative answer to the request which the students made last winter that I should stay at Princeton."

Between the lines of these letters you may read the rising of a better day for Princeton. And in the many letters of rejoicing that Henry van Dyke received when his resignation was withdrawn there are frequent allusions to his uncompromising stand as a vital factor in the new dawn. As a matter of fact the characteristically Dutch pertinacity with which he fought the issue through had no small root in his conviction that the welfare of the undergraduates, which he always put first, demanded a unified Princeton.

The following autumn as he took up again a fresh year's work he wrote cheerfully to Hamilton Mabie:

"You can hear the grass growing here. I hope it is on the grave of the academic hatchet."

And Professor John Grier Hibben who was shortly to be elected the new President wrote describing an intimate evening in his own home:

[233]

"We all agreed that no one has ever so completely portrayed the Princeton of our pride and of our hopes, as you have accomplished in such a masterly fashion in 'The Builders'. In the days of dissension and strife, Princeton men would do well to catch its spirit and illustrate it in their word and deed."

Chapter Sixteen

THE AUTHOR'S LITERARY CREED AND METHOD OF WORK

WHEN Henry van Dyke came to Princeton he combined in that move the two calls that had come to him during the years of his pastorate in New York: The call to associate himself with youth and the call to write. Already the essays of *Little Rivers* and *Fisherman's Luck* and a number of stories, notably "The First Christmas Tree," "The Other Wise Man," and "The Lost Word," as well as "The Toiling of Felix," a long ballad of Labor, and the six lyrics which were included in Stedman's American Anthology had made him a recognized figure in American literature. Now he began to write with great delight and a sense of freedom despite many other calls upon his time. At first in a little den off the big library in "Avalon" and later in a larger den which he added to the house and filled with the particular books which were the tools of his craft he was steadily at work. Especially he loved to write at night when he was secure from interruption and could lose himself in that complete concentration on the matter in hand which was always characteristic of him. When he did write he wrote with tremendous speed, but always these times were preceded by periods of intense preoccupation during which he read widely or wandered in his old garden full of flowers. Most of his stories, essays and poems originated from jottings in notebooks that he carried with him everywhere and in which he put down random lines that, often after the lapse of years, suddenly called for writing. Sometimes he began a story and discarded it as a false beginning; but in most cases, when he once took up his pencil to write, the story was so completely formed in his mind that except for the changing of a few words it came forth almost in its final form. Frequently when a story was finished in the afternoon or evening he would read it to the family and guests of the household. This was because he liked to share his own delight and because he felt that reading aloud was an excellent test of the story itself.

He began his own literary work in Princeton by completing the group of tales which were to make up his first book of stories, *The Ruling Passion*. Several of them had already been written, and the others were rapidly taking form in his mind.

In 1898 he had written his hearty thanks to Royal Cortissoz for a sympathetic review of one of his stories and on the last page had added:

"A Writer's Petition

Let me never tag a meaning to a story, nor tell a story without a meaning. Give me eyes to see the real, and a heart to feel the ideal. Let me catch the local colour, without missing the spiritual light. Teach me to hold the glass up to nature, but may it always reflect some rays from the eternal stars.

Grant me this, Master of all good workmen, for the work's sake."

This hastily penned scrap is worth recording here for some words which it elicited in Mr. Cortissoz's reply:

"The actual words in your letter mean much. More even, do I find in your proof that the critic can sometimes count on having understood, on being held acquitted of that insincerity and malice which it is so often the fashion to ascribe to him. He, too, conceives of his duty nobly, I hope; and, echoing your beautiful prayer, I thank you not only for sending it to me, but for an added stimulus in my work."

The incident further discloses the origin of the fuller paragraph which stood on the flyleaf of *The Ruling Passion* when it appeared in the autumn of 1901. From such incidents of personal relationship often sprang the most characteristic of Henry van Dyke's utterances:

"A Writer's Request of His Master

Lord, let me never tag a moral to a story, nor tell a story without a meaning. Make me respect my material so much that I dare not slight my work. Help me to deal very honestly with words and with people because they are both alive. Show me that as in a river, so in a writing, clearness is the best quality, and a little that is pure is worth more than much that is mixed. Teach me to see the local colour without being blind to the inner light. Give me an ideal that will stand the strain of weaving into human stuff on the loom of the real. Keep me from caring more for books than for folks, for art than for life. Steady me to do my full stint of work as well as I can: and when that is done, stop me, pay what wages Thou wilt, and help me to say, from a quiet heart a grateful Amen."

Another illustration of the personal experiences which lay at the root of Henry van Dyke's writing is found in one of these stories, "The Gentle Life," where he begins the account of his meeting with Izaak Walton by writing of his long time fishing companion Ned Mason. Would you know what lay behind it? Read this letter from Mason:

> "Balsam Lake Club,
> "March 11 or 12, 1898.

> "Henry, my dear young friend and beloved old crony; you riotous old hunter, you fastidious angler, you speaker of speeches, you writer of books, you lover of beauty, you seer and bard—in fact, you unmitigated durned old galoot, why not run up here for a few days, and watch dear Dame Nature awaken from her long sleep?
> Here we are, old man, F. and P. and i. Oh, what a bully time we are having! Comfortable, warm house. Plenty of fairly good grub. Wood fires. You know the place. We shall be here until March 20th or 21st—unless some accident happens. Come up to see us. . . The birds are here. Chipmunks are out. Snake killed yesterday. Snow going fast about 15 inches left on the level. Ice on the lake about 18 inches. Ther. yesterday and today 40 to 52. No frost last night.

> Thine
> Ned."

And enclosed with the letter a scrap of moss and a dry beech leaf.

The other stories in *The Ruling Passion* came from his camping notebooks many of them five or six years old and long-time meditated upon. A Princeton friend and neighbor of later years, Herbert

Adams Gibbons, with whom Henry van Dyke often spoke intimately, told me that one of those stories, probably "A Year of Nobility," sprang from a conversation overheard in the hotel at Roberval. "I couldn't understand the French Canadian talk without the greatest concentration," said Henry van Dyke, "yet I got enough to give me an idea for the story. The strange thing was I didn't know it was a story till ten years later when I wrote it."

And doubtless the earliest hint for the "Keeper of the Light" was the account (which in a sermon in 1885 he said he had somewhere read), of a light-keeper on a desolate Canadian shore who when the machinery failed gave his life to turn the light by hand.

"To tell about some of these ruling passions, simply, clearly, and concretely, is what I want to do in this book," wrote Henry van Dyke in his preface. "The characters are chosen, for the most part, among plain people, because their feelings are expressed with fewer words and greater truth, not being costumed for social effect. The scene is laid on Nature's stage because I like to be out-of-doors, even when I am trying to think and learning to write."

For the summer vacation of 1902 Henry van Dyke took his family to the island of Martha's Vineyard where he rented a cottage not far from the sea in what he always called "scroll saw city". At times he enjoyed playing on the beach or better still trolling for blue fish. But his mind was full of stories; and finally he wandered back into the hills, found a dilapidated old farm house which he hired from an equally dilapidated Portuguese farmer and there in the bare and empty hallway before an open door looking out over a wide rolling heath to a distant prospect of the sea he set up a kitchen table and spent his days preparing *The Blue Flower*. Five of the nine stories that made the volume were there written in a period of almost complete absorption and evident delight. The children and their friends vividly remember the evenings when the stories were read in the family circle with the sounds of passersby and the murmur of the sea floating through the open windows.

The central thought which brought the stories together had been for at least ten years in his mind,—"the search for inward happiness, which all men who are really alive are following." This he chose

[238]

to symbolize in the title of *The Blue Flower*, the phrase which Novalis had used to signify Poetry. The book embodies in the form of tales Henry van Dyke's interpretation of the meaning and significance of life. He always believed in happiness but as he often expressed it: "The place where the Blue Flower is most often found is near where the path of Friendship joins the path of Duty in the old-fashioned garden of Work." A profound and reverent sense of the mystery of human life and a stout conviction that joy lies at the heart of that mystery pervade the tales and touch many of the incidents with autobiographical reminiscences. At heart he was ever a mystic. He met events and later reflected upon his experiences as a man already convinced that they held some meaning of good—hard as it might be to find and recognize it. He was also a romantic, or more strictly a poet, in that he found symbolic values in certain spiritual experiences of his life which were out of all proportion to their external significance. For him the pilgrimage of the soul was the theme *par excellence*. But he not only looked in his own heart to write, he also looked at the world about him with a lover's eye and recorded it with the pen of an accurate observer and a devout artist. To him romance was never distance; it was rather the vital quality of being alive among men and amid the unfathomable wonders of nature. He was never an "escapist" in his dealing with life but he believed thoroughly that in order to keep alive a man must go back at times from the pressure of immediate action in order to revive himself at that source from which alone significant action is derived. "Realism," he often said, "is the life of romance; but exaggeration is its death."

If you seek Henry van Dyke's basic philosophy of life embodied in tales there is no place where you can find it more characteristically or more adequately expressed than in *The Blue Flower*. Here is his reverent acknowledgment of the greatest of all mysteries, the passionate sense of God beyond the reach of intellect. Here is his frank recognition of the dilemmas created by conflict and his sturdy faith that these dilemmas are to be resolved not in the abstractions of intellectual reasoning but on the field of generous action for the common good.

It was ten years later that his third volume of stories, *The Unknown Quantity* made its appearance. In order to see the significance of this book it is necessary to refer briefly here to some of the other writings and events of the intervening years the more important of which will be fully spoken of in other places. For several years following the completion of *The Blue Flower* he turned to poetry, writing two of his best odes and many of his finest lyrics. He was busy also with his introduction to the poetry of Tennyson and with the editorship of the Gateway Series of English Texts. In 1904 he took his two eldest daughters abroad, visiting his friends the Carnegies at Skibo Castle, Canon Rawnsley at Keswick, and Professor S. H. Butcher at the Lakes of Killarney. In 1907 he published another volume of discursive essays and fishing tales, *Days Off;* and made his long-anticipated trip to Palestine where he completed his poetic drama *The House of Rimmon* and wrote the travel essays *Out of Doors in the Holy Land.* The summers of 1908 and 1909 he spent with his family abroad delivering in the winter his lectures on *The Spirit of America* at The Sorbonne. Meanwhile he had published two small volumes of poetry *Music* and *The White Bees* and in 1911 he revised his poetry adding a number of new verses in the first collected edition of his Poems. During these years he was much engaged with his friends young and old and with his family. In 1908 his eldest daughter Brooke was married; as was his second daughter Dorothea in 1911. On February 24, 1912, Dorothea died with her infant daughter in childbirth. In the throes of this sorrow which never wholly left him he turned with passion to the completing of *The Unknown Quantity.* The strange providence which had broken the earthly tie to his "dear daughter Dorothea, ray of light, song of joy, heart of love" was not rebelled against. But it added a poignant personal note to his sense of the mystery of life. As he concluded his brief preface to the stories: "Without the Unknown Quantity life would be easier, perhaps, but certainly less interesting. It is not likely that we shall ever eliminate it. But we can live with it, work with it bravely, hopefully, happily, if we believe that after all it means good—infinite good, passing comprehension —to all who live in love."

At least three of the stories included in *The Unknown Quantity,*
—"The Music Lover," "The Sad Shepherd," "The Mansion," had
been already written and these three named had been already published before the spring of 1912; and so also with eight out of ten
of the Half-Told Tales—little stories "like etchings in which more is
suggested than is in the picture," a form of sententious writing
which he first attempted in 1911. But more than half the book, including at least five of the nine stories and two of the Half-Told
Tales were written chiefly during March, April and May 1912. Some
notes that I made at the time reveal the "streaks of writing" so characteristic of Henry van Dyke that their contents may be worth
recording here. On March 16th while staying in the New York
apartment of his beloved and now bereaved son-in-law, Guy R.
McLane, he was reading a book on the French Revolution. Suddenly the Breton legend which Anatole Le Braz had told him several years before began to take form in the story "The Messengers
at the Window." At ten o'clock that evening he began to write
spending much of that night over it and the whole of the next day.
In the evening of the second day he read the finished story to Guy
McLane and myself. And six days later he had finished "The Wedding Ring." On May 27th at Princeton he began the third of these
French Canadian stories remarking, "I have really begun the story
and cannot rest until it is finished." And on the afternoon of May
29th it was completed.

You are not to assume from this that the writing of short stories
or indeed of anything else was an easy and facile matter for Henry
van Dyke. But only that when he began actually to write, the story
was so complete in his mind that he was able to put it down on
paper with the almost incredible speed which perfect concentration
rendered possible. Behind the writing lay years of constant observation of people and nature, frequently months of study for particular
settings, and direct questions asked of experts on everything from
basic ideas to the smallest details. He was always a thorough workman. He strove not only for large effects as an artist, but concerned
himself with the minutest detail. I can recall the eagerness with

which he spoke of these two elements in artistic achievement as we stood before Rembrandt's pictures in the Rijks Museum at Amsterdam. Take for example a passage from a letter he wrote in 1897 to Dr. Cleland B. McAfee about *The Other Wise Man*:

"If the story itself came without effort, the writing of the story was a serious piece of labor. I cared for it so much and felt so grateful for it, that I should have been ashamed to put it off with cheap and easy work. I wanted to find precisely the right words, if I could, for every sentence. A clumsy phrase, a cloudy adjective, seemed intolerable—there are pages in the book that have been re-written ten times. For the brief description of the ride to Babylon I read nine volumes of travel, ancient and modern, in German, Greek and Latin—for the journey in the desert I made a day's excursion in the wilderness behind Assouan.

I am not ashamed to confess these things because I think a man ought to respect his work enough to be willing to try hard to make it as good as he can, and always to regret that it is not better."

Henry van Dyke was always a careful workman not only on all the elements of particular stories but on the language in which he wrote them. "The most valuable quality of style," he often said, "is clearness" and added to this was his profound sense of the association of words which he once summed up in an Academy paper on "The Fringe of Words." Simplicity and clarity were always characteristic of him. On one occasion, as Mrs. Alice M. Peaseley of the Maine Sea Coast Mission tells me, he was to read some of his stories and speak to a group of fishing folk on one of the islands. As Mrs. Peaseley put it: "I probably overdid it a little in reminding them that they were to hear a distinguished American author. When the meeting was over Uncle Allie came up to me and said severely: 'Well, I listened to your great American author and I sat right there and understood every word he said.'"

It would be impossible here to describe the way in which these books of stories took their places as "best sellers"; still less to report adequately the flood of letters which they drew not only from literary people but from folk of all sorts in mining camps, villages and cities, young and old, leaders and simple people.

A boy writes: "What beautiful stories and poems you write! I am only a boy of seventeen years, but if you knew how much pleasure they have given me and how much good they have done me, you would be glad not because they have done *me* good, but because they must have done others good also who are of more importance than myself."

A woman of seventy writes: "They have left a strange impression on my mind akin to that which has come to me sometimes since my widowhood, from still hours in autumn twilight when the sun had left a warm, calm, benignant afterglow in the western sky through which the evening star showed its serene beauty. A sense of divine protection and the nearness of God. And with these a reaching after the perfection which is assured at the end of life's faithful endeavor. I pray you to be grateful for what you have been able to do in the midst of this turbulent world."

From Brooklyn his old teacher, D. H. Cochran, writes:

"Yes, 'Henry', for I write not to Dr. van Dyke the well known author, but to the boy I knew and loved many years since in the Polytechnic . . . the stories are clean, the lesson clear and there are sentences as musical as the song of a brook. They make me happier and better and so will they many other old men whose work is done. When you left the ministry I thought you had made a mistake but now you have a larger hearing. Your work makes the world happier and better. These words require no acknowledgment and it can do you no harm to know the effect upon your old teacher of your teaching."

Another man wrote a delightful rambling account of how a second hand copy of *The Ruling Passion*, ("Just what I needed at that particular time,") came into his hands:

"The last carrier was an aged man of quiet mien, Asaph by name, a dealer in books that have a history, i.e. second-hand. Asaph, the Jew, gentle spoken, but knowing the weakness of the passerby called to me as I approached his stall. He wished to show me the volume he thought I would enjoy; as he spoke he turned the leaves affectionately; then when the bargain had been completed, pressed it lovingly between his thin hands full sixty seconds before parting with his treasure, speaking the while a good word for the author, hinting vaguely of the joy each must have experienced who had turned its pages during the long zigzag journey from the publisher to its latest possessor."

In a manuscript entitled "Etchings in Fiction," written at least in part in 1912 and of which no record of its having been published can be found, Henry van Dyke set down in response to persistent questioning by one of his former students, Wainwright Evans, his theory about short stories or, as he preferred to call them "tales." Beginning with "a kind of preamble with mild reservations," he attempts to put down "four marks of a good short story," admitting in advance that his standards "are not reached deductively, by reasoning from fixed theories. They are reached inductively by observation and comparison. I read what I like and then try to find out why I like it." The marks, though he added, "it goes without saying that a story may be good without having all of these characteristics," are "1. intentional brevity. 2. singleness of theme. 3. an atmosphere which enhances the value of the theme. 4. a symbolic meaning." The theory was illustrated with many references to the stories of Kipling, Zola, Bret Harte, Mrs. Wharton, Poe, Balzac, Hawthorne, Stockton, Stevenson, De Maupassant, Cable. As he said, the theory was inductively arrived at. It was based on a wide reading of the work of other authors and on *post factum* reflection upon the stories which he had himself felt compelled to write. His own stories, as must be obvious to any who have read them, were only incidentally the expression of a theory. Actually they were the intuitive recognition as material for tales of ideas that came to him frequently with whole sentences and paragraphs clearly formed, but usually requiring long periods of almost unconscious meditation and a great deal of work on the setting.

From the days of his youth poetry had been one of the passions of his life. And as soon as his first two volumes of stories were done he turned eagerly to writing the poems which through many crowded years had hovered about him. He was by nature a poet. The vigorous rhythm of his own days, his passion for melody and his delight in words, the pleasure that he found in observing and reflecting upon nature and human life, and his wide-ranging imagination and ready fancy marked him as a poet. In December 1901 he began work upon his "Ode to Music," a theme on which he had often reflected and spoken before, but soon laid it by. He was not yet ready for it, and there were too many things to be done at that time. But he could not wholly leave it alone. The theme possessed him and in odd moments he kept jotting it down. Finally in December 1902, he attempted to complete it and in January wrote his friend Edwin Mims: "It is just finished; that is to say it is done as well as I can do it,—really finished it will never be." A month later he went with his wife and the younger children of the family to the Sand Hills in Augusta, Georgia, and there, under the charm of a southern spring, the garden of poetry which was his heart and which constantly bore some bloom in it, thrust up a host of fresh spears. Here was begun "God of the Open Air," (which he always felt was among the best of his poems,) though it was not completed until more than a year afterwards. Here, too, were begun and in some instances finished a number of his most memorable lyrics. "Music" which he had thought was finished was revised again back at "Avalon" in May, and many of the poems which on that southern sojourn had begun to push their way toward bloom received in this and the following year their crown of flowers.

As a matter of fact "The Ode to Music" was not finally completed until 1916. Early that spring Henry Hadley wrote that he had selected this poem for writing the choral and orchestral work for the sixtieth Anniversary of the Worcester Music Festival of 1917:

"The beautiful contrasting words have given me genuine delight and they carry one through every gamut of emotion.

"Would it be possible, for the sake of bringing in a big *dramatic* force (musically) to add two stanzas, intensely turbulent, portraying the *Music of the Storm*—perhaps the ship-wreck—music of the fury of the waves; death and destruction at sea.

"I suggest this, my dear Sir, because I feel as I progress with the music that I have no dramatic number calling for the entire apparatus of the modern orchestra combined with a large chorus."

[245]

Henry van Dyke replied:

"It is extremely interesting to note your comment on the lack of a certain element of strife and tumult in the poem. How often a sincere note of criticism of this kind goes back into the actual history of the production of a piece of work. As a matter of fact, I wrote at least ten times as many lines for the 'Ode to Music' as those which I actually used. Among the strophes which were finally rejected and destroyed there was a long one on the music of War. This, if it had been retained, would have supplied the factor of turbulence and transient discord. I left it out, first —because I was not satisfied with it, and second—because I had a doubt in my heart whether noble music really belongs to war."

Nevertheless he consented to attempt again, though with his usual hesitation at this kind of undertaking, to write some strophes on "transient discord" and in May during some evening lulls amid the thronging duties of his service at the Hague in war time composed "War Music" and "Storm Music" offering them both to Mr. Hadley. Of the first Henry van Dyke wrote: "I have tried to write a new stanza indicating the idea that the object of the right kind of warfare is to put an end to the passion of military conquest." And of the latter: "The second strophe is meant to reflect the phase of storm in nature. It is there—We cannot evade it any more than we can entirely eliminate discord from great music. But it is not there permanently. It is there to be resisted, endured, conquered. And the art of really noble music is to recognize discord and overcome it and gain a certain strength from it, and finally dissolve it in the larger and more perfect harmony. As to the way of doing this, it is not for the poet to speak, but for the musician."

When Mr. Hadley selected the "War Music" for his interpretation, Henry van Dyke wrote:

"Upon the whole I am well satisfied that you have chosen the strophe entitled War Music. I am conscious of the faults in it, but after all it represents an effort to express what thoughtful people in this age think about war and its horrors and its justification when it is accepted in defence of a noble and righteous cause."

In 1920 when Henry van Dyke made his own last revision of his poetical works the War Music strophe was included as part of the Ode and the strophe on Storm Music was placed outside.

Poetry was never far from the heart of Henry van Dyke and the writing of it seldom far from his hand. He was able amid the pressure of constant activity to slip into his den and shut the door, or to sit down on a train or anywhere where he was free from interruption for a few hours, and put into form the poetic ideas which continuously thronged his mind. His work in other fields, far from inhibiting this activity, seemed to stimulate it. He discovered his poetry in the daily round though he found it necessary to shut the door when he sought to put it into form. But there were always certain periods when the writing of poetry or preparation for it was particularly active. Such were always times when he was much out of doors, in the spring and fall on his "Avalon" acres when he delighted to plant trees or wander in the garden or sit beneath the portico looking up into the great arms of the old elm; or on a summer vacation in the hills or by the sea; or on his longer lecturing tours across the United States especially on several visits in California; or on his regular fishing trips to Canada where he appeared to be totally concerned with fish and fisherman but where his unconscious mind was busily storing impressions and reflecting upon experiences.

In the spring of 1906 he delivered six lectures on the Percy Turnbull foundation upon the "Service of Poetry". Several times at the urgent request of his friend Ferris Greenslet he undertook to prepare these lectures for publication but always some necessity of creative writing or the pressure of immediate duties that called for action prevented the final work. The subjects of the lectures reveal clearly Henry van Dyke's view of the nature and function of poetry:

> What Poetry Is
> Poetry and Human Intercourse
> The Palace of Art
> Voices of Nature
> Marching Music
> Symphonies of the Immortal

From these pages constantly used on later occasions and frequently added to and recombined one learns that for Henry van Dyke poetry is to be approached not with a theory of how it is made but with a standard of judgment on the basis of which a man must be "ready to give a reason for the joy that is in him. He must not only be willing to be pleased, but also to tell why he is pleased." On this basis he offers the definition: "Poetry is the art which interprets nature and life through the imagination in beautiful language quickened by emotion and ordered by metre." From this he goes on to say that: "The diction of poetry differs from the diction of prose in the enhanced value which it gives to the colours, the associations, the suggestiveness of words"; and to defend his view of the importance of form in poetry by saying: "In every art the form, the gift of order which man's mind and hand bestow upon the substance, in secret, subtle obedience to a chosen law, is no less essential than the substance."

"Poetry," he said, "is by no means a mere pastime of man's leisure. It is an expression—perhaps the most intimate expression—of his hidden self . . . It is idealism set to music. And the world in which it lives, and into which it leads us, is real and will endure as long as love and patriotism and religion."

In concluding the lectures he said:

"I have not forgotten that they are delivered under the auspices of a great University which demands patient study and careful thought as conditions precedent to acceptable discourse; and if the technical terms and discussions which are familiar in literary criticism have been left out, it was because I thought it safe, with such an audience, to omit the processes and give the results. But I have remembered also that this University stands by the doctrine that the best learning is that which is most closely related to experience, and that culture is most precious when it teaches us how to live. I have spoken of poetry as an art; but not a remote, selfish, luxurious art, existing for its own sake. The glory of poetry is that it comes out of the inmost heart of man, and that it interprets the world in which he lives and the existence which belongs to him, in music of such beauty, such truth, such ideal nobility and splendor, that if we listen to it and take it into our souls, it makes life infinitely and eternally better worth living, for every child that is born of a woman, cradled in the arms of Nature, called to the tasks of duty, crowned with the glory of Love, and capable of entering Immortality. Therefore I believe that this troubled age has not passed, nor will the great world ever pass, beyond the need of the service of poetry."

Surely there is in this, as in his reflections upon the writing of stories, not only the formulation of a distinct theory of the art but the communication of a glowing conviction that any kind of literature can only be justified by its service to life itself.

In a brief article in the *Atlantic Monthly*, the substance of which was later embodied in the introduction to his selected and edited *Poems of Tennyson* (1903), he wrote:

"The reading of poetry, with the spirit and the understanding . . . is, in my judgment, one of the very finest instruments for the opening of the mind, the enlarging of the imagination, and the development of the character. . . . Even on the purely technical side, the study of metrical form and movement . . . trains the eye and the ear, enlightens the judgment and the taste, develops the faculties of careful observation and discrimination, and disciplines the mind, in the attempt to trace and verify the subtle laws, and to solve, at least tentatively, the interesting problems which we find in English verse."

From all this it is easy to see how Henry van Dyke both as a craftsman in metrical expression and because of his basic convictions about the function of poetry reacted from the rising school of poetry, especially that of "free verse."

"Have we got to revise all our judgments?" he wrote indignantly to Edwin Mims at Vanderbilt University. "Must real poetry go off with a bang and a fizz like soda water? or claim attention by its strong smell like Limburger cheese?"

"In the form of poetry," he often said, "I have long insisted that music is fundamental. That's why I hate this free verse stuff. Much modern poetry lacks a life strong enough to create its own forms. It leaves the material in a state of amorphous deliquescence." On one occasion when he was speaking in high dudgeon of the low estate of poetry he turned to me with a sudden laugh and said: "Anybody can write such stuff. Here it is:

"Look at me!
I am the banana.
Behold my beautiful skin.
But strip it from me
And throw it upon the pavement
And I can destroy
The mightiest intellect in Europe."

More carefully he wrote to Robert Underwood Johnson:

"I think with you about the productions of the so-called vers libre school. Most of it is not poetry at all, either in substance or in form. Some of it has the substance, but cannot properly be called poetry because it lacks the form which is the essential element. A little of it has both substance and form, and may be taken as an indication of the possibility of developing new metrical arrangements in English verse, which will have a measured and perceptible rhythm of their own. One thing which in my opinion is very much needed is to get away from the attempt to study English under the forms of classical prosody. They are utterly inapplicable and misleading, since our verse is based not upon a foot structure composed of long and short syllables, but upon an accent structure, which would therefore be measured not by feet, but by 'stresses.' As a matter of fact in reading English poetry aloud every intelligent person follows this method."

But he was never a poetic reactionary as must be apparent to any one who has examined the wide range of his metrical practice, from the old forms to new ones of his own, like "Autumn in the Garden," and reaching even to the rhythmic prose of the "Wayfaring Psalms." His taste and training, it is true, as well as the themes in which he was interested, drew him to the use of melodies that were more or less regular, and his regard for workmanship made him a careful master of detail. Mme. Sainte-Marie Perrin in one of the most adequate criticisms of his poetry (*La Revue des Deux Mondes*, November 1908), writes of *l'ampleur et la minutie* as one of the traits of his imagination. Despite concern for detailed workmanship there is certainly nothing small or conventional about the sweep of the verse and thought of the bulk of his narrative poems and odes or the rich and ample poetic drama, *The House of Rimmon*. It was only a few of his more slovenly critics, unable to distinguish between crudeness and strength, and overly preoccupied with his slighter versicles, who missed the vigour and power of his poetry. He never could see why roughness should be made synonymous with strength. Was a boor *ipso facto* stronger than a gentleman?

Moreover he found great delight in bearing tribute not only in lectures but in carefully discriminating poems to the older poets and to several of his beloved poetical colleagues. As late as 1921 delight in listening to Vachel Lindsay's rhythmic chanting of his own poetry led Henry van Dyke to write a colorful and sympathetic poem "Dream Peddler" on that memorable experience. His response to the poetry of anyone who struck the basic notes of sincerity and music was always quick and generous. Before the "yes" of his eager heart he was always ready to lay aside the modest theory that he drew from his own observation and reflection and practice.

Perhaps the clearest brief statement about what lay behind the writing of his own poetry is contained in *A Word in Prose* at the beginning of his "Poems; now first collected and revised with many hitherto unpublished" which appeared in 1911. I remember his saying to me as we read the proofs together: "What an extraordinary thing language is! There is my whole theory of poetry in the third and fourth paragraphs":

" 'Metre and rhyme have a deep relation to the rhythm of human emotion, of which I grow more sure the less I can explain it. Some call them a bondage, but the natural harmony of such laws makes for true freedom. Therefore, while using the older metrical forms with love and care, I have also adventured new ones, believing that English poesy has to win a larger liberty in those happy regions which lie between the formal and the formless.

" 'What I have seen and felt and dreamed beyond the horizon of prose, yet ever in the most real world, is here interpreted in verse. And if it speaks to you, gentle reader, it is yours as much as mine.' "

An even more intimate glimpse of the making of his poetry is contained in a sentence from a letter which he wrote to George E. Woodberry at this time: "As for my poems they were written to satisfy myself—which they did not, and to save my soul, which they did."

A comparison of the Collected Poems with the form in which they appeared in earlier books, and as they were again revised when he assembled the two volumes of poetry in 1920 for the Avalon edition of his works, reveals his passion for finished workmanship. But he was not one to sit mulling over his own writings. There was always something more important at hand to do than that. Besides no creative work of his ever went into print until he was satisfied that it was at least as well done as he could do it at the time. But once in a while when there was nothing new clamoring to be done and especially on the two occasions mentioned when he was inductively applying his theory to his own work, he found ways of improving a line here or there. The most noticeable feature of these changes is to be found in the poems of his youth from which he removed many adjectives and greatly strengthened the structure.

Following this volume Henry van Dyke published but one more book of poetry, *The Grand Canyon and Other Poems,* in 1914. In this appears the last of his long poems. "The Grand Canyon" was begun in 1905 on his first visit there but was laid aside. "I was too overwhelmed," he said, "and had to put it away." But he could not leave the impossibility alone. In 1913 again he stood before "the supreme and indescribable" marvel and again his imagination took fire. But he was on a lecture and preaching tour and there were many engagements to fill. At last in Pasadena he left the pleasant cottage where he was staying with his wife and two children and hired an office high in one of the city buildings where he had a glorious view of the Sierra Madre Mountains. There suddenly the vision took form and he wrote the poem—but not the story.

That autumn Henry van Dyke went as United States minister to the Netherlands. The War and many other immediate duties that followed kept him from ever undertaking any other sustained poetic effort though a number of his finest lyrics were composed up to the last months of his life. "To write poetry," he said, "requires a great *élan.*" And, as in the first years of his active pastorate so in the last twenty years of his life, he had little freedom from the duties which he freely undertook as a public servant. But this is not to say that Henry van Dyke found anything contradictory between the writing of poetry and other forms of public service. It is only to say that, as in the case of Chaucer and Milton to whom he often referred, the opportunity and inclination for the necessary literary workmanship was lacking in the midst of other activities. As a matter of fact, as we have already seen, his writing both of prose and poetry sprung directly from his conviction that the aim of literature was to "cheer, console, purify or ennoble the life of the people." When in 1910 he finally, after two previous declinations, delivered the Phi Beta Kappa poem at Harvard, "Who Follow the Flag," it took the form of a passionate protest in the name of the flag against child labor. Indeed, throughout his writing one catches the steady tone of that witness which unconsciously justified him in writing in a copy of one of his volumes for the Mercersburg School library: "To be entrusted with a message is a high honor, to deliver it safe and straight is a fine achievement—not something to be proud of, but something to be thankful for." This basic purpose combined with a genius for natural expression—"it is as if you went singing and chanting to yourself without thought of anybody by, beginning and leaving off as casually as an aeolian harp" wrote W. D. Howells —drew a flood of friendly letters from all sorts of people. To note here but a few,—though they are a vital part of the picture—his particular friend and neighbor John H. Finley wrote:

"I am thanking the Father of us all for what has come into my life through you. I cannot tell you all that I can tell Him, but perhaps He will translate it into a note or word of that great hymn of thanksgiving that you must be hearing in your heart. All that you do is, it seems to me, more beautiful than what went before."

Struthers Burt from his Wyoming ranch wrote:

"I have just returned from a pack-trip over into the Wind River country; across the Continental Divide; ninety miles from here. One day I came across a little deserted ranch up a creek known as Running Cottonwood, and on the wall of one of the log cabins I found this poem of yours (Spring in the South). I thought the incident might interest you.

You can imagine no surroundings much more different from those of a spring in the south—a little hidden valley in the midst of the Rocky Mountains; fir, pine, aspens; not a sound except Clarke's crows and magpies."

A farmer in the mid-west wrote a friend who had sent him Henry van Dyke's sonnet on "Life":

"I returned home yesterday p.m. tired and sweaty and dirty from helping a neighbor mow away clover hay in his barn and mercury hovering around 90°. My daughter had the usual batch of mail laid out upon the table which I gathered up and hied me away to the lawn swing under the grateful boughs of the tall maples. There among the mail was your very courteous letter and better than all, the coveted poem all so neatly typewritten upon clean crisp paper! I wish I could tell you how pleased I was and am for this. If you had placed in my hand a $10 bill it would not have pleased me nearly so well and I am very sure I should not have kept it so long as I shall keep this poem which in my present circumstances seems to go right to my heart. I sat there in the swing with farm papers and political papers and circulars galore lying all around me untouched holding and reading again and again van Dyke's poem on 'Life,' the tears falling like rain."

"Wish people I want and need," wrote James Whitcomb Riley, "would ever keep themselves adjacent! But they're *allus somers else.* And I'm not the only one who wants you in constant hand-reach, as you doubtless know. So say we every one."

Henry van Dyke was always more interested in living than in writing. In fact all his writing was in a sense a by-product. He could never justify himself for formulating a complete philosophy of life or for attempting to embody it in literary form. His lectures, speeches, sermons and all the varied forms of his writing were fundamentally "essays in application." "Self-observation in literary work," he often said, "has the same drawback that handicaps the Puritan practice of self-examination in religion." He could never be content in attempting to live in one department of life or be satisfied with one method of expression. His delight in writing and in public speech was constant but he was always something more than a man of letters or an orator. He was a man who found life good and who was convinced that he had a message—which was only partially his own—to make it better. As he put it in the preface to his typical *Essays in Application*: "I have tried to touch on certain points in education, in politics, in literature, in religion, in the conduct of life, from the standpoint of one who wishes to be guided in everyday judgments and affairs by a sane idealism."

Henry van Dyke was deeply conscious of the perils of this approach to his work. Even while his stories were among the "best sellers" and *Music and Other Poems* was passing through numerous editions and several of his books of essays were approaching the 100,000 mark and Mabie was declaring that he had "put himself definitely into the front rank of contemporary American men of letters," he was talking of his little company of Gentle Readers. Partly this was an expression of the inevitable loneliness of the creative artist; partly it came from what his sympathetic fellow worker in the Princeton English department, Charles W. Kennedy, described to me as "his habitual underestimation of the great number of people throughout America who listened and were glad of whatever he said or wrote"; partly it was the insatiable hunger of the human worker for more praise. But chiefly it was his own recognition of the fact that he was trying to write not for the fashion of the day (which his clear perception warned him was rapidly changing) but for the permanent meaning of life. As he wrote to Edwin Mims in reply to a friendly letter of encouragement:

"It is the conflict with conventional prejudice, and false culture, and pretentious ignorance, and strenuous frivolity that sometimes saddens me and sometimes stirs up my naturally quick temper. There are some of Wordsworth's letters and some of Lowell's that express my feelings precisely. When I feel this way again, I shall turn to these letters and read them over with sympathetic approval and say Amen."

And to Arthur H. Scribner he wrote in early 1914:

"So far as I know I am free from illusions about my work. To have a faithful company of 'gentle readers' satisfies my highest ambition. I have long ago realized that my chance for the future lies not in quantity but in quality, and I do not want to attempt anything beyond what I can do with a whole heart and a free hand. Writing for the market is not for me."

Before the arrival of the brazen age of literature and of standardless criticism Henry van Dyke saw the evil day approaching. But he refused to play with the fire upon his own altar. Sorrow entered deeply into his heart and at times it stirred him to indignant and not always considered utterance. But for his own work he chose to continue in his own way. As a writer the same thing might be said of him as Arnold said of Wordsworth that he did not so much "front the cloud of mortal destiny" as "put it by." Put it by, that is, not because he was unaware of it, but because he believed that there was a mightier power than mortal destiny and that from this mightier power came the real meaning of life.

On the only occasion where he spoke publicly of himself—the dinner in his honor at the Lotus Club he concluded:

Power of literature

"I should wish to see every page that I have ever written blotted out and burned rather than that one man should turn from what I have written with a mind degraded or defiled or weakened, disheartened and discouraged; and I should be most grateful if from any page or any verse that I have penned a man should draw something that would make it easier for him to meet life's vicissitudes and to do his duty and to love his fellowman, to rejoice in the world in which he lives and in the life which has been given to him. Two things have come to me that I am proud of: one, that my father for forty years took me into his closest intimacy and taught me the best that I have ever known; and the second, that through the work that I have done, poorly enough, here in this town for twenty years, I have won so many good and kind friends."

There spoke Henry van Dyke, poet heart and teller of tales, but above all the lover of men and of life.

Chapter Seventeen

AVALON: FAMILY, NEIGHBORS AND FESTIVE OCCASIONS

HENRY VAN DYKE'S exuberant nature immediately found great delight in coming to Princeton. There were many reasons for this. His creative spirit rejoiced in the freedom from the administrative duties of a large church while he was happy in continuing his personal activities as pastor at large. The University atmosphere (save for a sultry academic patch here and there) fascinated him as on earlier visits. In the social life of Princeton he was warmly welcomed and found great refreshment. The Clevelands, the Finleys, the Sloanes, the Morgans, the Marquands, the Armours, the Huttons, the Wilsons, the Phillipses, the Hibbens, the Scotts, the Schirmers, the Stocktons, Dr. West, his popular brother Paul van Dyke,—it would be impossible to mention everybody here or to recall the guests from everywhere that came and went—all provided a lively social milieu. They visited informally and dined each other with easy hospitality and eager conversation, serious and witty. Anything provided an occasion for summoning the neighbors. The sportsmen never ate venison or a bird or a fish alone. There was usually something new or, failing that, an anniversary to be celebrated. The children remember the cheerful sounds of those gatherings in various houses. Nor do they forget the frequent parties that celebrated their own returns from school or prepared their departures. Rugs were rolled up and everybody went to dancing—old as well as young. The students came to Avalon as boys more than as students. And not seldom a dancing evening would include an informal group of youngsters in the den listening to a new story or looking over some books.

In Avalon the *dea ex machina* was our mother. She was an expert housekeeper looking well to the ways of her household. Her collection of annotated and classified recipes bore witness to her mastery of diet and the symbol on all closets was neatness and cleanliness. Small but of almost uninterrupted health and by nature shy, sometimes to the point of retirement, she exercised a strong sense of duty and her moral precepts were sure. The deafness from which she suffered—while it was ever a great distress to her—was not noticed in her entertaining. Her swift and delicious response in social intercourse following her systematic provision for all details easily swallowed up her handicap—though the cost to herself may be better imagined than described. How eagerly the heart of her husband attempted to trace with her the lonely road of the deaf may be learned, so far as we are here concerned, from his long narrative poem "Vera." "Avalon," she used to say, "is a kind of glorified hotel. I am always welcoming the coming and speeding the parting guest." How she administered the household department, extending her care to the smallest details for each child and keeping her restless husband astonishingly fit and ready despite his multiple tasks, is one of those achievements of womanhood of which there is little to be said but much to be pondered. During the years before 1905 nine children (five daughters and four sons) were born of whom three sons died and the second daughter followed in the first bloom of womanhood. But these breaks in the circle, though they were never forgotten, were not allowed to cast a gloom over the family. The missing ones were remembered at family gatherings and often spoken of at quiet moments; and not seldom when the old house bulged with Christmas plans and guests it was as our household poet wrote it:

> "Dews of remembered happiness descend
> To bless us with the gift of Christmas tears."

It was a united and cheerful crew that inhabited Avalon. Boys and girls growing up are not, indeed, always merry. Nor are older people who have passed through deep waters consistently happy. But there was always something on foot in the household. No one felt that the dead were honored by cherishing sorrow. New experiences took up the treasurable memories of the past. One learned to look upon the living with deeper regard; and the parents led the way steadily forward.

Henry van Dyke was never a *poseur* but he believed vigorously in "playing the game." He said: "Don't be afraid of a thing being theatrical. 'All the world's a stage' and there's a little theatre inside of every man. I think it rather a good thing than a bad one." There was something about Robert Louis Stevenson whom he called "an adventurer in a velvet jacket," that appealed greatly to him and he was neither afraid nor ashamed to follow him in this. "Strange," he wrote, "that the most genuine of men usually have a bit of this in their composition; your only incurable poseur being the fellow who affects never to pose and betrays himself by his attitude of scorn." Henry van Dyke loved innocent merriment. A joke was seldom far off and he would laugh readily at any incongruity except when he felt that it represented something sacred to another man. His own foibles as well as those of other people were patent to him. Far from condemning them he only laughed genially at them insisting that they were merely a mark of exuberant vitality. For himself he took great pleasure in keeping a drawer full of brilliant neckties and socks and many striped and spotted waistcoats, and always insisted that Mark Twain's white suit was "all right, but I wore one long before he did."

Returning from a long southern lecturing trip once he told with evident amusement how he had been approached in the smoking car by a man in a checked suit and wearing a diamond scarf pin who said: "Excuse me, sir, but I see you're a sporting man too. Perhaps this would interest you," and handed him a sheet of racing news and other events. But though his black coat was worn only on formal occasions the minister's heart was always there. I wonder if that little vaudeville actress on the Texas express fulfilled her promise to write home? Certainly the promise was on her lips and the tears in her eyes when she left Henry van Dyke. He used to like to meet his daughters on their way through New York and carry them off in high feather to lunch at what he always called "The Walled Off

Hysteria"—a certain well known hostelry. He was unabashed in his enjoyment of the colorful human scene and of good food well served —though he was ever a light eater.

Many were his visits to his children in school and to his elder daughter in college. Into whatever was going on there he plunged with such whole-hearted pleasure that it always seemed to his children that the sermon or address that often accompanied these visits was mere spontaneous combustion—like the foolish verses or tales which were frequently on his lips. He liked people and had a passion for being liked by them. Always there was something of the laughing boy in him. One of his students once suggested to him that it would be an amusing trick to write a passage in blank verse or hexameters and print it as prose in order to draw from the critics an encomium for a marvellous flowing style. Henry van Dyke laughed and produced a passage of his own in which he had deliberately done that very thing. Only one critic had noted the fact and he had taken it as an unconscious imitation of something the author had been reading. "Your father," writes Wainwright Evans, "was as pleased over his flier in literary wickedness as a small boy who has rung somebody's doorbell and gotten away with it. He had deceived the very elect."

Henry van Dyke liked all sorts of people but as Struthers Burt has accurately observed: "He did not suffer fools gladly." Bumptious and pretentious people—no matter who they were or where they displayed themselves—were greeted with scorn. Tender as a woman to anything genuine he would waste no time on anything else. He could and did speak brusquely and sharply to triflers and busybodies. For such he believed thoroughly in Emerson's rough electric shock: Come out of that! Not seldom during his life he received letters from what he described as "female busybodies of both sexes" protesting their admiration of his beautiful writings and rebuking him for some rumor concerning him that had come to their ivory towers. "Dear Dr. van Dyke," wrote one, "I am told that you sometimes smoke. I cannot believe it possible that the author of etc., etc.," "Dear Madam," replied the indignant man with pardonable exaggeration, "It is not true that I sometimes smoke: I *always* smoke."

Throughout his life Henry van Dyke was never an abstemious man. He was by nature a hedonist. He used to say that the fruits of the earth were given by a good God for the use and enjoyment of man; but that it was always wrong for a man to use *anything* in such a way as to interfere with his working efficiency. There was usually something to drink in his cellar and not infrequently upon the table. He believed in the social and, under the counsel of doctors throughout his life, in the medicinal value of alcoholic beverages. The lesson, or rather the example, was not one of abstinence, but of temperance, with the clear acknowledgment that one man's food may be another man's poison. While he often went far to guard the weak brother against himself he never could see the justification for allowing the weak brother to establish the standards of living. Let each man decide what is good for himself, within the bounds of sane personal temperance and in reliance upon the sympathy and aid of his friends,—this was his principle. And it may be worthy of note here that though he was always outspoken in his opposition to Prohibition, as a method of dealing with the problem of intemperance, he never joined any of the societies for repeal. During the later years of his life while he watched with observant eye the development of the automobile and the coming of flying he found new social ground for his always steady insistence upon personal temperance.

Around him in Avalon he gathered through the years trophies and souvenirs of his varied experiences and relationships. The entrance hall housed the deer heads of Adirondack days, the great barren land caribou from Newfoundland, the black moose from New Brunswick and the big trout from the Nepigon. Signed pictures from many authors and several originals of illustrations for his stories illumined the library walls and over the bookcase that held his famous Tennyson collection stood William Ordway Partridge's classic bust of the poet. Here, too, he assembled his collection of Stevenson and his small but select fishing library. On the shelves were many books, new and old, chiefly poetry and fiction, art, history and theology. It is remarkable to note how many of these came from the authors themselves. Everywhere he went he made new friends and he rejoiced to dwell amid these reminders of them. But though he was ever a book lover he was never a litterateur. The winds of the world entered every nook and corner of his den. And he himself was always coming and going. He loved to sally forth to "his boys" at the University lecture halls. Until it was apparent that the automobile had superseded the horse he used to drive a strong pair of Adirondack horses, Whiteface and Hurricane, with a smart trap or sleigh to the lecture hall. The boys gathering for the lecture grinned delightedly at the swank picture but they were too honestly young to do more than tease him in the "Faculty song":

> "Here's to Henry, the brother of Paul,
> He's got a big head, but he's not very tall."

No account of Henry van Dyke would be adequate without a reference to the dreadful habit of personal publicity which was and still is one of the curses of American life. All through his days Henry van Dyke was beset with reporters. He was almost invariably a dramatic figure. His conversation and public speech were pungent. His versatile personality was ever alert to the signs of the times. He liked to talk and he had a sincere sympathy with reporters who were so often young men and women struggling to make their way in a difficult world. He found it hard to put aside these ambassadors of the insatiable American craving for personal news. Often they caught him with his guard down after some exhausting effort or when he had no time for considered utterance. The result was not always happy either for him or for the public. "A good press" in terms of the prevailing public taste was certainly not an unmixed blessing for a man with a message. But perhaps it was inescapable for one who was so vigorous and colorful an actor in the public scene.

In certain ways Henry van Dyke was at his best when speaking at those banquets in the conduct of which Americans are supreme. The social fellowship, the by-play of wit, the perils and opportunities of the particular occasions—all were exactly suited to his temperament. Many were the testimonial dinners and gatherings of various societies at which he held forth hilariously but always with a serious word dropped here or there. The Dutch, the Celtic or the Pilgrim spirit were not alien to him. He could address the sons of Ohio or of the South with equal gusto or thread his way with audacity through the intricacies of unknown political quantities, or bear heart-warming testimony to the achievements of his colleagues, or describe the foibles of the day until the room was dissolved in a laughter that left no sting behind it.

Once—and it is the only occasion I can find on which he ever expressed himself on the subject—he wrote his friend William Mann Irvine:

"As a general principle I regard after-dinner speaking as a kind of enlarged social conversation. The first thing that the speaker has to do is to get on good personal terms with his listeners, in order that they may not mistake his remarks either for an academic discourse or for a moving picture entertainment. Having done this, either by personal allusions, a humorous anecdote, or any other method which he deems appropriate and likely to induce a receptive frame of mind, he may proceed to develop whatever idea or ideas he has to give. But the presence of an idea in his mind is really indispensable. A string of anecdotes will not take the place of it. He must really have something to say, and he must say it with suitable clearness and force of expression. Suitable, I mean, to the essential conditions of the after-dinner speech, which should exclude all political and theological hostilities, all personal attacks, and all efforts to make capital out of an opportunity which is given to him on the basis of hospitality and good feeling. He may endeavor to make a favorable impression upon his hearers for a principle which he entertains or a sentiment he feels strongly. In fact I think this effort often lends an additional strength and interest to an after-dinner speech. But it must be made in the tone and under the conditions which properly belong to a social gathering, so that at the end neither good digestion nor sincere friendship will be interfered with."

On many such occasions he burst into verses, a few of which are rightfully preserved in the *Carmina Festiva* of his collected poems:
"A health, a health to all the world—and the solemn ass *outside*!"
Perhaps the most striking of these *jeux d'esprit* was at the dinner of the Periodical Publishers' Association when he confessed that he

had been meditating upon the best advice to give a young person who has firmly resolved to contribute to the magazines. First must be chosen a truly American subject. Take, for example, the clam,—the native, American, free-born, little neck Clam. We all know it. We all love it. Deal originally and vividly with the Clam. Next it must be presented in a form to suit the magazine for which you are writing. Each of the editors has his temperament, his aim, his ideal. Each of the magazines has its own keynote. How shall you strike this keynote with your Clam? If you can answer this question, you will be able to move "successward," as the Editor of *The Ladies Home Journal* puts it.

From this he goes on to describe how the subject should be treated for various periodicals of the day. For *Harper's* a scholarly, humorous article on "The Standard Pronunciation of the word 'Clam' "; showing first that it has no standard pronunciation; second, that there are three standard pronunciations; and third, that the proper American way to pronounce it is "quohaug." For the *Atlantic*, a superior magazine published in Boston, he suggests "The Cause of the Superiority of the Cod to the Clam." For *Scribner's* "The Under Clam"—but if your Clam dies you must make him die game—no weeping, no unmanly complaints! Just a silent, wholesome, heroic demise,—dying without tears. For *The Bookman* "The Link between the Poet and the Sea" with references to Whitman. For *The Century* you must remember that this magazine has two keynotes (which sounds absurd, but is nonetheless true), Italy and Tenement House Reform. If you try hard enough you can blend these two keynotes in the purest lyrical confusion, in "Il Mercatore Italiano della Clamma." For the *Smart Set* which likes things that are pretty and naughty and that show familiarity with the usages of sassiety, if you give your mind to it you can produce: "A Little-Neck Love Lyric." For *McClure's* Magazine you must expose the corruption of THE TRUSTS and strike the note of American Democracy—and strike it hard! Write an ode on "The Fettered Clam." For the *Outlook* (of which Theodore Roosevelt was then an editor), patriotism and moral inspiration are essential. "A Quatrain to a Recreant Clam" is indicated:

"Low dost thou lie amid the languid ooze,
Because thy slothful spirit doth refuse
The bliss of battle and the strain of strife:
Rise, Craven Clam, and lead the strenuous life!"

Thus did Henry van Dyke entertain himself and his hearers with sallies of penetrating observation clothed in laughing words. The solemn ass was left outside. Something significant must be said. But man must laugh or he will die.

Chapter Eighteen

A FAITHFUL SERVANT OF THE CHURCH

WHEN the Brick Church received the sorrowful news of the death of their new pastor, Dr. Maltbie Babcock, in the late spring of 1901, there was but one thought: send for Henry van Dyke. He came to the first communion service after the tragic loss and spoke brief words of comfort and peace. Nothing is more typical of him than his ready response to such a call; nor more revealing of his mind and heart than his utterance at such a time.

"There are two mistakes," he said, "that hide the comfort of God from us in the time of trouble. One is the idea that God is not in the world, but far away, unsearchable, unknowable, hidden from us, and that we are forgotten by Him. The other is the idea that God's way in the world is visible, open, comprehensible, easy to explain by a few formulas of predestination and providence, and that we are entrusted with His secrets. . . . For my part I am content with less knowledge of God's purposes and more trust in His character. . . .

What is it that God does for us even now to help us? Two things.

First, He sympathizes with us. Never a grief falls upon the innocent that God does not grieve with us. Never a shadow of death closes round a pure young life that God is not as sorry as we are. Jesus wept at the grave of Lazarus. He knew that Lazarus would rise again. But His tears were the pledge that the Divine Heart is touched with the feeling of our infirmities. 'In all their affliction He was afflicted, and the angel of His presence saved them.'

The second thing that God does for us in our trouble is to make them bear the peaceable fruits of righteousness. The tree shaken by the storm, sends its roots deeper and knits its fibres closer together. Faith tried and tested grows stronger and firmer. Sorrow cleanses the heart from passion, grief purifies the eyes from vanity, loss wakens the soul from idle dreams and makes it long to do as much good as possible in this brief and uncertain life. Weakness is changed into strength; bereavement is translated into consecration; the troubled life brings forth an ennobled heart, because God makes all things work together for good to them that love Him."

Promptly the Church asked his aid for the second time in procuring a pastor and in the autumn he consented also to become minister in charge. Hardly settled into his new tasks at Princeton he undertook the additional responsibility with joy and gave himself eagerly again to regular preaching and pastoral work. Meanwhile he was much occupied with his task as a member of General Assembly's Committee on revision of the doctrinal standards. In the spring of 1902 it began to be apparent in the Presbyterian Church that he was needed as Moderator for the General Assembly which was to meet in New York in May. His vigorous leadership for revision combined with his basically conservative position marked him as the man who could hold the Church together in the face of extremists on both wings. Oddly enough his own presbytery of New Brunswick in the face of all this failed to elect him a commissioner though he was named as first alternate. For several weeks ecclesiastical politics held sway. But Henry van Dyke ably counselled by his old friend Dr. John DeWitt waited patiently—not for the office though his father's record added keenness to his personal desire for it—but for the chance as a commissioner to defend the revision. It was a terrible ordeal for a forthright man of quick temper whose feelings were focussed to a burning point by the memory of how the Assembly of 1892 had wrecked the long labors of his own father for revision. At last one of the New Brunswick Commissioners, Dr. John Dixon, Assistant Secretary of the Board of Home Missions, wrote Henry van Dyke that he had declined his commission thus leaving it to the first alternate, and added: "I beg to assure you of my deepest appreciation of your noble courtesy in leaving me entirely free to reach such a decision as should seem to me right."

When the Assembly met a few days later Dr. William R. Taylor of Rochester nominated Henry van Dyke saying according to the

New York Times, "He stands for no party or clique. There has been no campaign in his favor." On the second ballot he was elected and as he took up the gavel said:

"I thank you with all my heart for giving me the privilege of standing in the place made especially sacred to me by the memory of my father. I do not deserve this honor, but I imagine many of those who voted for me thought they were voting for my father."

The Brooklyn *Eagle* editorially commented:

"His great father, Henry J. van Dyke, was moderator of the General Assembly which met in Brooklyn in 1876, the Centennial year of the republic. The son fitly succeeds the father, a quarter of a century later, in the highest honor which Presbyterianism can confer upon a clergyman of its number. This selection is not only satisfactory to the country, grateful to Presbyterianism and particularly agreeable to this community, but it is also an evidence of the growing strength of progressive influences within an intellectual and sanely conservative church. It is, too, a pointed rebuke and defeat of Bourbonish, reactionary, inquisitorial and vindictive tendencies within the same denomination."

Henry van Dyke at once took the helm of the Assembly as he was well qualified to do by virtue of his sane leadership, fairness and courtesy. The press both religious and secular as well as personal memories bear ample testimony to this fact. His moderator's sermon on "The Open Door" was a straight appeal for the inner life and outward service of religion. "Christ," he said, "must be your door, by whom you go in to God and out to man."

When the report of the Committee on Creed Revision, which had been two years in preparation, came before the Assembly there were those who expected a long and bitter debate. But it was not forthcoming. Every day since the report had been made public its constructiveness had won for it new friends. The committee of twenty-one had done their work thoroughly and in an irenic spirit. Representing many shades of opinion in the Church they had at first been divided into three camps: those who favored a revision of the Westminster Confession; those who desired an interpretative declaration; those who desired the substitution of another creed.

By a stroke of genius they combined the three things, offering a Declaratory Statement as to the sense in which the Westminster Confession was to be received, as the Presbyterian Churches of Scotland had done; amending the Confession in a few polemic phrases, and adding two chapters on the Holy Spirit and on the Love of God and Missions; and finally offering "A Brief Statement of the Reformed Faith for a better understanding of our doctrinal beliefs." The six candidates for Moderator, including Henry van Dyke by request, spoke for it in the course of an orderly debate and the report was adopted inside of two hours with only two dissenting votes. By this action the Declaratory Statement and other amendments of the Westminster Confession were sent to the Presbyteries to become effective only if approved by two-thirds of them; and the Brief Statement of the Reformed Faith was approved, not as part of the doctrinal standards but simply for a better understanding of them. In the second matter Henry van Dyke was peculiarly interested having long believed and said that "A statement of belief that can be used without a dictionary, understood by people who are not philosophers, and read in a few moments, would be worth having."

As the eleven day sessions ended Henry van Dyke said:

"Three great things have been done by this Assembly,

1. We have heard reports of the best year the mission boards have ever seen.

2. We have given a great, strong blessing to the work of evangelization throughout the bounds of our Church, and

3. We have passed by a practically unanimous vote the Revised Confession of Faith, and issued a new Brief Statement of the Reformed Faith for a better understanding of our doctrinal beliefs. All these three belong together. May all these things be ours for the coming year: The Open Book, the burning bush, and the uplifted Cross. May we have as our watchword, a plain Gospel, a loving heart, and a ready hand. Not a new Gospel, but more Gospel. The Church exists to help the Lord Jesus Christ save lost and sinful souls. All effort by the Church should be to help to bring men out of darkness into the love and fellowship of the Gospel of Christ."

This is not the place to tell the whole story of that General Assembly but the picture of Henry van Dyke would be too incomplete without reference to his words when the pioneer missionary, S. Hall Young, presented him with the walrus ivory gavel from the Yukon Presbytery: "I am glad that this gavel represents the outdoor life, and my firm faith is that it would be a good thing for our religion if we could get outdoors with it more." Or again to the verses which a new friend (and later fishing companion), G. A. Warburton, scribbled about him and which concluded:

"Of all inscrutable decrees
Which men can never understand,
The strangest, that in scenes like these
I hold a gavel in my hand;—
Give me a rod, a line, a fly,
And let me walk in quiet glade,
'I'm only wishing to go a-fishing;
For this the month of May was made.' "

And finally to the words of an old friend, George Foster Peabody, who wrote:

"Far beyond the height and breadth of the great Presbyterian fold will and does the influence of that vote (for revision) and all its surroundings reach, and much does it presage of hope and cheer for the one great all inclusive fold. I feel sure that in all communions it will have the effect of the fructifying wave which the sheets of water of some spring showers suggest.

You have given freedom to many minds held in bondage to some formula that they did not believe or dare to look into. A true and progressive emancipation has begun."

On the last Sunday morning the following October he concluded his year of volunteer service in the Brick Church and that afternoon took part in the installation of the new pastor procured under his guidance, Dr. William R. Richards. "Again," said the Church, "do we see this most delicate and difficult task tactfully and successfully accomplished, without division or even diversity of views as to the wisdom of his choice."

This was a year of tremendous work. His Princeton lectures to which he added an optional course in the second term at the students' request, his travels and sermons and other duties as Moderator of the Church kept him busy. There was much to do in seeing that Creed revision was not killed in the presbyteries. But though always moving rapidly on from one thing to another he was seldom hurried. He took rest by the way. Always he had time to see his many friends, and everywhere he went there was a home where he was a welcome guest. No matter how tired he was he could find prompt restoration. A friendly conversation, an hour's reading, a brief sleep, and he was ready to start out again. He relaxed easily and laughed quickly.

In early May he started West preaching and lecturing his way to California. When the General Assembly met in Los Angeles he preached the retiring Moderator's sermon. The press reported three thousand people crowded into Immanuel Church and nearly as many more unable to get in.

"Staid commissioners, local clergymen, distinguished missionaries and prominent church and society women formed a fringe around the edge of the pulpit platform. Famous doctors of divinity squatted on stairways and professors in theological seminaries sat tailor fashion in the aisles."

The atmosphere was electric and so was the preacher. With a basic dignity and yet with a verve that made inevitable several spontaneous outbursts of applause from the congregation he preached on "Joy and Power." Simple and clear to a degree the sermon was full of sharp turns and strong spiritual appeal. The preacher, the theme and the congregation were so perfectly united that each naturally played a part in the whole.

The *Los Angeles Times* wrote:

"It is but a soul speaking to other souls. Vibrant, intellectual, heartful —the words of his message ring firmly and gently into the mellow appreciative audience. Here is one who has felt, thought and conquered, who stands at the pivot and slowly turns a concentrated light on all the dark, hidden and mysterious places. He is the epitome of the modern preacher. He vitalizes the culture that has returned to nature and after examining the august recesses of the soul with the searchlight of criticism comes back to the beginning, relying upon simple faith and hope. A certain austerity about him betokens the intellectual child of Calvin, while the beaming light of the divine in his face says that experience with the frailties of mankind, as well as the incisive bidding of a keen brain, have told him to be kind and cheerful."

As chairman of the committee on canvass of the revision returns from the presbyteries Henry van Dyke reported an overwhelming victory for the overtures of the previous General Assembly. When after orderly debate the last effort to delay revision was voted down and the report as a whole was adopted by a rising vote with no negative, Henry van Dyke turned to the press representatives and said characteristically:

"Understand, brethren of the press, this revision of the Confession of Faith does not mean that the Presbyterian Church has changed her base one inch. It does mean that she has broadened and strengthened her foundations. It does mean that she has recognized the love of God, not in a single text quoted in a footnote, but in a full chapter in the Confession of Faith. It does mean that she has declared that our doctrine of divine salvation shall never be interpreted to mean fatalism. The Presbyterian Church stands still firm and unalterable on the doctrine of humanity, the inexhaustible love of God embracing all the little children of the world, and offered to all who will become as little children and accept God's salvation in Jesus Christ our Lord and Saviour."

"So the Confession was revised," reported the *Interior* with eloquent restraint, "and the struggle of fifteen years ended in a great festival of unmarred peace and fellowship." To Henry van Dyke the accomplishment had a peculiar poignancy. It was the vindication of his father's temporarily defeated efforts; it was the acceptance by the Church of his own strong reaction, beginning twenty years before, from what he felt were fatalistic implications in the Church doctrine. To that reaction the death of his first-born son in 1885 had given the earliest personal impulse, and now, in the inexplicable providence of God, the revision was complete two months after the death as an infant of his fourth son.

Out of overtures from the presbyteries of Denver and New York sprang another far-reaching action by the Church and a specific task for Henry van Dyke. We have already noted Henry van Dyke's long concern with public worship both in the Brick Church and as vice-president of the Presbyterian Church Service Society. Now the General Assembly appointed him and ten other ministers and elders to undertake the difficult task of preparing "in harmony with the *Directory for Worship* a book of simple forms and services, helpful and proper for voluntary use in Presbyterian churches."

The next three years were much occupied by this work. Long historical research was necessitated and careful literary judgment demanded. There were many in the church who reacted violently from the idea. The committee had to conduct a steady campaign of education lest their work be repulsed. Into all this Henry van Dyke entered with enthusiasm. In many ways he believed it the most important task of his life and often said so.

In 1905 the book was almost ready and he went to the General Assembly at Winona Lake to report. The *Interior* said:

"It had been an open secret on the Winona grounds from the opening of the Assembly that vigorous opposition to this report was brewing. It was alleged that the denomination is being insidiously led toward ritualism, and that this new volume of forms was at once a sign of this trend and an instrument intended to promote it. 'Presbyterian simplicity' was involved as against a tendency to elaborate the services of worship in our churches. There were in fact signs that in some 'nervous ganglia' of this feeling the sentiment of antipathy had grown almost violent. Dr. van Dyke faced all this opposition quite conscious of its extent and vehemence, and set himself deliberately to reason it down. His manner was the essence of frank sincerity. From step to step he proceeded to attack the adverse arguments that he had heard, and one could almost see the barriers melting away before his transparent logic. It was an instructive exhibition of the power of candor over reasonable men, and perhaps beyond that, an interesting evidence of Dr. van Dyke's personal magnetism. Before he was half through speaking it was evident that he had won over the Assembly and would carry the report."

The committee was enlarged by the addition of five men and authorized to publish the book "in order that the churches may have opportunity to consider and test the same, the Committee to make full report to the next Assembly." The final ordeal came at the Assembly of 1906 in Des Moines when holding a copy of the book gingerly in his fingers one commissioner flung it from him crying: "Faugh! it smells of priestcraft." Henry van Dyke, who a little before had been greeted by a veritable hurricane of applause grinned pleasantly amid the uproar. When he spoke it was quietly:

"I don't want to see a fight . . . this is not van Dyke's prayer book. It belongs to every member of the committee you appointed yourselves. . . . It's not a liturgy. It's not a ritual. It does not contain 'canned' prayers. It contains great live prayers of our fathers. Are you going to tell the man who wants to use this book that he can't have it!"

Finally as it became apparent that the opposition must fail they concentrated on the references to "the authority of the General Assembly" and demanded their elision. At once Henry van Dyke was on his feet. He was no contender for details. "I gladly accept the suggestion" he cried with both hands extended. The debate was over. Instead of "Published by authority of the General Assembly of the Presbyterian Church in the U.S.A. for voluntary use in the Churches" the title page was to read: "Prepared by the committee of the General Assembly of the Presbyterian Church in the U.S.A. for voluntary use." The opposition, chiefly composed of good but timorous souls, readily grasped the concession which in no wise affected the serviceableness of the book and besides left its origin clear. Henry van Dyke soberly declared: "It is no man's victory; we have all done what we considered best for our beloved church," and went cheerfully on to the next thing.

The outcome was a triumph for all the forces of decency and order in public church services and provided needed help for family and private devotions. The thing that particularly appealed to Henry van Dyke is represented in a letter he received from a commissioner at the Assembly:

"I have been trustee or elder in a frontier church for 17 years in Oklahoma and I know what we need out there. We hail this little book as a great boon and must earnestly request and beg Assembly to approve it.

I cannot speak in public but surely some one can speak for this great silent element, this great submerged silent force of the *Church at work*.

I as an elder have been called on repeatedly in the absence of a pastor to conduct a funeral service and I have found it very awkward and embarrassing because I did not know how to proceed, but this little book solves the problem and gives us *tongue-tied Moses* a chance to do our duty as we are called by our Master.

I have a copy for myself and am taking a copy to our minister who is a young man wanting experience. I would much prefer to use such a book of forms with the approval of the Assembly for I am a great believer in obedience and law and the will of the majority.

We may not be able to *say* what we want but we *know* what we need and we need this book of worship."

Henry van Dyke was by nature and conviction a pastor and preacher. He could never resist the temptation of a pulpit and by correspondence and personal relations he was constantly engaged in trying to help some one. Preaching and pastoral work were for him the necessary expression of the hunger of his soul. Never can I forget the evening in Wisconsin when he concluded an address on life and religion. Questions and answers followed: at last a young man rose and somewhat petulantly inquired: "If you believe all that why did you leave the Church?" Like a flash Henry van Dyke who had turned for a moment to the chairman of the meeting sprang to his feet. But as his eye fell on the pathetic figure of his questioner he softened into a smile. Looking round the audience he inquired gently: "Well, have I?" a ripple of laughter ran over the audience. Several cried out: "No, no!" As the youth sat down discomfited, Henry van Dyke began quietly to speak. As he went on the youth lifted his eyes, his defiance vanished, a look of awe transfigured his face. The audience sat intent while one soul spoke to the other.

But before the preacher had finished the audience had forgotten the youth and each man was occupied with himself.

Take his sermons during these years. The very titles indicate the contents (Henry van Dyke was ever fond of naming things—animals, places, houses—anything. Words to him were profoundly significant): The Gospel for an age of machinery; The things law cannot reach; The Seventh Sense; Positive Religion; The Higher Citizenship; The Good Old Way; The Battle of Life; Through Unity to Union; The Ideal Society.

Most of them were preached many times. Was it not George Whitfield who said that a sermon is not complete till it has been preached forty times? At any rate Henry van Dyke was constantly adjusting his sermons. Never did he preach a sermon twice in exactly the same way. Always there was a revision in it, something indicative of his meditation upon the new circumstances and his observation of the particular congregation.

In January 1910 again the Brick Church was left pastorless by the death of Dr. Richards, and again Henry van Dyke came to their aid insisting only as on the previous occasion that he serve without salary. A number of attempts to pay for his services and even to cover his expenses were firmly rebuffed. In November the Church officers informed him that they were "unwilling longer to accept his great services without some attempt at financial compensation" and invited him to continue as minister in charge for another year at a mutually satisfactory salary. Ever since his arrival he had been urging upon the Church the need of securing a new pastor. But many of the officers thought that by letting things drift along he might drift back to them again as regular pastor. They were keen enough observers to perceive some marks of his dissatisfaction with his position at Princeton. But only a few realized that a drifting policy would accomplish nothing with him. Matters came to a climax when his resignation at Princeton became public knowledge and a few days later on December 18th he announced that on Christmas Day he would conclude his services in the Brick Church. The officers of the three boards of the Church met at considerable incon-

venience on the evening of December 23rd and among other resolutions adopted one asking the chairman "to request Dr. van Dyke
to reconsider his determination and to ask him whether under any
conditions, and if so, what, he would be able to consent that a meeting of the congregation be called at which his election to the pastorate may be recommended and advocated." But though Henry van
Dyke felt personally much drawn to the proposal his clear view of
the needs of the Church and his concern in the issue at Princeton
which was now becoming more tense made him unwilling to accept. He did however consent to remain on the same conditions as
for the year 1910 until the new pastor was found.

In May the Church found a graceful way of expressing their gratitude when a loving cup inscribed

To

Henry van Dyke

For over twenty years our minister and always our loyal
friend this loving cup is presented by the people of the
Brick Presbyterian Church
in gratitude for his sympathy, wise counsel and generous
service, freely given and repeatedly renewed
New York, the tenth of May Nineteen Hundred and Eleven

was presented to him with an address by his friend Albert R.
Ledoux.

In the cup were two generous checks, one for the Grenfell Mission in Labrador and the other for the Edinburgh Medical Mission
at Nazareth in the Holy Land.

Meantime in the Sixth Presbyterian Church of Chicago where
he had quietly sat in the rear pew during a service Henry van Dyke
had found Dr. William P. Merrill. Matters went swiftly forward
and on October 8th Dr. Merrill was installed pastor of the Brick
Church. Henry van Dyke took part in the installation of his third
successor (who is still at work there today) and thus concluded
the official side of an extraordinary relationship between a church
and pastor. In January he returned for the installation of his former
colleague Dr. James M. Farr as pastor of the affiliated Christ Church
which Church commemorated "the loving and faithful service of

Henry van Dyke"; and many times thereafter he returned to preach in the Brick Church and its affiliated Churches. The last sermon he ever preached, on December 6th, 1931, when he had passed his 79th birthday, was preached in the Brick Church.

The recrudescence of what was popularly known as "fundamentalism" in a way reached its height in the Presbyterian Church in the General Assembly of 1910 when the famous "five points" were promulgated and an attempt was made to enforce them as tests of orthodoxy. Among the many young men who held that certain of these five points were both untrue and without authority in the Presbyterian Church was Henry van Dyke's son who was licensed by the Presbytery of New York in April 1913 under a minority protest. Henry van Dyke was in California at the time reading his poem "God of the Open Air" at the Easter service on Mount Roubidoux. Characteristically on his return he took up the issue vigorously. At his son's ordination in Christ Church where he had been working through his seminary years Henry van Dyke preached a strong sermon, "The Dead Letter and the Living Spirit." With scorn he pictured the method of "theological and critical inquisition" as if it were applied to the first apostles:

"Stay, Peter, before you go to proclaim the gospel to the Roman Cornelius you must tell us what you think about the ceremonial law of the Jews, and when it was written, and whether it is absolutely inspired. Stay, Paul, before you preach Christ to the Gentiles you must tell us what you understand by the virgin birth of Jesus and give a logical definition of the trinity. Stay, John, before you minister to the churches you must explain your views on Jonah and the whale, and tell us who wrote the book of Deuteronomy.

'Away, away,' I hear them answer, 'our gospel is not in these things. Men are suffering and dying. We must tell them about Jesus who came to save them from sin and death. We must tell them that He is the resurrection and the life. We must help the outcast and helpless to find God through Christ in the spirit. What are these things with which you trouble and delay us? The letter killeth but the spirit maketh alive'. . . '.

The world is hungry for a simple, straighter, more vital Christianity —a gospel that children can understand and strong men can live by. Real orthodoxy is not to be measured by definitions, but by the spirit that is in man. Religion is best served and promoted by those who express it simply, commend it warmly, and practise it daily. . . .

Whatever comes of the protest, I wish to take my stand with these young men. They are my brothers in the faith. If they are unfit for the ministry, I am unfit . . . I hold with them that the questions they could not answer, about the patterns of the tabernacle, and the literal interpretation of the virgin birth, and the physical death of Lazarus are not essential to the Christian faith. If I refused the right hand of fellowship to these young followers of Jesus I should be ashamed to look my Saviour in the face. If the Presbyterian Church should reject their service or cast a slur upon their sincerity she would cripple her own strength and betray her own cause. God forbid that such a thing should happen. Heresy-trials are the delight of the ungodly and the despair of religion. But if such a thing should come, let it be fair and brave and open. Do not try it on eager-hearted sensitive boys. Try it on a grown man who stands with them in the liberty wherewith Christ has made us free."

These were bold and sympathetic words of faith generously spoken. To them many responded with joy and, alas, some with bitterness.

The following letter not only speaks for those who grasped the significance of the sermon. It is also a sound tribute to the temper of Henry van Dyke's work as a faithful servant of the Church:

"92 Waters Avenue
West New Brighton, N. Y.
May 21, 1913.

"Edwin Markham, a watcher for the Dawn,
to Henry van Dyke, a watchman on the Towers—
Greeting:

It was a worthy thing you did when you stood up and fought those foolish ones who were striving to hold back the rising of the morning star. Your example will give heart and hope to all who are striving to draw the eyes of the world to the central principle of religion. We certainly need to put aside the non-essentials and join hands around the Vital Fact.

Grace and victory attend you in all your words and ways.

Edwin Markham."

Chapter Nineteen

THE IDEALIST IN EDUCATION, LECTURES
AND ORATIONS

IN HENRY van DYKE many qualities of the scholar, the educator, and the evangelist were blended in the unity of the natural
leader. His intimate friend, Hamilton W. Mabie, who has perhaps
best described the integrity of his diversified qualities wrote:

"In whatever medium of expression he works Dr. van Dyke goes
straight to the mark. Whatever he does bears the stamp of vigor of
thought, clear-cut purpose, and deliberate and thorough workmanship.
The facility he has acquired is 'the result of forgotten toil'; neither in his
face nor in his work is there any suggestion of the careless ease which is
an expression of temperament rather than of intellect. In prose and verse
he thinks clearly, and thinks to the end, before he touches pen to paper.
In his style, as in his voice, there is a certain quality of vibration suggestive of surrender to the matter in hand, and complete enlistment of heart,
mind, and will in dealing with it. . . . This vitality is a rare quality.
Most men live in one set of faculties; Dr. van Dyke lives in all his
faculties. He thinks clearly, closely, searchingly; he feels quickly and
profoundly; his will is virile and masterful. Hence his ability to speak
directly and authoritatively in verse, and fiction, in the essay, in criticism,
and in the sermon. Most men live in one sphere of action; Dr. van Dyke
lives in two spheres. Hence his first-hand knowledge of nature, of books,
and of men."

He delighted equally to work among his books, to meditate by
the fire in his den, or to go out among people for purposes of conversation or to bear his own message on formal or informal occasions. His power to assert himself was yoked with an equal ability

[280]

to receive from men and from nature—as indeed these talents always are yoked in sane and wholesome men.

Almost immediately upon coming to Princeton he took up the editorship of the "Gateway Series of English Texts" which had a wide influence upon the teaching of English both in colleges and schools.

"These books," he wrote in the General Plan of the series, "are treated as pieces of literature, rather than as philological diagrams, or grammatical puzzle-maps, or frame-works for theories of criticism. They are not overloaded with references and comments beyond the students' proper range. Simplicity, directness, sufficiency, vital interest and workmanship of the best quality within a very definite sphere—the entrance to the study of English literature, as well as the entrance to college—these are the ends which we wish, if possible, to reach in this series."

Here was a fresh and living note amid the arid wastes of college preparatory work—as the present writer, then a boy in school, can testify. And it may not be out of place to add that the van Dyke children were occasionally caught up into the study for brief and apparently accidental inquiries on some of the questions. Henry van Dyke liked to test his work and was adept at eliciting whatever opinions might be held about it.

But he was not only at work preparing the material, getting the right men to introduce and comment briefly on it, and setting forth a vital theory of the place of literature in education; he was also actively engaged in contending wherever he could get a hearing, for his broadly cultural view of education. It would be impossible and unnecessary here to single out all of his addresses on education or attempt to name all the colleges, schools, universities and teachers' associations where they were spoken. Indeed, as in his lectures and sermons, the central ideas of these addresses were being constantly used and developed and recombined. Henry van Dyke was never ashamed to say what he thought needed to be said merely because it was "old"; nor afraid to say something new because it was unpopular. From his first full length address on education, "Democracy and Culture" (which was delivered in its earliest form, I believe, at Vassar College about 1890 and which had some of its roots in his college oration on "The Allegiance of Culture") to his last great tribute to the unknown teacher in "Democratic Aristocracy" at the Phi Beta Kappa sesquicentennial in 1926, there were hundreds of addresses all bearing the same witness and each specifically directed to a particular audience. The chief contents of those addresses in one or other of their forms, with the exception of "Democratic Aristocracy" which will be described later—appears in Volume XIII of the collected works.

The gist of his convictions on education may perhaps be summed up in his declaration that though there are three prevalent ideas about it: the decorative, the marketable and the creative, only the last is entitled to serious consideration for it alone is an ideal. Further, his statement that education to be genuine must embody three results, instruction, emancipation and consecration, reveals his divergence from both the old school and the new school theory. As might be expected he was a vigorous believer in the great value of classical studies in a liberal education. To his friend Andrew F. West he wrote:

Value of the Classics

". . . First, they promote a more clear and thorough apprehension of the structure and significance of the various languages of mankind. All human languages are by no means of equal rank. Greek and Latin are certainly among the more perfect, if not altogether the most perfect of those vehicles of thought and feeling which have developed out of human intercourse and civilization. They are in a way norms and standards by which to measure the merits and demerits of other languages. This service is entirely apart from the value of Greek and Latin in helping us to a quicker understanding of words in the modern languages which are derived from Roman or Greek roots.

Second, a still higher value of classical studies lies in the opportunity which Greek and Latin literature give us to obtain a broader and better view of the permanent elements of human life and progress. It may be said that we could get this view equally well from translations. But that is not quite true. There is something in an Ode of Horace read in the original, which is never found in the translation, however good it may be. The sweep of the Virgilian thought may be imitated in English, but it cannot really be reproduced. To read a little of the classics in the original tongues makes an effect upon the mind, which, although it may be forgotten, is in my opinion hardly ever lost."

But he was not afraid to say: "I regard a living school of book-keeping as more valuable than a dead orthodox classical college. No scheme of education can ever be made perfect enough to do away with teachers who are alive."

He had no sympathy with mere encyclopedic information. "A walking dictionary is not an educated man"; he would say, "that's what we have reference books for. Forgetfulness is the result of overloading the mind with hat room checks for things that have never been received." To the very conclusion of his life he had a clear and retentive memory which I believe was founded on the fact that any information that entered his mind was at once absorbed and never allowed to go at loose ends. "A prig," he used to say, "is a person overeducated for his size."

Against the old memory system of education he spoke plainly saying especially of college entrance requirements at the beginning of the nineteenth century that there was "too much emphasis on acquisition and not enough on imagination and perception."

"No doubt," he said on Founders' Day at Lawrenceville School, "the beginnings of study must be chiefly exercises of memory. But at a certain point the reason and the imagination must awake and voluntarily come into play. As a teacher I would far rather have a student give me an incorrect answer in a way that shows real thought about the subject than a perfectly correct answer in a way that shows he has simply swallowed what I have told him and regurgitated it on the examination paper."

But equally he had only scorn for the laxness of superficial opinions. "Too wide a use of the elective system," he declared, "produces a sort of succotash effect."

His whole ideal of education revolved around the two foci of a live pupil and a live teacher engaged in the three arts of seeing (symbolic for the exercise of *all* the senses), reading and thinking. Though his own school and college education was classical rather than scientific, it had certainly included a vigorous study of the philosophy of science, and his own basically inductive approach to life made his views of education liberal beyond the conventional meaning. The doctrine of evolution he heartily accepted as the best explanation of the world of nature. His college studies with President McCosh, his life-long friendship with Henry Fairfield Osborn, his intimate conversations with Charles A. Young and later with Henry Norris Russell, Edwin Grant Conklin and Michael Pupin and others and his own general reading and interest in outdoor life kept him in touch with scientific thought. And though his actual activities in education were limited to the "liberal arts" aspect of it, his view of education always specifically included the scientific. In fact, his protest against exclusive specialization was constant and vigorous. For him the particular subjects through which a man sought to become educated were comparatively unimportant. The unqualified regard for truth wherever found and the full-orbed artistic approach to living were the basic requirements. To him the school, the college, the university and what went on there was not the only instrument of education. It was "The School of Life" (as he entitled his address in Smith College at his eldest daughter's graduation) that was the real educator of a genuine pupil.

"A certain openness of mind to learn the daily lessons of the school of life; a certain willingness of heart to give and to receive that extra service, that gift beyond the strict measure of debt which makes friendship possible; a certain clearness of spirit to perceive the best in things and people, to love it without fear and to cleave to it without mistrust; a peaceable sureness of affection and taste; a gentle straightforwardness of action; a kind sincerity of speech—these are the marks of the simple life. And wherever it is found it is the best prize of the school of life, the badge of a scholar well-beloved of the Master."

Education for Henry van Dyke meant in a special sense preparation for human service.

"I count a man cultured," he said, "who has a sense of the unity of human knowledge, and a feeling of the intimate variety of duty and a profound reverence for the naked truth and an apprehension of the significance of real literature and a wide sympathy with the upward striving dauntless mind of man."

In his ideal of creative education patriotism always occupied a large place. Though he was ever an internationalist he insisted strenuously that sound internationalism could only exist on the basis of a sound patriotism. Even a democracy required "ruling classes" which were to be kept alive and potent by education. "The educated men of the republic," he cried, "should be at once its conservative element and its progressive force."

Of the value of his own particular department in the obtaining of an education he was a firm believer. Next to men and nature he loved literature. He was truly a "teacher of reading"—especially of how to read, and incidentally of what to read. To state associations of teachers, to colleges and to groups of interested citizens everywhere he held forth on this subject with persuasive eloquence. To him reading was not an escape from life but an entrance into it. Books and literature belonged to the people. Even the specific study of them was something much more significant than a preparation for budding authors. If a student desired to write let him begin with the study of the masters of literature; but the art of reading was a vital element in anyone's education because it was the source of both instruction and pleasure. It was with such aims in view that with the assistance of D. Laurence Chambers he published his selection from the *Poems of Tennyson* with a full introduction, and with the assistance of Hardin Craig the four volumes of *Little Masterpieces of English Poetry*; and edited for children's libraries a volume on "Historic Scenes in Fiction" and another on "Literature" under the editorships respectively of Thomas Bailey Aldrich and William De Witt Hyde.

Furthermore Henry van Dyke took a great interest in the work of public, private and parochial schools. He was a frequent visitor to them and sometimes joined with a delicious mixture of satisfaction and embarrassment in their 'van Dyke programmes.' Many are the letters about these events in his files; and among them are fragments of correspondence with particular boys and girls. How surely these experiences sustained his faith that literature belongs to the people! A small boy in a frontier school wrote to thank him for his poem "The Ruby Crowned Kinglet" and concluded his appreciation by adding: "If it is not too rude I should like to know how much money you received for this poem. I think you should get a great deal, for it has made great enjoyment for us." In reply to Henry van Dyke's letter the boy launched out again:

"I have read another poem of yours called 'The Two Schools'. I like it but I do not like it as well as I do 'The Ruby Crowned Kinglet.'"

Then, dropping his inductive literary criticism, the boy fills his letter with a report on birds, and ends up:

"We go to school about a mile from home. There are ten pupils in our school. The postoffice is about five miles from home. There is a stage running from the post office to the railroad. I like to live out here. I should rather live in the country than in the city. We have very cold weather out here. It was about eighteen below zero last night. We have coyotes and wolves out here. They killed nine bucks and seven lambs one night not long ago. They have their dens in the hills near our house."

Or take a letter from Dr. A. Woodruff Halsey describing graduation in a public school on the lower east side of New York. All but one of the graduates were Hebrew girls. An item of the programme was a presentation of Henry van Dyke's story, "The Handful of Clay." One girl improvised at the piano. "Any one familiar with the story would have been able to follow it pretty accurately from her music."

"In the center of the room one young girl dressed in a long, flowing white gown stood on a raised platform, and as the speakers one after another gave the paragraphs of the story, she acted it in pantomime. This young girl had a beautiful face and her expressions as well as her gestures were admirable. She began with a handful of clay and as the story progressed she molded it and at the proper moment laid it aside and held up a common flower pot and later the pot with a lily springing up in all its beauty.

At the close of the story ten or fifteen girls, one after another, repeated selections from various authors, all illustrating the general theme of how the commonplace can minister to the beautiful.

It was most interesting to watch the faces of the parents as the story proceeded, and it was evident that the beautiful lesson was not lost on these uneducated men and women. One of the girls who did her part exceedingly well, came over from Russia some six years ago. . . . All who took part in the rendition seemed to do so with an enthusiasm and with an understanding of the root idea which made you feel that the truth had lodged itself in their hearts and lives."

Henry van Dyke had a natural aptitude for lectures and addresses and orations. He prepared them carefully and with delight and delivered them with evident pleasure. Always there was an element of intimacy in his speech and a ready seizing upon local conditions. His voice and manner were ever the mobile servants of the thought or feeling he wished to convey. He knew how to establish relations with an audience large or small in any part of the country. He was equally at home with a learned audience as on University Day at the University of Pennsylvania or at the dedication of the Rice Institute in Texas or at the southern, mid-west, or far western universities and with an audience chiefly composed of seamen and fishermen at the dedication of Grenfell's Seaman's Institute at St. John's in Newfoundland. Everywhere he had something to say and said it in a manner that was understood. He was one who believed that an audience played a real part, not indeed in his message at the moment, but in the manner and form of its delivery. Only once can I recall a lecture that went flat. We had arrived in a dingy town, and eaten at a lunch counter—the only place where a needed supper was available. The audience was flabby, listless. For the first five minutes Henry van Dyke sought the common denominator of laughter and tears and local interest. The audience sat stolid. Suddenly he turned to his manuscript and went faithfully through his lecture. Afterwards he said: "Well, I delivered it, but they couldn't receive it." The very next night less than a hundred miles away the very same lecture was received with great acclaim.

On these lecture tours on which he visited most of the states in the union Henry van Dyke had many and varied experiences. He was stalled in the snow in a western spring blizzard. On his first visit to one college he was left to shift for himself in a drab and dirty Main Street Hotel and told over the telephone: "You can take a taxi from the hotel when you come for the lecture tonight."

Characteristically he recalled the event: "I decided I'd go out for a walk. There was nothing else to do and I couldn't breathe in the hotel. Up on a corner of the campus was a cardinal bird. I'll never forget *him*. To hear him was worth putting up with any welcome. Whenever anybody mentions a cardinal I always think of him."

Of course he was introduced to audiences in many ways—not always with that restraint which he preferred. On one occasion when he was to deliver several lectures he endured the first ample utterance of the chairman and plunged directly into his task. But when at the second lecture another chairman proceeded in the same vein and Henry van Dyke noted a grin here and there in the audience he decided the thing must stop.

"I knew a man once," he began, "who kept a tame moose behind a stockade and charged visitors twenty-five cents to see him. One day a large buckboard drove up packed with children. The driver looped the reins around the whip, climbed down and knocked at the door. 'How much do you charge to see your moose?' he inquired. The owner of the moose looked at the flock of children and replied: 'I charge twenty-five cents a person; but I might make a special arrangement for your Sunday School'.

" 'Bless you,' returned the driver, 'that ain't a Sunday School; that's my family'.

" 'Say, stranger', said the owner of the moose, 'it won't cost you anything to take 'em all in. It's worth as much to my moose to see your family as it is to your family to see my moose.' "

The audience chuckled with delight—and there were no more introductions.

To catch a glimpse of the many engagements on these lecture tours consider this excerpt from a letter written from California in February 1913:

"Let me see if I can tell you about what I have done. Tuesday: a lunch with 'Bob' Burdette, and a dinner at C. F. Holder's. Wednesday: the really splendid banquet given by the Tuna Club, winding up with the presentation of an enormous silver loving cup. Thursday: the Princeton Alumni banquet at the Athletic Club, Los Angeles. Saturday: a motor trip to the field day of the George Junior Republic, sixty miles away.

Sunday preach in 1st Presbyterian Church to a throng. Monday: lecture before Ebell Club in Los Angeles. Wednesday: an honorific dinner at Valley Hunt Club, during which the club house was on fire, but we sat through it. Friday: address to the students of Occidental College and innumerable friends, and a musical reception this afternoon. All of these ceremonies have been enthusiastic and numerously attended, so that I should be in danger of thinking myself to be someone, if I did not know better.

Meantime there have been a good many hours for quiet work. The result has been that I have gone back to the wonderful Grand Canyon in thought; and you can tell what the thought was by the enclosed poem.

Next Sunday I am due in Los Angeles, and the Sunday after in Stanford University, with a half dozen engagements in between."

On one of these occasions in 1905 when he was lecturing in the crowded gymnasium of the University of California all the lights went out. As a natural rustle and buzz of apprehension broke forth, Henry van Dyke said quietly: "I am going to stay on the platform. Shall I ask for a candle and go on with the lecture?" The audience responded at once with cries of yes, yes, and by candlelight he continued as before until the repairs were made. I recall the pleasure with which he spoke of the long line of seventy-five or more ponies hitched outside the gymnasium by people who had ridden in from ranches to hear his literary lectures. "These people," said Henry van Dyke "are hungry for literature."

Under certain circumstances he was not averse to giving readings from his own works—especially the stories "A Brave Heart," or "The Keeper of the Light" and various selections from his poems always including "The Song Sparrow." He was especially happy to make the Easter dawn pilgrimage to Mount Roubidoux and read there his "God of the Open Air"—perhaps because his strong but never wholly defined faith in immortality breathed freest out of doors, and certainly because this event always included a happy visit with his friends "Father" Frank A. Miller and DeWitt Hutchings.

"A glorious morning, calm and bright," he wrote in a brief note on

[289]

one of these Easters. "Thousands of people streaming up the mountain at dawn, to the foot of the cross. Then silence, and the splendid sunrise over the eastern peaks; and then, rolling down upon the vast fertile plains, the groves, the silver threads of the river, and the habitations of men, came the flood of the New Day—the immortal light. Followed the hymns, the prayers, the words of the Good News of Christ Risen."

All his public appearances were inextricably mingled with the renewing of old friendships and the making of new ones, with outdoor experiences and the personal sharing of literary enthusiasms. To see the man one must view him not only on the platform or pushing his way through a staggering list of engagements, but one must take note of his presence with the Wheelers at "The Bend" on the McCloud river listening to "The First Bird o' Spring," or roaming through the early flowers on H. S. O'Melveny's ranch, or examining trees with T. P. Lukens or investigating fish with C. F. Holder. Or running off with J. P. Kennedy Bryan in Charleston, S. C., to lie under a tree in the magnolia gardens and recall college days but chiefly to listen to the birds. Or talking keenly with Clifford W. Barnes after a session of the Sunday Evening Club in Chicago. Or sharing enthusiasms among the book lovers with Madison Cawein in Louisville. Or conversing with Edwin Mims in Nashville about educational ideals. Or fishing Dickey's run with the Irvines and Archibald Rutledge after a lecture or sermon in Mercersburg School. Or refreshing himself after a lecture at "Yaddo" with his lifelong friend Katrina Trask and the whole fascinating household. Or spending a night with his Brick Church friends the Parsons, the Ledoux, the McAlpins, the Barbours, the Pyles, the Jesups. Or stepping into the Century Club for a stirrup cup of wit or a serious conversation. Henry van Dyke was always alive. He enjoyed the stress of life but he liked to salt it with quiet hours and especially with friendship.

He was indeed a popular lecturer whether before clubs or universities or the Brooklyn Institute or the New York League for Political Education. But though he was always entertaining he never failed to strike the serious note. What the *News and Observer* of Durham, N. C., said of his address there on "Literature and Life" may be taken as typical of the witness he bore: "The final impression gathered from the address was that of the personality of a man who has touched life at all points and who was himself the incarnation of the spirit manifested in his address. It may be said that the address will become one of those forces in the spiritual life of this section that are making for the development of the people."

Henry van Dyke was also on more formal occasions an orator of supreme eloquence. His powerful and flexible voice, his enormous vitality, his charm of manner, his sure command of language and the crystal clarity of his wide ranging mind were all elements in it. He loved to take a theme of vital concern or a personality to whom he could bear an honest tribute and after careful preparation pour forth an oration of impassioned speech. Such were his "Books, Literature and the People" at the first meeting of the National Institute of Arts and Letters, "Ruling Classes in a Democracy" at the Centennial of the University of Georgia, "Christianity and Current Literature" at the Pan Presbyterian Council in Liverpool, "The Chivalry of Lafayette" at the City Hall, New York, on the 160th anniversary of Lafayette's birthday, and the oration for the Century Association at the unveiling of Herbert Adams' bronze statue of Bryant in New York. On such occasions his vibrant eloquence compounded of solid thought and high imagination united orator and audience in the sustained sweep of lofty thought and impassioned feeling.

Perhaps the greatest of his orations was that at the University of Pennsylvania on "The Americanism of Washington and the Men Who Stood with Him." Delivered before a brilliant and enthusiastic audience in the Philadelphia Academy of Music it touched the heights of his ability in a tribute to a great man and a declaration of patriotism:

"What is true Americanism, and where does it reside? Not on the tongue, nor in the costume, nor among the transient social forms, refined or rude, which mottle the surface of human life. The log cabin has no monopoly of it, nor is it a fixture of the stately-pillared mansion. Its home is not on the frontier nor in the populous city, not among the trees of the forest nor the groves of Academe. Its dwelling is in the heart. It speaks a score of dialects but one language, follows a hundred paths to the same goal, performs a thousand kinds of service in loyalty to the same ideal which is its life.

True Americanism is this:

To believe that the inalienable rights of man to life, liberty, and the pursuit of happiness are given by God.

To believe that any form of power that tramples on these rights is unjust.

To believe that taxation without representation is tyranny, that government must rest upon the consent of the governed, and that the people should choose their own rulers.

To believe that freedom must be safeguarded by law and order, and that the end of freedom is fair play for all.

To believe not in a forced equality of conditions and estates, but in a true fairness of burdens, privileges, and opportunities.

To believe that union is as much a human necessity as liberty is a divine gift.

To believe, not that all people are good, but that the way to make them better is to trust the whole people.

To believe that a free state should offer an asylum to the oppressed, and an example of virtue, sobriety, and fair dealing to all nations.

To believe that for the existence and perpetuity of such a state a man should be willing to give his whole service, in property, in labour, and in life.

That is Americanism; an ideal embodying itself in action; a creed heated in the furnace of conviction and hammered into shape on the anvil of life; a vision commanding men to follow it. It was the subordination of the personal self to that ideal, that creed, that vision, which gave eminence and glory to Washington and the men who stood with him."

To Henry van Dyke such events were not mere occasions for the orator; they were above all opportunities for sharing with the people the ideals from which he drew his own abundant life. Oratory like literature was for him a means through which he sought to emancipate and ennoble the life of the people.

In the spring of 1908 he was invited by Harvard University to become lecturer for the following winter on the James Hazen Hyde Foundation at the University of Paris. The adventure appealed greatly to him as an opportunity for carrying his message still wider and for gaining first-hand knowledge of France and also as an educational experience for his four young daughters. At once and characteristically his mind began to work on the lectures. He took counsel among his friends and assembling a few books of reference sailed with his family for France in the early summer. After a few days in Paris busy with seeking advice he retired to a little house in the village of St. Gervais in Savoy and while the children delighted themselves amid the natural beauties he set to work on his lectures. Encouraged by Mme. E. Sainte-Marie Perrin, the daughter of René Bazin, and who had already translated a volume of his stories into French, he determined to speak on the "large and simple" subject of the "Spirit of America." It was a happy choice thoroughly in accord with his natural patriotism and one for which he was well qualified by his earlier studies and his experiences in all parts of the United States. But the preparation of the twenty-six *conférences* was a difficult task. Keeping steadily before him the creation of a better understanding between France and America and recognizing clearly the limitations inherent in all the circumstances he went enthusiastically ahead.

When he rose to speak at the first lecture in the amphitheatre Richelieu he faced a crowded audience and his success was instantaneous. Raymond Recouly in *Le Temps* wrote:

"A spiritual quality, a burning idealism animates this man, short in stature, of reserved appearance, but who becomes singularly impressive when, with perfect power and precision he set forth his ideas. There is about him something I cannot quite define of the apostle and the poet. One feels the former pastor who has become a man of letters and later a professor and who brings into literature living moral concern and an ardent hunger for his mission."

And Maurice Leudet in *Le Figaro* added: "All at once he won his audience by his uncommonly perfect diction, by his persuasive eloquence and by his humour. English and American humour is truly pungent."

As was to be expected Henry van Dyke had taken to heart Hamilton W. Mabie's sage counsel: "Speak slow and distinct, Henry; them French don't ketch our language easy."

He took delight in his success; he was too honest not to. Besides, success in this sense always seemed to him within the grasp of a man who was willing to join himself with his audience in frank recognition of a common humanity, and at the same time willing to do the work that the undertaking required. Perhaps the same thing could be said of him here as Mme. Sainte-Marie Perrin wrote in a brilliant critique of his poetry:

"It is perhaps injudicious to say of a writer that he has not sought for success, but one can say with confidence of this man that success has left his sincerity intact."

Henry van Dyke was doubtless entertained to know that *Le Jockey* announced among other sporting and society events that attendance at his *conférences* was "fort à la mode." He went the round of receptions and *soirées musicales* and enjoyed some of it too. But his vital interest was rather in what his long-time friend William Milligan Sloane had written him:

"Your colleagues in the Sorbonne will treat you royally and you will find their kindly simplicity of life fascinating. I trust you to get below the surface: study the provinces and the left bank of the Seine in Paris— the rest is the same scum you know all about in New York, or London, or Berlin, or wherever a metropolis sacrifices to Moloch."

While he spoke twice a week for the better part of four months and made many other addresses including a notable speech "From Washington to Lincoln" at the American Club, he was much occupied with the life and education of his daughters and with the pastoral opportunities that always followed him wherever he went. He was not too busy to get a sick American in the hospital and cheer him through his illness; nor to follow up on behalf of distracted parents in America several students who had ventured into what they thought was the life of Paris. Dr. Chauncey W. Goodrich writes me:

"The winter when he was in Paris as Sorbonne Lecturer he and all the family were most faithful in attendance at the Church on the Rue de Berri and showed the utmost interest in all its activities. Christmas time, a heavy season for every Pastor, was particularly so in Paris because of all that we did for missionary organizations throughout the city. Just after New Year's your father came to me and said: 'I know that you must be very tired. Just take a week off and go anywhere you like with Mrs. Goodrich and I will look after the church.' The temptation was too much for me and Mrs. Goodrich and I went away for four days spending Sunday at Rheims where I think that I attended every 'Office' in the Cathedral which was then in its splendor with stained glass and tapestries. We came back greatly refreshed and with a gratitude to your father for his thoughtfulness which has never ceased. That incident I know is typical of many in which your father showed his alertness to render friendly services and in any picture of him that side of his many-sided character should not be forgotten. Probably you have heard many testimonies of this kind.

I cherish also his friendliness in little ways. I can still see him, as I was saying Goodbye after a call on your father and mother, dart into his study from which he emerged with a tin of——cigarettes (not always easy to get in Paris) from which he stuffed my overcoat pocket. It was a slight but absolutely characteristic gesture."

In the spring he visited and lectured at many of the Universities in the provinces, Nancy, Lille, Dijon, Rennes, Poitiers, Lyon, Bordeaux—though some of his other engagements had to be cancelled because the lecturer was overtaxed. On these occasions he attended numerous receptions and banquets frequently speaking in French to the delight of his hearers. Marcel Knecht's comment was much quoted: "M. van Dyke parle française très bien avec un accent un peu exotique." Doubtless this was a reference to the French-Canadian origin of his French—of which Henry van Dyke was not at all ashamed. At any rate the newspapers noted his sure grasp of the French speeches he heard and his ready replies expressed with a "nice sense of the *nuances* of our language."

He and his wife refreshed themselves with a happy visit to their friends the Hills at the American Embassy in Berlin. A little later followed a time of great anxiety over the serious illness of one daughter. As usual, Henry van Dyke sat by her bed through the nights of crisis and, as often, when such things were past, he transmuted the experience into a lyric of peace and victory.

At Oberhofen on the Lake of Thunn and at Gstaad during the summer he led many jovial picnic expeditions, went fishing and wrote poetry. As his heart began to turn toward America, whither he returned in early September, he wrote those singing lines with the unforgettable refrain:

> "O it's home again, and home again, America for me!
> My heart is turning home again, and there I long to be,
> In the land of youth and freedom beyond the ocean bars,
> Where the air is full of sunlight and the flag is full of stars."

His lectures had not only achieved a natural *succes d'estime*. They had "produced a real and very wholesome impression in this country," as the American Ambassador wrote him. "How sweet the English language seemed to me when you spoke it. I did not care very much for America but now it is quite different," wrote a French student.

Those of the lectures, which most specifically interpreted the spirit of America were translated by Mme. Sainte-Marie Perrin with a preface by Alexander Ribot into French to meet an obvious demand. In fact throughout the course one could not but be impressed by the widespread interest evidenced not only in the French press but in that of Britain and Spain. Not only the raciness of speech and manner in which they were delivered but the serious content of what he had to say on education and will power and especially on those untranslatable American phrases *self-reliance* and *fair-play* excited great interest.

When he got back to America he found to his surprise that the Americans also desired to hear this interpretation. And after repeating the lectures in several places he published them in *The Spirit of America* with the warning "to remember its origin." The book in fact is typical of Henry van Dyke's method of dealing with public questions. He was never a reformer hammering incessantly at any one particular problem. He had no panacea. Nor did he believe it necessary to be dull in order to be serious. His method was to pick out any good that he could find and to emphasize this against the background of the evil that he never failed to see though he often chose to say nothing directly about it. His silences were fully as significant as what he said. He himself has described these lectures as "a report, made in Paris, of the things that seem vital, significant, and creative in the life and character of the American people."

A year later Emile Boutroux, between whom and Henry van Dyke a firm and lasting friendship had sprung up, wrote that the cross of knight of the Legion of Honor had been conferred upon him. Thus was set a seal upon Henry van Dyke's admiration for France which, beginning in his early studies of the history of his own country had advanced through this new experience, and was to flower again, though as yet he knew it not, in time of war.

Chapter Twenty

LOVER OF NATURE AND INCORRIGIBLE
FISHERMAN

HENRY VAN DYKE took naturally to the out-of-doors. It was in his blood; in his own adventurous character; in the simple delight that he found in the exercise of his sound senses. Furthermore he had been raised by a wise father, with the indulgence of a sympathetic mother, in the strictest sect of trout fishermen. The outcome was his own choice; it was also inevitable.

To be out-of-doors remained for him not merely a way of "keeping fit" for other tasks. It was a prime necessity of his nature. Fishing—and all that goes with it—was not a hobby; there was nothing delicately deliberate about it; it was a passion. It did indeed take him away from his immediate work. But far more it irradiated his whole life. Love of Nature, a passion for land and water was part —and no small part—of his preaching, writing, friendships. He was an out-door man. He loved the city—above all New York— and in its swirling tides of humanity he found delight as well as opportunity for the work he loved. But even there, as his understanding friend, John H. Finley, has emphasized, he was a fisher of men. The attitude of fishing was the bent of his soul. For men or for fish he cast a line upon the waters with equal hope. If he had followed the first inclination of his youth he would have become an Adirondack guide. But like most youthful passions its earlier form had to be filled up with the higher purpose of his life intent. Out-door life and fishing was always the web on which he wove the many-coloured pattern of his days. He loved and had a genuine understanding of horses and dogs as his tales record and as letters from friends of those faithful servants of mankind bear tribute. His appreciation of the natural scene made its appeal to all sorts of people. The story is told by Mrs. Peaseley of the Maine Sea Coast Mission that she read his verses, "A Snow Song", to a young coast fisherman. After demanding its re-reading twice more the young man asked: "Who is this man and where does he fish?" The bird songs to which he gave expression especially in his early poems at once captured the attention and praise of nature lovers like Frank Chapman, John Burroughs, Olive Thorne Miller, Mable Osgood Wright, Ernest Thompson Seton. The poems had a considerable influence in the establishing of nature study in the life of the American people. As a fisherman Henry van Dyke was early known as a skilful fly-caster and was renowned for his ability to find fish. Until 1905 he was an excellent shot with a rifle and not a few trophies fell to his aim. With his brother Paul he went to Newfoundland and each brought back, if memory serves, two handsome caribou heads. In New Brunswick one fall he shot a large and very black moose. I recall one day as we went down the trail on the Batiscan river two caribou, disturbed in the marsh below, dashed through the thick spruces. He fired a snap-shot at a range of 250 yards and the leading animal leaped and fell at the single shot which struck just behind the shoulder.

In 1906 in *The Illustrated Outdoor News* Harry V. Radford making a list of America's greatest living sportsmen named first Charles Hallock, second Caspar Whitney, third Theodore Roosevelt and then added seven names in alphabetical order:

> John Burroughs
> George Bird Grinnell
> William T. Hornaday
> Alexander Starbuck
> Henry van Dyke
> T. S. van Dyke
> W. Austin Wadsworth

Several times Henry van Dyke made preliminary plans for hunting sheep, and elk and grizzlies. Once a plan was made with S.

Hall Young for an Alaskan hunt in which Roosevelt was to join. But the plans fell through. Characteristically Henry van Dyke found that his duties as Moderator of the Presbyterian Church prevented. He was after other game. About this time he laid aside his rifle in favor of his rod; but this was a matter of personal preference —not a change of heart. To a gentle critic who sent him a lovely drawing of a deer with the dubious motto: "Thou shalt not kill" he replied expressing pleasure at the gift and suggesting as a more adequate motto: "Rise Peter, slay and eat." He was always as one would expect a merciful but never a half-hearted hunter and fisherman. If an animal were hit but not brought down at first he would not abandon the trail. Two such occasions I recall, having been with him at the time. Once six hours on the trail gave him another shot with which he brought down the caribou. Another time a long afternoon following a moose convinced him that the animal had been but lightly fleshed by his first shot. As he saw the huge beast running off in the dusk across a meadow too far for a sure shot he gave up the chase. We spent that night far from camp sustained chiefly by a handful of blueberries, a bite of chocolate and our pipes while we fought off the savage onslaught of mosquitoes.

A dozen times I have seen him hold fire as the game moved off, within range, but too distant for a likely shot. He wanted to kill but he hated just to hit. As for fishing, he used to argue affably that tackle adjusted to the expected weight of the fish was a sporting proposition for the fish as well as for the man. "If you want to enjoy sport," he said, "give the game a fair chance." Occasionally he would denounce the "pathetic fallacy" of ascribing human feelings to the fish. But for the most part he felt that fair fishing needed no defense. He always liked to kill his fish with a swift rap on the head when they came to net or gaff. Perhaps this was another reason why he did not find so much enjoyment in sea fishing with a hand line. Sometimes, when camp was supplied with all the fish that could be used or preserved by smoking or salting, he might try a few casts with barbless hooks. But though he loved to catch "his limit" he would often reel up at the height of the rise saying: "That's enough, for today." Once on the Grand Cascapedia fishing for big sea trout in September he found himself fast to a late run salmon (which was estimated to weigh nearly 25 pounds). He was fishing with his 4 ounce trout rod and, of course, there was no net that could hold a fish of that size. After an hour's skilful play the fish, now utterly exhausted, was beached and under the fisherman's direction two men seized him gently in the water and released the hook. "He was so tired out," wrote Henry van Dyke in describing the incident "that he rolled over on his back like a dead fish. He had evidently fainted away. So we tried a method of revival. We steered him gently into a swift little current and held him there with his head upstream so that the water could flow through his gills in the right direction. Presently the gills began to move. He breathed very slowly at first, then took two or three long breaths (it almost seemed as if we could hear him sigh), gave a couple of weak wriggles, then a strong one, and finally he dashed up the stream splashing water upon us as he went. It was an interesting experience in life saving."

His following of the outdoor life and fishing took him to many parts of the United States from Maine to California and back to Florida, to Ontario, Quebec, Nova Scotia, Newfoundland, New Brunswick, the north and south shores of the St. Lawrence. He made fishing expeditions to Scotland, Norway and New Zealand and on visits primarily for other purposes to England and to many parts of Continental Europe, Japan, and Palestine he took days off and went fishing. One could name a hundred comrades of these happy experiences beginning with his father and his brother, Paul, "My Lady Greygown" for whom he wrote in the bewitching dedication of *Fisherman's Luck*: "In all the life of your fisherman the best piece of luck is just *You*," his son and daughters, the men of the Swiftwater Preserve, the Mercersburg Academy, the Ste. Marguerite Salmon Club and the Fly-fisher's Club of London, and a host of the friendly tribe of fishermen whom he met here and there. And always his little 4 ounce split-bamboo rod with the sumac butt, the "wand of enchantment" given him in 1894 for his first fishing poem "An Angler's Wish," was his inseparable companion. If that rod could speak what a tale it could tell! But like a genuine fisherman it exercises a due reserve. Perhaps because, as Solomon Singlewitz (Henry van Dyke's *alter ego*) wrote in *The Early Life of Jonah*: "When fishermen tell the truth, they do it well."

To describe Henry van Dyke on his little rivers is beyond the pencil of one who was nevertheless happy to share many of his expeditions for more than thirty-five years. The story is one for the camp fire; it can only be suggested in a book. You may observe the nature of the fisherman's soul in *Little Rivers, Fisherman's Luck, Days Off, The Travel Diary of An Angler, A Creelful of Fishing Stories*. It is further portrayed in a full and ardent correspondence with British and American fishing friends. One gets a revealing glimpse of him in Charles Dudley Warner's request of 1897: "I should like to give a little tang to your vacation by having you do something useful. We want about a thousand or twelve hundred words on Izaak Walton. I do not know anybody who has more of the vein for doing this moralistic sportsman than yourself. If Walton were living, I would ask him to do the paper on you for the *Library*."

One sees him again on an expedition to the Grand Falls of the Humber River to watch the salmon leap the twelve foot falls and to take a few in the pools below. J. A. MacDonald one of the companions on this trip wrote in *The Continent*: "To me van Dyke was more interesting than the river or the salmon. It was when night came on and the gleaming camp fire burned a hole in the encircling darkness that we got closer together and unseen hands felt for the common chord. A few songs—college glees, negro melodies, folklore ballads, perhaps a Gaelic lament, or an old English Methodist fragment from Warburton and the blinds were drawn back on the windows of those interior rooms in which a man lives and thinks and is himself. A glimpse into these inner chambers of a real personality, when the gloaming round the camp fire shuts out the intrusion of the vulgar everyday world—the sights and sounds of garish day have no match for that." Or take the lovely picture that Archibald Rutledge, ofttimes his companion on Dickey's Run, gives in "The Art of the Old Master" in *Outdoor America* for October 1926.

"One characteristic of the Old Master is his alertness to notice the things of nature along the stream, and to describe them felicitously. I recall his description of the Columbine's flowers as 'red chalices'; of the field sparrow's singing at dusk as 'a song of the spirit'; and of the shadowy waters of a deep pool as 'a huge amethyst.' His awareness of the wild life about him, even while he is absorbed in sport, may be judged from the fact that the only rose-breasted grosbeak I ever saw in this country he pointed out to me in an old sycamore overhanging the stream.

His remarks about life, casually spoken, as some little incident made him think of its relation to human experience, are eminently shrewd and profound. I remember him saying that nearly all human misery can be traced to someone's lack of self-control. I remember him saying that no man who really knows nature and understands her can possibly doubt the existence and the essential goodness of God. And I recall this: 'Sophisticated people pride themselves on knowing too much, whereas the real trouble with them is that they know too little.' . . .

Henry van Dyke caught his largest fish from this stream under a little wooden bridge. In mid-afternoon he had located the leviathan, and he had had from him one or two savage but bickering rises. We fished perhaps a mile downstream, and I thought that we were then ready to start home, for the sun was among the black pines fringing the mountain-ridge. But a fisherman has a vivid memory. As my companion turned from the stream, I could see that something was on his mind.

'Arch,' he said, 'that big one under the bridge is still there, and he shouldn't be.'

It was the kind of sentiment with which I can always quickly agree. Together we returned to the crude stream-crossing, with the sun down and with the first mist of evening beginning to rise from the brook. The Master stood far back to one side of the bridge and made a long crooked cast under it—like a long 'hooked' drive in golf. I heard a splash, saw the line tighten, heard the reel sing. To play a fish under a bridge amid old snags and trash is really an art, and I saw the feat performed that evening. It was a gallant fight, between two expert veterans, and the fish lost. He was close to eighteen inches; and he was taken on a fourteen hook, to which was tied a Queen of the Water. It takes a queen to humble a king."

How he loved to set off on a long and often adventurous expedition. Till 1897 his Lady Greygown was his constant companion. After that she turned with naturalness and an uncomplaining sense of duty to the care of the growing children. She no longer sat with him by the camp fire or floated with him in a canoe but bade him farewell and hailed his return on the doorstep—though several times in the latter years they revived old memories at Swiftwater and once in Norway.

Take a handful of snap-shots from various memory albums:

His ruddy face intent beneath a broad brimmed fedora with the hat band full of flies he is wading the rapids at sunset below Virgin Falls on the Nepigon river. His cast drops delicately on a deep pool below a submerged rock. There is a flash in the water. The line tightens; the four ounce rod bends. When he comes into camp an hour later at repeated shouts of "Supper!" he lays down two brook trout—each something over six pounds. At night by the camp fire with his companions and Ojibway guides he listens to the visiting medicine man chant the tales of Hiawatha.

Again he is off with his eldest daughter and her school-girl friend —the strenuous life is for girls, too, he insists—on a coasting steamer from Quebec down the north shore of the St. Lawrence. They are scouting for salmon in the regions where the great Napoleon Commeau is the guardian spirit. How he observed people and events may be noted in his poem, "Gran' Boule", which a little later recorded the fate that befell the captain of the vessel. In a fur trader's house Henry van Dyke is asleep on the floor outside the door of the girls' room. A drunken Indian lifts the window, but after he gazes sadly into Henry van Dyke's cocked and ready rifle he departs muttering: "Dis be de wrong house."

From Struthers Burt's ranch he goes forth on the Snake River one hot sunny day to find the cut-throat trout. The fishing had been dull—a few small fish now and then. But when he returned he had fourteen trout, the largest five pounds. Though I saw it done I shall only say that it was "fine and far-off," almost all the fish taken in one glassy pool where he knew the fish were and where he experimented with flies till they came.

You may see him in many lands beside his little rivers. In England on the Barle and the Up-Exe or in the lush meadows along the Itchen with G. E. M. Skues. By the gray glacial waters of Switzer-

BAR BC RANCH

STE. MARGUERITE

DICKEY'S RUN

"THE OLD MASTER"

FATHER—JOKE—SON

land, along the streams of Luxembourg with goggle-eyed villagers following at a respectful distance to watch the trout come to the mysterious flies. On the Vosse-Elv in Norway where on an angling furlough from his war duties at The Hague he brought in on the last day two salmon weighing 32 and 34 pounds apiece. He had refused the customary method of "harling" and used his light split bamboo salmon rod with flies.

Again he appears coming in from some little stream after a "poor" fishing day with one or two trout in his creel, a bunch of bishop's caps and orchids in his hand and a couple of bird songs in his heart, well content. He was not a "record fisherman"— though he was keen to hold a place among his brother anglers.

You must see him also as he came and went constantly during twenty-five years along the Ste. Marguerite River among friendly fishing comrades and with his excellent canoemen Ezide and Henri Gravel. How he would burst into song as he shot down the rapids past Brackett's point and approached the club! How he loved to yawn himself asleep in the hot noons reclining on the porch of Chateau, the lodge that had about it something of the air of a small-scale ancestral mansion dreaming beneath its elms. How eagerly he sallied forth at Rocky Bar to tease a huge salmon to rise at the foot of the long glassy pool while Ezide, perched high in a spruce top, guided his long casts with suppressedly explosive counsel.

There were long talks with the canoeman—not only about fishing—and not seldom Henry van Dyke was called as a judge to settle the short-lived sharp quarrels among *les enfants des bois*. And after the delicious formalities of dinner at the club there were yarns and philosophy before the fireplace with the lovely steel engraving of Ste. Marguerite and Walton's motto:

> We'll banish all sorrow and sing till tomorrow,
> And angle and angle again.

Henry van Dyke made some famous catches on the river in the salmon season. But he loved equally to return with a companion when the sea trout were running in August and go up river with his lightest tackle—occasionally as if bent on exterminating the trout which he knew were destructive of salmon fry and eggs, but usually "to cast the fly, and loaf and dream." How swiftly he would revive there from all the stress and strain of his always strenuous life. And what a companion he was—wise and witty and full of understanding sympathy with youth and age.

Perhaps the most characteristic of his out-door experiences was the trip through the Holy Land where he rode and camped his way with Doctor and Mrs. John Knox McLean from Jerusalem to Damascus not seeking "to make any theological theory, but simply to ride through the highlands of Judea, and the valley of Jordan, and the mountains of Gilead, and the rich plains of Samaria, and the grassy hills of Galilee, looking upon the faces and the ways of the common folk, the labours of the husbandman in the field, the vigils of the shepherd on the hillside, the games of the children in the market-place."

This journey was indeed an epitome of his whole out-door philosophy. Christianity was to him always "an out-of-doors religion" and he rejoiced in the fact. The journey had also another meaning for him for it was in part planned that he might there complete work on his long-meditated poetic drama *The House of Rimmon*.

One sees the whole significance of the journey not only in his volume *Out-of-Doors in the Holy Land* with its wayfaring Psalms, but in such a letter as that he wrote from Banias (Caesarea-Philippi) to John H. Finley, poetic ministering angel to the writing of the drama of Naaman and Ruahmah:

"How often I have thought of you on this delightful journey and wished you here to share it. We have been in the Holy Land just four weeks and not slept under a roof one night. We have ridden from Hebron (where there was a fierce thunder-storm with hail that whitened the hills), to Dan, where we lunched yesterday beside the biggest spring of the Jordan—a river springing full-grown from the foot of a hill. Today we are passing a quiet Sunday at the most beautiful of the Jordan's fountains, where a river, but little smaller than the other, bursts from the side of a mountain and rushes down clear and foaming through a lovely valley crowded with wild figs, oleanders, wild grapes and fragrant flowering shrubs. Our tents are under the olives, broken columns around us, and in front the great rock cavern where the Sanctuary of Pan and the Nymphs stood, and where Herod built his temple to Augustus Caesar.

I have traversed the caverns of Naaman and Ruahmah [the leading characters in the drama on which he was working], by Beth-Shan and Jezreel and Dothan and Samaria. I have found among the mountains the very pass where their tents stood, looking down on the city of Israel's king. I have camped beside the flowing spring of Dothan at the foot of the hill where Elisha dwelt, and ridden over the ground from there to Jordan. The drama all seems doubly real to me now.

We had a fine week east of the Jordan, among the mountains of Gilead. Jerash is a wonderful ruin—the most striking I have ever seen. I have swum in the clear, cool waters of the Lake of Galilee, and caught many fish there with the fly—also in the springs that feed the Jordan. All has gone well, the weather ranging from 45 degrees at Hebron to 106 degrees in the Jordan Valley, and our camps from 3000 feet above the sea-level to 1000 feet below it.

But the most wonderful thing has been the new sense of the reality and meaning of the Old Testament narratives and of the Gospel Story. Among these flowery fields, over these opalescent mountains, beside these flowing brooks, the presence of the Master has been an unseen companionship. This was the northernmost place that He visited, and from here He set His face steadfastly to go to Jerusalem, knowing the end. Here Peter made his confession; and here, I think, on some spur of the snowy Hermon above us, Jesus was transfigured. How glorious it all is. I wish you were here with me under the olives and beside the singing little river Jordan.

Tomorrow we start on our way for the top of Hermon (if the snow is not too deep) and for Damascus. Give my love to Mrs. Finley and keep a friendly thought now and then for

> Your friend
> Henry van Dyke.

If any one tells you that Palestine is disappointing, be sure he has gone the wrong way, or his heart has not been there."

. . . .

No account of Henry van Dyke as an out-door man would begin to be adequate which did not accent his concern in the preservation of game and of the natural beauty of land and water. His own conduct as a sportsman and lover of Nature out of which this particular activity sprang has already been indicated. But there was far more to it than this. He saw the need for cooperative public action. He was not one of those "sportsmen" who, so long as they are able to escape to outlying regions of wilderness or to make use of private preserves, care not what befalls more circumscribed citizens. His fundamental democracy appears in this too.

His earliest writing on the subject is a letter to the *New York Tribune* December 19, 1883. He pleads for preservation of the Adirondack region of forests and waters "in its pristine beauty," calling attention to its value as a recreation ground for the people and denouncing the irreparable damage done by damming "the once lovely Racquette River, the fairest, wildest stream I ever floated on, . . . now changed into a dismal and desolate canal flowing through the graveyards of a noble forest." The story of the victory over predatory interests that preserved this region for the people need not be recounted here. The crusading zeal of Gifford Pinchot for the American forests; the influence of President Theodore Roosevelt's famous Country Life Commission culminating in the whole Conservation Movement was now opening a new day for out-door life in the United States. Henry van Dyke took his part in that movement. Let us examine a few illustrations:

On November 11, 1907 he was made chairman of the first convention of the North American Association of Honest Anglers. He produced letters about fish protection received from President Roosevelt and from ex-President Cleveland remarking as he read them that "this is probably the only topic which could bring harmonious opinions from these two men."

The New York *World* obviously in the language of an enthusiast but hardly that of a fisherman reported: "The Doctor threw a wily line. They rose eagerly to his fly. It was one of his own manufacture painted with the sober colors of the true sporting spirit. After a brief hour's play he gaffed the great catch of the evening, the appointment of a committee to form the nucleus of a national organization for the protection of food and game fish in American waters."

"In three things," he declared, "the sportsman of today must be an advance on his ancestor with the barbed arrow and the pronged spear:

1. The true sportsman must recognize that the supply of food which nature provides in the woods and waters is something to be guarded and protected for human use. He must favor the enactment of wise and stringent laws to prevent the waste and extermination of these natural resources either directly or indirectly by the pollution of waters and the destruction of the forests. He must favor these laws and keep them himself.

2. He must hold himself to a strict account for the use of his own game and fish. He must not be greedy or insatiable. He must not be a game butcher or a fish hog.

3. He must recognize that his sport is for him not a matter of necessity, but a recreation, and therefore he must follow it as a game with rules that equalize the chances, and make success depend upon skill and good judgment and perseverance."

In California in 1913 Henry van Dyke joined in the campaign for fish protection headed by the veteran angler Dr. Charles F. Holder. He had a real share in the enactment of the three mile law; was elected an honorary member of the Tuna Club, though, as he whimsically declared: "I never caught a tuna, and am not worthy to catch a tuna." The silver loving cup which the club presented to him at the hands of one of his former pupils, Robert Freeman, was a tribute to him as a sporting angler whose interest covered the whole field of fishing, though he never took any of the large game fish from the sea. His sporting spirit was expressed, after the manner dear to fishermen, in the phrase: "The fish like a lady should be given the opportunity to say Yes or No. Sometimes, like a lady, she means Yes when she says No."

A little later he regaled the San Francisco Fly Casting Club with stories and tales in which he always abounded. He could spin the yarn of the Red, White and Blue trout, or of Ahazuerus, the Educated Fish, and countless others, as well as report more objective facts with gusto. To him angling and the association with anglers was always an exuberant delight.

In 1921 and 1923 at the invitation of Struthers Burt aided by those two other distinguished conservationists, Stephen T. Mather, the Director of National Parks, and Horace M. Albright, then Superintendent of Yellowstone National Park, Henry van Dyke made extended visits to the whole Yellowstone region and took an active part in the struggle then on foot for the defense of the Parks and the protection of game and fish throughout the district. With his rod in his hand he investigated the fishing and talked carefully with many hunters and fishermen. He travelled the whole region, some of it in a car, the back districts on horseback and afoot along the lakes and streams. It was a characteristically thorough piece of work. The fruits of it appeared in articles in the *New York Times*, September 18, 1921, "Nature and the New Campers," and September 25, 1921, "The Nation's Heirlooms of Beauty" and in the *New York Herald*, October 21, 1923, "Angling Problems in and around Yellowstone." There were also many letters about the issues raised. He fought the bill for the damming of Yellowstone Lake, made valuable observations on the spawning habits of the fish and offered a proposal: "Establish by law (at least for the streams and lakes in these high altitudes), a closed season of protection for red throat trout, and grayling, beginning when the ice goes out, and ending about July 15th, or at any rate not earlier than July 1st. Give the fish a chance to do their best at the proper time, and to rest and fatten up after they have done it!" He took an active and important part in the campaign to extend Yellowstone Park to include the Teton mountain district—a region against which the exploiters were in full cry. For this purpose he traversed the country on horseback and drew a studied line upon the map and supported his opinion with vigorous cogent letters.

Meantime his pen and personal influence were busy in the founding of the Izaak Walton League of America. Perhaps Walton might say to us, he wrote: "Trust me, scholars, the gentle sport of Angling shall be safe in your country for many a year, if every man among you will but learn to love his neighbor's fishing as his own." And he rejoiced when the General Federation of Women's Clubs endorsed the League's proposal for a National Preserve on the upper waters of the Mississippi: "Let us get into our minds and into theirs," he wrote, "the constructive idea of a Savings Bank for our Country's resources of natural beauty and healthful out-door life. The mothers of America can do even more than the fathers to bring this idea home and make it work." He refused to take part in the quarrels between sportsmen's organizations: "The odium theologicum will not be beneficial in the realm of sport any more than it has been in the realm of religion." Here, too, he was an open honest fighter despising cant and holding his eye on the main objective.

In 1926 he wrote for the National Parks Bulletin an article in which he asked:

"Why should we not regard our National Parks as the *Out-Door University of the United States?*

The State Parks would be local colleges. The Municipal Parks would be playgrounds and pleasances.

I do not mean that the Parks should be organized in academic fashion, with faculties and classes, entrance examinations, grades, diplomas, and degrees. Heaven forbid! We have enough of that already,—for my taste perhaps a little too much. . . .

A National Park, if it is used as Yellowstone is, should be as sacred as a temple."

A little later he joined in the successful defense of the seldom-visited southwest section of Yellowstone Park—where he had ridden in 1923—against a well-organized commercial raid. For *The Outlook* at the invitation of Ernest Hamlin Abbott he wrote "A Meadow that Belongs to the People" and elsewhere also presented first-hand testimony on behalf of the Park.

His service as a conservationist and his status as an out-door man were recognized when in 1927 he was made a member of the National Parks Association's "Advisory Board on Educational and Inspirational Functions of National Parks" (a title which it is needless to add Henry van Dyke did *not* suggest).

A letter from John C. Merriam, President of the Carnegie Institution of Washington bears authoritative testimony to Henry van Dyke's share in keeping America aware of her birthright:

"As I think I remarked to you in conversation, I consider your contributions to interpretation of certain aspects of some of the national parks as among the most important materials available in America. Your poem on the Grand Canyon I recognize as an outstanding piece of literature, presenting an interpretation of the Canyon of paramount interest to everyone."

In his reply to this letter you may see that for Henry van Dyke religion and nature were the conjugate foci of a genuinely good life:

"I have long been of the opinion that our nature, at least in its present stage of development, is a composite thing to which both body and soul belong. Its welfare depends upon keeping both in good working order and in their right relation to each other. An aspiring soul in a neglected and crippled body is a failure. But a well nourished and flourishing body which houses a starved, frustrated, unhappy spirit, is a still greater failure. It seems to me that a real fellowship with nature in the joy of beauty and the vigour of free out-door living, is the best prophylactic against both these forms of degeneration."

Henry van Dyke's love of nature and passion for fishing were the fruit of a natural delight and a profound conviction. "Man," he used to say, "is not a part of nature, but he is united to her by marriage." Never a specialist in any one field, his knowledge of fish, flowers, birds, trees, water and land, was often surprising. Even during the years when there were many literary nature fakers loose in the land he was never tempted by the obvious rewards to join their shoddy company. That was why wherever he went he made friends with out-door men—simple folk as well as famous sportsmen. He received a letter one day from an unknown man who expressed an ardent desire to go fishing with him. The simple letter bore the indescribable signet of the out-door man and Henry van Dyke went. When he returned happy from the adventure he remarked: "I won a bet for that fellow. His wife bet him I'd never even answer the letter, but I did, and we caught fish too."

Henry van Dyke's songs of out-of-doors, fishing tales and essays, are more than classics; they are found in many a simple home and camp across the great America which he loved. For wherever he went he was out-of-doors in the holy land and carried the breath of it into everything that he did and said and wrote.

Chapter Twenty-one

AN ADVENTURE IN DIPLOMACY

HENRY VAN DYKE was always a great admirer of Woodrow Wilson from the day when he heard Wilson make his great oration on "Princeton in the Nation's Service." Nothing was more characteristic of those two doughty American idealists than their refusal to allow anything to interfere with their sound personal relations. Though on certain questions they were agreed to differ they were equally resolved—if not at all times to love—at least steadfastly to respect each other. Neither was averse to a good-humored laugh at the other's foibles. While they had been heartily at variance in the method of dealing with problems at Princeton they were certainly united by a basically democratic ideal. Henry van Dyke, although he was subjected to not a little criticism for it, cheerfully and whole-heartedly hailed the rising of Wilson's political star in 1911. Here was a man who out of sound scholarship and profound human sympathy was expressing with beauty and power the aspirations of a burning patriotism. It was impossible for Henry van Dyke to refrain. As an old-fashioned Democrat by birth and training, and as a man keenly interested in the public affairs of his own day, he could not fail to join that marching music, for it was already in his heart. When the nation's response carried Wilson into the Presidency, among the many "literary Americans" whom he selected for diplomatic posts was Henry van Dyke. This appointment to the Netherlands and Luxembourg had an element of magnanimity in it. It was also a just appraisal of Henry van Dyke's mettle as a contender for peace, as he had shown it in the Princeton affair. The appointment was popular at home and abroad according to newspaper reports and a flood of letters from all sorts of people.

Perhaps Henry van Dyke was most affected by a sheaf of letters from the girls of Public School 188 in New York, where he had been a recent visitor; by the remark lightly attached to a serious letter: "I have reliable information that the rates of life insurance on fish in Dutch waters have materially advanced in the last few days"; and by such notes as that of John H. Finley who wrote: "You are the whole of Holland to me and an ambassador to the rest of Europe" enclosing a "map of the New New Netherlands" which he had drawn to represent Henry van Dyke capped and gowned, and hooded with orange, skipping across the Dutch provinces. The word of children, a sly dig at his fishing propensities, the expression of friendship, especially when it was not solemn, strengthened his heart. He liked to take up heavy responsibilities like a woodsman shouldering his pack with a laugh.

When after a busy summer of preparation, which included a couple of weeks' fishing on the Ste. Marguerite River, and which was crowned with a little dinner among his friends, Henry van Dyke sailed with his family in September 1913, his chief motive as he himself described it was "the desire to promote the great work of peace which had been begun by the International Peace Conference at The Hague. This indeed was what the President especially charged me to do."

Peace reforms were certainly in the air of those days. Bryan's "Stop—Look—Listen" treaties were much to the fore. Carnegie's Peace Palace at The Hague was just completed. On Henry van Dyke's appointment the Carnegies had cabled him, "Hurrah rite man rite place see you opening peace palace sure." The Palace was dedicated on August 28th but Henry van Dyke characteristically had obtained a delay in going to his post in order that his predecessor, Lloyd Bryce, might conclude his services at this hopeful event.

His voyage was made both delightful and profitable by the presence on the ship of Jonkheer John Loudon who was returning from Washington after a brilliantly successful period as Minister to the United States to become the Foreign Minister of the Netherlands.

In fact, the beginning and whole duration of Henry van Dyke's incumbency at The Hague was marked by the most friendly, personal and official relations with that cheerful and able diplomat.

When the family arrived and took up residence in Count Bentinck's house which served as the American Legation on the beautiful Lange Vorhout, all was serene. Henry van Dyke noted with satisfaction the charm of the scene.

"Holland was at her autumnal best. Wide pastures wonderfully green were full of drowsy, contented cattle. The level brown fields and gardens were smoothly ploughed and harrowed for next year's harvest, and the vast tulip beds were ready to receive the little gray bulbs which would overflow April with a flood-tide of flowers. On the broad canals innumerable barges and sloops and motor-boats were leisurely passing, and on the little side-canals and ditches which drained the fields the duckweed spread its pale-emerald carpet undisturbed. In the woods—the tall woods of Holland—the elms and the lindens were putting on frosted gold, and the massy beeches glowed with ruddy bronze in the sunlight. The quaint towns and villages looked at themselves in the waters at their feet and were content. Slowly the long arms of the windmills turned in the suave and shimmering air. Everybody, in city and country, seemed to be busy without haste. And overhead, the luminous cloud mountains —the poor man's Alps—marched placidly with the wind from horizon to horizon."

Promptly he presented his credentials to the Queen at the summer palace of Het Loo; and later to the Grand Duchess in Luxembourg. The usual "rounds of ceremonial visits were ground out. . . . There were dinners and dances and court receptions and fancy-dress balls—all of a discreet and moderate joyousness which New York and Newport, perhaps even Chicago and Hot Springs, would have called tame and rustic." Mrs. van Dyke, who had come to the Netherlands with great misgivings because of her deafness, was soon recognized as a gracious and charming hostess and behind the scenes, as a real housekeeper. Her fluent and graceful French, learned as a girl, was another of her assets.

They were the guests on brief visits with the Theodore Marburgs at the American Legation in Brussels where there was much conversation about world peace, and with the Walter Hines Pages in the London Embassy. On the latter visit Henry van Dyke also preached in Oxford at the American Thanksgiving celebration. Christmas was spent with the Chauncey M. Depews at their Chateau d'Annel in the forest of Compiègne with many other guests among whom was Rudyard Kipling and his family. Henry van Dyke wrote:

"Kipling is a tremendous but a very despondent imperialist: He firmly believes that there will be a civil war in England before long. I think that his interest in modern machinery, automobiles and flying machines, has somewhat overshadowed his interest in human beings, so that his imagination is more synthetic and less sympathetic than it used to be. But he is a most interesting fellow and very good to talk with.

"We had a lot of French people to dinner every night as well as an Indian Prince who came on Sunday. On Christmas afternoon there was a big Christmas tree in the ballroom at which all the people of the village with their children assisted and received gifts. The curé of Longueil, a very intelligent man, was there and I had a good deal of talk with him. He told me that he had been twenty-eight years in charge of that parish and that he had a hard time owing to the difficulties raised by the anti-clericalism of the government. I think that anti-clericalism is a bad thing and that ecclesiasticism is almost equally as bad. We have every reason to be thankful for the absolute freedom which exists in America. If religion cannot take care of itself, it is not worth taking care of."

There were many strings to Henry van Dyke's bow. He always had a voluminous correspondence and he never failed to find time for his friends. To Dean West he despatched some orange tulip bulbs for the garden of the new Graduate College at Princeton. Mr. and Mrs. Harry F. Reid, beloved brother and sister-in-law of Mrs. van Dyke and himself, were their first guests at the Legation. Henry van Dyke wanted to write but there was no time. On leaving America he had counted on being able to assemble the novel which for several years had been in his mind. *Scribner's Magazine* had announced for 1914, "A Famous Writer's First Long Novel." But even in that first year at The Hague he could not get at it. It was not the weight of his sixty-one years, which he carried easily, that prevented. It was rather his conscientious devotion to the pressing duties of his office and his characteristic inability to refuse any immediate opportunity that was presented. Recognizing that diplomacy depended much for its success upon right relations between diplomats he spent a great deal of time with his colleagues and sedulously cultivated their understanding and good will.

Duties connected with the President's Peace Plan of April 24, 1913; preparations for the Third Hague Peace Conference, which had been considerably neglected by all the nations, and, for the Third International Opium Conference; an important International Convention on Education for 1914; and problems arising out of the opening of the Panama Canal and the repercussions of the Mexican situation made his hands full. He was alert on his international watch tower, industrious in acquiring a particular knowledge of the Netherlands and its people even to learning the language—which he soon read easily and spoke with ready inaccuracy. "This afternoon," he wrote in early January, "Paula (his daughter) and I buckled on our skates and started to Delft by a canal through the meadows. Everybody is on the ice now. It is interesting to see how naturally the Hollanders take to it and how jolly and good-humored they become as soon as they begin *schaatsenterijden*. We asked our way to Delft in Dutch, and got many smiles and sufficient information. . . . If the ice holds I want to get away for two or three days as soon as possible to skate the round of the eleven cities of Friesland."

Before he was well settled in the Legation he had begun work for the Third Peace Conference. It was both the first task of his office as the President had charged him and the thing nearest to his heart as plainly appears in his letters, despatches and other activities. In a few weeks he sent a despatch to the Secretary of State accurately pointing out the difficulties in the way and offering two suggestions for their possible solution. These suggestions, both of which were adopted by the United States Government, proposed first—in order to carry out the expressed judgment of the American commissioners to the Second Conference that the Third Conference should not be under the control or dominance of any one nation,—that the Queen of the Netherlands as chief of that country whose hospitality the Conference would enjoy might be invited to take the initiative in calling it; and second "that the Permanent Administrative Council of the Court of Arbitration at The Hague (which is composed of the Netherlands Minister of Foreign Affairs and the diplomatic representatives of the contracting Powers accredited to The Hague), might serve, with the authorization of the respective governments, as the 'preparatory committee', recommended in the final resolution of 1907."

The whole matter was exceedingly difficult and required the most careful handling. Andrew Carnegie was greatly disappointed over the doubt prevalent about the holding of the Conference. He wrote forthrightly but with complete disregard of diplomatic procedure, that perhaps Henry van Dyke would go to Berlin and with Ambassador Gerard secure the aid of the German Emperor to assure the holding of the Conference. Meantime Henry van Dyke industriously was discovering that there were not only practical obstacles in divergences of opinions and procedures to be overcome but—what he had not suspected when he first came to The Hague—a real disinclination to work for peace in certain quarters. Some of the storm signs were already apparent in the inner circles.

Against these difficulties he contended vigorously with heart and mind. Often in after days he recalled with delight his frequent conferences on these matters with Mr. Loudon, the Netherlands Minister for Foreign Affairs. The picture of these two men, so different in their personal appearance and their previous experiences and yet so similar in their essentially cheerful and hopeful natures and united in their wrestling for peace, is unforgettable.

"They went about their greatest tasks like noble boys at play."

In America the popular impression gained ground—due apparently to Henry van Dyke's well-known activities—that America was to have the honor of calling the Conference; but Henry van Dyke was working at a far deeper level than the popular impression. He felt the urgency of the situation to such a degree that the question of who was to have the honor of proposing this or that was to him merely a pawn to be traded for the promotion of world peace.

When March came the outlook seemed to him much brighter and he even wrote hopefully about his contemplated novel to E. L. Burlingame, the Editor of *Scribner's Magazine*:

"I understand and feel all that you say about the magazine that lives in the future. My sense of loyalty to it is strong and I do not forget my obligation. I appreciate the way in which you put the matter, making allowance for the changed conditions which have arisen out of my appointment here. Fortunately these conditions are now becoming a little easier. . . . I feel that it will be right to take things a little more easily and literature begins to look up in that poor assemblage of fragments which I am accustomed to call my mind. I have already gotten four or five interesting and delightful books which bear upon the subject of the story about which I am thinking, and as I read them the tale itself seems to be dimly moving behind the scenes. It may stand out clearly one of these days, but before I can write it, I must visit Brittany and go over the ground carefully. This is all that I can say about it at present. But it means at least the survival of a hope deferred."

Alas, the novel was not to be. Never again did he seriously consider writing it. Despite the efforts of peace lovers all over the world events were coming to a head and the policies of blood and iron were inexorably prevailing. The embryo of the novel lies in a note-book neglected from this time forth. Even in later years the pressure of something immediate that needed doing prevented him from taking it up again, until at last he knew that it had definitely passed into the limbo of unrealizable dreams. Perhaps also the feeling which he several times voiced, that the novel was not his *métier* had something to do with it.

But even amid the constant pressure of events and official duties he could not altogether lay down his pencil. At night and in brief pauses through the days he meditated as a poet upon the kaleidoscopic world about him. "The Standard Bearer" written in February 1914 expressed the struggling of a soul amid the peril of uncertain ways, and "Stain not the Sky" with prophetic insight uttered the peace lover's plea for the preservation of the one realm as yet unviolated by war.

Meantime he served as an extra-canonical Warden of the English Church at The Hague, frequently read the lessons, preached a number of times for the Rector, Rev. Herbert Ratford, as well as in other churches, and found time to lend his support to the Dutch and English boy scouts. "The world supposes and says," he wrote me in March, "that I have accepted an honor and abandoned my calling. Not so, as God is my judge! I have come here to work for a definite end in the service of my Master,—the coming of peace on earth. All the other duties connected with my office, and they are many, are accepted as means to the end. . . . For myself, I want no credit or honor,—only to get the work done. It will be a long job, to do away with war. I have no illusions on the subject. But I have a hope, and a forward-reaching faith."

To keep himself fit for his work—fly-fishing was not easily accessible—he even took up golf at which he was always inept and which with a mixture of disgust and wrath he denounced as "a game invented by demons for the torture of imbeciles." But though the diplomatic golf was fearful to observe the companionship was good and the lovely greensward and the North Sea breezes were a delight. All his letters too are full of expressions of pleasure in the stately forests of The Hague and in the acres and acres of flower fields which heralded the spring.

The peace plans would not move beyond a certain point. Something puzzling, baffling, mysterious was in the way. At a court function in Luxembourg in March he found further support for the feeling which he had gathered in The Hague that the Germans were distinctly indifferent or even hostile to peace. But it was in early June, when he went again to Luxembourg to gather material for a report on the steel industry and to get some trout fishing by way of resting his greatly over-taxed eyes, that he became wholly convinced that Germany was ready for war and intended it at the first convenient opportunity. At a luncheon given by Prime Minister Eyschen he heard that redoubtable gentleman say with great good humor to the French and German ministers that doubtless one of their two countries might march an army through the famous Luxembourger Loch before long, and then with inquiring inflexion to the German Minister: "Most likely it will be your country, Excellency?" And a few days later fishing over the German border he watched the innumerable trains of German soldiers on their "Pentecost vacation" to Trier. It was at Wasserbillig, seven miles from Trier, on the Luxembourg frontier, that the German forces entered the neutral country August 2nd on their march to Belgium.

Back in the Netherlands again he went to the tercentenary celebration of the University of Groningen as the delegate of Princeton University, and, on behalf of the delegates of ten American Universities and two Academies who were present, made a brief but ringing speech in Dutch. As the Latin epistle which he was also to present was delayed in the mails he secured the aid of the daughter of the Burgomaster and together they concocted a noble scroll of parchment decorated with flowing orange and black ribbons which was presented "without explanation and with a manner which indicated that it was the most important document of the day." The following morning the delayed epistle replaced its makeshift substitute, but the smile between the conspirators remained.

About the middle of July Henry van Dyke in his indefatigable habit of looking at his task from every angle gathered his family, after meeting his son in Antwerp on July 10th, and set out for further travel in North Holland to visit some of the dead cities of the Zuider Zee and tour Friesland and Overijssel. It was in the dreaming city of Enkhuizen one beautiful night as we walked the quiet streets under the tinkling of the carillons that we spoke of the European outlook. "The situation grows more ominous," said he, "I will go back to see that everything is in order in the Legation." The presentiment seemed impossible in that atmosphere and even after we had been several days in The Hague Henry van Dyke wrote on July 30th to John H. Finley: "Next Monday we are expecting to go to Luxembourg for a couple of weeks of rest and a little fishing." But he added, "provided a general European war does not break out between now and then, which I do not expect." The last phrase was rather a wish than a judgment. Henry van Dyke's clear mind had brought him back to his post though his heart still beat incessantly: *War cannot be*. In his judgment the die was cast when he read in the Legation on July 24th the Austro-Hungarian note to Servia, and said to me: "That means an immense war. God knows how far it will go and how long it will last." Events rushed on like a nightmare. And on the very day before he had hoped to go fishing in Luxembourg the German army entered the Grand Duchy, rolled into the ditch the motor van which the Luxembourgers had drawn up across the road and which they declined to move at German orders, and the march on Belgium was begun.

Henry van Dyke was not at all incognizant of the complex factors that had led up to the outbreak of war, but one cannot understand his clear position from the very beginning without recognizing that from his first-hand observations he was convinced that Germany had deliberately chosen the method of war to settle her problems. As he saw it the plans of the world to substitute the methods of arbitration, conciliation and adjudication for the arbitrament of the sword were repudiated by Germany and the hopes of mankind for peace temporarily destroyed. He never thought the issue was that of the angels against the demons but equally he never doubted that nothing could be done for peace until those whom he was convinced had chosen the sword were stopped. Amid the horror and repugnance of feeling that these events aroused he turned calmly and with immense concentration to his particular duties. Promptly the Legation was organized to meet the oncoming rush of travellers. Henry van Dyke immediately saw that the Netherlands was "the neck of the bottle through which must pour the flood of home-going Americans." Carefully selecting volunteer assistants he set them at desks throughout the spacious rooms of the Legation and was ready with an organization capable of meeting every need when the horde of bewildered people arrived. Among those with whom he manned the new posts were first of all Professor George Grafton Wilson who was promptly confirmed by the Department of State as Counsellor of Legation and who was always a tower of strength and wisdom for the perilous and heavy weeks that followed. Others were Professor Philip M. Brown, Professor F. J. Moore, Hon. Charles H.

Sherrill, Charles Edward Russell and Mrs. Russell, Alexander R. Gulick, Van Santvoord Merle-Smith and Tertius van Dyke. These added to the regular staff: Marshall Langhorne, Secretary of Legation, Captain A. H. Sunderland, and later Captain Arthur Poillon, Military Attachés; G. Evans Hubbard, and J. J. Heldson Rix, long time clerk of the Legation and his daughter, Miss Agnes Rix, who was afterward the Minister's invaluable private secretary in America, and Miss Irene Rix, equipped the legation.

So Henry van Dyke was ready not only with a well-organized Legation but with a clearly defined understanding that the Legation was to be free of outside interference by itinerant visitors from Washington. With exact correctness he proposed to keep entirely in his own hands the exercise of his office. His own relations, official and personal, with the Netherlands Minister of Foreign Affairs were sound and cordial—not to say affectionate. He had learned to admire Mr. Loudon's courage, skill and tact, and as the days went on more and more he recognized the greatness of mind and heart of the Foreign Minister of a state entirely surrounded by belligerents. There can be no doubt that the relationship between these two men is in large part the key to the steadfast defense of human rights that was made at The Hague.

The most pressing problem at the Legation was the securing of funds for the stranded Americans who straightway poured into the Netherlands from all over Europe. Professor Wilson has described in the New York *Evening Post* for October 3, 1914 the brilliant plan made by the Minister to meet the emergency:

"Declaration of war caused general and financial panic. Runs immediately followed on a majority of the banks, some of which temporarily stopped payment. No foreign bills were bought. Letters of credit were useless; likewise travellers' checks, except those of the American Express Company.

Dr. van Dyke at once conferred with the Dutch Foreign Minister regarding the situation, with the purpose of securing relief for Americans. The Foreign Minister expressed a willingness to give financial aid, and to that end an arrangement was made whereby checks and drafts on letters of credit endorsed by Dr. van Dyke would be cashed by the Netherlands Bank, or, that failing, by the Treasury of the Netherlands.

This undertaking on the part of the Netherlands Government was made at a time when there was no assurance that checks and drafts would be taken up in gold in the Netherlands, and at a time when collections on drafts were impossible in England, because of the then existing moratorium, and seemingly impossible in America because of the uncertainty of communication and the risk to be incurred should gold be shipped. The necessary confirmation and authorization of the United States State Department was secured on August 3, at which date the endorsement of checks and drafts on letters of credit began until gold was received from the Relief Commission and gold from the American bankers came. Checks and drafts to the amount of about $50,000 were endorsed by the Minister for strictly necessary requirements.

On September 5, the paper held by the Netherlands Bank was taken up by the American Legation in American gold on the authorization from the Government. The Netherlands Government asked no interest.

This important financial transaction had its inception in the mind of Dr. van Dyke, and was by him carried out. The entire credit is due him in affording the means of relief for the American citizens. The plan fully met and entirely settled a very difficult financial situation, one that caused great embarrassment, not only at The Hague, but in London and Berlin. There was no precedent.

Nothing could have been accomplished except by one enjoying the fullest confidence of the Foreign Minister of the Netherlands and that Government. Dr. van Dyke had and has that confidence to the fullest degree. Moreover, Dr. van Dyke's handling of the whole affair shows business ability of a high order. His decision to draw drafts directly on the banks and bankers issuing the letters of credit instead of through London correspondent banks and bankers, as usually done, was a wise one, and one highly approved by the representatives of the American bankers who came to The Hague.

"Because of the moratorium in England, serious delay, embarrassment, and privation would have resulted during the period between declaration of war and the arrival of relief from America, had it not been for the prompt action of the American Minister at The Hague."

Henry van Dyke disliked to deal with finances. But when the Banker's Committee arrived on the battleship *Tennessee* some weeks

later they were more than surprised to learn that there were no
financial difficulties to straighten out at The Hague. And when they
heard what the Minister had done one of them remarked to a member of the staff: "That's pretty damned good for an amateur!"

Van Santvoord Merle-Smith and Tertius van Dyke were appointed
to interview those who asked for endorsements on their checks and
letters of credit. Most of the time they were much affected by the
courageous conduct of all sorts of Americans under great stress. But
once in a while they were surprised. A resplendent lady approached
one difficult day with the demand for an endorsement for $1,000.
According to instructions I asked as mildly as I could for what purposes the money was required. The conversation proceeded to a
point where to my fellow workers' delight I was addressed as a
young upstart coupled with a demand to see the Minister. I took the
lady's card to the harassed Minister who ordered me to wait as the
complainant entered. "But I want to tell you about him," she protested regarding me with hostility. "That's why he's waiting" said
the Minister affably. So he listened gravely while the lady described
how she felt about me, and dismissed her by saying: "That's his job:
to keep endorsements down to amounts for absolute necessities," remarked to me with a laugh after she swept out: "Now you *know*
what you are," and turned to his desk. Late that afternoon the lady
who had toured all places of credit without avail returned to secure
endorsement, but through Van Santvoord Merle-Smith, for $150.
There was simply no money to be had anywhere except through the
plan set up by the Minister.

Endless incidents of the events of those early weeks of war spring
to mind. Amid them all stands the steady figure of Henry van Dyke
always thinking ahead of new situations and with good humor and
common sense straightening out the constant tangle of affairs. I see
him in the morning sunlight outside the Legation addressing a
throng that the ever helpful Dutch Boy Scouts were struggling to
handle, as wild rumors were making them unmanageable: "Aren't
we all Americans here?" he began smilingly. "When those inside
the Legation are attended to you'll each get your turn. There's plenty
of time. I'll see you're informed of any danger. Enjoy the air. The

Hague is a beautiful city and as safe as any place in the world. So long. We'll see you inside soon." He waved his hand and went in. Some one laughed. Another cheered. The trouble was over. I see him again at Rotterdam as he went down to the sailing of each ship with Americans aboard. What speeches he made and how he radiated assurance as he went about. "Remember, there's a war going on so don't be too angry if you get a boiled egg when you asked for a fried egg," he admonished. "Be thankful, be thankful," he cried, "and do your bit." When he could get hold of anyone who was spreading rumors or frightening the helpless he was furious. Any such got short shrift and biting words.

Passport questions were always difficult especially as The Hague teemed with spies. One day a group of American Indians who had been stranded in Hamburg with a Wild West Show won their way somehow to the Legation. As Henry van Dyke heard their plain unvarnished tale with its evident truthfulness he turned to his Counsellor Wilson with a twinkle in his eyes. "I guess," he said, "if anybody is entitled to an American passport, these are the people." So they were returned home with smiling faces and guttural thanks.

Nothing was more useful in keeping order among the throngs who besieged the Legation than Professor Wilson's system of handing out numbered cards to the people. Once in a while some one got the idea that he was above the system. "Do *I* have to have a card?" would reverberate an indignant voice. And then, if the rooms were quiet enough, would be heard the suave voice of the Counsellor: "But surely you approve the American system of equality?" A rustle of approval from those who were waiting their turn, and the incident was over.

It was hard for some people to realize that war was in progress. A lady who was returning to America via England was for long unable to understand why the Legation would not correspond with the British Foreign Office to secure the lifting of the regular British quarantine on dogs. That her poor little Fido should have to return alone to America on a Dutch vessel was certainly a matter for diplomatic intervention.

Some unauthorized person hearing that there was an excellent communication system running at The Hague—a system that brought news of families divided by the inexorable sword of war— thoughtlessly let loose an avalanche of mail upon the Legation. One such letter is unforgettable. A long screed from a man in the North of England to his German sweetheart was accompanied by a brief explanation for the Minister: "This letter is written in poor German, but I think she will understand it."

General Sherrill who patiently dealt with such letters and the mass of telegrams about "lost" Americans rose quietly one day as some fellow attempted to display his own importance. "I used to be somebody too," he said, "but in war time I'm satisfied to be a communications clerk. And if you'll leave me," he added sitting down, "I'll go on with it." Nor can one forget Mr. Gulick's glittering eye as he limped over to a neighboring desk to report that a fellow who had been pestering him over a florin's cost for a telegram had "compromised the matter by contributing $100 to the relief fund."

From morning to night the Legation hummed with activity. But a deliberately staged hour in the afternoon when tea was ceremoniously served in the garden broke the day for workers and visitors. On these occasions Mrs. van Dyke and her daughters played a part that had to be experienced to be appreciated. Certainly this social half-hour was no small factor in maintaining an air of serenity and confidence amid the steady strain. Frequent night conferences of the staff kept the organization in smooth running order. Sleep had to fend for itself, and it was commonly said that the Minister slept on his way upstairs, so frequent were his returns to his desk after retiring. Again and again he was found at his desk by those who were on duty to receive the night messages. On August 21st Henry van Dyke reported that "Americans are arriving in flight from Germany at the rate of from four to six hundred a day," and that "we have despatched from Rotterdam last Saturday about two thousand passengers on the S. S. Noordam, and tomorrow morning fully as many will go off on the S. S. Rijndam." To keep these people distributed so that they could find places to stay while awaiting passage, to keep them supplied with needed money, to prevent them from becoming the prey of the rumor-mongers, to put a stop to the unneutral activities of some and the unneutral speech of many, to bring separated friends and families together was a large order. Henry van Dyke described it laconically in a despatch: "Americans in this country have been perfectly safe and entirely comfortable— except the nervous ones."

But he had far more to do than this. As an American observer in a neutral country he watched with keen eyes the turn of events and reported pungently and frequently about the preservation of neutral rights wherever affected. He saw at once the advantages of the neutrality of the Netherlands not only to America and the Netherlands but to "the maintenance of that intercourse which is essential to the progress of civilization" and he cooperated vigorously with the Netherlands programme for that purpose. In addition eternal vigilance was needed to prevent the planting of spies in the Legation or the use of communications for war purposes. On August 15th the newspapers of a belligerent country reported that certain warnings had been transmitted through the intervention of a neutral power so sure were they that they could "use" the Legation at The Hague. Unhappily for them the announcement was premature—for even while the presses were printing the announcement the Minister was suavely expounding the law about neutral obligations to the disappointed agent of a hopefully naïve nation—and refusing to transmit the warnings.

Meantime Henry van Dyke was watching closely the matter of neutral rights and of international law regarding wars, and reporting carefully on all violations. On the basis of a first-hand report by Captain Williams on the bombing of Antwerp on August 24th he reported: "I believe that a firm protest against such clear violations of the common law of humanity among nations is the only hope of checking the spirit of ferocity and scientific blood-thirsty barbarianism which seems to be growing in this conflict." To the President he wrote on September 10th, 1914:

"In all my despatches to the Department of State, and in the advice which I have urgently given to Americans here, I have followed strictly your admirable declaration of neutrality.

But in view of the uncertainty of human life I feel that it is my duty to leave with you personally a simple statement of some impressions which have been deeply made on my mind by the conflict which is now devastating Europe. Pardon me if the effort to shorten the statement makes it seem too plain.

I. The beginning of the war belongs to Austria and Germany. Not only did they make the first declarations, they also made the first active preparations some time before. e.g.,

1) On the first of *June*, while fishing on the border of Luxembourg, I saw the hundreds of trains crowded with soldiers, who were being massed along the line between *Cologne* and *Treves*.

2) Thousands of German Reservists were called to the colors from *Brazil* in June. [Here follows a reference to certain confidential conversations with Colleagues.]

II. The conduct of the war has been marked by great atrocities. I believe no newspaper stories. But eye-witnesses have told me of the aerial bomb-dropping on Antwerp, the ruin of Louvain, and the utter devastation of numerous Belgian towns. It seems clear that Germany is waging this war with a purpose of making Terror her ally.

III. The talk of a race-conflict, 'Teuton against Slav', is utterly misleading. This is really a clash of systems: militarism against democracy. The strong hand claims the right to prevail. Austria refused Servia's offer to accept her ultimatum on all points but one, and to submit that one to the Hague Court. Germany refused England's proposal of a four-power mediation between Austria and Servia, for the purpose of limiting the war. Germany invaded the countries of Luxembourg and Belgium, whose neutrality she herself had guaranteed. In justifying this action the German Chancellor said in the Reichstag, 'Necessity knows no law.' The 'necessity' is the German purpose to rule Europe.

IV. The United States has no part in a European war. Our present duty of strict neutrality has been admirably defined by you. But our interests,—not merely commercial interests, but vital interests,—are necessarily affected by this conflict. We can hardly ignore the future possibilities and consequences of the war. Germany has already conquered Belgium and holds the greater part of its territory as a province. She aims now to crush France which stands between her and England. She does not wish to visit Paris again. She wants to go to London this time. The next station beyond London is on the shores of the new world.

V. German doctors of philosophy have been the most scornful critics of the Monroe Doctrine. They call it obsolete. The German propaganda in the United States is immense and subtle. The German ambition in South America is well known. [Here follows reference to confidential conversations with Colleagues.]

It is true that many United States citizens have been treated with almost flattering courtesy in Germany. Some were stripped naked, searched, and imprisoned in the early weeks of the war. But this seems to have stopped. Now, *trains-de-luxe* are provided; flowers and hot coffee are brought to the cars containing American refugees, and they are provided with copies of the German 'White Book'. This is very pleasant, but it does not alter the facts upon which a judgment of the international situation must be based.

I can not withhold from you, my friend and my Chief, the strong conviction which is pressed upon me.

The domination of Europe by the sword of Germany would be a menace to the United States.

This war is the greatest argument for peace that the world has ever seen. But it can not be a peace based upon conquest."

To Hamilton Holt he wrote on September 16th:

"I am killed with work here. This is the open door for Europe, the funnel through which Germany, Austria, Switzerland, Russia, pour their American refugees. In addition we are looking for the lost and wounded of every nation. I have organized an international banking bureau, a correspondence bureau, a registration office, and a department of consolation for nervous folks, as annexes to the diplomatic task which is heavy enough in itself.

"But after all, this kind of work is what America stands for. Blot out the race-feud. Serve humanity. Resist tyrants. Make the war-god obsolete. Show the world a more excellent way. For that cause a man should be glad to face death, in the field, or in the place of work."

By October most of the Americans passing through the Netherlands were gone except for the difficult cases of the "lame ducks" that inflicted themselves upon the Legation and the Consulates. With the fall of Antwerp came the vast movement of Belgian refugees into the Netherlands. On October 14th Henry van Dyke reported more than 400,000, almost all of them in a state of extreme poverty and distress.

"Nothing like that sad, fear-smitten exodus has been seen on earth in modern times," he wrote. "There was something in it at once fateful, pathetic, and irresistible, which recalled De Quincey's famous story of *The Flight of a Tartar Tribe*. No barrier in the Holland border could have kept that flood of Belgian refugees out. They were an enormous flock of sheep and lambs, harried by the Werwolf, and fleeing for their lives. But Holland did not want a barrier. She stood with open doors and arms, offering an asylum to the distressed and persecuted."

In administering funds given by generous Americans for their aid Henry van Dyke worked with the highest satisfaction with Mr. Th. Stuart, President of the Netherlands Relief Committee, and with Baron van Tuyll van Serooskerken, the Queen's General Commissioner.

Characteristically he made a tour of the ruined cities and villages even unto Antwerp. He saw the shell hole in the great cathedral in the very wall where, until it was hastily removed for safety, had hung Rubens' "Descent from the Cross."

Beside the as yet unburied corpses of men and animals he conversed with those who were salvaging what remained of their ruined homes in towns and villages across the desolate countryside. In the orderly refugee camps in Holland he was a frequent visitor encouraging the workers and bearing them aid, and forgetting not amid the tragedy to carry pockets full of bijoux and candies for the children too young to know what had happened to them. A sense of horror and of repugnance battled within him. He hated the awful mess. But he did what he could. With controlled but nonetheless burning indignation he reported to the State Department on October 20th, the effort of Germany to evade the responsibility of providing food for impoverished Belgium. When the Commission for Relief in Belgium under Herbert Hoover took over this responsibility in the name of humanity Henry van Dyke as a member of the Commission was kept busy holding open the door through which all supplies had to pass. He made protests, remonstrances and polite suggestions about what would happen if the flow of food were interrupted. There were perilous days for that great enterprise. The actual dispatch of food into Belgium several times hung upon the ability of one man to win the consent of those who feared that it would be diverted from its proper destination. When the *S. S. Coblenz* arrived on November 1st he ordered the delivery of this shipment placed in the hands of the Secretary of the Legation, but the doubts and hesitations of the Allied Officials were not finally dissolved until he remarked: "That food goes to Belgium tomorrow if I have to put an American *with an American flag in his hands* on top of each load." The cargo went through after a stormy interview. As Henry van Dyke wrote to the former Counsellor of Legation. "I think it is time for ———— and others to find out that neutrals have certain rights which must be respected, and that the U. S. proposes to attend to its obligations of humanity without reference to any outside interference." This also was a time when it was important to see that the out-pouring of humanitarian impulses was rightly directed lest gifts be misused and the givers discouraged. It is too long a story for these pages. Let it suffice to say that Henry van Dyke listened carefully to the reports of the competent investigators sent by the Red Cross and other organizations, was in constant touch with the delightfully indefatigable Mr. Th. Stuart, regularly visited all work to which he directed gifts, kept himself accessible to any who had actual information to convey, and conducted a large correspondence with America on the basis of the knowledge he acquired. Accurate information conveyed with the interpretation of the human touch was the theme of that correspondence.

Occasionally he wrote personally to some of his friends of his "deep impression of the horror, hatefulness and essential insanity of war." Yet he felt that there was a moral distinction between the combatants in this particular war. To one who wrote him sadly of the vanishing of all that is gentle and urbane and kindly and tender in the world he replied:

"There are still some Philip Sidneys left on the battlefield, and there are millions of quiet, faithful laboring people who desire peace and in the end will obtain it. The war-madness is frightful. But even in its worst paroxysms we must distinguish between those who fight merely for the bare assertion of power, and those who fight for honor and fidelity to pledged obligations. Times like these try men's souls and women's souls too. They bring out the difference between those who believe in fundamental righteousness and human kindness, and those who have no aim except ambition and the increase of wealth. It is the tone which dominates on one side or the other, which determines the moral quality of the strife."

After three months of constant and diverse activity the work of the Legation began to settle down to a more or less steady routine and Henry van Dyke realized that he was even more tired than he felt and that one of his eyes which had troubled him for six months was practically blind. He received permission to return to New York for treatment and wrote Hamilton Mabie:

"It makes me glad to think that I may see you soon, provided we do not get caught by a mine on the way over. About that I do not care a cent. In fact a little touch of danger is refreshing after this terrific grind of work and perfectly safe work which we have had here."

On his return he found the country full of rumors beginning with one to the effect that he was bearing a peace proposal to the President. "Dr. van Dyke Back, Interviews Himself" ran the headline in the *Evening World*. He avoided leading questions and yet held attention on neutral rights and the hope of world peace. As he left the White House arrayed in his characteristic black cape coat and tall hat an eager newsreel photographer approached him saying: "I have orders to get a hundred feet of you." With a wave of the hand Henry van Dyke passed by: "Humph, there is only five feet six inches of me."

At the White House and the State Department, though of course this was not public knowledge at the time—he bore witness to his strong conviction that no peace proposal was worth considering that did not include evacuation of violated neutral territory and reparation for damages, the submission of all war-claims for indemnification to a non-partisan tribunal, and the bringing of the original *casus belli* before an international court. Upon the doing of these things the great issue of disarmament must wait.[1]

[1] The statement is made by Henry van Dyke in *Fighting for Peace* (written in the hectic summer of 1917) that he bore to Washington at this time (late November 1914), "a personal, unofficial message" from Sir Edward Grey which concerned America's part in the

He found refreshment and rest among his friends. At the Lotos Club dinner he said with a barely disguised sigh of relief: "I came back to have my eyes patched up. It's done them good already to see you. I'm glad to see that there are no submarines nor mines in the waters where the Lotos blooms." In a speech at Alexander Hall in Princeton he reminded the audience that "after their madness the nations must return to the Palace of Peace at The Hague." Though he was thoroughly convinced of Germany's primary responsibility for the outbreak of war he rarely failed to note that war itself was insanity and he never failed to hold attention on the day of peace that was to follow.

Back in The Hague just before Christmas 1914 his outspoken admiration of the President whom he frankly regarded as the chief

council of peace after the war and her attitude toward "a league of nations pledged to resist and punish any war begun without previous submission of the cause to international investigation and judgment."

This statement, several times repeated in addresses and letters, cannot be verified from outside sources. Unfortunately it was never discussed by Henry van Dyke and myself,—I having assumed, until after his death when the systematic study of his papers was begun, that the message of September 7, 1915 (see below page 339) was his first specific message to Washington about the League.

I am particularly indebted to the following persons whom I have consulted on the matter: Mr. Ray Stannard Baker writes that there is no record of the 1914 message in the papers of President Wilson. Neither Mr. Marshall Langhorne, then Secretary of the Legation at The Hague, nor Henry van Dyke's private secretary have any recollection of it. The Hon. Theodore Marburg, author of the historic volumes, *The Development of the League of Nations Idea* has no corroborative evidence; nor has Professor George Grafton Wilson, formerly Counsellor at the Legation. The only record I can find at the Department of State is of the 1915 message. Lord Tyrrell (Sir Edward Grey's secretary in 1914) and Sir Eric Drummond can throw no light on the matter. Sir Samuel Hoare, the present British Principal Secretary of State for Foreign Affairs, informs me (after having a search made) that there is no record of such a message in Sir Edward Grey's private papers or in the official correspondence, and no record of a meeting between the two men at the time in question.

In my opinion the probable conclusion is that Henry van Dyke in the stress of the summer of 1917, when he was writing *Fighting for Peace*, became confused as to the date of his 1915 message the contents of which later message is practically identical with the presumptive 1914 message, yet contains no reference to it.

It must however be equally frankly said that if this is the case it is the only confusion of important dates that I have found in Henry van Dyke's careful records; and it must furthermore be admitted that "a personal, unofficial message" might have been conveyed without ever reaching the records.

It is recorded that on December 2, 1914 Henry van Dyke was a guest of the President at an informal luncheon at the White House.

hope for the restoration of peace, his imaginative sympathy with the sufferings of plain people everywhere, and his clear understanding of the responsibilities of his office held him neutral in conduct; though in private he could never forget what he had seen and learned on trusted authority about the origin and conduct of the war. Concentrating on the defense of neutral rights he did not fail to protest against the British interference with the American mails as well as with the German interruption of his official correspondence with Luxembourg. He launched the protest that put a stop to the imposing of German taxes on food imported into Belgium by the Commission for Relief, insisting that the neutral character of that work must be maintained at all costs. The tax already collected was returned. He wrestled daily for the defense of the rights of neutral commerce:

"A practical stoppage of that commerce," he wrote the State Department on March 6th, "either by the sinking of merchant ships by submarines, or by the imprisonment of such ships in belligerent harbors, would amount in effect to an unlawful attack upon the economic life of neutral nations.

It would therefore not be merely a measure of reprisal between belligerents. It would be also a measure of damage to neutrals, and thus an illegitimate pressure upon them to take sides in the war, since a peaceful abstinence would no longer secure them the benefits of non-contraband trade under international law.

The Declaration of Paris would thus be abolished. The right of property of non-combatants on the sea would be subject entirely to the will and the alleged necessities of the belligerents. . . . In my judgment thoughtful public opinion here looks to the United States for leadership in a firm, united maintenance, by pacific means, of the common rights of neutral nations in commerce during the time of War."

After receiving word from the Prime Minister of Luxembourg that a bread famine there was imminent, Henry van Dyke began a lengthy correspondence seeking to find a way to secure supplies for the helpless Grand Duchy.

Finally at the end of April 1915 he went there with his son to investigate personally. It was a significant journey and threatened the end of his diplomatic service. According to German instructions we were met at the German frontier by a fine German officer, Captain Von Mumm who was to "show the best roads for travel to Luxembourg." Henry van Dyke grinned but accepted the necessity. But when we arrived at the Luxembourg frontier he turned politely to the Captain and remarked: "Being safely and pleasantly conducted by you through German territory I now have the honor of inviting you to be my guest in the sovereign territory of the Grand Duchy to which I am the accredited American representative." The Captain saw that the tables were turned and accepted gracefully. The German doctrine of "the occupation of Luxembourg for purposes of transportation only" was carefully investigated. As we sat one evening with one of the military commanders and his staff the commander politely asked Henry van Dyke: "Do you hear any objections to the conduct of my troops?" "O, no," replied the Minister promptly, "no objections to their conduct—but plenty to their presence." There followed a blank silence which the American found it unnecessary to interrupt. To cut short the tale of an interesting journey to many towns where we saw the remnants of the wheat supplies under guard in the town halls and watched in the streets frail children with baskets begging for scraps from door to door, and heard full reports from the government—Henry van Dyke wired the State Department:

"After six days careful investigation of conditions in Grand Duchy of Luxembourg, I am convinced that there is danger of a famine within six weeks unless work of the Belgian Relief Commission can be extended to the Grand Duchy of Luxembourg. The Grand Duchess has requested me personally to telegraph the President:

'I appeal to the well known chivalrous sympathies of the President for an interest in my unhappy and innocent country to the end that the Belgian Relief Commission may bring us food for the civil population of the Grand Duchy of Luxembourg. We will pay for it. We accept beforehand all conditions imposed.'

I earnestly request to endeavor to secure consent to carry out this humane work."

But something mysterious was in the way. The Department of

State would not act except as the Commission for Relief in Belgium indicated and although Henry van Dyke appealed directly to the Commission there were "insurmountable obstacles." Finally informed by the Department that he had done all that duty required or the conditions made possible in the matter of furnishing food to Luxembourg, and learning that his zeal was being unfavorably commented upon, he wrote the President offering to retire if the President felt any lack of confidence in his service. A friendly letter from the President put an end to that idea. On July 5th he wrote his son who had just returned to America:

"You will have seen by the newspapers, probably, that my efforts to get food for Luxembourg were more successful on the French side than on the English. After the Department of State politely told me (on somebody's suggestion) that I had done enough at London, I began to talk with my French colleagues here, and found a very sympathetic reception. The result is that a small, but I hope sufficient amount of flour is going through from Switzerland with French consent every fortnight."

Henry van Dyke was not one to stop working when he was convinced that he had a good cause. Besides he always had toward the charming Grand Duchess something of the attitude of the old dragon fighter rescuing a lady in distress.

Meantime the naval and air operations in and around the North Sea and the Channel were increasingly imperilling Belgian relief and neutral trade. The Legation at The Hague was smothered with incidents demanding prompt and vigorous action. Americans with legitimate and delicate missions were constantly coming and going and seeking aid, while others with axes to grind boldly demanded assistance. Henry van Dyke held to his task. He administered the supplies for relief that poured upon the Legation. To a lady who had adopted eleven Belgian families to care for he proposed taking one more "to make it an even dozen," and she agreed. He even stood for several hours among a forlorn band of children to give them dolls from America, and, accepting the children's command to name them, obediently brought forth name after name and was rewarded with shy smiles.

But his spirit rebelled within him. "I have my days of tempestuous neutral emotion" he wrote his brother, Paul van Dyke. He could not see why the real business of the world should be at the mercy of violence. My diary hastily jotted down at night records his growing conviction that the catastrophe of war was forcing upon the United States the necessity of coming to the side of the Allies. On March 24th, 1915 he completed a brief article "Plain Words from America to Sister-Nations in Europe" which on May 12th was published in *The Outlook* under the nom-de-plume of *Cives Americanus*. It was a typical expression of Henry van Dyke's conviction of the personal responsibility of national leaders for their country's conduct. As twenty years before in New York he had insisted that the real source of municipal troubles was bad men in office, so now he argued that the German and Austrian leaders were primarily responsible for the war.

To David Jayne Hill he expressed his hatred of the universal dangers that war creates. This was about the time when several Dutch children playing on the shore had been killed by a mine that broke adrift.

"You say this is a bad time for historical work, I can assure you that it is an equally bad time for literary work. Even if I had some time free to give to it, the constant pressure of the nightmare of this war seems to make all writing futile. The course which affairs have taken is so stupid, so brutal and so bloody, that the power of ideas seems to be almost paralyzed, and nothing is left but a sense of force and fury working almost at hazard among the children of men. Think of this bomb dropping from aeroplanes, and this filling of the sea with drifting shells of death ready to explode at the touch of the first innocent traveller. Is it not all an appeal to chance in its worst form? Can it by any stretch of language be called 'civilized war'? It is hard to understand why one man should hate another man and wish to kill him because their views on the tariff or on the proper 'brand of culture' differ. But even suppose you grant that such a difference is a sufficient ground for hatred and enmity, the most that you could justify under that supposition would be the effort of one soldier to kill another soldier on the other side. But to launch death without an aim and in such a form that you cannot possibly know whether it will strike man, woman or child, is an act worthy not only of a savage, but also of a maniac. It looks to me as if the world had thrown away in this year a good part of what it had gained in three centuries of painful progress."

After carrying on his work from his bed for some weeks in July he received leave for a change and rest in England where he visited many old friends. On September 7, 1915 from his post he wrote a significant letter to the Secretary of State in which he reported:

"At a private dinner of six friends on September 1st, Sir William Tyrrell, secretary to Sir Edward Grey, talked with me apart and confidentially, with such evident intention that I feel that you should know what he said. The substance of his conversations was as follows:

He felt that Great Britain could not possibly consider any peace propositions, which did not include as a first term the full restoration of Belgium and Northern France. If I understood him correctly, he believed that compensation for damages by Germany should also be made. After that, he said, he thought that a 'league of nations' should be formed, to prevent the recurrence of such a war as this: to guarantee the respect of established neutrality and the maintenance of the general principles embodied in the Hague Conventions (here the details were not more closely defined), *and to punish future infractions and violations.* He said that in his opinion, if America were favorable to an idea of this kind, her good offices, mediation (call it what you like), would be welcome when the consideration of terms of peace became possible.

There was nothing formal or official in his conversation, which lasted for nearly an hour, but I felt sure that he had not spoken without reflection. He gave me a personal friendly message from Sir Edward Grey, who had gone to the country for a fortnight's vacation on account of his health."

And on September 29th he wrote Theodore Marburg:

"The war is in fact an interruption by violence of the peaceful development of the world. As long as violent men exist, such interruptions will always be possible. It is for that reason, I believe, that peace-loving men and nations should bind themselves together in agreement to punish such violations of the common interests of mankind, and should provide themselves with a force sufficient to carry out this idea of civilization against the opposition, studied or spasmodic, of those who reject it and trample it under foot. I do not suppose that such an idea will be easy to realize, but it is certainly not impossible, and it seems to be the guiding star of the efforts which should be made from this time on. I am not sure that peace can be 'enforced'. But I believe that it can be more surely protected."

Meantime an American newspaper correspondent who had been relieved by the British at Dover of certain official Austrian and German correspondence came to The Hague. Acting on instructions from Washington Henry van Dyke took up his passport and sent him back to the United States to report to the Government. There was much indignation over the incident which was thoroughly aired in the American press. Several papers with German sympathies renewed their outcry for the recall of Ambassador Page and Minister van Dyke. I remember the latter's wry smile as he remarked: "Funny how these pro-Germans think that neutrality consists in keeping an even balance between belligerents—as if there were no such thing as neutral rights and responsibilities!"

Henry van Dyke was satisfied that the cause of the Allies embodied the only hope of peace for the world. But he did not fail to note all violations of neutral rights. When the American mails were taken from the *Nieuw Amsterdam* on December 23rd, he wired: "I am convinced that a peremptory protest to the British Government is necessary to prevent recurrence of this act of violence and to protect the dignity of the United States. If the protest is disregarded, I believe reprisals should be made" and referred to his previous milder protest against a similar action in 1914.

In January 1916 he was summoned to Washington to discuss the trade situation and left with the Legation careful instructions that the policy of welcoming the Ford Peace Expedition as "American tourists" should be continued. In Washington he bore his witness in official circles to the necessity for the vigorous maintenance of American rights under international law; and in the pulpit of the Brick Church in New York he preached "Peace on Guard," a sermon that declared the reality of the inward peace which not even war could destroy—for those who fight to resist the exercise of violence. His short poems: "Lights Out" and "Remarks about Kings" which had been read at the Academy meeting in November, showed where he stood in the dilemma which faced America. "It is quite possible that the publication of either of these poems may get me into trouble—but I don't care," he had written Robert Underwood Johnson. A peaceful attitude combined with military preparedness, he told the Sons of the Revolution, was the only sound policy under the conditions. For himself the die was already cast, although he recognized the grounds for the French satisfaction in the fact that the United States was not actually in the war. As to what the United States would do if events continued their present course he believed with unwavering loyalty that the President both because of his knowledge and moral leadership could best speak, and he expressed himself freely about the extremists on both sides who were attacking the President.

At his post again and harassed by the demands of business men whose trade was caught in the terrible uncertainties of war he kept on pressing for protests against atrocities in the name of humanity, pleading for a united neutral front against all violations of international law, and arguing for the formation of an American Overseas Trust to deal with American trade in the same efficient manner as the Netherlands Overseas trust.

In June he wrote Professor George G. Wilson whose unforgettable services as Counsellor in the Legation in 1914 and whose friendship he constantly cherished:

"This frightful war will [result in] a clear conviction by experience that the general disregard of international law in which the belligerents have indulged is a very bad thing for the world at large. If that conviction is thoroughly inwrought we may hope that the aforesaid world, which after all holds together and keeps going only because it has a certain amount of common sense and right feeling, will resolve to put international law on a stronger basis than ever before, and to surround it with such safeguards as the combined nations will be able to devise and achieve. In other words, I believe in a 'League for the Protection of Peace.' We shall probably not be able to get it at once. And even when we get it, it will probably not be a universal cure for all the evils that affect mankind through the mistakes and misconduct of rulers. But at least it will be a partial safeguard, and it will strengthen the appeal to the moral consciousness of mankind, which is after all the foundation of all government."

[341]

In July 1916 he received a month's leave of absence and went fishing in Norway with his wife and two daughters. On the way he visited Maurice Francis Egan, United States Minister at Copenhagen who wrote: "It was a red letter night when he came to dinner. We forgot politics and talked of Stedman and Gilder and the elder days." So did these men put aside momentarily the strain of responsibility in order the better to bear their burdens.

By the middle of August he had determined to resign. The state of his mind is reflected in a friendly letter of August 22nd to Brand Whitlock in Brussels:

"How tiresome it all is, and how much it makes one wonder why it had to come,—all this carnage, and waste, and hatred, and sorrow, and bitterness! I am not speaking now of the political and military responsibility for the war. I am thinking of something very much larger;— of its significance to mankind at large, its relation to the education and upward movement of the race, which it seems to have interrupted so violently; of its bearing upon the problems of social betterment and the physical and moral improvement of the race. Did the world need this cleansing by blood and tears? Had men grown so mean and soft and cruel that something violent was demanded in order to shake them out of the sloth in which they were rotting? Had the world forgotten God, and must it be reminded? Yet how can God be seen in this particular form of reminder? I think that it is much more philosophic and probably much more true to look for the origin of this great catastrophe in the selfishness, shortsightedness and real incompetence of certain ruling classes, for whose mistakes and misdeeds the people must suffer. But again the old question comes back: Why?"

On September 6th the resignation was written in a formal letter to the President, the purely personal reasons being reserved for a private letter. The time when the resignation should become effective was left to the President's judgment and convenience. The fact was that Henry van Dyke wanted to speak out and act out. He felt that the time for restrained talk was past. When his own decision was made the convictions of his heart burned into poetry. Within a few days he wrote "The Glory of Ships", "The Bells of Malines", "The Name of France", and "America's Prosperity". Beneath the rhythmic words and sober thought beat an eager heart convinced beyond a shadow that the cause of the Allies was the cause of peace, and yearning unspeakably that the cause might be maintained without blot. The poems were widely quoted and commented upon in America, England and France. On November 28th he gave an interview to the *New York Times* on "certain points which are matters of public knowledge." Stressing the desire of the President and the Government for peace he pointed out that the offer of mediation as made by the President was not an unfriendly act and that there was need "to know more clearly the causes and aims of this bloody conflict. Many explanations have been offered from both sides, but every one of them contained at least one vague undefined term; this is what needs to be made clear." He went on to speak of the proposed league of peace, saying "It is not a league to enforce peace now, but a league to defend peace when restored."

Shortly after the President's note of December 18th, asking all belligerents to state their aims, had been published, Henry van Dyke in a statement to the Associated Press said without much regard for diplomatic amenities, though he insisted that it accorded with the proprieties: "The Entente Powers have already done this with some clearness, and will probably soon do so even more clearly. The Central Powers have politely, even affectionately, but very practically declined the President's invitation to state their terms. That is the deadlock on peace-talks at present. When both sides are equally frank the world can judge whether the peace which all just men desire is near or far away."

As Henry van Dyke prepared to step out of his post into more direct action he gathered the American Consuls and their families in the Legation for a cheerful Christmas dinner. The following weeks were crowded with lunches and dinners, official and unofficial, which his Dutch friends offered him. Ample in food and bounteous in friendliness, after the Dutch fashion, they were for him a delightful reminder of the many personal friendships which crowned his stay in the Netherlands. On January 7, 1917 he preached a farewell sermon on "Patience" in the English Church. And on January 9th lectured at the University of Leiden on "The Poetry of Nature". "It is well," he said, "to remember the great things that existed before the war was begun and which will certainly endure after it is ended."

Just before he left there came to him from Germany the first copy in book form of the translation into German of his *Story of the Other Wise Man*.

On the evening of January 14th the Netherlands Minister of Foreign Affairs and Mrs. Loudon, the Burgomaster of The Hague, and a host of court officials and members of the diplomatic corps and other friends,—except the Germans—waved farewell as he passed through a crowded station on the way to Flushing and England. He was through with diplomacy's struggle for peace and eager for the next adventure.

Chapter Twenty-two

FIGHTING FOR PEACE

STOPPED first by a German submarine and an hour later by two British submarines, and threading a way through large flotillas of ships of all nationalities—including several Belgian relief boats with banners and insignia of their calling plastered all over them,—we reached Gravesend in the evening. A few hours later before a dingy fire of slate-like coal in darkened London, Henry van Dyke remarked: "I believe utterly in the cause of the Allies. It is a question of the preservation of civilization. Might or Right: that is the question. I'm not saying there was no justification on Germany's side, or that there is no wrong mixed with the Allies' right. But the choice of war lies with Germany, and the Allies must beat her at her own game."

It was this oft-uttered conviction which now made Henry van Dyke an outspoken proponent of America's joining the Allies and which determined his activities throughout the war.

Despite the pleas and warnings of many of his British and American friends he was determined to see the front for himself. The battle which had raged at Verdun since 1916 and the famous French watchword "On ne passe pas!" were to him symbols of the real significance of the war and nothing would do but that he should see the war with his own eyes. As in October 1914 he had entered Belgium that he might write as an eye-witness of the sorrows of the homeless refugees, so now his heart was for France to see for himself the resistance of the Allies to the German plans. Characteristically he demanded first hand knowledge of that on which he wished to speak and write. On January 19, 1917 wearing lightly his sixty-four

[345]

years he disappeared on a troopship into the mists of the Channel; went first to the battlefield of the Marne at Senlis and Compiègne and after visiting a hospital within a few kilometres of the front wrote:

"The contrast between the imminent noise and the quiet work was immense and comforting."

Along the Marne he visited the *Marais de St. Gond* where in 1914 Foch stayed the German advance. At Verdun, "no more a city of habitation but a mouthful of broken teeth," he saw the trenches and field-hospitals, watched an eminent French surgeon operating to save the life of a wounded German, was caught under fire, and lunched in the citadel in a cave under thirty feet of earth and stone with General Guillaumat and his staff.

"Everybody (officers and men)," he wrote, "is calm, cheerful, sober, resolute and confident of the result—namely Peace with the Victory which is necessary to obtain it right. . . .

The weather was *arctic,*—bright sun, snow everywhere,—afternoon wind full of snow dust, and night full of stringent stars. Cannon shots about once in five seconds during the day—in the white night, silence! . . . It was just an ordinary day in the long battle,—*relativement calme.*"

As Henry van Dyke returned to London February 3rd he rejoiced in the breaking of American diplomatic relations with Germany but carefully noted that historically such a rupture did not always mean war. Struggling with the effects of a heavy cold and exhaustion he went on seeing people and listening to all serious and measured speech about the war. Much as he yearned to be back in America he could neither be persuaded to leave till all his consultations were finished, nor would he rest. The inevitable happened, and suffering acute pain in the inner ear that at times made him delirious, he was taken by Sir Maurice Abbott Anderson, M.D., and his son to a nursing home. After two weeks of constant uncertainty and struggle he was recovered sufficiently to go to Brighton where he bewailed the working of his "poor old mind like a saw log bumping down a stream." He was utterly exhausted and could not rest. For five weeks more the matter of an operation hung in the balance. But somehow the crisis passed, thanks to good doctors and nurses and the indomitable will of the patient—and I can vouch for the fact that nothing availed more in that achievement than the patient's concern in writing two poems: "Liberty Enlightening the World" and "The Oxford Thrushes". Back in London for "America Day", April 20th, in celebration of America's entry into the war he attended the service in St. Paul's Cathedral, listened with sober joy to Bishop Brent's noble sermon, and noted with amusement that the American flag beside the British flag in the chancel had only forty-five stars! A few days' dry fly fishing in the lush meadows along the Itchin at Winchester as the guest of G. E. M. Skues of the Flyfisher's Club crowned his convalescence. On May 7th he went to Oxford as the guest of Sir Herbert Warren and the following day, in the crowded Convocation Hall, received the University's D.C.L. at a simple but moving ceremony.

Crossing the muddy Mersey the next day to take the *S.S. Baltic* for America he remarked: "Well did Shakespeare say: 'The quality of *Mersey* is not strained.'" He was in high feather personally and a cheerful shipmate as the vessel zig-zagged for safety across the Irish Channel and laid to for three days in Red Bay while the British and American navies sought and sank an enemy submarine outside. On May 22nd we were in New York and after reporting to Washington he set to work. "They're not awake yet in this country," he cried, "the trouble with democracy now is that it is not organized for war, and yet, if it can't fight, it will go out of existence." More than twenty years before this Henry van Dyke had written:

"Milton's catastrophe was the civil war, sweeping over England like a flood. But the fate which involved him in it was none other than his own conscience. This it was that drew him, by compulsion more strong than sweet, from the florid literary hospitality of Italian mutual laudation societies into the vortex of tumultuous London, made him 'lay aside his singing robes' for the heavy armour of the controversialist, and leave his 'calm and pleasant solitariness, fed with cheerful and confident thoughts, to embark on a troubled sea of noises and harsh disputes.' His conscience, I say, not his tastes: all these led him the other way. But an irresistible sense of duty caught him, and dragged him, as it were by the neck to the verge of the precipice, and flung him down into the thick of the hottest conflict England has ever seen."

Now Henry van Dyke was to find himself similarly snatched from his career by an inexorable conscience. The Potsdam gang was in the Footpath to Peace and their defeat was the first business on hand. Vigorously and ceaselessly on the platform, in the pulpit, through articles in the magazines and newspapers and through a voluminous correspondence he pressed the issue:

> "A willing, gray-haired servitor
> Bearing the Fiery Cross of righteous war."

At the Madison Barracks, on July 4th, he spoke for the first time to American soldiers. In the open air on a breezy day of bright sun he struck the note typical of all his later addresses. The theme was: "Conscientious Objectors, Fourth of July Type"; and the argument ran:

> "1. We object to the existence of this war.
> 2. We object to the manner in which Germany has conducted this war.
> 3. We object to the way in which the German government has forced this war on our peace loving country."

During July and August he made a careful study of his own experiences and of the official documents concerning the origin and conduct of the war and wrote with great intensity the articles published in November in a volume, *Fighting for Peace*. The articles included "A Dialogue on Peace Between a Householder and a Burglar" and concluded with "Pax Humana." The former had the realistic irony of one of Raemaker's cartoons; and the latter spoke simply of the steps by which mankind's deathless hope of peace might be realized. With this hope in view he joined Theodore Marburg and Talcott Williams in a brief but crowded trip through western New York. Three times a day they pleaded and argued in support of the waging of war but always they held before their audiences the ultimate peace toward which they believed the prosecution of the war was the first step.

Following this trip Henry van Dyke went on as a free-lance, speaking wherever he could get the chance on the cause, meaning and issues of the war. On October 19th his date-book bears the scribbled record: "36,500 people addressed this week."

The record of those days in America is the record of the power of voice and pen to stir a nation to almost unbelievable action. The propaganda both for and against the war is available both in newspaper files and in a number of books. This is not the place to discuss it. Only this much must be said in describing Henry van Dyke's active part in the propaganda for war: he was speaking out on the basis of his honest convictions, he was seeking a chance to get to the front in some capacity, and he several times deliberately took long chances to deliver the message with which he was charged. Through it all he wrote many gentle explanatory letters to troubled souls, but on the field of controversy he gave and asked no quarter.

In the late autumn, as the Honorable Josephus Daniels, then Secretary of the Navy, writes me, Henry van Dyke went to Washington and called on him at the Navy Department:

"He said to me," writes Mr. Daniels, " 'I am the most unhappy man in America. You know that for months I have been urging Woodrow and talking with you and trying to convince you both that America could not save its soul unless it took part in this struggle to end imperialism. Now that we have gone in, I do not find any place where I can serve my country. Is there not something you could give me to do?'

I said: 'If your age did not prevent, I could make you a Chaplain in the Reserve Corps of the Navy.'

'What is the age limit?' he asked.

'35 years,' I replied.

With a quizzical smile he said: 'I was once 35, and in my heart I am not over that now.'

'Very well,' I said, 'I will enroll you as a Chaplain in the Naval Reserve.'

Your father was very happy and said: 'I will be eternally grateful for the opportunity to serve with the brave boys of your arm of the service.'

I said: 'There is one preliminary to your enrollment.'

He said: 'What is it? I will do anything to get in the Navy.'

I said: 'You must stand an examination in theology.'

That seemed to astonish him and he asked: 'Who conducts the examination?'

I said: 'I do. Wait a minute.' I rang the bell and told the messenger to call Chaplain Frazier, who was the officer in charge of the enrollment and assignment to duty of Chaplains. You may remember that he was Dewey's Chaplain at Manila. When Chaplain Frazier came in I told him that I wished Dr. van Dyke to be enrolled as Chaplain in the Reserve Corps. He said: 'But, Mr. Secretary, the age limit is 35.'

'I know that,' I replied, 'and I officially declare to you that Dr. van Dyke is of the proper age.'

Then I turned to Dr. van Dyke and said: 'I will now conduct the examination in theology. Stand up.'

You know how erect your father could stand, and catching on to my spirit, he stood up as if he were at assize.

'The first question I ask you,' I said, 'is, do you believe in Calvinism?' He said: 'No, and I never did.'

I said: 'You pass the examination creditably, but it is very fortunate that you are being examined by a Methodist and not by Woodrow Wilson or my wife. Those Presbyterians would give you a cipher and you could not secure the commission.' "

So Henry van Dyke was commissioned and attached to the First Naval District of which Admiral Spencer S. Wood was Commandant. Boy-like he cherished the hope that this might lead to assignment to sea duty in European waters and vainly applied for it several times. Instead he was sent to deliver his message on "The Causes, Meaning and Issues of the War" at Naval Stations from Maine to Florida, from South California to Washington, and on the Great Lakes. He rejoiced at this opportunity of working directly with men engaged in the conduct of the war, and made many friends among officers and enlisted men.

His interest in naval matters included all sorts of details. Mr. Daniels writes further:

"At the time your father was enrolled, the Chaplains in the Navy had no rank and there was no gold braid on their uniforms as there was on those of the officers of the line. In fact the insignia of the office was black instead of gold. Every time I saw him, your father said with a smile:

'When are you going to take me out of mourning? I do not like it. You ought to let me wear gold braid.'

Afterwards I issued an order giving military rank to the Chaplains as well as others on the staff corps. I think your father was the first one to buy himself a uniform with gold braid."

The rank of Lieutenant Commander was conferred upon him, and he wore his uniform and insignia with serious mien and un-alloyed delight. Equally he performed his often arduous duties with enthusiasm. Pegasus was cheerfully harnessed to make popular verses. The only time when his health gave way under the incessant strain he wrote, in March 1918, during a few days in hospital at Jacksonville, Florida, "Easter Road" a few lines of which better than much argument reveal the purpose and spirit of his warfare:

> "O my soul, my comrades, soldiers of freedom,
> Follow the pathway of Easter, for there is no other,
> Follow it through to peace, yea, follow it fighting.
> This Armageddon is not darker than Calvary.
> The day will break when the Dragon is vanished;
> He that exalteth himself as God shall be cast down,
> And the Lords of War shall fall,
> And the long, long terror be ended,
> Victory, justice, peace enduring!"

Even the few short stories that he wrote in odd moments and which were gathered in *The Valley of Vision* (published in March 1919) dealt with the ironies of conflict and war—though in all of them was the secret heart of peace. Of one of these, "The Primitive and His Sandals", Theodore Roosevelt wrote him on August 13, 1918:

"I wish it could be read as a tract by every half-baked and every wholly baked parlor Bolshevist in the land! Preferably I should like it read once a week after nightfall in penitential garb, by the light of torches made in each case out of the entire edition, for that week, of the New Republic."

The forthright pungency in Henry van Dyke's voice and pen as he bore the flaming torch of war was met with equal vehemence by those who disagreed. There is no need here to attempt to stir up the ashes of each particular controversy. The record is written—but it is not worth speaking about, save to remind ourselves of the Apostle James' solemn word: "The tongue is a fire". To Henry van Dyke the main issue was perfectly clear; and as a controversialist he was not one to mince words in talking about it.

But it would be a mistake to overlook the fact that for him the necessary business of winning the war was only the first step toward the greater task of establishing world peace. One gets a glimpse of the spirit in which he moved among his naval duties from such little incidents as that at the Rockland, Maine, Naval Base in the summer of 1918. With the Commandant, Lieutenant Kidd, and his his wife and their two-year-old son, James, Henry van Dyke had made a trip around the Base ending with a little island excursion. He had been much drawn to the boy, and together they had stood on a lofty part of the island and gazed upon the sea with mutual awe and delight. When Henry van Dyke returned to Boston he sat down at a hotel desk and wrote some verses for "Admiral James Stark Lawrence Kidd of the Grand Fleet of Youth":

> "I'll tell you 'zactly what we did
> One morning,—me and Jamie Kidd!
> We sailed upon the ocean blue,
> With Jamie's Pa and Mother too.
> The C'mander's gig she went so fast
> She scared the sea-gulls flopping past;
> And then we came unto an Island
> And climbed upon a little highland.
> A house was there, all trim and neat,
> And friends who gave us things to eat.
> We saw the dog, the sheep, the trees,
> And many cu-ri-osy-tees.
> But what we thought most *fine* and *grand*
> Was a reg'lar crow-nest on the land;
> So up we climbed, Jamie and me,
> And looked across the shining sea."

It was a small incident but typical of the eagerness with which

Henry van Dyke turned at every opportunity to share a child's delight and wonder.

The day before the Armistice he preached in Trinity Church, Boston, on Isaiah's word: "My sword shall be bathed in heaven." Concluding a solemn considered defense of the righteousness of the war he said:

"After long suffering, Peace draws near. The sword bathed in Heaven has beaten down the sword forged in Potsdam and bathed in Hell.

What shall this glorious victory mean to us and to the world?

That is the question of the hour.

It must mean not vengeance but justice. . . .

The religious lessons of this last world-war are unforgettable. Above the peace of mankind, for which we fought, must shine the sword bathed in Heaven."

In December at his own request he was retired to the inactive list of the Navy and wrote Secretary Daniels

"I want no pay. If the regulations require it to be drawn, I shall give it to the Naval Academy at Annapolis. It has been for me a sufficient reward to know, to admire, and to love the officers and men of the splendid United States Navy."

The Secretary replied:

"I wish you to know how much I have appreciated the spirit of your high services, and how your ministrations have been helpful in the great War. While it is true that no war can be won without munitions and men on the firing line, it is equally true that the spirit of a nation is the determining factor. Your addresses, your sermons and your writings have been inspiring and helpful, not alone to those in the naval service, but to the whole country, and the men fighting across the waters."

The pay which he was required to draw was turned over to the Naval Academy as a trust fund, the income of which provides annually a gold watch for that member of the graduating class who submits the best original article on any naval or equally patriotic subject.

True to the ideals which had led him into active service in the war Henry van Dyke did not retire after the Armistice. He concerned himself vigorously with the making of the real peace for which he believed the war had been waged. At the Memorial Service in the Princeton Chapel he uttered in his Ode "Golden Stars", not only a solemn Threnody for the dead but also proclaimed the duty of keeping faith with the dead. To the end of his days he contended conscientiously for the keeping of that faith. The idea of a league of nations seemed to him the heart of the issue. Henry van Dyke had been corresponding about the League to Enforce Peace before its birth on June 17, 1915, and after his return from the Netherlands often took active part in it,—though he steadily insisted that "The League to *Protect* Peace" was a more accurate description for the ideal.

"This war will be worse than wasted if we forget its moral meaning. This victory will be turned into a defeat if we let it separate us from our religion," he warned at the League of Nations' meeting in Pittsburgh in December 1918. "Yet there is danger that both of these things may happen, if we are satisfied to hurrah without thinking, or to make our plans without praying.

The defeated and discredited doctrines will surely seek to regain what they lost in the arbitrament of battle by an appeal to the superficial sentiments and passions of a victorious hour.

One of these heresies is *militarism*—the theory that might makes right. The other is *pacificism*—the theory that right has no claim upon us to defend and uphold it against an unjust and tyrannous might. Both of these theories are false and treacherous. Both begin to show their snakey heads among the laurels and the palms with which the hour of victory is adorned. Against both we must be on guard. . . . To secure this end it is not necessary to have a complete reorganization and federation of all the nations of the world. The time for that, in my judgment, is not yet ripe. The difference of education and character among the motley tribes of earth are too great for a world confederation on the basis of equal votes for all. The more advanced nations must be, as President Wilson says, 'Trustees of the peace of the world'."

With the distinct understanding that he was supporting the President's proposal for a league of nations he took part in the speaking tour to the Pacific Coast conducted by the League to Enforce Peace with Taft, Morgenthau, Lowell, Wickersham, George G. Wilson,

Filene and others. It was strenuous work though there were lighter moments mixed with the campaign. On one occasion when Mr. Taft had a sore throat he went to the rear platform of the train to address an assemblage at the railway station. "We want Taft!" yelled the crowd, drowning out all attempts to explain. Suddenly Henry van Dyke shook his fist and shouted "Shut up!" Momentarily nonplussed at this address the disturbers were still. "Now," said he, good humoredly, "do you want Taft dead or alive?—because if he speaks now he'll be dead." Some one laughed and he got the chance to continue with another question: "What did we go to war for?" An old man cried: "To beat dot dom Kaiser!" "Yes," said Henry van Dyke, "and for what else?" And a young man said: "To make peace for the world." "There," cried Henry van Dyke, "you have it all: First lick the Kaiser and then establish peace."—and he went on with his uninterrupted speech.

Already the political movement against the President was taking violent form. Henry van Dyke sensing the perils of the situation went to see the President and endeavored to persuade him to take to the Peace Conference certain distinguished Republicans as members of the American delegation. A friend (Reverend W. E. Brooks) to whom Henry van Dyke spoke of his interview reports that Henry van Dyke described Mr. Wilson as "obdurate" as he shook his head in constant refusal and finally said: "No Henry, whoever I took would betray me to Lodge."

Against what Henry van Dyke felt was a partisan attempt to prevent the United States' entry into the League of Nations he struggled with voice and pen. "I am against ratification (of the Covenant) with the rude and ruinous Lodge reservations. I favor urging patriotic senators to compromise on reasonable reservations interpreting treaty and covenant and then to vote for a real ratification without delay." In the League to Enforce Peace he contended strenuously for the re-issue of one of its earlier definite public statements in favor of the League of Nations. But the proposal was defeated in the violent personalities of the approaching presidential election, and the League to Enforce Peace which had done so great a work was started for the scrap heap. Henry van Dyke on September 20, 1920,

wrote Theodore Marburg, who from 1914 had been an active proponent of the League idea: "When an issue like the League of Nations clearly rises above the ordinary questions of partisan politics,
it seems to me the duty of a man of honor to follow his conscience
both in speech and in action. These instances may be rare, but when
they arrive they are absolute and commanding."

When the League of Nations non-partisan Association was proposed on November 12, 1922, he gladly consented to serve on the
sponsoring committee. To the end of his days he felt that a great
patriotic and humanitarian movement in America had been interrupted by the failure of certain leaders of the nation to support the
League of Nations' idea. Against those who he was convinced had
betrayed the cause he spoke and wrote vigorously. But his chief
concern was to support as a loyal American every movement looking
toward entry into the World Court or any association of nations for
the maintenance of world peace. He supported "as a *beau geste*" the
successful movement for America's signing of the Pact of Paris, and
at the League of Nations' dinner in Baltimore on January 17, 1929,
he added the typical remark, "But if this pledge is kept it will be, it
must be, the first step of the greatest democracy on earth toward
the World Court and then towards an honorable entrance with all
our rights of sovereignty into the League of Nations."

Honors came upon him which he received thankfully and gaily.
By France he was made Commander of the Legion of Honor, and
the King of the Belgians conferred upon him the medal of the first
class of the *Comité National*. He took part in the welcome home to
the fleet in New York Harbor, and served on several committees
for the arriving army divisions. And always with voice and pen to
soldiers and sailors and citizens he cried: Now that liberty has been
defended, show that you know how to exercise it rightly.

His enemies of the *vae victis* stripe accounted him weak—because
he pleaded for vindication, not vengeance; and the now burgeoning
movement of theoretical pacifists denounced him as a mere fire
eater, because he insisted that, despite the awfulness of war, there
was a point at which it became necessary to defend by the sword
rights attacked with the sword. To understand Henry van Dyke's

position in the war and in the controversies that surrounded the attempt to turn the armistice into an organized peace two things must be kept in mind: first, that in dealing with men his judgments were based on an unmitigated realism; and second, that he believed that ideals where they existed were as real as anything else in the world. What he objected to was the theoretical attributing of ideals to those who lacked them, or the neglect of the factor of ideals in determining the treatment of those who possessed them. Perhaps the simplest exposition of his views is to be found in the thesis of his address *The World to Be*: 1. A new world improbable; 2. A stand-pat world impossible; 3. How to make things better. Here he stands revealed as neither an optimist nor a pessimist but as a working meliorist. "The day is coming," he concluded, "when men will know and accept the laws of nature and live according to them. The day is coming when capital and labor will cease their mad strife and work together for the good of mankind. The day is coming when nations will no longer regard one another as embattled foes, but as friends and allies in the maintenance of peace. The day is coming when man shall see eye to eye with man, and all eyes shall look upward reverently to God.

Distant is that day. But we look and work toward it, in the spirit of our Master, Jesus Christ."

During these years he was beset by requests for his opinion on all sorts of questions: Should Santa Claus be suppressed? What did he think of the value of the radio telephone in education? What was his recipe for success? What was his opinion of the newspapers? of the Theatre? Do animals reason? How did he feel about the reproduction of Bible scenes on the screen? For a while he tossed back good-natured replies, but soon he surrendered the job of involuntary sage which was never to his liking.

The personal integrity with which Henry van Dyke contended in these war years is written in the record. That his activities in those strident times were not the unbridled conduct of a man released to unaccustomed action is further evidenced by his return with unabated zest to the exercise of his calling as teacher, preacher and poet. When the sword was drawn he believed it must be met by

[357]

the sword, but the things by which mankind advanced along the upward way were religion, education, and the arts.

No better expression of his attitude toward war and peace can be found than in his tale, "The Hero and the Tin Soldiers." Here is his unaffected reverence for the man who answers his Country's call when war has come; and here also is his conviction that the armies of tin soldiers must be demobilized in the interests of humanity. War may become a grim necessity. But for nobody, child or adult, should war be allowed to become a game.

Chapter Twenty-three

A MELIORIST CARRIES ON

IN THE fall of 1919 Henry van Dyke resumed with delight his regular teaching in Princeton University. To a former pupil and assistant, the Reverend William E. Brooks, he wrote:

"It is a happiness to me to know that you think of the days when you were in my class,—my intimate class,—with pleasure. Those days are very far away, and yet they do not seem so very distant, now that I have taken up the work of a teacher of reading again with the students here, and find it just as congenial and rewarding as ever. Do you know, there is a very curious thing about this first class that I have had since the war. They seem so much more mature than the fellows of the same age were before the war.

My hope in regard to them is that I may be able to do for them what I have tried to do for all my classes,—to teach all of them to love reading, and to help those of them who are fitted for writing to do it with more joy and with more power.

After all what one man can do amounts to very little. But perhaps in the sum total of human effort it may count for something."

To President Hibben he insisted that his first year's salary be turned over to the Endowment fund and expressed the hope that it might be used "to increase the pay of other professors and instructors, especially in the department of which I am a member." His enthusiasm for "teaching young men to read" was as great as ever, and his courses alternating between British and American Poetry and British and American Prose of the 19th Century were again very popular. In 1921 his colleague Professor George M. Harper wrote him: "In reading the essays from the men in my preceptorial

[359]

sections of the class in 19th Century Poetry I have been impressed by their efforts—in some cases very successful, and in all respectable— to appreciate poetry and write about it in an appropriate manner. The result has been most gratifying, and since it is apparent to me that your lectures had much to do with it, I am glad to tell you the fact and what seems to me to have been a principal cause. On the whole, it is, I think, the best miscellaneous collection of essays that I have ever received from seniors."

Henry van Dyke also communicated his enthusiasm for reading to a wider audience through correspondence and addresses. He answered at length Chaplain Frazier's inquiry about books for the sea libraries of the Navy and submitted a varied list in accord with his belief that everybody likes to read good books. He made numerous addresses, such as that on "Talking, Reading and Writing English in America" at Columbia University in which he voiced his conviction about the message of English Literature:

"The two main qualities of English literature, in its English and American branches, are its romantic spirit and its moral significance. Every great writer in English has ended by trying to teach something about life. Stevenson said: 'I would rise from the dead to preach'; Kipling loves and thumps his pulpit; Barrie never lets you go without a gentle incitement to faith, hope and charity. In America, perhaps, the new writers have been more timid or uncertain. But Emerson and Hawthorne were not ashamed to teach. And the best of our young men (whom I do not name, fearing the odium of omission) have taken courage to say that life has a spiritual meaning, and that the meaning is interesting and good—which is the great message of English literature."

On less formal occasions he did not hesitate to express his scorn of the "new fireworks school of criticism" or to speak of those "young critics who have in their bones all the gouty prejudices of an antediluvian conventionality." Certainly he was heartily out of sympathy with the bulk of American writing at this time. To his mind it betrayed lack of faith and careless workmanship, both of which he considered utterly destructive of significant writing. Believing ardently that the only way to overcome darkness was to light a candle, he could not endure those who however sincerely went about beating down whatever lights remained. The slip-shod use of language, too, hurt him to the quick. Seriously he pleaded for accurate speech with due regard for that fringe of meaning which gives words their real significance. Exuberantly, as in his skit "The Generalcy of Normalcy," he ridiculed all use of high sounding verbiage, and continued to argue for the revival of the study of Greek and Latin as an aid in the correct use of English. He believed vigorously in the value of a liberal education as the best preparation for service in all the professions and occupations of life.

As he took up in his teaching again he began to gather and revise the harvest of his own pen for the "Avalon" edition of his works.

"Far have I travelled from these walls," he wrote in his beloved study, "yet always on the same quest, and never forgetting 'the rock whence I was hewn.' Now I come back to gather up the things that I have written in my voyages of body and of spirit.

The realities of faith are unshaken; the visions of hope undimmed; the shrines of love undefiled. And while I sit here assembling these pages, —an adventurous conservative—I look forward to further journeys and to coming back to the same home."

The work on this Collected Edition of his writings received the same detailed and enthusiastic attention which he had always given to his books. But though some things were omitted and rearrangements effected he found few changes to make except in the two volumes of poetry which show a careful selection and revision of the poems old and new which were included. To the *Studies in Tennyson* he added a brief preface that tells the story of his undying interest in the poet. And for the volume of sermons, *Counsels by the Way,* he selected sixteen sermons from a great mass published and unpublished. "A few sermons," he said, "easily represent the message of all." The edition was announced as "personally edited and arranged by Dr. van Dyke himself to contain all of his writings that he wishes to live." But though the sixteen volumes were later increased to eighteen there still remain typical stories, essays, addresses, and short poems of his later years outside the edition.

With renewed emphasis at this time many friends urged him to write his reminiscences; but he always refused. One may remember in this connection that he had written in the preface to *The Poetry of Tennyson* in 1889: "the best biography of Tennyson will always be found in his works"; and that in *Days Off* in 1907 he makes his "Uncle Peter" remark: "Autobiography is usually a man's view of what his biography ought to be." The fact was as he put it: "My mind was not built that way." As late as 1932 he wrote: "I have no intention of writing my autobiography, being still too busy with work which is worth while." During the last four or five years of his life he did some work organizing his voluminous papers but it was distasteful labor to him and only done at urgent request. He was not averse to conversational reminiscences of his experiences while talking of the affairs of the day, and careful notes made after many of these conversations during more than twenty years have been used in the present volume. Call it what you will, this unwillingness to write systematically about himself was the mark of the man of action more than ready to let the past speak for itself while he had something new to do.

In March 1920 he took his daughter Paula and sailed from San Francisco for the One Hundredth Anniversary celebration of Christian Missions in Hawaii. With the eagerness of an alert boy he took in the new experiences of people and scenery and events. "It's a dream of beauty. But I can't work," he wrote, but that was only his way of saying that he was a little puzzled at finding himself fully content without the urge to write. In "Tomorrow's Message to To-day," flavored with pithy slang and sober epigrammatic wisdom, he made his chief address in the form of a super-wireless dialogue. Commenting pungently upon the high lights of the American scene he insisted that America must learn to distinguish tomorrow from the Millennium; and was not ashamed to declare simply that the hope of the future lay in better men and women, sane in mind, sound in body, and democratically educated. He preached or spoke frequently and finally wrote with enthusiasm an account of the great centenary pageant with glimpses of the colorful island of Oahu. For the rest he enjoyed the easy hospitality of the John E. Waterhouses, swam in the "warm, silken caressing waters," rode the surf in the long out-rigger canoes, and "caught some of those Joseph's coat fish—not very large (he confessed) but colorful", and strove laughingly to eat *poi*, native fashion with his fingers. When the twenty days were past, in fulfilment of an old promise, he went on with his daughter (named for the trip "Little Fuji San") to Japan. Henry van Dyke was well aware from his diplomatic experiences that the Far Eastern question was rapidly moving toward the centre of world affairs. Characteristically he wished to gain some personal knowledge of it and to see the Japanese and their country, not through the eyes of a conventional tourist, or of a man with a particular axe to grind, but through the eyes of a friendly traveller. He always preferred to forget the honors and titles which had come to him; but his daughter recalls the skill with which, when the occasion required, he employed a carefully prepared calling card with a full record of his status on it. This, too, was characteristic of him.

Among those whom he always remembered with gratitude as helping him to a better understanding of Japan were Viscount Kaneko, Baron Yamagawa, President of the Imperial University, Dr. Saiki of Kyoto, a renowned physician, Mrs. Kei Ozaki, a distinguished author, Mrs. Charles Burnett, poet in English and Japanese, and wife of the American Military Attache in Tokyo, Mr. Kosuke Hiromasa, a well known writer and graduate of Princeton University, and Dr. Tasuku Harada, ex-president of Doshisha University. With the intimate conversation of those who knew and loved Japan to interpret their journeys, they started leisurely to see certain carefully selected places. They stood by the Red Bridge at Nikko and heard the temple bells, and the waterfalls; they went up the river to Lake Chuzenji and to the foaming Dragon Tail falls above, and fished three days for trout in the stream below Lake Yumoto. They approached Kyoto by boat through the swift flowing canal from Lake Biwa that passes under the mountain. There was a walk at Kyoto to Kurodani, the Ginkakuji and the grave of Dr. Niishima, a visit to the Cherry Blossom Dance and to the stately Noh Drama. Through the forest they climbed with the Shivelys to the temple on Mount Hiei. At Yamada-Ise they spent a day and night visiting the two chief Shinto shrines. Around the temples and the pagoda at Nara they walked among the deer, and on the sea

[363]

coast at Toba they watched the pearl divers; and at Gifu went out at night to see the fishermen with their cormorants taking fish by the flare of torches. At the Inn of Eight Thousand Pines by the Sumida they passed a day in quiet converse. There were ceremonial teas and dinners on one of which occasions the Minister of War Tanaka writing his name for the guest committed himself to *Bushido* above his signature. Was this a tribute to the right of the pen to compete on equality with the sword; or was it a tribute to the warrior in the American poet? At the Imperial University Henry van Dyke lectured on "Poetry and Patriotism" quoting two of the Emperor's poems which were made known to him in Mrs. Burnett's translation; and as usual seized the opportunity on several other occasions to speak in interpretation of America and the Christian religion. Seven times during his stay he caught up in short lyrics the impressions of beauty and power which he felt about him.

The visit was brief—less than two months in Japan—but the experience of the Japanese spirit was neither small nor insignificant. From this time on Henry van Dyke said frequently that two qualities of the Japanese must be kept in mind in attempting to maintain friendly relations with them: first, that they are both proud and sensitive—"almost as much so as Americans"; and second, that they have the genius of self-organization which constitutes them the natural leaders of the Orient. In both these judgments, history records that he spoke as a prophet,—though as usual the prophet was without honor.

Soon after returning to Princeton Henry van Dyke was spoken of in several quarters as a good candidate for the New Jersey Senatorship or Governorship, but when directly addressed on the matter replied that he had never and did not then desire any public office, being content to write and speak as opportunity offered for the principles of democracy. In this he judged himself wisely, for he was already exercising considerable public influence in many directions. Following up his official action in 1915 as delegate to the opium conference in The Hague he was taking active part in the Narcotic Drug Control League. He became identified with the National Committee on Mental Hygiene as a result of reviewing Clifford W. Beers' classic, "A Mind that Found Itself." After visits to Yellowstone Park with Superintendent Albright and to the ranch of his friend Struthers Burt, he threw himself vigorously into the campaign for the defense of the people's rights in the National Parks against the grabbing policy of particular groups and interests and wrote many articles about the protection of American game fish. He devoted not a little time to strengthening and directing the interest of boys in out-of-door life through the Woodcraft League and the Boy Scouts. In the confused and tumultuous political scene he took part as a free-lance democrat battling realistically for the League of Nations idea and joining with enthusiasm in the establishment of the Woodrow Wilson Foundation. Indeed Henry van Dyke's tributes to that great American both before and after Wilson fell, mortally wounded in the struggle for the League, are among the finest of his writings. Preaching frequently wherever he got the chance he stedfastly refused to align himself with what he considered the inflated movements then agitating the Protestant churches. He preferred to concern himself with "the old-fashioned gospel"—which to him meant bringing the appeal of Christ to bear directly upon each man for his personal decision. In newspaper articles that were widely syndicated he wrote brief comments on Bible texts. A little volume of seven hymns, "Thy Sea is Great, Our Boats are Small" gave expression to what he described as "the thoughts and feelings of Christian people today in the light of the new knowledge which has changed so many of our conceptions about the processes of nature and the social progress of man, without in the least degree altering the central realities of our faith in God and Christ."

As the anti-Jewish movement began to show its ugly head in Europe and then in America, Henry van Dyke spoke plainly: "Anti-Semitism is one of the most dangerous forms of anti-Christianity"; but he was equally outspoken in saying that "certain renegade Jews" were at the bottom of much of the world's unsettlement. "Prohibition" he denounced as a fake. He considered it the theoretical victory of a militant minority who substituted sumptuary law for faith in temperance education. But he never consented to align himself with

Two great reform societies; The Church and the United States

any of the movements against Prohibition. When asked by an interviewer: "Are you a member of a reform society?" He replied: "No, I belong to no reform society—except the Church and the United States of America."

Henry van Dyke hated shams, especially those founded on unreal concepts of human nature. But he hated them because he loved the ideals that had one foot planted in a realistic knowledge of men. Concerning a certain theoretical idealist he used to say: "He's a lovely fellow, but he has no feet." His faith in the rising generation based on a wide personal friendship with young men and women was enthusiastic. But with neither of the two extremist views of the day could he agree. The counsels of despair uttered by the children—not all of them young—of the Jazz Age and the delusions of grandeur of the announcers of the New Era were to him equally silly. The real issues of the day were "the perpetual crises" that beset men of goodwill and intelligence in any age and for which genuine spiritual religion and education offered the only hope.

The controversial spirit of the days of the World War was still abroad in the land. And in deliberately taking his part in the public questions of the day Henry van Dyke gave as well as received heavy blows. It may be interesting to conjecture what would have been his influence at this time had he stepped out of the arena of popular discussion. But the conjecture would be futile, for Henry van Dyke never could breathe in the ivory tower of aloofness. At no time in his long life was his writing a flight from life. It was always, as he described it, "an escape *into* life." And so now he carried the questions of the day into his study at "Avalon", or into "Green Door," the little bungalow for writing that he had built on the rocks near his summer cottage at Seal Harbor, Maine, or attacked them on trains or boats as he travelled. In several new lyrics, "Salute to the Trees", "The Ballad of Princeton Battle" (read at the dedication of the Battle Monument) and others, and in two new books, he put forth the eager convictions of his heart centered as always around the two unchanging foci of his thought—the human needs of the hour and the demands of eternity. *Camp Fires and Guide Posts* included a series of travel papers and divers essays on the interpretation of life and four exquisite tributes to friends who had passed beyond the veil of sight. *Companionable Books* was made up of essays new and old on "books worth taking with you on a journey, where the weight of luggage counts, or keeping beside your bed, near the night-lamp." Of the latter volume, which included the notable essay on Stevenson, "An Adventurer in a Velvet Jacket," Sir Sidney Colvin wrote: "Dr. van Dyke's work at its best. That best to the minds of some of us at any rate, is also the actual and positive best which the craft of criticism in the English language has in recent years produced. Such praise may sound superlative but is not the less deliberate."

Amid these many activities and preoccupations Henry van Dyke made time to speak at the two hundredth anniversary of his former church, the United Congregational Church of Newport, and at the unveiling of the memorial gateway in Saratoga Springs to his lifelong friend Katrina Trask. In 1921 for six weeks by the bedside of his desperately ill wife he joined the doctors and nurses in a day and night struggle for life. Apparently never doubting the outcome he radiated confidence to all and finally carried her off in triumph to convalesce in Maine. Twice he went across the ocean with his daughter Elaine who had developed a penchant for visiting out of the way portions of the world. His seventy years were swallowed up in his zest for life; and his delight in action and people was irrepressible. Veritably he was living,—as Wordsworth said man does live, "by admiration, hope and love."

When the time for his retirement from the active duties of his professorship came in 1922 Princeton asked him to remain another year. This invitation he gladly accepted with the understanding that "at the end of the next academic year the Trustees will accept my offered resignation and allow me to turn, not indeed to the generous allowance of the Carnegie foundation, but to other work for which I hope still to be fit." To this he added a request for permission to contribute the salary of an additional instructor in the short-handed and over-tasked English department. The proposals

[367]

were promptly accepted. His colleagues delightedly recognized the defiant note in his remark that he would never allow himself to be retired or pensioned, and freely expressed their admiration. Here was no dry academic stick but a bough still full of sap and green.

When his resignation was accepted in early January 1923 the chairman of the English Department, Dr. Charles G. Osgood, wrote a resolution recording appreciation of "his confidence in us, his friendship toward us, and his ready and effective cooperation with us at all times" and voicing "the pain which we feel, individually and personally, at this separation." And a number of gracious letters from colleagues, alumni and students rejoiced his heart.

On January 30th, 1923 he went to McCosh Hall to give the last lecture of his ever popular course. To his surprise, and at first confusion, he had to thread his way through a crowd of more than 600 students who were perched all over seats and floor and window ledges and thronged the door and stairway. The Vice-President of the class received "what was left of the floor" and, as Henry van Dyke described it later to a friend,

"made some remarks which indicated that the boys thought me younger than I claimed to be and that they had survived the lectures without serious resentment. Thereupon he presented a silver humidor as a gift from the class and a token that they knew at least one of my failings—which is always a bond of sympathy."

There were resolutions presented by the class Secretary.

"Well after that," recalled Henry van Dyke, "you can imagine what trouble I had in saying goodbye with dry cheeks. The whole thing was so unacademic, young, straightforward, that it warmed the cockles of my heart—better than any university degree."

He was invited to give occasional lectures for the whole student body and was appointed by the Trustees Murray Professor of English Literature, Emeritus, and University Lecturer on English Poetry. Thus came to a conclusion his twenty-three years of regular teaching to successive Princeton classes interrupted only by the years of his service in France, at The Hague, and in the United States Navy. An editorial in the *Daily Princetonian* on January 9, 1923 reveals in its gentle familiarities and its personal tribute the genuine affection subsisting between the old teacher and the young pupils:

"OF US, FOR US AND WITH US

. . . . We rejoice in the glory that he has won for himself, for Princeton, and for America. But we see much more than his titles, his degrees, his literary triumphs. We recognize in him a friend, a companion,—an ever sympathetic and understanding spirit. We admire his scarlet doctor's robe; but we love the warm heart beneath it.

To the undergraduate the mark of Henry van Dyke's genius is not his poetry, his essays, his stories, or his sermons, splendid and fine as they are. It is something much more intangible and much more compelling. Without effort, with as easy naturalness as he writes, Doctor van Dyke personifies, with all its dignity and courtliness, the grace of a gentleman of the old school; and at the same time he radiates infectiously all the ardor and enthusiasm and joy of optimistic youth."

IV

ONE ADVENTURE MORE

Lame, I hobble cheerful on:
Old, my armor has no rust:
Death can't take what life has won:
God alone I fear—and trust.

H. v. D.

Chapter Twenty-four

SOMETHING STILL TO BE DONE

IT WAS utterly characteristic of Henry van Dyke that he would not allow himself to be retired at Princeton in 1923 but insisted upon resigning for himself. He would not wait for the official axe to fall but anticipated even that impersonal action. If he had to admit his years it was done almost defiantly, for he was confident that "the ravages of *anno domini*" were still alien to him. As if in answer to a challenge, he crossed the sea for some fishing in England and in the summer rode on a stiff pack trip through the seldom visited southwest district of Yellowstone Park. Indeed the next six or seven years record a great deal of his most characteristic activities in travel, speech and writing. He was by no means through with life but with an increasing adaptability that excited the admiration of those closest to him his mind began to make ready for the brief sunset of his own years. Against the physical limitations of age he rebelled passionately to the very end. But his soul approached the final adventure with equanimity and at last with eagerness.

Meantime he had things yet to do. In an age when many were acclaiming science as the new messiah, and when fanatical extremists were wrangling for possession of organized religion, and when utilitarianism was distorting education, and when literature without standards was loudly praised (if carelessly read) and when many cried: Who shall show us any good?—he continued to be an undismayed liberal. Neither in despairing retreat upon the past nor in a feverish grasping of the exclusively new could he see hope. The eternal verities he found unchanged and the task of the day he saw as their embodiment in the life of the day. To this task he continued

[373]

to devote himself without stint in what was one of the most vigorous periods of his life. Indeed, except for the lengthening of his regular fishing expeditions he went on at his usual pace.

In a vain attempt to head off an obscurantist view of the relation between science and religion Henry van Dyke joined a group of scientists and religious leaders in preparing and issuing a statement:

"The purpose of science is to develop, without prejudice or preconception of any kind, a knowledge of the facts, the laws, and the processes of nature. The even more important task of religion, on the other hand, is to develop the consciences, the ideals, and the aspirations of mankind. Each of these two activities represent a deep and vital function of the soul of man, and both are necessary for the life, the progress, and the happiness of the human race."

But the obscurantist campaign once launched was like a forest fire. With the devout and astute William Jennings Bryan leading on, it advanced through the Protestant churches and later flamed high at the Scopes trial in Tennessee. Henry van Dyke, though he grieved at the realization that the old battles were to be fought again, rose like a veteran and cheerfully resumed his place with those who contended for Christian liberty, peace, and unity. In the pulpits of the Brick Church and the Park Avenue Presbyterian Church in New York on June 3, 1923, he preached on "The Perpetual Crisis in the Church" denouncing "the declaration of war between science and religion," and as a Presbyterian refusing to accept the famous five points "taken from a declaration of opinion made by the General Assembly of 1910" and now foisted upon the Church as "new tests of orthodoxy." Referring with deep feeling to his fifty-five years as a member of the Church, he solemnly protested the injustice of the attempt to eject all except the members of one party from the Church.

He entered upon a long and polite but utterly inconclusive correspondence with Dr. Clarence E. Macartney upon the subject. For *The Outlook* he wrote, "The Religion of a Liberal Christian" with the suggestion much too direct to be accepted by the literalists:

"Why not sweep away these two silly and misleading names, 'Fundamentalists' and 'Modernists'? They only becloud the issue and confuse the minds of plain folks. The real difference (which I pray may not become a division) is between the *Literalists*, who interpret the Scripture according to the letter, and the *Liberals*, who interpret according to the spirit."

In one of his Half-Told Tales, "The Only Infallible Soap," he related the story of a humble stranger who, for his clean hands and pure heart, was welcomed into the celestial city. Meantime the many soap makers who had sought to capitalize the requirement of cleanliness, each one for the benefit of his own particular brand of soap, were left arguing which kind of soap the man must have used "else he could never have entered."

The "perpetual crisis," in its violent form, continued for several years. Henry van Dyke dramatically marched out of the Princeton Church one Sunday in protest against the preaching of the Stated Supply and made public his reasons for giving up his pew with no uncertain sound. He became controversially engaged with several other leaders of "the obscurantists" and received a flood of denunciatory letters—many of them anonymous. To understand the vigor of feeling and conviction to which Henry van Dyke gave free expression in this controversy it is necessary to recognize the nature of the attack and the character of the men attacked. Many of these men were well known for their Christian lives and were his personal friends. It is well also to note that Henry van Dyke with his realistic judgment of men once remarked of some of the trouble makers: "They are not great theologians, but they have a tremendous sense of the value of real estate. It is in fact the same trick that the Wee Frees tried in Scotland." By degrees the attack subsided and finally died down as common sense revived throughout the churches. Henry van Dyke with a sigh of relief, returned to the positive promulgation of Christian faith in a turbulent world. In sermons and articles and voluminous correspondence and frequent conversations he pleaded eagerly for meeting the problems of the day by the personal following of Christ. "Christianity," he said in the teeth of the new humanists, "is theism plus Christ." But his faith was not that which divided God from his world. "I don't believe

[375]

in the *supernatural*," he declared, "but I do believe in the *super-human*." Human problems originate, he said, in "my old friend T. D." (total depravity)—which means "not that all men are equally bad or that any one man is totally bad, but that we all have a twist in our human nature." Amid the clash of the defeatist policies of the obscurantists and the wild schemes of those who proposed to make a new religion without God he stood firm. He pleaded everywhere for liberty and tolerance in the exercise of faith. "Sin is strong," he said, "but divine grace is much stronger."

But he was not to be allowed to continue long with this quiet activity. As the Presidential campaign of 1928 approached the horrid monster of religious bigotry awoke and Henry van Dyke took up arms both as a citizen in defense of the Constitution and as a man in defense of religious liberty. He wrote indignantly and cogently—sometimes with a touch of provocative vehemence—to the Protestant religious press where he saw the trail of the monster. Through a pamphlet, "In Defense of Religious Liberty," and on October 3rd, in a radio address, "For Freedom of Conscience," he spoke plainly of the "widespread cabal to keep one of the candidates for the Presidency from election because he is a member of the Catholic Church." Declaring that this was "far and away the most important question before the country today" he pointed to the Constitutional guarantees on the subject, reviewed the sorrowful history of similar movements, defended the Americanism of men of various religious affiliations who had exercised high office, and declared that the present movement was intolerable as an invasion of the rights of conscience and was to be resisted at all costs.

His resounding defense swept across the country and brought to him many words of commendation and a pitiful flood of abuse. At seventy-six he was beyond greatly caring. He had spoken his convictions as an American citizen and as a believer. The life-long champion of liberty and fair-play was still undauntedly at work. He was, as a matter of fact, the only Protestant minister of distinction who took an outspoken stand on the issue.

But Henry van Dyke was never a man of a single track mind. If he worked with passion and frankly delighted in battle when it

[376]

was unavoidable, he turned with equal conviction and zest to un-disguised play. Travel always fascinated him. He loved the beauty of the world and delighted to meet new people and see new places. He found himself at home everywhere, made friends easily and came home refreshed and bubbling over with acute observations on scenery, people and manners.

For a number of years as a result of conversations with his British friends and lured by tales of huge rainbow trout he had been long-ing to visit New Zealand. In January 1926 his desire was fulfilled. To a friend he said:

"Like Ulysses I must have one adventure more. But I'm doing what old Ulysses never did—I'm taking two unmarried daughters with me!"

From the boat he wrote:

"We have been steadily rolling through the blue Pacific, with a stop of 12 hours at Tahiti, and one of 24 hours at Raratonga. They are beauti-ful volcanic islands, green and mountainous and fruity. But, frankly, the tropics do not enchant me,—nor the people in them. There is something deliquescent about it all. The heat, while not intense, is like an obsession. The saving trade winds make me want to sail-away! The flying fish are the most enviable creatures,—swimming and skimming till a shark gets them. Mangoes are a despicable fruit and a good apple is worth a ton of them."

In both the north and south islands of New Zealand they travelled far around the curving shores, among the crystal lakes, into the Alps at Mt. Cook, to the geyser district of Whakanewarewa and the Maori village where they watched the *haka* dance—terrifying but no longer dangerous, in the Town Hall,—and spent some time in three cities. As usual Henry van Dyke found chances to preach —and took them. He also talked at length with New Zealanders and assembled much information about what he has described as "the foremost experiment station of state socialism without a tinge of red in it." But the real business was fishing and picnics and out-door delights with young and old. He noted the beauty and variety of the landscape and wrote in particular of the songs of several birds. Along the Temuka River he waded with the feeling of being in England. At Lake Roto-ehu standing in water to the hips he took a dozen rainbows through the day from 4 to 8 pounds each. Conducted by State Superintendent of Game Moorhouse he went on to Lake Taupo, lived in a Maori cabin, and often fished at dusk along the Waihaha with the friendly Maori chief. Here at the stream mouth he took his largest fish a 16½ pound rainbow that leaped four times out of water before he came to the gaff.

Henry van Dyke was never quite sure when the fishing was ended, or when he had gone as deep as his waders permitted. It was on the Tongariro River, where he rejoiced in the fellowship of three friendly anglers, that he forgot the perils of icy water in his zeal for fish. The event was without drama. No big fish to mark it. Nothing but cold water—over the top of his waders. It was all in the day's fishing. But as a result he spent a week flat on his back; and ever afterwards his left leg had a hard time to keep pace with his right. He took it gamely, and refused to allow it to keep him still; but it was ever a distress to him and not seldom a pain.

The next winter he was again eager to go somewhere. One of his good neighbors at Princeton was Herbert Adams Gibbons. So these two cronies of unequal ages but equal sympathies put their heads together. At first they were for Greece. "But, see," said Henry van Dyke, "that's an old story for you. Let's go where neither of us has been." And so they settled on South America. They made the journey as two men who loved the world and each other's company and were out to be happy. Take what is written and hinted at in Henry van Dyke's letters to catch the tone of mellow youthfulness:

". . . The company is agreeable: Bishop ——, General ——, Colonel ——, three very charming girls; four or five talkable ladies, etc., etc. Gibbons and I have been in general circulation.

The feature of the voyage has been *birthday dinners*. We began with Lincoln, and have had at least one every day. Also a fancy dress ball. Also a grand tournament of deck sports . . . We have had lots of fun and spent a thoroughly idle fortnight, without injury to anybody or serious damage to the universe. I tried to write one of my stories but gave up at the third page. Weather too sticky. Your cigarettes were fine.

The Bishop and the Captain begged me to preach today. So I did and enjoyed it as usual. If you go deep enough everybody wants religion, even in calm weather. . . .

You might send this epistle of an errant grandfather to (the family at) Princeton and Washington."

Or take the picture he described as he sailed away from Rio:

"The town itself is picturesque,—architecture varied and striking,—baroque, mauresque, modern French, Colonial Portuguese, semi-hemi-demi-classical,—houses of all colours, pink, blue, green, brown, white and red,—pillars, domes and pergolas. But the glory of the place is its natural situation. It is built on a great bay with many arms running up into a land of bewitched hills of the most fantastic shapes. At the foot of these hills the sea breaks on silver crescent beaches or dashes over huge black rocks. The valleys between are filled with a superb tropical forest, palms and banyans and mahogany trees; creepers, ferns and orchids,—blossoms of blue and gold and red and white; plantations of bananas and little straggling villages of yellow and pink houses. Through this wonderland we motored over winding, precipitous roads for a day and a half. When we got back to the ship I was so satiated with eye-pleasure that I could hardly see."

At Buenos Aires they found Carnival in celebration and spent a night driving through it:

"Long stands with open boxes had been erected in the main streets and the plaza. In these and in the circling cars the youth and beauty of B.A. were gathered: many were in fancy dress, some masked, all armed with flowers, confetti and smiles. It was a merry glamorous scene. I did not see one drunken, or one disorderly act. Good humour was universal and politeness ruled. The two ladies in our company were young and pretty and were almost buried in confetti and flowers."

They were entertained by the authorities in several places; and visited missions, schools and colleges. Once Henry van Dyke launching into a sermon found himself suddenly at the end of his strength. Turning with a smile to his travelling companion, he said: "At this point Dr. Gibbons will continue our sermon." They exchanged places—so ready was the understanding between them—and the sermon was completed. It is done on the football field—so ran their argument in recalling it later—so why not in the pulpit?

[379]

Again in 1927 Henry van Dyke returned to California to read "God of the Open Air" at Easter dawn on Mt. Roubidoux, (for the second and last time in person, though the poem is always a part of the service), to lecture five times for the benefit of the local hospital and to visit many friends. It was a typical episode of mingled work and play such as was always dear to his heart.

Meantime, though resigned from his regular teaching, his concern in education was undimmed. Against extreme specialization for utilitarian purposes he continued to maintain the practical values of a liberal education. He spent a month at the Gunnery School of which his son-in-law Hamilton Gibson was Head Master, teaching and inquiring into English instruction.

At the 150th anniversary of Phi Beta Kappa at the College of William and Mary on November 27th, 1926 he delivered what was in many ways the noblest oration of his career. Certainly he never wrote or uttered with greater *élan* the conviction of his heart. The theme was: "Democratic Aristocracy: its needs, its quality, and its ideals." Moving with dignity and clarity through the tumultuous scene of the day and lightened with characteristic sudden flashes of humor the oration progressed to its climax in the unforgettable tribute to the unknown teacher:

"And what of teaching? Ah, there you have the worst paid and the best rewarded of all the vocations. Dare not to enter it unless you love it. For the vast majority of men and women it has no promise of wealth or fame, but they to whom it is dear for its own sake are among the nobility of mankind.

I sing the praise of the Unknown Teacher.

Great generals win campaigns, but it is the Unknown Soldier who wins the war.

Famous educators plan new systems of pedagogy, but it is the Unknown Teacher who delivers and guides the young. He lives in obscurity and contends with hardship. For him no trumpets blare, no chariots wait, no golden decorations are decreed. He keeps the watch along the borders of darkness and makes the attack on the trenches of ignorance and folly. Patient in his daily duty, he strives to conquer the evil powers which are the enemies of youth. He awakens sleeping spirits. He quickens the indolent, encourages the eager, and steadies the unstable. He communicates his own joy in learning and shares with boys and girls the best treasures of his mind. He lights many candles which in later years will shine back to cheer him. This is his reward.

Knowledge may be gained from books; but the love of knowledge is transmitted only by personal contact. No one has deserved better of the Republic than the Unknown Teacher. No one is more worthy to be enrolled in a democratic aristocracy, ——

'King of himself and servant of mankind.'"

The oration was not only heard with enthusiasm. It was reprinted and quoted all over the country, and on the wall of many a school to this day hangs the tribute to the Unknown Teacher.

How the oration came to be written is an interesting story and typical of its author. Fortunately it can be told in his own words from a letter to Mr. J. W. Crabtree:

"The first idea that came to me in connection with it was to pay a tribute of gratitude to my old teachers in school and college, who did so much to awaken and train the mind of a rather unruly and adventurous boy. My debt to them is one that can never be fully paid. Although with the possible exception of President James McCosh of Princeton they were not 'famous men' in the worldly sense of the phrase, they were faithful, patient, enthusiastic workmen, and by their personality communicated to their pupils the vital spark of the love of learning. Meditating upon this subject I became convinced that it was properly the concluding part of an address which must have a broader scope, including both 'scholarship' and 'friendship,' the two fundamental factors of the Phi Beta Kappa creed. This idea at once raised the question of the part which scholarship and friendship have to play in the upbuilding of a great republic. From this I was led inevitably to the theme which is the title of the oration, 'Democratic Aristocracy.' In this age, when vulgarity is so rampant and domineering, it seems to me that this is a subject worthy of our consideration.

My regret is that the awkward limitations of the English language prevented me from making it clear that when I was speaking of the teachers as 'men,' I was thinking also of those thousands of fine women who have done such splendid work in the profession of teaching. But perhaps after all intelligent people will recognize that when a speaker says 'he' or 'him,' he is simply using the generic masculine, in which 'she' and 'her' are included."

[381]

Five times between 1924 and 1929 Henry van Dyke as University Lecturer on English Literature gave short series of lectures in Princeton. At first hesitant because doubtful whether the crowded schedule would permit the students to attend, he finally yielded to the invitation of the Trustees and the urgings of his Colleagues, old and new. Beginning with his constantly revised series on "The Service of Poetry" he went on to three new series, "Lights in Poetry," "Problematic Natures in English Literature," and "Four Noteworthy Modern Novels." Most of the authors discussed were of the Nineteenth Century but there were entirely new lectures on "The Morning Star" (Chaucer), "A Dark Lantern" (Edgar Lee Masters) and "The Bridge of San Luis Rey" (Thornton Wilder) and "Death Comes for the Archbishop" (Willa Cather). And through all the lectures ran a vein of pungent comment on literature and life, comparison and contrast between the old and the new. Never had the old "teacher of reading" been in better form. Students and Professors crowded the hall till the lectures had to be moved to a larger one. Professor Henry L. Savage in the *Princetonian* wrote:

"Undergraduate Princeton has seldom received such enlightenment on literary matters. The Doctor's criticism was delicate, liberal and kindly, but it was also trenchant, keen, pressed down and running over with humorous common sense. To listen to him quote poetry was to remember it for days afterwards.— Many of my colleagues have acknowledged their indebtedness to these Friday afternoon lectures."

On January 21, 1929 he gave the last of the series. Though he was afterward invited and urged to take up lecturing again he would not. Perhaps it was because of his closing words that winter afternoon in McCosh Hall. He had finished recounting the moving tale of "Death Comes for the Archbishop":

"So the Archbishop lies on his narrow bed a-dreaming of a green field in his native land, and of the two young men who found brotherhood there, and made adventure together—until at last he falls asleep to wake elsewhere."

The Lecturer paused, and then went on:

"After all what profit is there in a sermon after a great story? Actions

[382]

speak not only louder, but often clearer than words. Define less and do more. Religion is adventure not in theory but in practice. What we need now is not a new set of Ten Commandments from a professor of sociology, but a truer understanding of the old ones and a stronger will to keep them in the spirit. What the modern age lacks is not a new concept of God scientifically defined, but a deeper sense of His vital presence in the world and in our hearts, and a more courageous resolve to make Him known to our fellowmen through Christ."

As he stopped there was a hush upon the room. Then the audience rose to applaud. It was a tribute to the lecture but above all it was the spontaneous recognition of the man behind it. Even those to whom his faith was alien acknowledged its power in the cheerful, alert, keen spirit, and in the slight but straight form that bowed gravely and marched off limping like Jacob after wrestling with the angel.

In June with a grateful tribute in his heart and on his lips he spoke at the Commencement of the Polytechnic Institute of Brooklyn from which he had graduated 60 years before. His speech, the *New York Times* reported, "had all the audaciousness and pugnaciousness and sentiment of the Brooklyn boy who was father to this optimistic septuagenarian citizen of two continents—preacher, teacher, philosopher, diplomat, poet and fisherman."

The fact was that nothing could daunt his zest for life. He was constantly in touch with young men in the Church, in literature, in business. They were frequently running in to see him and his correspondence with them was full of affectionate sympathy and hope. For himself he met the "ravages of *anno domini*" with a joke. Dr. Curt Kayser tells me that as he completed a reconstruction of Henry van Dyke's teeth the patient climbed gloomily out of the chair and uttered one word: "appurtenances." As the delighted doctor noted the clear enunciation Henry van Dyke laughed happily and added: "You see I still have something to say."

I recall one of the last times he went fishing on the Ste. Marguerite. Coming down the river to the Saguenay there was a stiff wind and the canoeman labored to keep the big Gaspé canoes afloat on the bay. As we clambered aboard the motor boat to take us to Tadousac huge black waves crowned with flying scud leaped against the cliff which we had to pass. The captain was willing. "Maybe we make it," he grinned. "Let her go," said Henry van Dyke and lighting his cigar seated himself on the floor of the cabin with his arm around a stanchion and a slicker wrapped around him. There was one grave moment when, as the boat bounced and buffeted her way along the cliff in a smother of foam, the engine sputtered. We exchanged a look, but a moment later the engine picked up and we slammed past the ledge so close that the wave which bore us slid up the cliff like a wall of water and rolled the boat flat on her side. She righted herself and yawed her way down the turbulent river to safety at the Tadousac dock.

This natural vitality and resilience of body and spirit was ever typical of Henry van Dyke. "Danger is sweet when you front her," he had written and he believed it and practiced it. Old age was not so bad with a youthful spirit, and death was already conquered. His one real sorrow was the passing of "the old familiar faces." Manfully he wrote sympathetic and always discriminating tributes to them. Again and again he wrote and spoke of Woodrow Wilson interpreting him eagerly to the American people and acting as Chairman of the Princeton University Committee that drew up the classic memorial for the Alumni. Cheerfully he composed long pastoral letters to men and women who inquired at the door of his own faith. With new friends and old he foregathered as he had strength and with distant friends, old and young, he corresponded whimsically, even gaily. He wondered whether Cicero who perished at "the paltry age of 63" was ever a fisherman. How much fishing had Walton done after 70? What was a good *new* detective or mystery story? He liked to be up to date in this important field.

When the new "Sunbeam" for the Maine Sea Coast Mission (of which he was long time President) was launched at Damariscotta he was there with a poem. When the new Princeton Chapel was dedicated—although he had agitated vigorously but unsuccessfully for "a chapel which by its very form and atmosphere shall invite simple and orderly worship, hearty congregational singing, plain and vigorous preaching, and a spirit of reasonable and united reverence in the Sunday service"—he was there with a hymn, "Living Temples," and offered the prayers of invocation,—one of St. Augustine's, another of John Calvin's, concluding with the Lord's Prayer. Always ready to give himself to the support of movements for the common good where his own interest agreed with that of his friends, he headed the New Jersey Audubon Society's campaign for the protection of birds; shared in the dedication of the new chapel at Mercersburg School where he had long been a regular preacher; and spoke at the rededication of Carnegie Hall, and at the big celebration of the People's Liberty Chorus. He participated personally in Helen Keller's courageous campaign for the blind and she gave him a true title when she wrote:

"I know that you are an architect of happiness, and in your hands are precious materials which still build, strong and sure, stairways for groping feet to climb up into the sweet satisfaction of usefulness and self-respect."

His enthusiasm for the people and the institutions that enriched the common life was boundless. Sunday after Sunday he preached in one or another church with evident delight. During the long and happy summer vacations on Mount Desert Island he preached regularly in half a dozen churches. A carpenter, who had made a spar for Henry van Dyke's boat, told me:

"I always went whenever he preached and so did every one else. He was the only man I know who could *rightly* make a joke in the pulpit. He was the kind of fellow that you *wanted* to hear preach,—or go fishing with."

During the last years he used to stay for a winter holiday at a little inn on the west coast of Florida at the mouth of Charlotte Bay. Here Samuel Hopkins and Chester S. Lord and Henry van Dyke, familiarly known as The Three Musketeers, fished and talked and rejoiced together.

Through the dreamy days on the silvery waters of the Bay they contended indolently for the biggest fish, the most fish and the unique fish. At table the contests were judged and reports were received from the golfers, as Henry van Dyke scornfully observed,

[385]

"1000 words to 9 strokes." But there were occasions when the dream of action was laid aside and the reality of words held sway. Especially in the evenings they talked—how they talked! Any one who had the chance of listening to their sporting yarns and philosophical comments on events old and new received a fresh conception of what years may mean to men. Occasionally Henry van Dyke wrote a serene lyric—"The Onward Voice," "Foresight"—and frequently he penned brief but memorable letters. And each year in one of the little churches he preached vigorously, tolerantly, stipulating as his only terms that the collection should be divided between the Baptist, Methodist and Catholic churches. It is said that on the last of these occasions the Catholic Bishop postponed a parish meeting till the afternoon in order that the people might hear the sermon.

During the years after his resignation from regular teaching at Princeton Henry van Dyke turned eagerly to writing. But he approached the publication of each of his volumes with some anxiety. He was well aware that both the principles behind his writing and the manner of it were in conflict with the prevalent fashion of the movement. Against that fashion he was still ready to contend. He wrote to a school teacher:

"To me clearness has always seemed the most necessary quality (in writing), and force the most vital, and beauty the most delightful. Eccentricity is a monkey trick. Artificiality is a cosmetic. Dullness is a kind of dope. And carelessness is an insult to the reader. Some of our modern self-styled critics seem to value these qualities very highly, and to regard them as the marks of genius."

To Arthur Scribner he wrote of

"the 'Literary Gilders,' whose aims appear to be, first, the extermination of the worthy tribe of booksellers,—especially in towns and small cities; second, the establishment of the absolute dictatorship of the critical firm of Winkin, Bunkum and Pog, whose censorship of manuscripts will prevent the publication of books guilty of morals, manners or grammar; and third, the standardization on a commercial basis of what used to be called in a hopeful spirit, American Literature."

Concerning a picture submitted for a frontispiece for one of his volumes he wrote stringently:

"I do not like it at all. It seems not only weak, but quite out of tune with the book which does not contain a single painful monk or sad young man in a bathrobe."

Needless to add the picture was rejected.

With regard to his own writing Henry van Dyke was constantly on guard. "I don't want to overstay my welcome," he said again and again. His publishers and other friends were frequently consulted on this question. To John Hall Wheelock he wrote:

"I think I remember a scriptual warning somewhere against the idea that a man shall be read for his much writing. May a kind Providence save me from a scribulous old age."

Indeed, it is clear that many of his last stories and essays and poems —a number of which are among the best examples of his work,— would never have been undertaken save for wise and friendly encouragement. Not that Henry van Dyke was himself doubtful about his writing. The same zest and assurance as in earlier years went into the writing and he still exercised a strict judgment over his own work. A full waste paper basket bore evidence that he was a vigorous critic of himself. But when he was satisfied with a story and had that judgment confirmed by a friend or two he was ready to contend for it. "A man always wants his youngest child," he said, "to have the best possible chance in life." When one Editor "turned down" his latest story he wrote scornfully:

"I desire to state, however, since he is now going in for realism in his old magazine, that the most incredible details of this story—are extremely realistic ——,"

and he went on to describe how he had himself seen the events around which the story centred.

He faced the changing world with an extraordinary combination of courage and docility. His heart was often sad but he still had his message and the will and skill to deliver it. The same realism in the factual basis and the details of his stories was still there as was also the romantic element of interpretation.

"Life means more than we can understand, much less describe. Symbols help us, fables and parables are illuminating, little incidents throw a far light."

In 1925 his volume of thirty *Half Told Tales* was published. Brief and pithy, hard as diamonds on the realistic side, they flashed long rays of fire into the mysterious side—the side which in one of his late lyrics he called "The Side toward the Sky."

The Book was dedicated—in the same style in which it was written—

> "To Arthur H. Scribner
> forty years my Publisher
> and still my Friend."

In 1926 he set himself with deep absorption to write a number of the longer stories that still called in his fertile mind for expression. Two of them came from meditation upon Biblical stories, but the seeds for the others were his own far-flung experiences at home or abroad and tales that he had heard from all sorts of people. Wherever he went, whatever he saw, whoever was speaking, Henry van Dyke's mind was eagerly looking and listening for anything that might throw light on the meaning and significance of life. The slightest hint he retained and turned over and over in his mind to see if there were a story in it. First at his desk in "Avalon" and later at his writing table in "Green Door" among the spruces while the summer sea came and went beside him, he wrote steadily, "with a sense of freedom and fresh human interest." Eleven of the twelve stories that were gathered in *The Golden Key* and published in the autumn of 1926 were written in the first nine months of that year. As usual with Henry van Dyke in preparing a book of tales there was an underlying theme that united the diverse stories.

"It appears," he wrote in the preface, "that these are all stories of deliverance from some kind of peril or perplexity or bondage.

The book could have had as a motto: *There is always a way out.*

But this might be too sweeping,—misleading to light readers who look for a 'happy ending' in tune with their own desires.

Life is not made that way. The doors of deliverance are often different from what we expected. Sometimes one that looks dark leads into liberty. However that may be, I believe that in all God's world there is no hopeless imprisonment nor endless torment.

So instead of a motto I have chosen for this book a symbol: *The Golden Key.*"

The book was dedicated:

> "To my friend George Foster Peabody
> who has brought deliverance
> to many that were bound."

In a time when the disillusionment of the age was issuing in a literature of dull despair the book was a bright example of courageous faith. The basic style was that of his earlier stories but there was in this volume a greater emphasis on the irony of life—an emphasis to which his friend Maurice Francis Egan has particularly called attention. In a few newspapers the book was reviewed with enthusiasm but for the most part it faced an indifferent, sometimes a hostile, press. And yet even those who complained of its moral insistence—oblivious to the fact that despair is as much an assumption as faith—admitted somewhat grudgingly the too frequent truth of the tales and the author's adeptness in simple and direct narrative.

Henry van Dyke who had suffered from forebodings of this reception took the shock cheerfully, commented caustically but without bitterness on the situation, and was much gratified by the letters of his friends and the news that in the first four months 15,000 copies of *The Golden Key* were sold. But his chief satisfaction was in his own realization that once more he had sent a well-aimed arrow at the unchanging mark.

In 1927 he was much occupied with bringing out the cheap popular Sylvanora Edition of ten of his volumes—a plan proposed by Mr. Scribner and which Henry van Dyke accepted with delight. An "edition of economy" instead of an edition de luxe was exactly to his liking and he gave himself eagerly to selecting the poems for the single volume, "Chosen Poems," which was included, and as usual to all the details of illustrations and format.

His *Story of the Other Wise Man,* published more than thirty years before by Harper and Brothers, had now passed the 800,000 mark in its English form and had been translated into all the European languages and into most of the languages and many dialects of the Near and Far East. About this story Henry van Dyke always had strong feeling. He was content to have it translated into foreign languages without receiving royalties. He permitted its use for benevolent and religious objects where no admission was charged. He felt that the story had been "given" to him—not indeed by "direct inspiration" as he was frequently and wrongfully described as claiming—but *given to him* in the sense that the idea for the story came to him "suddenly and without labor" in the long watches of the night. The writing of it was another matter involving months of research and careful writing. A steady flow of letters from all over the world asking permission to dramatize the story for particular occasions finally led William H. Briggs to suggest that the message of the book could best be safeguarded if the author himself should make the dramatic version. The idea was a sound one and was promptly carried out with the aid of suggestions from the publishers. Henry van Dyke was much relieved to take this new step in defense of the integrity of a story which he felt had a message for the world as it had for himself and about the possible distortion of which he was often anxious. Some day the account of the travels of that story and its strange vicissitudes will be assembled. It will be a wonderful tale and a surprising report on the basic unity of mankind.

During these years Henry van Dyke received many pleas for stories and poems. But he would not write to order. Always he insisted that the invitation must coincide with one of "those impulses of the spirit which come to us unsought." But sometimes a plea offered the occasion to an unformulated impulse. His last Christmas Story, *Even Unto Bethlehem,* came in just this way. In his own words he said of it:

"I had resolved to write no more Christmas stories. But then a request came from a friend, and suddenly, without premeditation, the idea flashed upon me: why not write the story of the first Christmas? It was certainly a wonderful adventure for Mary and Joseph,—a shining example of a woman's courage when her heart is full of a great purpose. A journey in the open air through unknown hardships and perils, to a beautiful and triumphant goal. So I tried to tell that story as it was given to me, and I had more joy in writing it than in anything that I have ever done."

It was characteristic of Henry van Dyke that he went to write the greater part of the story in the study of his life-long friend Katrina Trask at "Yaddo,"

"She has gone," he wrote, "from that quiet room to the country of 'the river clear as crystal.' But her presence still inhabits there. I felt it quite distinctly and it made the writing of the story very happy."

Out of the plea of a friend, the flash that answered it, and the quiet work in the room of his friend, came one of the best of Henry van Dyke's Christmas stories. In it a keen sensibility to human pain and sorrow is transfigured by a serene faith in God in and beyond all travail.

In 1929 he undertook to prepare his new Princeton University lectures for publication. With the generous help of John Hall Wheelock, to whom he dedicated the book, the task was swiftly completed. *The Man Behind the Book* he called it with his never failing capacity for pointing to illimitable ideas with a clear and precise phrase. Life in the rich full-bodied sense still drew him and books were dear only as they opened doors into life.

When Eugene V. Connett, III, came along with the charming suggestion that two or three scattered fishing essays must be waiting patiently for companion pieces to be gathered into a special fisherman's volume, Henry van Dyke rose gallantly to that fly and with the greatest exuberance produced *The Travel Diary of An Angler*. Through the pages, which record fishing trips from Norway to Japan and New Zealand, from Wyoming to England, from Canada to Palestine, were scattered, after the quaint manner of fishermen, many philosophical observations. The volume closed with a chapter, "Dedicated to Sainte Marguerite," the little Canadian river where for twenty-five years he had fished almost every season. Recounting the tale of the capture of a 20 pound salmon that several times seemed lost as the long line tangled in the spikes of a sawyer bobbing in the pool, he concluded with the characteristic observation:

"Never give up your fish until you are sure he is gone.
So long, kind reader! And good
luck to your fishing!"

Henry van Dyke's heart was still strong for life. He responded swiftly and naturally to people and events. Somehow he found time without hurry for all sorts of things. A youthful war veteran, Kenneth Humphrey, long confined to the hospital, wrote Henry van Dyke a grateful letter about his writings, "as different from most of the modern books as Handel's Hallelujah Chorus is from 'Yes, we have no bananas.'" There followed a long drawn out correspondence with exchange of views on books and life. Once Henry van Dyke received back one of his own letters marked *undeliverable.* As he spoke on the radio the following night he referred gratefully and sorrowfully to his friend. But it was all a mistake. The indomitable young veteran was at the moment listening to the radio and the correspondence was joyfully resumed.

With Jedediah Tingle (after his death discovered to be William E. Harmon) Henry van Dyke had a characteristically delicious correspondence as he joined in the scheme "to bring smiles and tender thoughts to the great in heart—in high and low places—to comfort and cheer those who do exceptional things, or suffer."

Meantime Henry van Dyke was giving himself eagerly to his family. He joined the "tribal" Christmases at Washington, Connecticut, where most of his grandchildren lived, cheerfully announcing that "the old man can be moved easier than the young sprouts." By the fire with the Christmas tree at his elbow he sat while the bewitched children listened to wonderful tales and shouted with laughter at his nonsense rhymes. Not seldom the community Christmas began in one of the village churches where he read one of his stories or delivered an inimitable brief sermon.

When the first week of May came round he picked up his Bible and fishing rod and started for Mercersburg School Chapel and Dickey's Run. This was an almost annual event for twenty-five years, a cherished period of the calendar, when in the School and along the stream his steadfast friendship with the Irvines and Rutledges blossomed in serious talk and laughing by-play. "Reading like other pleasures," he wrote for the School book-plate "strengthens or weakens us."

At "Avalon" on his birthdays, when he was not off speaking, his wife liked to surprise him with a little dinner of friends, young and old. In the big library they received the guests with delight,— "My Lady Greygown" all dressed up (including her delicious smile) and Henry van Dyke beaming upon her while he declared: "My dear, you look *beautiful*." Sometimes on his birthday Henry van Dyke, deeply touched by the messages which poured in upon him from all parts of the country, consented to say a word for the newspapers. You get an impression of the temper of the man in these words on his seventy-fifth birthday:

". . . At 75 a man can't expect many more joyful surprises; but he can be happy enough in an Indian summer kind of way. His health has been spared and he has 'a reasonable, religious and holy hope.' He can still enjoy books and music and good talk. The morning air is sweet to him and the evening shadows have no fear in them. He can still hook and play and land a big salmon or a basketful of trout, and a clean pipe still tastes sweet to him. His memories of the old familiar faces are clear and bright. Surely he has nothing to complain of and much to be grateful for, even in an era when gratitude seems to have gone a little out of fashion.

The trouble with the 'Smart Aleck School' of writers and talkers today is that they demand too much from life and don't give enough to it. That is why they are old when young.

Of course I'm not satisfied with the use I've made of these 75 years. Who could be? But I'm thankful to have lived in a most interesting time, and to be still alive, with a good bit of work before me if the lamp holds out to burn, and brave young friends to comfort me for missing the old ones who have gone into the world of light ahead of me.

Looking back, the best things that have come to me seem to be these: twenty-five years of work in the Christian pastorate; twenty-five years of teaching in Princeton and preaching around the country; four years in the diplomatic service and one in the navy during the great war; forty years of writing about worth-while things and finding many gentle readers; sixty years of joyful intimacy with the big out-of-doors; and most of all, a family of five children and nine grandchildren, who inherit their good qualities from my wife.

You see, I am not an optimist; there's too much evil in the world and in me. Nor am I a pessimist; there's too much good in the world and in God. So I am just a meliorist, believing that He wills to make the world better, and trying to do my bit to help, and wishing that it were more."

His former colleague, Stockton Axson, accurately summed up the temper of these years when, recalling earlier experiences, he said that Henry van Dyke still showed,

"the same unconquerable courage of living, the same candor in speech, the same honesty in thinking, the same impatience with cant."

But there was still another adventure which Henry van Dyke was eager to undertake. For a number of years he had felt that *The Book of Common Worship*, prepared in 1903-06 by a committee of which he was chairman, might profitably be revised and expanded. The great usefulness of the volume together with comments about it that he heard as he went everywhere among the churches led him increasingly to that conviction. Suddenly the opportunity came, and Henry van Dyke promptly seized it. On June 9th, 1927, Dr. Lewis S. Mudge, Stated Clerk of the General Assembly, sent him, as an ex-Moderator, the invitation to be the guest of the General Assembly meeting in May, 1928 in Tulsa, Oklahoma. On June 10th Henry van Duke accepted the invitation and added:

"At some time in the fall I should like to have the privilege of consulting with you about the propriety of a revision of THE BOOK OF COMMON WORSHIP, which was published by the Presbyterian Board of Publication in 1906. It has now been under the test of use for more than 21 years, and it is not only possible, but probable, that some improvements could be made in it. Of the original committee of sixteen which was appointed and instructed by the General Assembly, five ministers and one or two ruling elders are still living. With the addition of some new members in sympathy with the conservative and historic spirit of the book, a committee might be formed to carry on and complete the work. I should like very much to talk with you about this idea."

The plan met with hearty support and he prepared himself to bring it before the church.

When Henry van Dyke rose to address the 140th General Assembly on May 25th, 1928, it was a tense hour. The so-called Fundamentalist-Modernist Controversy was in full swing and the anti-Catholic movement in the Presbyterian, as in other churches, was not far-off. Henry van Dyke was well aware of the dynamite in the situation. As usual he made no compromises but spoke straight to the issues with characteristic courage and persuasiveness. As usual also, his speech was not a party utterance, but an expression of universal Christianity. "Your masterful address," wrote Dr. John McDowell, a former Moderator, "was the keynote of the Assembly and a real contribution to the future of the Church." The theme was "Faith of Our Fathers." Beginning with "An expression of that antique emotion, gratitude, which is so much out of fashion among the professional cynics, gloom-casters, and revilers of Creation who now becloud our literary horizon," he turned to a moving tribute to his own father who had been Moderator of the General Assembly of 1876. It would be difficult to say who took most delight in the tribute—he who was uttering the ever blazing admiration of his heart; or the General Assembly which always hears with approval the praise of spiritual greatness and loves the lessons of home.

After recounting briefly the history of the first *Book of Common Worship* he concluded:

"But the committee had no idea that the book on which they had labored so long and so earnestly was perfect. We felt it was likely that the test of use and experience would show that there was room for improvement in certain points, without changing the spirit and tone of the book. Personally, I envisaged that period of trial at about ten years. Twenty-two years have now elapsed. Again the Assembly meets in the Middle West, in a sovereign State which has come into being since the book was adopted. I humbly venture to suggest that this would be a good time and place to ask for a small committee, consisting of the (six) surviving members of the former committee and an equal number of new members,

[395]

to consider whether and where the Book of Common Worship needs improvement. Their conclusions should be submitted to the Assembly for its approval, and if that were obtained the book would be sent out anew, for voluntary use in public and private devotions in that branch of the Church of Christ which follows the Presbyterian rule and order.

This suggestion is made in the belief that men and women are enlightened, uplifted and confirmed in the faith not only by sermons, but also by the prayer and praise in which they habitually unite to draw near to their Heavenly Father, through His Son Jesus Christ, in the fellowship of the Holy Spirit."

The proposal was promptly approved. The six surviving members of the first Committee and eleven new members, with Henry van Dyke again as Chairman, were appointed "to consider the revision of *The Book of Common Worship* and, if such revision is found desirable, to proceed with it."

As the report to the next General Assembly states, the first meeting of the committee unanimously voted the desirability of revision and further discovered that,

"the average age of the Committee was too high. Most of the men appointed by the Moderator, if not past their prime, were certainly past middle age. This was evident as we looked at one another, though each may have failed to recognize and admit it in himself. But what we specially wanted and needed in this important work for our Church today, was the counsel and help of the younger men, the active pastors who are in close touch with that indispensable, blessed, and foolishly-feared element of our Church life, 'the younger generation.' The wisdom of age may be salutary —but the generous impulse of youth is vital."

Thirty ministers in close touch with youth were made advisers to the Committee and the work got under way with their replies to a questionnaire.

It is neither possible nor indeed is it needful here to recount in detail the many meetings and the long researches entailed in the completion of this work during three busy years. There were differences of opinions, of course. Some of the Committee, rightly disturbed over the prevalence of divorce, desired a charge to the bride and groom inserted in the marriage service. As the Committee debated the matter Henry van Dyke remarked:

"You can't give advice at a wedding ceremony; it's either too late, or too early."

Some of the Committee laughed, but they all decided to leave the marriage service unchanged.

Dr. James H. Snowden who was a member of the Committees of 1903 and 1928 writes me of Henry van Dyke's part in the work:

"I was associated with your father as a member of the First and then of the Second Assembly's Committee that prepared The Book of Common Worship. He was chairman of both committees and gave his mind and heart to the work and the book bears the impress of his hand more than that of any other member of the committee. He is really the author of the book as he prepared most of it and guided and inspired all of it, and it is his gift to the Church and perhaps the most important work he did for it in its service. During the twenty-five years that I was thus associated with him I saw him grow in grace in a remarkable degree. In the work of the First Committee he swayed it by right of his chairmanship and of his literary distinction and his sharply marked individuality displayed itself in dominating but not in domineering ways. Always courteous and gracious, he was yet positive in asserting his views and the committee felt he should have his way and I recall only one instance in which he was outvoted in the final decision.

In the work of the Second Committee he showed that he had ripened and mellowed in spirit and his open-mindedness to every suggestion and his eagerness to accept every proposed improvement disarmed and charmed the committee and he had his way without asking for it. While he was easily the master of the committee in literary art and taste, yet he was the most modest of them in expressing his view. The grace with which he presided over the committee was beautiful to see and it was a privilege and delight to sit under him."

It is true that many of the prayers and services were given to the Church through the heart and hand of Henry van Dyke. The marriage service "based in order and in language on the first edition of the Directory for Worship (1645)" and the five litanies and many prayers were of his composition. But as he always eagerly said:

[397]

"The book is in no sense a one man piece of work." He liked to bear frank witness to the labors of his "true friends and fellow workers" of the Committee and often spoke of the fine work of Dr. Louis F. Benson in particular.

As the work on the book approached its conclusion an event intervened which nearly ended Henry van Dyke's part in it. The story belongs to the next chapter.

Chapter Twenty-five

INTO THE SUNRISE

THIS is the record of the last three years of life of a man already past his 77th birthday. He was looking eagerly over the rim of the world into the sunrise but he was by no means through with the things of the world, and especially not with the people among whom he moved. To the end he paddled his own canoe with a masterful if sometimes a weary paddle. Against the limitations of the flesh he rebelled, but with increasing good humor. For the things in which he believed he still contended vigorously. What were the chief events, internal and external, of those three last years?

The first year began with a sudden crisis that turned through steady recovery to advance into new strength. The second was a time of busy and eager completion of tasks. The last was a period of unhurried activity and grateful remembrance ending with a brief farewell. His preparation for death consisted not in dropping his paddle to drift but in thrusting his canoe over the shining rim of the world.

. . . .

On January 15, 1930 following a family Christmas in Washington, Connecticut, Henry van Dyke set out to join in the prolonged annual meeting of The Three Musketeers at Boca Grande, Florida. He was in high feather and promptly started in fishing. On January 21st he spent the morning and afternoon on the water. As he strolled from the dock back to the Inn suddenly his physical heart failed. His beloved fishing comrade, Samuel Hopkins (the other member of The Three Musketeers not yet having arrived), Dr. Henry Wallace, the House physician and Mrs. Beth Dunn, cheerful and competent nurse, soon had him in bed. His illness was promptly diagnosed as a coronary thrombosis or occlusion. "The distress is almost unendurable" wrote the Doctor "and hard to witness. I shall not go farther into details." Several members of the family alternated in staying with him, and the two months struggle for life began.

For a number of weeks the outcome was more than doubtful. And then, thanks to good care and the will of the patient to live, recovery set in. The whole Inn was considerately solicitous. One day a bellboy took a member of the family by the arm. "Excuse me," he said, "but we've got to know how the Doctor is. He was sort of one of the family, you know. Everybody likes him." Henry van Dyke gradually began to converse in cheerful vein and wrote brief letters to his friends from "Bedlands-with-the-windows-open." He liked the sounds and the feeling of life. Scornfully he declined to use a wheel chair, but as soon as the doctor permitted began taking carefully limited walks. He used to like to eat his lunch on a secluded corner of the porch in the open air and top it off with a little nip and a nicotine-free cigar. Late in March, when his son-in-law, Hamilton Gibson, "dear to me as a son," had come to bring him home, Henry van Dyke wrote:

"Climbing up from the Valley, is slow and rather painful, but I seem to gain a little from day to day. Yesterday I walked with Hamil to the bathing-beach and back. There was a fine surf running and the waters of the Gulf sparkled far out towards the westering sun.

Hamil and Sam Hopkins went on a picnic with the Meiers today and have just come in, full of fun and oysters. H and Mrs. Dunn will escort me homeward on Saturday (29th). Homeward for sure, however the journey goes."

Safely back in Princeton he came under the medical guidance of a veteran friend Dr. William S. Schauffler; and a little later the cheerful Mrs. Wane Johnson joined the household; for there were now no children regularly at "Avalon." Henry van Dyke and "my Lady Greygown" were coming upon their reminiscent years. But the past was by no means everything. The mistress of "Avalon" still held the decorous administration of the household in her hands; and the old master was as scornful as ever about retiring. To someone who remarked to him that he was looking remarkably well and strong he replied with spirit:

"I'm doing pretty well for a fellow with a spliced rod! I remember going fishing for ouananiche at the falls of the Metabechouan. Someone forgot the rods. There was a fellow living nearby who had an old rod spliced in two places. If you held it right it would play a fish, but if you got it wrong it would give—like that! Well, with that rod I made the best catch of ouananiche of my ill-spent career!"

With steadily renewed strength he set himself to catch up with his neglected correspondence; and at the friendly suggestion of John Macrae, he undertook the writing of an essay on Gratitude. When Charles Scribner died he wrote an affectionate and discriminating tribute with the characteristic touch:

"I have few memories more delightful than the sessions of friendly talk in the offices of the House. If it was in Charles' room Arthur would join us. If it was in Arthur's room Charles would drop in. And when Burlingame or Bridges or Brownell or Chapin or Marvin came along, it was like adding a new log to the fire on the hearth."

"You have been a true friend to us both," wrote Arthur Scribner, "and such instances make publishing more than a mere business—something higher and more worthwhile. I cannot tell you how much I personally value your friendship."

Eagerly he took up again his interrupted work on the revision of *The Book of Common Worship,* devoting much thought to the writing of the litanies. With Dr. Charles R. Erdman he prepared a statement about the nature and progress of the work and himself offered a characteristically frank paragraph addressed to objectors:

"We can see no force in the thoughtless opposition to such a book which is represented by the rather irreverent phrase, 'canned prayers'. The Bible and the service books of Calvin, Knox, and the other reformers, all contain written forms of prayer. All our hymns are written. Yet no one is foolish and crude enough to protest against 'canned praise'. The effectual fervent prayer of a righteous man is acceptable though it be written."

Unhappily the calmness of those days of recovery and fresh work was interrupted. Dr. Clarence True Wilson of the Methodist Board of Temperance, Prohibition and Morals in a report which was read before the Senate Lobby Committee with reference to the shifting of prohibition enforcement from the Treasury Department to the Department of Justice, made some derogatory references to Henry van Dyke and to his father. With understandable vehemence Henry van Dyke rose to the defense with a public statement:

"I have protested, and still protest, and will protest as long as I live, against the tyranny of an inquisitional church in American politics. That is treasonable. I am a protestant.

But when Dr. Wilson goes beyond my insignificant personality to attack my beloved father in his grave, it is impossible for a man of honor to keep silence."

And he went on to expound his father's record as has already been given in the earlier pages of this volume. Dean Christian Gauss of Princeton also came boldly to his support. The defense rested with the citation of the record. There was no reply. It was a painful experience for an old man, but not without an element of satisfaction because it afforded him the chance to bear fresh witness to the indissoluble bonds between his father and himself. Of the mass of cheering and a few condemnatory letters that followed he said: "There's the credit and debit sheet for speaking the unpopular truth."

His mind soon turned to other things. He had the same capacity as ever for finishing up one job and then moving on to the next thing. During a long summer with family and friends at "Sylvanora" he voyaged serenely among the fresh sea islands, his "Lady Greygown" and a grandchild or two with him when the waves were calm. She disliked as much as he liked a tossing sea. Even the sturdy motor boat, "Eileen",—which he "named as near Ellen as her femininity would allow"—would not tempt her to join him when the breezes blew.

Henry van Dyke either kept his whole mind deliberately at work, or else occupied the conscious portion of it with some pattern of activity. When he lacked the strength for full thinking, or felt that he had done his day's stint, he did not let his thoughts run loose. He turned to endless card games of solitaire or read rapidly a flood of light fiction, mystery and detective stories. So far as one can judge these two pastimes served equally to hold his attention but left the subconscious free for its perpetual activity. He was not always serene. I can see him now receiving an armful of books from the hopeful Mrs. Johnson and flinging them one by one on the floor as he growled: "I've read them all; can't you find any new ones?" But such irritabilities were momentary. He might speak brusquely or glower and then it was all over. He was incapable of sustained unhappiness. Like all sensitive people he had moods, but they evaporated promptly before the steady sun of an unconquerable will. Sometimes he chose to follow up sad thoughts but as he himself put it "I have never regretted anything though of course I have found it necessary to repent." He liked to think practically about his family and friends and talk about them quietly. He always said *yes* to life, though he occasionally uttered keen criticism on the fashion of the day.

Save for the happy "interruptions" of small social gatherings, the regular round of preaching, and his duties as President of the Maine Sea Coast Mission, he spent much time meditating and writing at "Green Door." Here he wrote with great satisfaction and the old incredible speed his essay on *Gratitude*, full of honest thought about the experiences of life, redolent of literary and personal memories, and expressed in language pure and clear. In the fall it was published as a booklet dedicated: "To Josephine and Henry Morgenthau with Gratitude." Here, too, he wrote his promised chapter, "De Maximis," for *The Book of the Fly Rod* and sent it to Hugh T. Sheringham with a note:

"If you really and truly like it, it is yours. Otherwise it is still mine, and you'll send it back. Speak frankly if you love me, 'honest Injun!' What an old man needs from his friends is affection, correction, and a firm hand on the chatterbox.

The 'thoughts-come-to-me' passages are included according to your suggestion. If they seem preachy, they can easily be left out. You have full authority to amend errors. I swear it on the sumac hilt of my old split bamboo fly-rod!"

One afternoon he recalled a tentative promise for a Christmas lyric for his friend Eleanor Carroll. "Last night," he said, "the idea came and here it is." He handed me a sheet of his neat hand-writing. There were three or four erasures in the eighteen lines. He had written it almost exactly as it was published with but three descriptive adjectives in the crystal and unutterably moving lines, "How Jesus Spoke." The will, the power and the grace of the poet were still in him. Life ran red and free in his veins.

As he came back to Princeton he took up again the meetings of the Committee for *The Book of Common Worship.* On November 2nd he journeyed to Philadelphia to bear tribute at the funeral of his friend of forty years, Dr. Louis F. Benson, "the foremost hymnolo-gist that America has produced."

". . . We think too much of death as the end of mortal life. Let us think of it more as the beginning of heavenly life. I doubt not that the spirit of my friend, set free from all infirmities and burdens of the flesh, now takes part in a joyful worship of God in praise and prayer, more pure and perfect, more musical and gracious, than that which he desired and labored to promote on earth in the name of Jesus our adorable Redeemer."

Soon thereafter came one of those public outbursts which al-ways revealed the strong convictions of his mind and heart. At the Germantown Business Men's Luncheon Club on November 28th Henry van Dyke commented unfavorably on the award of the Nobel Prize for Literature recently made to Sinclair Lewis. The press re-ported that he had said it was "an insult to America" but this he publicly denied on November 30th.

"I never said that the award of the Nobel prize for literature to the author of *Main Street* and *Elmer Gantry* was an 'insult' to America. I said it was a back handed compliment. This was a mild statement, when you consider the view of America given in those books. The author's name was not mentioned. There was nothing personal in my remarks."

The matter was widely bruited in the newspapers and Henry van Dyke received a flood of letters most of them supporting his view and thanking him for saying what needed to be said. From his replies to these letters and from notes made on his conversations about it the grounds for his disapproval of the award plainly appear.

"My comments . . . were not based on moral grounds, but on literary and philosophic grounds. An out and out pessimist cannot be a really great writer any more than an out and out optimist can be. This is because, as Kipling says, 'human nature is contrarious'. Also because it is mixed. As Chesterton said the other day, you cannot really describe Main Street if you ignore the sunny side."

"It isn't the darkness of his views I object to, it's the meanness of them. Take Howells' *Rise of Silas Lapham*. That's dark, but it's true to the heart of American life."

"I have visited and stayed in the Main Streets of thousands of American towns and villages, east and west, north and south, . . . while of course I have met many dull people, some mean people and a few slippery people during these peregrinations and habitations, I have also met many interesting people, lots of generous people, and some men and women who deserve to be called sons and daughters of God. These, in my opinion, are the people who have made and are making America. But there is no trace of their existence in the book called 'Main Street', or in 'Babbitt', or in 'Elmer Gantry'. Therefore, these books seem to me, in addition to their dullness to present a cock-eyed view of our country."

"We have at least a dozen American writers of fiction who are more deserving of such an honour. Among them I would name Miss Willa Cather, Mr. Booth Tarkington, Mr. Hamlin Garland, Mr. Struthers Burt, and Mr. James Boyd. The list could easily be enlarged."

When Sinclair Lewis made his long and vigorous speech as he received the award in Stockholm he made an extended reference (The *New York Times*, December 13th, 1930) to

". . . a learned and most amiable old gentleman who has been a pastor, university professor and diplomat. He is a member of the American Academy of Arts and Letters and no few universities have honored him with degrees. . . . This scholar stated, and publicly, that in awarding the Nobel Prize to a person who had scoffed at American institutions as much

[405]

as I, the Nobel committee and the Swedish Academy had insulted America. I do not know whether as an ex-diplomat he intends to have an international incident made of it, and perhaps demand that the American Government land marines at Stockholm to protect American literary rights, but I hope not.

I should have supposed that to a man so learned as to become a doctor of divinity, a doctor of letters, and I do not know how many other imposing magnificences, the matter would have seemed different. I should have supposed he would have reasoned: 'Although, I personally dislike this man's book, nevertheless the Swedish Academy has in choosing him honored an American by assuming the Americans no longer appear as a back-woods clan so inferior that they are afraid of criticism, but instead a nation which has come of age and is able to consider calmly and maturely the dissection of their land.' . . ."

Expressing his gratitude to "the fishing Academician" for having "given me the right to speak as frankly of that Academy as he has spoken of me" the prize recipient observed: "It (the Academy) does not represent literary America today; it represents only Henry Wadsworth Longfellow."

The New York *Herald Tribune* commenting in an editorial on this long and pithy speech referred to "Mr. Lewis in his hour of awful nakedness at Stockholm." And Henry van Dyke cheerfully remarked:

"Who would be so unkind as to interrupt the bubbling joy of the author of 'Elmer Gantry' in receiving the Nobel prize for literature? Why send the marines to Stockholm to interfere with the Babbitt? Just tell it to them; that is enough."

Having borne witness again to his faith that good literature must have "a human aim,—to cheer, console, purify or ennoble the life of the people" he dropped the controversy. He was willing to let the people choose.

Deeply he felt the changing public taste in books which ran counter to what he believed were the standards of lasting literature. To Arthur Scribner he wrote:

"Thank God you do not change. Even when book sales are declining you remain loyal, considerate and encouraging to the author's heart. . . .

Some of the new books hardly seem to me worth the expense of launching and exploitation. But of course this is by no means true of all of them."

He was watching with sorrowful, but unblinded eyes as a world disintegrated about him. It was a hard experience, not made easier by his years. But the most notable features of his attitude were his swift recognition of standards in some of the new books and his steady witness to the human values which he ever insisted were basic to good literature. He was sometimes discouraged, but never querulous. There is a characteristic note of mingled defiance and confidence in the verses found after his death in a drawer of his desk:

To Thersites

You seem to hate me. Well, what does it matter?
I do not have to read your peppery patter,
Nor you my books! Let's take our ways apart,
And follow each the guidance of his heart.
You say God's dead, and life's a bawdy tale;
I think God lives, and goodness will prevail.
You mock mankind with lewd ungainly mirth:
I find a lot of folks to love on earth.
On prejudice you feed and nurse your spleen:
I'd rather have more wholesome food, and clean.
You write a language hitherto unknown;
To Shakespeare's tongue and faith, I fealty own.
So ride your road, Smart Aleck, gaily ride;
I keep my path; the future will decide.

On December 15th he rose to speak affectionately at the funeral service of his old friend George Alexander, "here in our dear old dusty, crowded, noisy New York . . . a tranquil shining angel of the Divine Mercy." Thus was fulfilled the pledge exchanged between them almost fifty years before as they began their youthful work as city pastors: whichever survived was to conduct the funeral of the other.

Less than a month earlier Dr. Alexander had written:

"I expect to be the beneficiary (of our compact). It frees me from that

dread which haunted the soul of James Russell Lowell when he sent for
Professor Norton and said: 'I don't want any parson spouting over me'.
Yours to the end of the road—and beyond."

Truly there were no spouting parsons at that service—only the quiet
voices of believing friends giving thanks for a mighty believer. For
Henry van Dyke the event was an exhausting effort but above all
a genuine blessing.

His gaze was now reaching eagerly into the unknown country
but, as ever, he saw it not by looking away from this world but by
looking into the world. He was still ready to question Professor
Albert Einstein's widely quoted approval of the statement that "the
only deeply religious people of our . . . age are the earnest men
of research." He published an article in *The Presbyterian Magazine*
defending the status of religion in a broader field than that of
research and emphasizing the fact that the basis for science itself
must ever be found in a "real relation" between God and man.

In January 1931 he went to spend a winter holiday in Bermuda
near his daughter Paula and her family. As he left he wrote to
James Kerney in reply to a friendly letter:

"I fancy that you and I are in a very similar condition, cloistered but
still cheerful and trying to earn our living.

Let's not take the veil after all!

I hope that the God whom we both love and trust much more than
we understand Him will soon restore you to full health that we may still
have some good times together here on this whirling globe."

In Bermuda he took in his surroundings with delight despite a
blustery season:

"Have I told you about this apartment? It is called the Ship Room. All
the decorations—pictures, andirons, curtains, bed-spread, fire tongs, ink-
stand, and two brass anchors beside the hearth,—are maritime. I feel like
a Marlinspike or a binnacle. So when the gale roars, as it does almost
every day, I just hug the harbor and wait for the clouds to roll by."

Despite days of weakness he was fully capable of innocent merriment and laughed in the face of old age even better than he had been
able to laugh in his youth under the burden of doubts. In fact this

sojourn was a gay interlude. Several younger writers were there,—his son-in-law Henry Chapin, Hervey Allen, Louis Untermeyer, Thomas S. Matthews; and they all played about together in vacation style. Mr. Untermeyer has recalled the scene:

"Yes, I remember vividly those weeks at the Cambridge on the little island of Somerset. And I remember even more clearly the first night your father arrived. I had pictured him not so much as an old fogey as Old Fogey Himself with a brace of thunderbolts in one hand and a set of bristling obiter dicta in the other. I was both afraid of him and fascinated by what I thought him to be. I suppose I considered him an arch reactionary, and I have no doubt he pictured me—if he thought about me at all—as a red-eyed revolutionary. I think we appraised each other warily for a day or two. And then I completely succumbed. It was not his literary judgments which convinced me, though these were far more tolerant than I had allowed myself to believe they might be, nor was it his *Weltanschauung*, though, curiously enough, it was not so unlike my own. It was, first of all, the unmistakable charm of the man, the quick sense of sympathy, the unexpressed camaraderie, which won all the members of that little community.

I remember our evenings full of raillery and anagrams. I had grown so fond of your father that I determined to be generous and give the elderly gentleman a chance to win by overlooking the possibilities of certain key-letters. After the first round, however, I made no more 'noble' gestures; it was all I could do to hold my own against his quick eye and quicker brain."

On his return to Princeton Henry van Dyke gave an interview to Harry Goldberg of the Philadelphia *Public Ledger*. It is a clear picture of an undismayed liberal, a Jeffersonian democrat:

". . . The first fact which we must face is not 'a new world', but the same old world of imperfect human beings, working under new conditions." Pleading for "a more humane spirit in the conduct of business" and "a special kind of leadership in national matters . . . experts who understand the intricate currents of industry and international trade; men who have the courage and the intellectual power to modify traditional methods and policies, if necessary, in order to achieve the welfare of the public," he concluded:

"Good will, common sense and mutual helpfulness will enable us to pass through this depressed valley without panic. And 'in the long run', as Grover Cleveland phrased it, I reckon that American courage, hopefulness, idealism, intelligence and grit will bring us out, chastened but not broken, into a new and saner time of true prosperity, earned by the free labor of all and fairly shared by all according to the service they have rendered to the Commonwealth.

These are my humble views of 'What's Ahead for America'. They are old fashioned but progressive. Let me add one thing: Our country will never see her great desire of a secure and lasting world peace until She takes an active hand in providing a rational substitute for the ancient and futile horror of war."

Was there anyone in those convulsive days who spoke more sanely and directly than this upon the central human issues of the day?

In his quiet study he wrote metrical versions of two Psalms and composed some verses which he read at the unveiling of a memorial doorway in Trinity Church, Princeton, for the late Rector, Alfred Britten Baker.

Equipped for the possible emergency which now regularly attended his steps, he left for Pittsburgh on May 31st to make his final report on the revision of *The Book of Common Worship*. After three years of steady work the book was ready. As he was warmly welcomed to the front of the platform in Syria Mosque by the Vice Moderator, President Cheesman A. Herrick, there was prolonged applause and all empty seats on the floor were promptly filled from the buzzing lobbies. With a voice that rang easily into the back of the gallery he read a brief report in which he expressed gratitude for his share in the work "as the last labor of my life." For the Book he asked approval with permission for the Committee and the Board of Christian Education to complete the Psalter and other responsive readings later to be included. He had come to make the report perfectly aware that it might be *literally* the last labor of his life. But as he spoke the weight of emotion that he bore lightened. He always accounted his share in *The Book of Common Worship* the most important work of his life, but his manner as he now submitted it to the democratic test of the General Assembly can only be described in Wordsworth's phrase, "solemn glee." A great hush was on the house as he paused and looking around added: "If you will say Amen"—and then with the incorrigible twinkle in his eyes—"or even Āmen, to these two requests, we shall be abundantly rewarded." The house and the speaker were united in heart-easing laughter.

"Will the chairman answer questions?" called a commissioner. "Certainly," he replied affably; and there followed a few minutes of that swift and vivid exchange which was ever dear to his heart. When the vote was taken it was unanimous, and the Assembly rose to applaud as the Moderator, Dr. Hugh Thomson Kerr, expressed appreciation to Henry van Dyke for "his lifelong service to the Presbyterian Church." Retiring with a happy smile Henry van Dyke remarked: "I can't help being a Presbyterian; I was born that way."

It was quite typical of him that as he revived from the effort of this last report he insisted upon going to call on a friend and member of his last Princeton class of 1923, Le Moyne Page. And as the train bore us eastward again he said to his son: "Old man, we ought to go fishing now." To which the only reply possible was: "Young fellow, we will."

At the Orchard Lake Club we were guests of Alexander R. Gulick and floated idly on the still mirror of the Lake while Henry van Dyke wafted his flies, now under the branches of the tall trees where the tanagers and grosbeaks sang, now beside the reeds at the source where the red-winged blackbird gurgled his kon-ker-ree. The trout came well to his tiny Queen of the Water; but occasionally he would reel up with a little sigh and sit listening to the birds.

Later in the summer at "Sylvanora" he wrote "Tic-Tac-Toc," a story full of verve and feeling though strangely enough the manner of it, as he himself confessed, was like that of Hans Christian Anderson's tales. We discussed this style at length but there was no accounting for it. His reading outside of the Bible, and there chiefly in Genesis, was light fiction. The style had no traceable origin. "Perhaps," he said, "it just belongs with the nature of the story. That's the way it ought to be, anyhow."

Here, too, he began work (later completed at "Avalon") on "An

Act of Worship in America commemorating the 200th anniversary of George Washington's Birthday" which included a new litany of Patriotism.

Another event of this summer of 1931 deserves particular note. He said nothing about it at the time but the facts reveal that he was well aware of what he was doing. As the date for his regular sermon in the Union Church at Seal Harbor approached he prepared a new sermon, "The Truth in Christ." Not that the theme was new, but it was freshly prepared, in notes which lie before me now, on the text: "To this end am I come into the world, that I should bear witness unto the truth."

"Unlike many others in his day and in the present time, the truth to Christ was supreme. He believed it, spoke, lived, died for it. It made him strong, confident, calm, triumphant. It made him obedient, kind, considerate, forbearing. He was willing to listen to all who spoke sincerely. Willing to help all who sought the truth. Willing to forgive all who sinned through ignorance.

His manner of teaching was his own. It was not as the Scribes by arguing, defining, syllogizing. It was direct, with authority, simple and strong as sunlight. . . . He *bore witness*. He was sure.

Did not claim *omniscience* in his earthly life. Admitted that some things He did not know. . . . But He claimed *certainty* in what He taught. Consider some of these things:

1. God is not a dream, theory, definition, but a person, Spirit who must be worshipped in spirit and in truth . . .
2. Jesus came forth from God to reveal Him to men . . .
3. Man is sinful but not damned. Needs to be saved and can be saved. . . . Jesus is messenger of this forgiving love. . . .
4. Truth as Jesus sees it is not static. Dynamic, advancing, unfolding. . . .
5. World beyond this world; life beyond grave. Not a dream, a perhaps, a pious hope. But a reality, a certainty. . . .

Our world today is full of confused noise and smoke of warring theories and carbon monoxide gas of universal doubt. To pass from these to truth in Jesus, is like passing from danger and turmoil of one of our unlivable city streets into a quiet place full of heavenly music.

I hear the voice of Him who spoke as never man spoke saying:

UNITED STATES LEGATION AT THE HAGUE, AUGUST 1914

THE AMERICAN ACADEMY CELEBRATES HIS 80TH BIRTHDAY,
NOVEMBER 10, 1932

GOLDEN WEDDING, AVALON, 1931

'Come unto me all ye that labor and are heavy laden, and I will give you rest. Take my yoke upon you and learn of me; for I am meek and lowly in spirit and ye shall find rest unto your souls.' "

This was his last sermon, preached four times: in Seal Harbor July 12th, in Bar Harbor, August 9th, in the First Church Princeton, October 18th, and in the Brick Church, New York, December 6th. The preacher's last word was *The Truth in Jesus*. He uttered it eagerly in the churches where he was regularly accustomed to preach; he delivered it last in the church of his vigorous middle years. Never again did he speak in public save once to acknowledge birthday greetings; and then the note on which he concluded was the same.

On December 14th—a day late to leave Sunday free—the children and grandchildren and a host of neighbors and friends poured into "Avalon." It was the Golden Wedding celebration. Through the rooms among their friends Henry and Ellen van Dyke moved hand in hand and when the last guest was gone and the grandchildren were raiding what remained in the dining room they were found still hand in hand content as they sat side by side upon the library sofa. How beautiful was the Golden Honeymoon that rose upon the faithful but not always untroubled years of this born leader of men and his elusive but vivid and devoted wife.

The winter passed quietly in the mellow serenity of "Avalon." Children and grandchildren, friends and neighbors, came and went. The old grandfather clock in the hall chimed the timeless hours of peace. Henry van Dyke was invited to give another lecture on Tennyson, "Humph," he growled pleasantly, "I love Tennyson too much. A man must stop before he makes a fool of himself." The fact was that he had decided not to appear in public again.

Regretfully acknowledging his inability to attend the Princeton dinner in New York he sent a friendly message praising President Hibben's "wise, fruitful and peaceful service of twenty years at the head of Old Nassau." He wrote many brief letters about personal religion, about the Church, about literature. Scornfully he declared, in answer to a question: "I do not believe in 'proletarian literature' any more than I believe in 'capitalistic literature'." To a

[413]

young friend who wished to write he sent a careful criticism of his work together with an annotated list of twenty-six "great writers who have 'made their living' by other means than writing." He busied himself happily with the task that Arthur Scribner suggested to him—the assembling of notable brief fishing stories and the writing of introductory paragraphs.

In late May 1932 with his son he celebrated the thirty-seventh anniversary of their first fishing trip by a second visit to Orchard Lake. As we drifted along the dam one calm afternoon he looked down to a still shallow pool on the stream below where several trout were rising briskly. "You know," he said slowly with the familiar incorrigible look on his face, "I've been told 'no more stream fishing', but don't you think those trout need my fly?" Like bad boys we climbed out of the boat and eased our way down the bank. Delicately, accurately he made his casts. When one shining trout came to net he was satisfied. He had taken a fish and proclaimed his liberty!

Once more at Tunk Lake in Maine his faithful friend Theodore Marburg took him to the still waters with a rod where as he gaily expressed it he "caught the limit of trout with barbless hooks." He might be satisfied to "cast the fly and loaf and dream," but he much preferred to take fish.

The summer passed with scarcely differentiated days. As the news of the death of René Bazin reached him he wrote an exquisite tribute to his long-time friend whom he had first met through the latter's daughter, Mme. Sainte-Marie Perrin.

Though much delighted by what he called the "brave and honest" stand against Prohibition just taken by his Seal Harbor neighbor, John D. Rockefeller, Jr., Henry van Dyke refused an invitation to write about Prohibition.

"You know," he remarked, "how much I dislike Prohibition. At the same time it isn't so important as the controversialists have made it. I'd like to see it repealed, but there are lots of things more important. And I really think (with an eager smile) I'd rather concern myself with them." He was measuring his strength carefully.

When he returned to "Avalon" a trained nurse, Miss Maud Collins, brought her serene strength and wisdom to the household. The beautifully printed and decorated volume, *A Creelful of Fishing Stories*,—the last book venture of himself and his publishers,— shortly made its appearance and was followed by many friendly letters from fishermen all over the world. It was a fitting conclusion to a publishing relationship begun nearly fifty years before with the printing of the first essays of *Little Rivers*.

From his den Henry van Dyke wrote often to his friends. Two of these letters are quoted here for the interesting views they express and as illustrations of his clear mind and steady heart:

On October 31st to Dr. Nicholas Murray Butler:

"Your interesting letter of October 27th was duly received, and has been under careful consideration.

The task of selecting the 'six outstanding names in American literature' to be carved on a building devoted to letters, which is now being erected in the City of New York, is certainly not an easy one. I am glad that it is in your hands. The counsel for which you ask is herewith at your disposal, but it represents, of course, only an individual point of view.

Certain principles may be taken for granted:

1. The selection is to represent as far as possible permanent literary values, and not publicity records or prize awards by foreign academies.

2. The selection is to be made not according to the judgment of past generations, or upon our guess of the judgment of coming generations which is a thing that no man can find out; but upon our own judgment today. By that I mean not the judgment of the crowd, but of those who have knowledge and understanding and standards of excellence.

3. It must be remembered that the selection is only temporary for no building in New York, except a church, is likely to last more than fifty years.

Bearing these principles in mind I have studied your list of twelve names with a view of recommending six of them to your consideration.

[President Butler's letter had given the following names: Bancroft, Bryant, Cooper, Emerson, Hawthorne, Irving, Poe, Longfellow, Lowell, Mark Twain, Whitman and Whittier; and added: "From this list, or from this list enlarged in such a way as you may advise, a selection of six names must be made."]

It seems to me that Bancroft may be safely omitted; even if his work is 'history' it is certainly not 'literature.'

Bryant, with a few lovely lyrics and some sonorous blank verse remains memorable more as a journalist than as a man of letters.

The same thing may be said in the main of our beloved Mark Twain.

The two men who may be fairly ranked as the beginners of American literature are Irving and Cooper and it seems to me that their names should head the chosen six.

Next to them, I think, should come Longfellow as a poet and Emerson, the philosopher.

Following them, I think, should come Hawthorne, the lonely genius who conceived and wrote in pure English the greatest American romance of universal significance,—'The Scarlet Letter'.

That makes five names. For the sixth in my judgment the choice would lie between Whitman and Poe. The greater part of Poe's work was disordered and confused by his hereditary physical infirmity, but he wrote half a dozen wonderful short stories of mystery and terror and perhaps half a dozen lyrics of exquisite verbal beauty. The bulk of Whitman's work outruns his undoubted genius; some of his dithyrambs are deadly dull and a few are slightly indecent. But beyond a doubt he rendered a great service to literature in claiming for English verse a larger freedom, not from metre (for everyone of his best poems has a subtle metrical structure of its own) but from the bondage of monotony in the use of metre. His genius in exercising this freedom produced many superbly beautiful lyrics and lyrical passages.

If the choice lay with me I should choose Whitman rather than Poe for the sixth name. But I should feel a sincere regret that I could not include them both. The same regret I should feel in regard to the omission of Lowell and Whittier."

On November 8th in acknowledging a warm birthday letter from Dr. Lewis S. Mudge, Stated Clerk of the General Assembly of the Presbyterian Church, he wrote:

"Since early youth I have had a feeling of unworthiness for the high calling of the ministry. But my father, who was a friend of your father and your grandfather, told me that it was not a question of personal fitness but of an inward call and willingness to serve. On that basis, with all my faults, I went ahead and have had lots of hard work and great joy in the service of Christ. But believe me, in spite of all your kind words, our Church has done more for me than I have ever been able to do for our Church.

Being as you know a Liberal Presbyterian I have never found any restrictions in the way of studying nature and human nature and writing about worthwhile things in the best English that I could command. I have often followed St. Peter's example and gone a-fishing, and have always tried to live by St. John's advice and 'love the brethren'.

I am grateful to you for your counsel through which I was led to devote the last three years of my life to the revision and completion of the Book of Common Worship. It was a happy task which brought me into close fellowship with men whose company did me great good in heart and mind. Some of them have gone before me on that journey in which I expect before long to rejoin them. Meantime, while the area of my faith has shrunken a little and the number of things that I believe is slightly smaller, I am more convinced than ever that the essence of Christianity is to think, and feel, and act, according to Christ Jesus."

On the same day he went to the polls and, as recorded in his date book, voted Democratic.

Henry van Dyke was never quite satisfied that any members of his own family could drive a car. Perhaps this was because he had always refused to learn to do it himself. Nevertheless he consented to the risk on November 10th and we all drove up to the American Academy meeting in New York which was to conclude with a celebration of his 80th birthday. There was a greeting from William Lyon Phelps, "An Illustration of the Good Life"; a sonnet by Robert Underwood Johnson—to whom Henry van Dyke had written in anticipation: "You may not recognize your old friend when he arrives, for he has grown a beard during the summer. But it is a very little one and in no sense a rival to yours." The singing of Henry van Dyke's Academy Hymn by Inez Barbour Hadley accompanied by the Composer was the last event before "the birthday child," a slight but trim and erect figure, rose to speak. In a voice at first shaken with emotion but shortly settling into its vibrant tone, Henry van Dyke replied:

"An old traveller thanks you for your friendly greeting at the 80th mile-stone on his foot-path of life.

If there is anything in the world for which a man deserves no credit it is his birthday. This is true of his first and of his last. Both come without his choice. Only for the years between is he responsible. It is a comfort to know that you think my years between have not been altogether wasted.

Many tasks of different kinds have met me on the way. None was accepted without a real claim of service. I have not written for the market, but because certain things seemed worth writing about. If they came in prose, they were written in prose. If they came in verse so they were written, hoping that they might be poetry. A poet must keep his eye on the object and his imagination beyond it. What he does not see and feel he can never make into a poem. If a thing is worth writing about, in prose or verse, it deserves the best, clearest, most fitting words that a man can find. That tribute I have gladly paid to the art of letters.

As the only minister who has been admitted to the Academy, I am grateful for your tolerance towards my simple faith and for encouraging me to live up to it better. That faith is not at war with art or science. Truth is its friend, beauty its ornament, goodness its aim. Its door is open and its windows wide. It knows not hate or fear. It is in fellowship with all who deal justly, love mercy, and walk humbly with their God. To these sailors, homeward-bound,

'The port, well worth the cruise, is near,
And every wave is charmed.' "

The words had been carefully written but not once was the paper looked at. It was the heart of Henry van Dyke speaking and every faculty was in his command.

Ellen Reid, "My Lady Greygown," sat not far away. During the earlier part of the Academy proceedings, before the celebration for which she had come began, she was restless and even wondered audibly "why *do* these old men talk so much?" Of course she could hear nothing. But when the *real* celebration commenced she leaned back contentedly and watched her man upon the platform with un-wearied eyes. When it was all over she said with one of her spar-kling smiles: "I *knew* it was all good."

The next day Henry van Dyke was up as usual and busied himself

[handwritten margin note: man deserves no credit for his birthday]

writing his thanks to those who had made his birthday happy. To Professor Harper he wrote: "I value especially your words about Mrs. van Dyke without whom, as you very well know, I could have done nothing."

Christmas passed brightly at "Avalon" with neighborly visits and messages. Elaine arrived seasonably from a long sojourn in India, and Katrina and her family came on from Chicago, and all the families visited "Avalon" during the holidays. Henry van Dyke's heart was made glad by the devoutly simple message from his old canoeman on the river Ste. Marguerite:

"Que nous sommes heureux de pouvoir encore cette annee venir vous souhaiter heureux et joyeux Noel. Nous nous portons à merveille encore et vivons toujours sous l'esperance de vous revoir. En attendant ce moment si longtemps desiré, la volonte de Dieu le permettant,
Nous demeurons vos humbles serviteurs.
Messieurs Henri Gravel et Ezide Gravel."

But there was one more struggle which must be mentioned here. He was still capable of rising to the defense. The serenity of his last months had been badly broken late in November. *The Book of Common Worship,* first published in 1905 and on the revision of which the Committee with Henry van Dyke as chairman had long worked, was published in April, 1932. Now he received notice of another book of Church services bearing the practically identical main title of *Book of Common Worship.* At once he was up in arms. He knew, of course, that book titles cannot be copyrighted but he was sure that there was a genuine ethical consideration at stake which should apply even in the case of religious books. He entered upon a pointed and indignant correspondence with the editors and the publishers. Curiously—perhaps naturally is more accurate—the publisher promptly wrote that if he had known of the similarity of the titles he would have insisted upon a different one and expressed genuine regret. But the clergyman-editors had a different idea to the effect that the title was a general one and sufficiently differentiated in the sub-title. Henry van Dyke concluded the matter in January with a cogent letter to one of the editors pointing out that he had previously sent copies of the report on *The Book of Common Worship* to the editors of the new volume at their own request: that "no permission had been asked or given for the use of a title which was, and still is, distinctive"; and further that in the preface to their book there was absolutely no mention of *The Book of Common Worship*. "It is natural to conclude that this strange omission is intentional. . . . I am sure you could have found a more original title and a franker preface if you had been asked to do so."

To Dr. William C. Covert, his fellow worker on the Presbyterian Book, he wrote on January 3, 1933:

"The interests of *The Book of Common Worship* are entirely in your able hands. Being old and tired I shall write no more upon the subject. All letters referring to it will be sent to you."

Was it all a tempest in a teapot? It was not. It was the same old issue that he had found as a young man when he copied Shakespeare's lines into his book of thoughts:

"Rightly to be great
Is not to stir without great argument,
But greatly to find quarrel in a straw
When honour's at the stake."

As Dr. Covert wrote him on January 6th:

"I think you have administered in a highly dignified way a much deserved rebuke to —————. They seem to have run amuck at many points. A little wisdom . . . would have saved them from much embarrassment. You have said not one word too much, and what you have said has been so marked by the code of a gentleman that it must bring the brethren to an understanding . . ."

A few more things needed to be done. As the New Year advanced Henry van Dyke composed a poem for the 80th birthday of the "Venerable young man", Robert Underwood Johnson. Gratefully he acknowledged a friendly greeting, with a pussy willow attached, from Frank Chapman at Little Rivers, Florida. In the *Daily Princetonian* he wrote enthusiastically of "The Princeton Spirit in Athletics". "One thing is certain—no American University can prosper or do its work without athletics. The question is not whether we will have them, but how we shall best conduct them."

He uttered his enthusiasm and hope in the new Democratic administration in a poem for President Roosevelt, "To Our New Pilot", in the New York *Times* of March 19th and received with delight the President's personal letter of thanks. At the invitation of the Williams College *Record* he wrote a brief article voicing his faith in the widening of "lucid intervals" in the relations of men and nations: "I have a vague and comforting impression that the greatest safeguard against another war in Europe will be the unwillingness of the plain citizen—'the forgotten man'—to have his substance wasted and his life destroyed by another armed conflict."

On March 29th he inscribed a copy of his *Chosen Poems* and sent it to Ranger Edd. W. Cummings at the Grand Canyon. He had been informed by a visitor that the man had a well worn copy of Henry van Dyke's poems in his saddle bag.

"For years," wrote the Ranger in expressing his thanks, "I have carried your collection, 'Songs Out of Doors', and when alone on the trails have read it many times. Also when on camping trips with parties have asked some one in the party to read your poems to the others. 'Grand Canyon at Daybreak' and 'God of the Open Air' are my favourites. How often I have read the two and thought, 'How can a man believe there is no Maker, and how can a man live at the Grand Canyon and see its beauties and not believe in Him.' "

"Every week brings an ebbing of strength, an increase of pain and mortal weakness," he wrote to his neighbor and classmate Joseph H. Dulles regretfully reporting that he would not be "physically able" to have the Anniversary Dinner of the Class of 1873 at "Avalon." But the next day he rose and wrote his promised brief introduction for the book on *Worship* by Shackelford Dauerty who had been one of his able young helpers on *The Book of Common Worship.*

As, he expressed it whimsically: "I've got Anno Domini,—but Anne Gina hasn't got me yet."

For long Dr. Charles R. Erdman had been a faithful pastoral visitor and they spoke often as fellow believers about the mystery toward which he now began to move eagerly. The words of Scripture were often on his lips and in moments of mortal weakness he prayed audibly. But he was much refreshed when his former Princeton pupil and medical adviser, Dr. Davenport West, came on April 4th to see him and to consult with Dr. Schauffler. After the examination, as the two Doctors were reporting to the family, Henry van Dyke on his nurse's arm entered triumphantly to say with smiling emphasis: "It does *my heart* good to see you all." That evening he sat for the most part silent in his den looking occasionally at the familiar things, spoke a few words of faith and affection to us, and went upstairs for the last time to his room. On Friday his former Secretary, now Mrs. Ralph Downes came, as often, to inquire. "Take two letters," he greeted her in the old manner with flashing eye and dictated his last letters. The same evening his eldest daughter brought a night nurse and the brief vigil began. Sunday he took an affectionate farewell of his brother Paul and of each member of the family. As night came on he was ready for the last adventure. Dr. Schauffler spent the hours at his side. As the first streaks of dawn lightened his wide open eastern window the robins were in full song in the maple trees. The family stood by his bed. The nurse's little candle was guttering in the candle stick. Henry van Dyke's candle of life was burned to the socket. He had no more need of that candle. It went out as the breath of dawn touched it.

"And when at last I can no longer move
    Among them freely, but must part
From the green fields and from the waters clear,
Let me not creep
Into some darkened room and hide
From all that makes the world so bright and dear;
    But throw the windows wide
    To welcome in the light;
And while I clasp a well-belovèd hand,
    Let me once more have sight
Of the deep sky and the far-smiling land,—
    Then gently fall on sleep,
And breathe my body back to Nature's care,
My spirit out to Thee, God of the open air."

WHAT DOES THE PARABLE MEAN?

WHAT then is the meaning of the parable of this man's life? I cannot tell. The story has been told honestly as we agreed it should be done. But it has always been and still remains true that:

> "None can truly write his single day,
> And none can write it for him upon earth."

When the soul has completed its mortal journey the man is most adequately interpreted by his works and by the spiritual relations of which he has become (or failed to become) a part.

As in the case of all significant men, there was always something paradoxical about Henry van Dyke. Basically a lover of peace, he could fight briskly, but he never brawled. He had the soul of a poet and many qualities of the colonel of a cavalry regiment. By nature an aristocrat, he was in his personal relations a complete democrat. His manner at court was the same as his manner in camp. He was an opportunist with principles. You could count on him for consistent action, but he was never within reach of obvious classification. By nature a hedonist he was by character a cheerful moralist. His sympathy with all sorts of people was boundless. One who knew him well under all kinds of circumstances said: "I never knew a man of more concentrated humanity." Bumptiousness, cant, pretentiousness drew from him expressions of utter scorn. But in the face of trouble or sorrow his sympathy and helpfulness were without limit. He was vividly conscious of himself and not above dramatizing himself *for a purpose*, but he was never self-conscious. What his enemies denounced as pose was fundamentally his poise in view of human need. He honestly liked success, but he preferred to fail rather than to surrender his ideal of independence. His scorn for laziness was fully equalled by his love of indolence—at the proper time.

[423]

He liked genuine people wherever he found them. Nobody who met him ever forgot him. He was a great household friend as a man and as an author. Many were the children who hailed his arrival with cheers.

On the whole—though he never used the phrase—he believed in a "man-run world"; but he clearly recognized woman's vital part in it. He was strenuous in defense of women's rights and heartily opposed to women's "equality" with men. Like all sound men he delighted greatly in the society of women, and had deep and lasting friendships with some of them. He responded promptly to feminine beauty, but he turned away abruptly unless it was matched with grace and vigor of mind. He hated to waste time with nobodies, and no one was more competent than he to put an end to what he adjudged an unprofitable relationship of any kind with man or woman.

Positiveness and clarity were his unmistakable marks. His public appearances were ever noted for a fine reserve and assurance. The battle lay behind them. He was a combination of realist and idealist fused into integrity in the mystery of personality. But he was always more of an artist than a reformer, of a poet than a scientist. As a realist he was a keen observer of men and nature. As an idealist he emphasized the good instead of criticizing the bad. What he omitted to say was fully as significant as what he said. Irony was one of his tools, but he had no use for satire. Consequently he failed to appreciate some of the critical idealists. As a natural-born and a thoroughly-trained leader he could always find something good that needed to be done; and delighted to undertake his own particular task and to help others undertake theirs.

The outstanding qualities of the man were courage, sensitiveness, sympathy. He was alive all the time.

Henry van Dyke was never tempted to become an exclusive specialist in any one field of his many interests. He was always an amateur,—a lover,—not a professional. *Solvitur ambulando,* he often said, was his motto. His career was subsidiary to his life.

Perhaps, when the history of the period during which he lived comes to be written in terms of the men who truly represented that period as well as deeply affected it,—instead of in terms of reports on classifiable groups of professionalists,—Henry van Dyke will find his rightful place in it. At least it will be found to be something less than critical to have neglected his influence and achievements in any particular field because he had also a record in other fields. The versatility that arises from vitality and broad human interest cannot long keep a man from being seriously considered,—provided we honestly desire to apprehend the meaning of human life, individual and social. In any case, Henry van Dyke's tales, essays, poems, oratory, teaching, preaching and pastoral work were what they were because he declined to become a specialist where it interfered with his remaining a human being. And whatever be the judgment of time as to the significance of his various works, that judgment must take notice of the fact that in whatever he did, said, wrote, he was first, last, and all the time a man.

In conclusion, it is worthy of note that the power that carried him through the varied experiences of a long and full life was that of which he spoke when he preached, during his twenty-fifth year, in his father's church in Brooklyn on the evening of June 10, 1877:

"I have seen the strong man in danger and difficulty, in the heat and burdens of the day, the old and weary pilgrim whose friends have all passed over the river of death, but who still waits on this shore for the summons to enter into rest. I have seen the young and the old, the weak and the strong, the brave and the timid, all leaning upon the love of Christ, and I know that it is real and living and faithful unto death, and that for this world and the next it passeth knowledge."

THE END

BIBLIOGRAPHY

I

BOOKS BY HENRY VAN DYKE IN ORDER OF PUBLICATION

(First American publication date at left of title; publishers, foreign date, etc., following.)

(Author's name in a number of the earlier books is Henry J. van Dyke, Jr.)

1884 *The Reality of Religion.* New York, Charles Scribner's Sons. London, Unwin, 1885.

1887 *The Story of the Psalms.* New York, Charles Scribner's Sons.

1889 *The Poetry of Tennyson.* New York, Charles Scribner's Sons. London, Mathews, 1890. (Complete rev. in *Studies in Tennyson* 1920.)

1890 *God and Little Children.* New York, Randolph.

1893 *Historic Presbyterianism.* New York, Randolph.

1893 *Straight Sermons.* New York, Charles Scribner's Sons. (See *Sermons to Young Men*, 1898.)

1894 *The Christ Child in Art.* New York, Harper & Brothers.

1895 *Little Rivers.* New York, Charles Scribner's Sons. London, Nutt, 1895.

1896 *The Story of the Other Wise Man.* New York, Harper & Brothers. London, Harper, 1907. Sydney, Australia, Cornstalk Pub., undated. (Translated into most Europ. langs. and many langs. and dialects of Near and Far East. Ital. version pub. Harper 1912.)

1896 *The Gospel for An Age of Doubt.* New York, Macmillan Co. London, Hodder, 1899.

1897 *Ships and Havens.* New York, Thomas Y. Crowell Co.

1897 *The Builders and Other Poems.* New York, Charles Scribner's Sons.

1897 *The First Christmas Tree.* New York, Charles Scribner's Sons. (Mag. title, *The Oak of Geismar.*)

1898 *The Lost Word.* New York, Charles Scribner's Sons. London, J. Clarke, 1899. Paris, Fischbachen, 1903. (Le Noux Perdu.) (Mag. title, *A Christmas Loss.*)

[427]

1898   *Sermons to Young Men.* New York, Charles Scribner's Sons. London, Dickinson, 1901. (New and enl. ed. of *Straight Sermons.*)

1898   *The Toiling of Felix.* New York, Charles Scribner's Sons. (125 copies privately printed.)

1899   *Fisherman's Luck.* New York, Charles Scribner's Sons. London, Low, 1899.

1899   *The Gospel for a World of Sin.* New York, Macmillan Co. London, Hodder and Stoughton, 1899.

1900   *The Toiling of Felix and Other Poems.* New York, Charles Scribner's Sons. London, Hodder and Stoughton, 1911.

1900   *The Poetry of the Psalms.* New York, Thomas Y. Crowell Co.

1900   *The Friendly Year.* New York, Charles Scribner's Sons. (Sel. from writings of H. v. D. chosen and arranged by George Sidney Webster.)

1900   *Books, Literature and the People.* New York, Cadmus Press. (Privately printed.)

1901   *The Ruling Passion.* New York, Charles Scribner's Sons. Paris, Calmann Lévy, 1908. (La Gardienne de la Lumière.)

1902   *The Blue Flower.* New York, Charles Scribner's Sons.

1903   *The Open Door.* Philadelphia, Presbyterian Board. (In the Presby. Pulpit Ser.)

1903   *Joy and Power.* New York, Thomas Y. Crowell Co.

1904   *Music and Other Poems.* New York, Charles Scribner's Sons.

1905   *The Childhood of Jesus Christ.* New York, F. A. Stokes Co.

1905   *Essays in Application.* New York, Charles Scribner's Sons. London, Hodder and Stoughton, 1906. (Ideals and Applications.)

1905   *The School of Life.* New York, Charles Scribner's Sons.

1905   *The Spirit of Christmas.* New York, Charles Scribner's Sons.

1905   *The Van Dyke Book.* New York, Charles Scribner's Sons. (Sel. from writings of H. v. D. by Edwin Mims with intro. by ed. and biograph. sketch by Brooke van Dyke. New ed. rev. with intro. by Maxwell Struthers Burt, 1920.)

1906   *The Americanism of Washington.* New York, Harper & Brothers.

1907   *The Battle of Life.* New York, Thomas Y. Crowell Co.

1907   *The Good Old Way.* New York, Thomas Y. Crowell Co.

1907   *The Music Lover.* New York, Moffatt, Yard & Co. (first pub. as Prelude to *Where Speech Ends*, 1906. See below p. 431.)

1907   *Days Off.* New York, Charles Scribner's Sons. London, Hodder and Stoughton, 1907.

1908   *Counsels by the Way.* New York, Thomas Y. Crowell Co.

1908 *The House of Rimmon*. New York, Charles Scribner's Sons. (A poetic drama.)

1908 *Out of Doors in the Holy Land*. New York, Charles Scribner's Sons. London, Hodder and Stoughton, 1908.

1909 *The White Bees and Other Poems*. New York, Charles Scribner's Sons.

1910 *The Spirit of America*. New York, Macmillan Co. London, Macmillan, 1912. Paris, Calmann Lévy, 1909. (Le Génie de l'Amérique.) Pref. by A. Ribot.

1911 *The Mansion*. New York, Harper & Brothers.

1911 *The Sad Shepherd*. New York, Charles Scribner's Sons. London, Harper, 1912.

1911 *Poems of Henry van Dyke*. New York, Charles Scribner's Sons. (Now first coll. and rev. with many hitherto unpub.) London, Bird, 1913. (Also a new and rev. ed. with many hitherto uncollected. Scribner, 1920.)

1912 *The Unknown Quantity*. New York, Charles Scribner's Sons. London, Harper, 1913.

1913 *Ars Agricolaris*. Jenkins. (Privately printed.)

1914 *The Grand Canyon and Other Poems*. New York, Charles Scribner's Sons.

1914 *The Lost Boy*. New York, Harper & Brothers. London, Harper, 1914.

1915 *Prayer for Christmas Morning*. New York, E. P. Dutton & Co.

1917 *The Red Flower*. New York, Charles Scribner's Sons. London, Hodder and Stoughton, 1918.

1917 *Fighting for Peace*. New York, Charles Scribner's Sons. London, Hodder and Stoughton, 1918.

1919 *The Valley of Vision*. New York, Charles Scribner's Sons. London, Hodder and Stoughton, 1919.

1919 *The Broken Soldier and the Maid of France*. New York, Harper & Brothers. London, Harper, 1919.

1919 *Golden Stars and Other Verses*. New York, Charles Scribner's Sons. London, Hodder and Stoughton, 1919.

1919 *What Peace Means*. New York, Fleming H. Revell Co.

1920 Works. *Avalon Ed*. Vols. 1-8. New York, Charles Scribner's Sons. Little Rivers, Fisherman's Luck, Days Off, Out of Doors in the Holy Land, Ruling Passion, Blue Flower, Unknown Quantity, Valley of Vision.

1920 *Studies in Tennyson.* (Complete rev. of *The Poetry of Tennyson.*) New York, Charles Scribner's Sons.

1921 *Camp Fires and Guide Posts.* New York, Charles Scribner's Sons. London, Hodder and Stoughton, 1921.

1921-22 Works, *Avalon Ed.* Vols. 9-17. New York, Charles Scribner's Sons. Poems, 2 vols., Pro Patria, Studies in Tennyson, Ideals and Applications, Evangel, Counsels by the Way, Camp Fires and Guide Posts, Companionable Books (Golden Key added as vol. 18 in 1927).

1922 *Companionable Books.* New York, Charles Scribner's Sons. London, Hodder and Stoughton, 1923.

1922 *Songs out of Doors.* New York, Charles Scribner's Sons.

1922 *Thy Sea is Great, Our Boats are Small.* New York, Fleming H. Revell Co. London, Hodder and Stoughton, 1922.

1924 *Six Days of the Week.* New York, Charles Scribner's Sons. London, Hodder and Stoughton, 1925.

1925 *Half Told Tales.* New York, Charles Scribner's Sons.

1926 *The Golden Key.* New York, Charles Scribner's Sons.

1926 *Light My Candle.* New York, Fleming H. Revell Co. (With Tertius van Dyke.) London, Oliphant, 1927.

1927 *Chosen Poems.* New York, Charles Scribner's Sons. London, Bird, 1928.

1927 Works. *Sylvanora Ed.* (An ed. of economy.) Blue Flower, Chosen Poems, Days Off, Fisherman's Luck, Little Rivers, Out of Doors in the Holy Land, Ruling Passion, Unknown Quantity, Valley of Vision, Companionable Books. New York, Charles Scribner's Sons.

1927 *The Story of the Other Wise Man.* (A dramatic version by the author.) New York, Harper & Brothers.

1928 *Even Unto Bethlehem.* New York, Charles Scribner's Sons.

1929 *The Man Behind the Book.* New York, Charles Scribner's Sons.

1929 *The Travel Diary of an Angler.* New York, Derrydale Press.

1930 *Gratitude.* New York, E. P. Dutton & Co.

1932 *A Creelful of Fishing Stories.* New York, Charles Scribner's Sons.

BIBLIOGRAPHY

II

BOOKS IN WHICH HENRY VAN DYKE HAD A PART

1892 *Henry Jackson van Dyke*. Mem. vol. ed. Henry van Dyke and Paul van Dyke. New York, Randolph.

1895 *Responsive Readings*. (Rev. and enl. from bk. orig. prep. for Chapel Harvard Univ.) Boston, Ginn & Co.

1897 *The Age of the Renascence*. By Paul van Dyke. Intro. Henry van Dyke. New York, The Christian Literature Co.

1900 *Women of the Bible*. By Eminent Divines. "Miriam" by Henry van Dyke. New York, Harper & Brothers.

1900 *Counsel upon the Reading of Books*. By H. Morse Stephens. Intro. Henry van Dyke. Boston, Houghton Mifflin Co.

1901 *Young Folks Library*. T. B. Aldrich, Ed. in Chief, Vol. 19, "Hist. Scenes in Fiction," intro. Henry van Dyke; also vol. 8 in *Vocations,* "Literature," intro. Henry van Dyke, 1911. Boston, Hall and Locke.

1903 *Poems of Tennyson*. Chosen and ed. with intro. by Henry van Dyke. Boston, Ginn & Co.

1903 *Poems of Tennyson* (Athenaeum Press Series) ed. by Henry van Dyke and D. Laurance Chambers. Boston, Ginn & Co. (enlargement of the above vol.).

1903 *Not in the Curriculum*. By O. F. Gardner and F. L. Janeway. Intro. Henry van Dyke. New York, Fleming H. Revell Co.

1904 *The Gateway Series of English Texts*. Gen. Ed., Henry van Dyke. Also Henry van Dyke ed. with intro. and notes: Idylls of the King, 1904. Sel. Essays R. W. Emerson, 1907. New York, American Book Co.

1905 *Little Masterpieces of English Poetry*. 6 vols., ed. by Henry van Dyke and Hardin Craig. New York, Doubleday, Doran & Co.

1906 *Where Speech Ends* by Robert Haven Schauffler. Prelude, "The Music Lover" by Henry van Dyke. New York, Moffatt, Yard & Co.

1906 *The Book of Common Worship*. Prep. by a comm., Henry van Dyke, chairman. Philadelphia, Presbyterian Board.

1908 *The Whole Family*. A novel by 12 authors. New York, Harper & Brothers.

[431]

1909   *The Poetry of Nature.* Henry van Dyke, comp. New York, Double-
        day, Doran & Co. London, Heinemann, 1909.

1912   *Once Upon a Time Tales* by Mary Stewart. Intro. "The Way to
        Once Upon a Time" by Henry van Dyke. New York, Fleming
        H. Revell Co.

1917   *The World Peril.* By members of the faculty, Princeton Univ.
        "American Rights Imperilled," by Henry van Dyke. Princeton
        University Press.

1918   *The Faith of France.* By Maurice Barrès. Foreword by Henry van
        Dyke. Boston, Houghton Mifflin Co.

1918   *The Navy Chaplain's Manual* by John B. Frazier. Intro. by Henry
        van Dyke. New York, Federal Council of the Churches of Christ
        in America.

1919   *A Book of Princeton Verse II.* Henry van Dyke one of editors and
        wrote pref. Princeton University Press.

1921   *The Story of a Poet: Madison Cawein* by Otto A. Rothert. Reminis-
        cences by Henry van Dyke. Louisville, Ky., John P. Morton & Co.

1922   *Just Nerves* by Austen Fox Riggs. Foreword by Henry van Dyke.
        Boston, Houghton Mifflin Co.

1922   *The Princeton Battle Monument.* "Ballad of Princeton Battle," by
        Henry van Dyke. Princeton University Press.

1923   *Little Masterpieces of Poetry by British and American Authors.*
        Ed. by Henry van Dyke with Hardin Craig and A. D. Dickin-
        son. New York, Doubleday, Doran & Co.

1924   *Recollections of a Happy Life* by Maurice Francis Egan. Intro. by
        Henry van Dyke. New York, Geo. H. Doran Co.

1925   *Academy Papers* by Paul Elmer More, etc., "The Fringe of Words"
        by Henry van Dyke. New York, Charles Scribner's Sons.

1926   *An Outline of Christianity* by many writers. In Vol. I ed. by Ernest
        F. Scott and Burton S. Easton. Chap. II "The Birth and Child-
        hood of Jesus" by Henry van Dyke. New York, Bethlehem Pub-
        lishers, Inc., Dodd, Mead & Co., Distributors.

1929   *The Poetic and Dramatic Works of Alfred Lord Tennyson* (7 vols.)
        Intro. by Henry van Dyke. Boston, Houghton Mifflin Co.

1931   *The Book of the Fly-Rod* ed. by Hugh T. Sheringham and John
        Moore. Chapter I "De Maximus" by Henry van Dyke. London,
        Eyre and Spottiswoode. Boston, Houghton Mifflin Co.

1932   *The Book of Common Worship.* (The 1906 vol. rev. and enl. by a
        committee with Henry van Dyke again chairman.) Philadelphia,
        Presbyterian Board.

III

PAMPHLETS AND LEAFLETS BY HENRY VAN DYKE

1888 *The National Sin of Literary Piracy.* New York, Charles Scribner's Sons.

1891 *Man Better than a Sheep.* Princeton, Robinson & Co.

1891 *A Brief for Foreign Missions.* New York, Woman's Board of Foreign Missions of the Presbyterian Church.

1893 *The True Presbyterian Doctrine of the Church.* New York, Wm. C. Martin.

1893 *An Historic Church.* New York, Wm. C. Martin.

1893 *The Bible As It Is.* New York, Wm. C. Martin.
Is This Calvinism or Christianity? (Privately printed.)

1895 *The People Responsible for the Character of Their Rulers* (sermon to the Sons of the Revolution).

1898 *The Cross of War.* (Privately printed.)

1898 *Sea, the Men Upon it and the God Above It.* (Sermon to American Seaman's Friend Society.) New York.

1898 *The American Birthright and the Philippine Pottage.* New York, Charles Scribner's Sons.

1898 *Salt* (Baccalaureate sermon). New York, Columbia University Press.

1899 *Liberty* (a chap. from *The Gospel for an Age of Doubt*). New York, Macmillan Co.

1902 *The Three Best Things.* New York, Outlook Co.

1904-5 *Footpath to Peace.* New York, Dodge. (Also Donohue, Elder, Barse and Hopkins.)

1904-5 *Love.* New York, Dodge.

1911 *Who Follow the Flag.* New York, Charles Scribner's Sons.

1912 *Christmas Greetings.* Barse and Hopkins.

1913 *Immortality.* Barse and Hopkins.

1913 *The Angel of God's Face.* Philadelphia, Presbyterian Board.

1915 *Texas: A Democratic Ode* (at Rice Institute, 1912). Houston, Texas.

1928 *In Defense of Religious Liberty* distrib. by Democratic National Committee.

1928 *For Freedom of Conscience* (Radio address Oct. 3) distrib. by Democratic National Committee.

INDEX

INDEX

[436]

INDEX

INDEX

INDEX

INDEX

Essays, 86 f., 92, 168 f., 235, 348, 366 f., 391 f., 403; literary criticism, 92, 158 ff., 203, 244; religious, 156, 179 ff., 182, 240, 361; criticism of art, 88, 92, 150, 153

Poetry, 23 f., 38 ff., 61, 85 f., 165, 167 f., 173, 194, 240, 244 ff., 253, 278, 319, 340, 342, 347, 351, 361, 365, 366, 384 f., 386, 404, 411, 420, 421

Tales, xiii-xiv, 166, 167, 194, 236 ff., 240, 244, 344, 351, 358, 375, 388 f., 390 f., 415

Characteristics of, xiii-xiv, 423-425; *courage*, 21, 49, 60, 77, 101, 230, 256, 332, 345, 349, 367 f., 376, 383, 387 f., 410, 418, 422; *sensitiveness*, 16, 22, 35, 49 f., 64, 75, 155, 213 f., 222, 226, 255, 338, 352, 387; *sympathy*, 17, 60, 75, 103, 108, 199 ff., 225, 259, 312, 335, 342, 369, 385, 392; *clarity and positiveness*, 3, 18, 36, 41, 44 ff., 47, 53 f., 62, 78, 82, 99, 103, 109, 137, 166, 201 f., 229 f., 242, 340, 341, 345, 354, 355, 365 f., 386, 401, 410; *thoroughness*, 26, 29, 69 f., 236 f., 241 f., 250, 280, 337, 360; *humor*, 9 f., 31 f., 52, 58 f., 65, 120, 144, 145, 151, 174 f., 208 f., 259 f., 262 ff., 288, 302, 309, 321, 333, 336, 347, 366, 397, 408 f., 414, 417; *vitality*, 20, 25, 31, 41 f., 47, 50, 55, 57 ff., 70, 86 f., 92, 108, 121, 143, 151, 155, 176, 186, 202, 216, 259, 271, 280, 290, 298, 310, 322, 325, 327, 330, 383 f., 393 f., 399, 420 f.; *combativeness*, 17, 20, 22, 60, 82 ff., 138 f., 231 ff., 278 f., 313, 351 f., 365, 366, 374 f., 402, 404 ff., 419 f.; *belief in freedom*, 13, 41, 55, 61, 111, 122, 414

Children of:

(Fanny) Brooke. *See* Gibson, Mrs. Hamilton

Roger (Andrew) (d. 1885)

Tertius (Henry J., 3rd)

Bernard (d. 1897)

Dorothea (d. 1912)

Elaine

Paula. *See* Chapin, Mrs. Henry

Anthony Ashmead (d. 1903)

Katrina. *See* Brush, Mrs. Murray Peabody, Jr.

Family refs., 144 ff., 148, 150, 175, 214, 252, 257, 258 ff., 281, 296, 301, 314, 321, 392, 394, 400, 402, 413, 422 (specific refs. under full names)

van Dyke, Mrs. Henry (Ellen Reid), first meetings with H. v. D., 56, 63; engaged, 90; married, 91; shows interest in Tennyson, 92; goes camping, 92; happy in N. Y., 99; with H. v. D. to consult Paul van Dyke about Andover call, 141; care of children, 145; camping trips, 148 f.; Christmas exped. with children, 175; in Calif. with H. v. D., 252; deafness of, 258; *dea ex machina,* at Avalon, 258; fishing companion of H. v. D., 301, 303 f.; at The Hague, 315; in war time, 327; desperately ill, 367; arranges birthday dinners for H. v. D., 393; household manager, 400 f.; on "Eileen," 402; golden wedding, 413; at American Academy celebration, 418

van Dyke, Rev. Henry Jackson, born Abington, Pa., 8; youthful characteristics, 8; pastor Bridgeton, N. J., 8; pastor Germantown, Pa., 9, 14; death of two sons, 9, 14; birth of Henry, 9; pastor Brooklyn, N. Y., 14 ff.; as preacher, pastor, 15; family life, 16; Kate born and dies, 16; Paul born, 16; to Europe and Florida, 17 f.; anti-abolitionist, 20 ff.; courage, 21 f.; called to Nashville, 48; moderator Gen. Assembly, 56 (268); belief in sports, 59; at First Pan Presby. Council, 67 f.; Talmage incident, 82 ff.; growing liberalism, 123; member Gen. Assembly com. on creed rev., 124; elect. Prof. Union Theol. Sem., N. Y., 127; death, vii, 128; relations with H. v. D., xiii, 13, 16, 17, 19, 20 ff., 29, 35, 38, 49, 52, 57 ff., 64, 65 ff., 69, 74, 76, 81, 82 ff., 88, 90, 93, 99, 103, 105, 127 f., 145, 159, 223, 256, 298, 301, 425

van Dyke, Mrs. Henry Jackson (Henrietta Ashmead), 1845 marries H. J. v. D., 8; ancestry of, 11-13, described by H. v. D., 16; reads to Henry, 19; takes Henry to Charleston, 20; takes Henry to Philadelphia and visits him in college, 35; seriously ill, 48; letters to Henry, 71-72; excited at Henry's installation, 81; visits Henry's family, 145; indulges his fishing, 298

van Dyke, John C., ix, 4, 5

van Dyke, Kate (younger sister of H. v. D., died as child), 16, 17

van Dyke, Paul, with H. v. D. only surviving children of H. J. v. D., 16; "born good,"

[443]